MW00535037

Minnesota's Iron Country
Rich Ore, Rich Lives

by Marvin G. Lamppa

Lake Superior Port Cities Inc.

©2004 Marvin G. Lamppa

All rights reserved. No part of this publication may be reproduced or transmitted in any form or by any means, electronic or mechanical, including photocopying, recording or any information storage and retrieval system, without permission in writing from the publisher.

First Edition: June 2004

5 4 3 2 1

Published by
LAKE SUPERIOR PORT CITIES INC.
P.O. Box 16417
Duluth, Minnesota 55816-0417
USA   888-BIG LAKE (244-5253) • www.lakesuperior.com

Publishers of *Lake Superior Magazine* and *Lake Superior Travel Guide*

Library of Congress Cataloging-In-Publication Data

Lamppa, Marvin G., 1933-
    Minnesota's iron country / by Marvin G. Lamppa. – 1st ed.
      p. cm.
    Includes bibliographical references and index.
    ISBN 0-942235-56-8
    1. Minnesota – History. 2. Minnesota – History, Local. 3. Iron ranges –
Minnesota – History. 4. Frontier and pioneer life – Minnesota. 5. Iron miners –
Minnesota – History. 6. Iron mines and mining – Minnesota – History. 7.
Minnesota – Economic conditions. I. Title.

F606.L29 2004
977.6 22–dc22   2004048279

Printed in the United States of America

 Editing: Hugh E. Bishop, Konnie LeMay, Paul L. Hayden
 Design: Matt Pawlak
Printing: Sheridan Books, Chelsea, Michigan

Dedication

To all Iron Rangers,
wherever they may be.

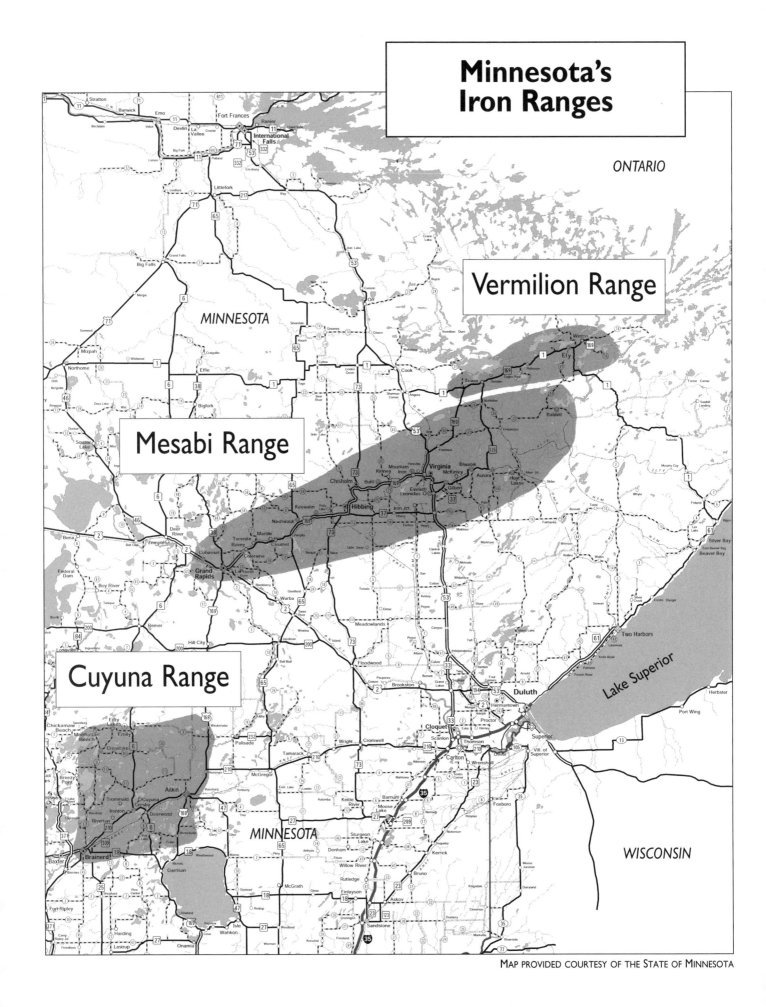

Minnesota's Iron Ranges

Vermilion Range

Mesabi Range

Cuyuna Range

MAP PROVIDED COURTESY OF THE STATE OF MINNESOTA

Table of Contents

Introduction

There were ore trains running through Embarrass, Minnesota, when I was a boy. On summer nights, I listened to the powerful steam-driven Mallets as they began their slow ascent of the Mesabi heights and fell asleep to the long melancholy of their whistles. There was daily passenger service, too. A 15-minute ride on the noon train would find me in Soudan at my Aunt Elina's, where there would be boat rides to the island cottage, swimming at McKinley Park and where my lifelong affair with Minnesota's Iron Country had its start.

Soudan had all the appearances of a mining location in those days: company-built houses, fenced-in yards – no private businesses. The only place where you could get an ice cream cone or, for that matter, buy anything at all was at the "Oliver Club" on the corner of Centre Street and Main, across the street from the hospital. High above the town was the mine – remote, unapproachable, its steel headframe silhouetted against the sky, sheaves continually turning, ore rumbling through its crushers. It seemed as natural as life itself and as permanent as the hills around it. I think it was the same for many of the men who worked there. The mine was there when they became miners – it would be there when they were gone.

My grandfather spent a good part of his life as a barman in that mine. His job was to tap the hanging wall of a stope with a steel bar after a blast in order to drop down loose rock, making it safe for miners to enter. After he retired he came to live with us in Embarrass. Although he talked more about his boyhood days in Finland than about the mine, he did present my parents with two huge mineral specimens. My mother used one of them to hold the back door open on hot summer days. It was on one of those summer days that I discovered my first ghost town.

I don't remember exactly how it happened or who was with me, but a few friends and I learned that a seldom used dirt road a short distance from my house led to an old abandoned mining town. We left early and within an hour were bicycling over unmaintained corduroy toward the Mesabi heights. It was a surprisingly short trip – the road turned rusty red and we were there. The place was like nothing I had ever experienced.

At the top of an empty hill was a two-story brick building with the words "Village of Mesaba" etched in stone above the door. One section of the building had windows with bars. A jail! The building reminded me of village halls that I had seen in Aurora and Biwabik, except there was no town surrounding it. The decaying remains of a boardwalk led to a street overgrown with grass. On what was once a corner, a rusting sign read "Broadway and …." I couldn't make out the rest. Farther down the way, like some movie of the Old West, was a saloon – at least we thought it was a saloon – with its door hanging half open on a single hinge, windows broken and interior covered with rubble and dust. Imaginations soared. My interest in history grew.

As I look back now, the most incredible discovery came when we found out the town wasn't entirely abandoned. One house was occupied; there was still an old-timer in town. He said he was the last mayor of Mesaba and was more than willing to tell us about the town. He talked long into the afternoon about lumberjacks, miners, immigrants and entrepreneurs. He described long-vanished hotels, restaurants, saloons and gambling halls. Hours passed and then, as we pedaled homeward in the evening dusk, I was aware of a feeling of connectedness with the past, a sense that something special had happened and I was

somehow part of it. It was on that day that I became a "Ranger."

Years later I came to understand that I had glimpsed vestiges of a passing era, one that is becoming increasingly obscure. I had by then come to value the documented certainties of history books and was well on my way to a teaching career. However, I sometimes think that my lifelong inquiry into the region's past would never have begun had it not been for my boyhood experiences and the urging of my mentor and graduate advisor, the late Doctor Maude Lindquist, who was determined that I should write a paper about Mesabi Range ghost towns. It was at a time when the region's natural ores were thought to be gone and there was talk of dying towns and the promise of taconite.

During my early research into the region's past, I encountered a limited, but diverse and often conflicting, body of writings. The Iron Range was described in terms of everything from a vital appendage of the steel industry, where tonnages measured success, to a place of strikes, unrest and exploited immigrant miners. Most of the published works were by non-Rangers: scholars, economists, professional writers and journalists – outsiders who saw the Range on their own terms and according to their specialties.

Characterizations of the region's people varied and sometimes reached mythic proportions. In a 1927 article published in *The Outlook* describing the visit of Princeton-trained Presbyterian missionary William J. Bell, writer Fred Eastman began with the words, "Good-by God, I'm going to the Iron Range."

If there were accounts written by people who lived on the Iron Range, people, for example, who knew what it meant to be a contract miner at the Genoa Mine or a boardinghouse cook in Hibbing, they were difficult to find, if not impossible, or their stories were buried among the pages and footnotes of technical writings, books on other subjects and biographies of successful entrepreneurs.

Thanks to the leadership of the late Minnesota governor, Rudy Perpich, whose insightful belief in a people's right and need to access and understand their past, a change

came over the state beginning in the mid-1970s. The facilities of the Minnesota Historical Society were expanded and its archival and manuscript capabilities improved, a survey of the state's historic sites and structures was carried out, regional research centers were established and the collections of the St. Louis County Historical Society, including valuable accounts of the early years of mining, were placed in the Northeast Minnesota Historical Center located on the campus of the University of Minnesota-Duluth and made available to the public. At Chisholm on the Mesabi Range, an Iron Range Research Center with a state-of-the-art archival unit was added to the Iron Range Interpretative Center and began collecting manuscripts, public records and other primary sources related to the three Minnesota iron ranges.

A wealth of primary sources collected at these centers make it possible for the general public to join historians and researchers in the exploration of countless subjects related to the history of the state and region and has contributed to a growing interest in northeast Minnesota and its mining past. During my time as director of the Iron Range Interpretative Program, the most frequent question I encountered was, "Where can I find a general history of the Iron Range?"

This book is written in response to that question. It surveys the region's past, from formation of its iron ores billions of years ago to events of the late 20th century and places the iron mining story into the broader context of a larger region. Iron mining directly influenced the economy and history of nearly every community in the northeast portion of the state. Cities like Brainerd, Grand Rapids, Duluth, Two Harbors and Silver Bay owe much of their development to iron ore. It is therefore not so much an "iron range" around which this story unfolds, but rather an "Iron Country," one that includes the entire Arrowhead region and most of northeast Minnesota.

The book draws its inspiration and much of its substance from the labor of others: the late Doctor Michael Karni, known for his publications and his pioneering efforts in rescuing the records of

northeast Minnesota's Finnish-American community, and the efforts of the late Doctor Matti Kaups, whose detailed studies of settlement patterns contributed much to an understanding of the region. I am proud to say that I had the privilege of working closely with both; they were an inspiration to me and I have counted them as my friends.

I also wish to credit the late Doctor Edward W. Davis whose work in taconite development as described in his book, *Pioneering With Taconite*, contributed much of the substance in Chapter 12 and the late Robert F. Harney of the Multicultural History Society of Ontario, who taught me about *tuteshi* and made me realize that "Iron Rangers" do exist. My deepest appreciation and many thanks go to Doctor David Walker, author of *Iron Frontier*, who read and critiqued an early draft of this writing and forced me to rethink some of my all-too-quickly drawn assumptions and formulations. Dr. Walker's own study of the entrepreneurs, developers, speculators and industrial consolidations during the formative years of Minnesota's three iron ranges set a standard for academic research that is difficult to match. Equally important, I think, was his reminder that "men and women create history," not "inanimate institutions."

There are others, although they may not be aware of it, who contributed greatly to my knowledge of the region: certainly the authors of published works, theses and dissertations credited in my notes; the staff and volunteers of the Itasca County Historical Society, Iron Range Historical Society, Hibbing Historical Society, Lake County Historical Society, Virginia Area Historical Society, Ely-Winton Historical Society and Tower-Soudan Historical Society; people outside of the field of history; geologists, engineers, librarians, teachers, students in my classes, fellow Iron Rangers, names too numerous to mention.

There are a few who were directly instrumental in making this book happen: Edward Nelson, Iron Range Research Center archivist, who helped me with illustrations and whose insistence on the need for a history of the region brought me out of retirement; Jim Marshall of Lake Superior Port Cities Inc., who believed in me,

encouraged my work and asked that the company have the chance to publish it; Donn Larson, who helped me sort out the changing roles of the region's many mining companies; my son, Robert Lamppa, whose sketches and diagrams are part of this book; Debbie Fena at the Iron Range Research Center; Pat Maus at the Northeast Minnesota History Center; Lake Superior Port Cities' Hugh Bishop, Cindy and Paul Hayden and, most importantly, my wife, Carolyn, who read drafts of my writing, and whose patience, support and encouragement helped to make this book a reality.

Finally, I'll take credit for whatever is left, including any omissions or whatever seems misguided and, if my work appears a bit "Iron Rangerish," I'll take credit for that and happily agree!

Marvin Lamppa
Birch Lake
June 2004

CHAPTER 1

The Time Before History

This is a story about a place, a region of the country that is famous for its iron mines and recognized for its significant role in building America's steel industry. Sprawling crescent-like across a large portion of northeastern Minnesota, 60-some miles inland from the port city of Duluth, it is today a place of abandoned mines, sophisticated taconite processing plants and small towns struggling with change.

The region received the attention of the world at the end of the 19th century, when some of the largest and most accessible deposits of iron ore ever discovered were found on what came to be called the Vermilion, Mesabi and Cuyuna iron ranges. By 1925, the region's 272 active iron mines had shattered all records of production and children in schools across the nation were reading about the great "iron ranges" at the far end of the Great Lakes. Today, mining takes place only on one, the Mesabi, but the three iron ranges – and most of the surrounding countryside – are often lumped together as "the Range" and most people who live there are referred to as "Rangers."

The development and settlement of the three mining districts are only part of the larger and more ancient story of "Minnesota Iron Country," a region forged from the most common metal on earth and as old as the planet itself. It speaks of unimaginable ages, when the ores that were so quickly consumed were laid down and ingenious methods devised to wrest the last of the iron from the rock. It describes the workings of ancient miners, the builders of mysterious mounds, rice gatherers, hunters, trappers, explorers, prospectors, miners and immigrant families in search of a new way of life – a procession of peoples whose lives were intertwined in some way with this region and its iron-laden hills.

This is also a story of mining, an art as old as Iron Country itself. At first it was simple, but as human living became more complex it expanded and diversified. Pits dug for jasper, flint and quartz became copper mines. Ways learned to mine copper were used for lead, tin, gold and iron. When Iron Country's ores were first discovered, mining was already a highly sophisticated practice. A thousand or more years of experience had produced tried and tested ways of winning the ore. The men who came to develop the mines of the region were expert technicians, schooled in the arts of stoping, top slicing, caving and a hundred other ways to get the ore out of the ground.

The land they entered abounded in metals and minerals, but it was iron in the form of hematite, a compound of iron and oxygen – ancient rust – that opened the region to mining. The ores were old beyond belief, formed when the first land rose above the primeval waters. All about lay the remnants of this first land: greenstone, jasper, slate and schist, rocks formed during the earliest era of Earth's history, billions of years ago when the planet's crust was still solidifying and much of the world was covered by a tepid sea.

The story of Minnesota's Iron Country begins in this primordial time.

Creation
In a time so distant it is impossible to imagine, land rose above a strange and alien sea. Here and there, islands of cooling lava floated on an ocean of magma while giant meteorites of rock, iron and ice rained down from the sky. Dusty clouds darkened the sun, steam and poisonous gases poured out from the interior and iron mingled with the elements of a world far different from the one we know today.

There passed a very long time. The meteoric bombardment slowed, the dust settled, it rained and water spread across the

A lofty mountain range appeared and with it came the minerals of Iron Country.
ROBERT LAMPPA

planet's surface. Volcanism was intense and lava pillowed beneath boiling waves, molten basalt was turned into greenstone and particles of corroding rock and iron were washed into cracks and crannies in the slowly rising land. A lofty mountain range appeared along the outer edge of a vast horseshoe-shaped island. A large part of North America had made its appearance and with it came the minerals of Iron Country.

One can still make out the outline of this ancient island. Any topographical map of the continent will show it as a vast plateau surrounding Hudson Bay. On some maps it's labeled Laurentian Plateau, on others Hudson Bay Shield, but no matter what it's called, the plateau, which slants gently toward the bay, is the oldest part of the continent. The mountains stretched from the Arctic's Beaufort Sea to the Lake of the Woods and across Minnesota, Wisconsin and Michigan into eastern Canada. Geologists call them the Laurentian Mountains, but they aren't on any map now because they disappeared ages ago. A billion years of wind and rain wore them away until only parts of their rocky iron-rich base remain.

The Vermilion Range

Some of this iron-rich base is seen on the Vermilion Range located in St. Louis and Lake counties. The range is about 25 miles long and a mile or two wide. The heaviest concentrations of iron were located in the vicinities of present day Tower and Ely.

In its original state, the region's iron formation probably contained a fair amount of iron, but it was not yet iron ore. It would take another billion years of erosion and a million or more years of mountain building to squeeze the ancient sediments together and leach out their impurities, creating the high grade Vermilion Range hematite that brought iron mining to Minnesota in the 1880s.[1]

The hematite took the form of "lentil shaped deposits distributed in a complex geology containing several kinds of iron-bearing rock." They were located in a vertical formation of Ely greenstone and "encapsulated within a hard irony rock known as 'jaspelite.'"[2] Nineteenth century mining men labeled it the Soudan formation.

Early mining captains called the hematite deposits "lenses" and took pride in their ability to locate them. The lenses descended vertically to great depths and varied in size and shape. Some are said to have been the size of a pebble, others a hundred feet thick and a half-mile long. The largest, called the "Ely Trough," gave rise to six producing mines.[3]

The Mesabi Range

About a billion years ago, but long after the Laurentian Mountains were gone, another mountain building event began, creating what geologists call the Algoman Mountains.[4] Iron-rich slates and sediments were thrust upward to distances of two or three miles. Twenty miles south of the Vermilion Range, where stands the long granite ridge of the Mesabi, one can imagine a range of snowcapped peaks. Then this second mountain range eroded away. It boggles the mind to think of how long that took.

It was during this long period of Algoman erosion that the Mesabi's Biwabik Iron Formation began to evolve. Around 700 million years ago a shallow sea spread across much of what today are Minnesota, Wisconsin and Michigan. Geologists call it the Animikie Sea. Soluble iron oxides, silica and mud from the eroding mountains thickened the sea's water and gradually settled to its bottom, building beds of iron-rich silt hundreds of feet thick. As the sea dried, new mud and silt covered the beds and during the next 100 million years or so they were compacted, heated and recrystallized by new volcanic intrusions to form the lean magnetic taconite being mined on the Mesabi Range today.[5]

Although the sea didn't last long in terms of geological time, more than a million years would have been needed to create the 700-foot-thick beds of slaty iron, chert and taconite that make up the region's extensive Biwabik Iron Formation.[6] Dipping gently beneath the land's surface to the southeast, it stretches westward to Pokegama Lake in Itasca County and eastward to Birch Lake in St. Louis County, where it disappears beneath a layer of younger rock only to re-emerge near Gunflint Lake on the Canadian border.

Five hundred million years of wind, weather and rain followed and the formation did what all iron does when exposed to the elements. It rusted. Circulating surface waters deposited the rust into folds and fractures in the formation, creating pockets, sometimes very broad pockets, of oxidized iron and silica. In many places the water also dissolved out the silica, leaving only soft, dark iron-rich hematite.[7] This was the Mesabi Merch that made the range famous. No processing was needed. Steam shovels could load it directly into waiting trains for immediate shipment to steel mills.

The Cuyuna Range

It was probably during the time of the Animikie Sea that sands were deposited in what today is Crow Wing County, 40 miles southwest of the Mesabi, creating the quartz lenses often seen in the Cuyuna Iron Formation. Much of the formation is a greenish magnetic slate with an iron content of around 30 percent. The rest consists of cherts, iron carbonates and hematite. Although parts of the Cuyuna Range appear to have a geological past similar to that of the Mesabi, not much is known about the relationship between the two ranges. Exploration in the area that separates them has been scant.

The Cuyuna's iron ore deposits were suspected long before they were discovered. A layer of 15 to 300 feet of glacial drift covered them and the entire area appeared as a relatively flat plain with only a few low hills and many lakes and bogs. Hematite was found "just below the glacial drift in the form of deeply pitched and very irregular lens-like deposits." They were sometimes broad, sometimes narrow, but always irregular and never predictable.[8]

Like the Mesabi, much of the Cuyuna's hematite was formed by circulating surface water. The highest concentrations of iron were usually found near the top of a deposit and the percentage tended to drop as a mine deepened. Good ore was seldom found below a depth of 450 feet. The ores were mostly red and dark brown hydrated hematites. Some contained significant

Ice

Ice Free Corridor

Ice

MINNESOTA

WISCONSIN

Glacial Retreat

About 12,000 years ago in Northern Minnesota, the last remnants of the ice sheet that once covered most of the state were receding. Iron Country was then part of an ice-free corridor that extended well into Canada. It was a treeless and windy barren of melt water, tundra and rock.

amounts of manganese and were much in demand during the first decades of the 20th century.[9]

The Great Ice Sheets

The iron deposits of all three ranges were gradually covered with the sands and gravels of 100 million years of weather and erosion. Seas advanced and retreated leaving behind silts and muds. Soils were enriched by the remains of a thousand species of bacteria, mold, mushrooms, green plants and strange creatures. Eons passed. Then the surface materials were ripped away by the first of a series of advancing sheets of ice.

No one knows how many glaciers there were, but geologists tell us at least four pushed across Iron Country during the last million years. They describe four glacial epochs, each lasting something like 50,000 years. The Nebraskan began a million years ago; the Kansan, 475,000 years ago; the Illinoian, 300,000 years ago; and the Wisconsin, 60,000 years ago. Most scientists believe there is no reason to think there aren't more coming.

The ice is thought to have been as much as 1 to 2 miles thick at the height of each glacial advance. The enormous weight and force of each of these slowly moving sheets of

ice were enough to destroy most of the features of the previous landscape. The already worn-down mountains of Iron Country were scraped clean of surface materials and only the hardest of rock formations – the granite, jasper and taconite – avoided complete destruction. An entire land surface was picked up by the moving ice and deposited hundreds of miles to the south. Likewise, surface materials from the north were deposited in Iron Country in the form of rounded boulders, gravel and clay. The glacial debris covered the ice-scraped rock and iron formations and formed an entirely new landscape.

Each glacial epoch seems to have been followed by a long period of mild climate lasting thousands of years. The ice of the last glacier is thought to have melted away something like 11,000 years ago. Time enough for humans to enter the region, hunt the animals, fight wars, mine the iron and build towns, highways and airports. It is doubtful anything like this followed previous ice sheets, but if it had, all evidence would probably have been ground into dust by the glacier that followed. We appear to be in the early stages of a mild period now. We are less than 12,000 years removed from the ice and during that time occurred all the events we know of as history.

The First Iron Rangers

Remnants of the last glacier were still around when the first humans arrived in Iron Country. Very little is known about these first people. What is clear is this: On a geologic time scale, the entire period of human occupation would seem no more than a fraction of a second and the history of Iron Country is even shorter. It covers a period of no more than the last 350 years. Humans had been in Iron Country for at least 8,000 years before history began.

History is a study of written records. The period of time humans occupied a given region but kept no written records is referred to as "prehistory." Although much has recently been learned about prehistoric peoples in northeast Minnesota, the story of Iron Country's earliest inhabitants remains somewhat less certain than its geology.

What we do know about these people is pieced together from artifacts found near the tops of hills, along the shores of lakes and streams and close to exposures of iron, jasper and quartz. Ancient fire pits, mysterious stone hammers, knives of copper and quartz, jaspelite points and scrapers and thousands of pieces of broken pottery have been discovered and identified by archaeologists. From their work emerges a fascinating story.

The Time of the Hunters (6,000-12,000 Years Ago)

Twelve thousand years ago, Iron Country was a treeless, windy barren of tundra and rock. The Wisconsin ice sheet was waning but there was still enough ice around to block the natural flow of water to the north. Shallow lakes of meltwater covered parts of the region. Most of iron country was free of ice, but not far away two glacial lobes remained. One covered much of what today is Lake Superior and the other

was a few hundred miles to the northwest in Rainy River country.[10]

Mosses and lichens growing along the shores of the region's shallow meltwater lakes were a natural attraction for migrating herds of caribou. Along with the caribou came the first humans – clans of hunters carrying their belongings with them as they moved. Using carefully crafted stone-pointed darts and throwing sticks, they hunted with a skill and brilliance unmatched to this day. Their numbers were small, they were constantly on the move and the animals they hunted were undoubtedly the focus of their lives. They had no use for heavy objects or permanent building materials – they valued only those items that they could carry with them as they moved. Their stories are forgotten, they left no monuments to mark their passing.

But they did leave signs that tell us they were here: the remains of a few campsites, a

Almost 12,000 years ago, along with herds of caribou, the first humans appeared in Iron Country, carrying their belongings with them. Living in clans, they hunted with a skill and brilliance unmatched to this day. ROBERT LAMPPA

Explorer George Stuntz was convinced formations like these on the Embarrass River were the remains of prehistoric stone dams. **Bottom:** This copper point was found near Pelican Lake. It is of a type associated with an Eastern Archaic people believed to have been in the region as early as 5,000 years ago. They differed from the hunters in both tools and reasons for being in Iron Country and may have been the first miners to inhabit the area. PHOTOS BY AUTHOR

small number of stone points of excellent workmanship and some scrapers for tanning hides. Scant evidence, but enough for archaeologists to say with authority that someone was hunting big game in Iron Country more than 10,000 years ago. Experts think that these hunters might have been descendants of earlier peoples who crossed to North America from Siberia when sea levels were lower. They call them paleo-people and identify their descendants as modern day Native Americans.[11]

Iron Country's hematite outcroppings and bluffs of taconite probably had their uses, even in those ancient times. From their heights, hunting parties could track the migrating herds. Although their time in Iron Country was passing, the hunters could not have been aware of it. To them the great mountain of ice was as permanent as the hills of hematite and the rainswept treeless tundra. But slowly, imperceptibly, the herds were moving north. So were the hunters.

The First Miners
(3,000-6,000 Years Ago)

About 8,000 years ago, the climate changed abruptly. It became warmer and drier. Meltwater disappeared and lakes and streams dropped to levels far below what they are today. The warm dry period seems to have lasted for a very long time, possibly thousands of years.[12]

At some unknown time during this long warm dry spell, the first Iron Country miners arrived. These people, called Eastern

Archaic or, more romantically, "Old Copper Indians," differed from the earlier hunters in both tools and reasons for being here. Artifacts associated with them include finely polished stone gouges for woodworking and an array of hunting points, axes, scrapers, knives, punches and drills of copper, quartz and jaspelite. They appear to have known how to make dugout canoes, which were probably used to reach Iron Country from some unknown place east of Lake Superior, hundreds, possibly thousands, of miles away.[13]

Anthropologists do not dispute the fact that Lake Vermilion was part of a navigable waterway connecting the Great Lakes and Lake Winnipeg, even during times of lower water levels.[14] The arrival of these ancient miners in Iron Country seems to be tied to this water corridor and the quartz and jasper outcroppings of the Vermilion Range. The

copper for their tools, however, appears to have been mined in northern Wisconsin and upper Michigan. The Eastern Archaic people were the first in North or South America to make metal tools – at about the same time that the ancient Egyptians were using copper for the same purposes. However, while the Egyptians progressed from copper to bronze, the use of copper for tools in the region surrounding Lake Superior seems to mysteriously stop about 3,000 years ago.

These people are not just recognized for their use of copper, they are also noted for a distribution of jaspelite points and tools found all along the water corridor from northern Wisconsin to the Winnipeg River. Jaspelite has been described as an extremely hard "jaspery taconite" found in abundance on the Vermilion Range. Beyond this particular distribution, the use of jaspelite for tools is not often seen.[15]

North of the Soudan Mine near Tower, 1,000 feet or so from the shore of Lake Vermilion, is a mysterious excavation into the face of an outcropping of jaspelite. It was discovered in 1865 by Duluth land surveyor George R. Stuntz, who was in the area prospecting for gold just after the Civil War. In 1884, he reported his find to the Minnesota Academy of Natural Sciences.

"On the north side of the bluff in Section 27, Town 42, Range 15, is an excavation made in solid jasper, one of the hardest rocks known, and exceedingly tough and consequently difficult to break. The depth of this cut is not known, as the sides have given away and the pit is partially filled. Here masses of rock, from 3 to 10 cubic yards in size, have been detached and removed out of the cut to the dump. There are no marks to indicate how these immense blocks of jasper were detached, or what mechanical appliances were used to hoist them out of the cut and place them on the banks…. A gravel walk is still visible and in tolerable repair, leading from the cut to the dump. This was evidently built for carrying out the materials from the mine."[16]

At the west end of Lake Vermilion's Stuntz Bay he found a second excavation.

"About 40 rods from the canoe … a quartz vein, 8 feet in width, with slaty iron walls on each side. Subsequent explorations of this vein showed the east end of it to have

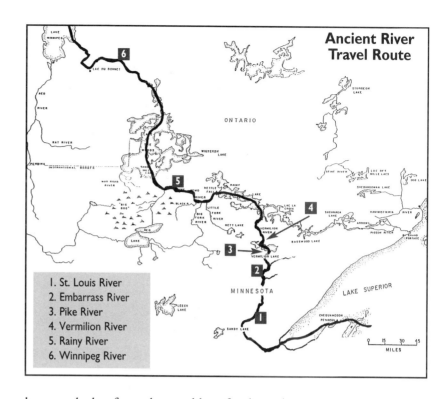

Ancient River Travel Route

1. St. Louis River
2. Embarrass River
3. Pike River
4. Vermilion River
5. Rainy River
6. Winnipeg River

been worked as far as they could get for the water. I ran a stick as far as 10 feet below the natural surface of the ground. This trench had been worked for 30 or 40 rods but had been filled in, either by nature, or by the operators, with intent to cover up their work. The masses of rock had been tumbled back."[17]

These and other discoveries convinced Stuntz that "at a very remote age" a "race of semi-civilized people" constructed dams and improved the waterways leading to Lake Vermilion and the "northeastern portions of the state and Canada" where they mined for "ochers, precious metals and copper."[18]

In a 1974 publication, Winnipeg University anthropologist Jack Steinbring, who made a study of the distribution of prehistoric copper and jaspelite artifacts along Manitoba and Ontario waterways, suggested that Stuntz's discoveries be given a closer look.

According to Professor Steinbring, "There is evidence – the distribution of Lake Superior artifacts and the unique oolitic jasper, for example – that the historic waterways between Lake Superior and Lake Winnipeg were utilized in very ancient times."[19] Oolitic jasper is another name for jaspelite.

Jaspelite is hard and when broken holds a very sharp edge. It seems an ideal point for an ancient hunting device known as an atl-atl. The device consisted of a throwing stick and a dart made up of three parts: a stone

The ancient St. Louis-Vermilion river travel route in Northeast Minnesota connected Lake Superior to Lake Winnipeg. Copper and red jaspelite artifacts found along this water route indicate that it was used for travel in very early times. Red jaspelite is found in abundance on the Vermilion Iron Range.

There are several prehistoric burial mounds in the vicinity of Esquagama Lake near Biwabik. Marvin Lamppa

point, foreshaft and main shaft. The stone point was fixed to the foreshaft and the foreshaft fit into a carefully carved out hollow on the main shaft. When the dart was thrown and an animal hit, the main shaft dropped off and could be easily retrieved for future use. Because the shaft was short, a hard sharp jaspelite point might have increased the effectiveness of the dart. The search for materials for a better point for an atl-atl might well have helped bring the first miners to Iron Country thousands of years ago.

The Mound Builders
(350-3,000 Years Ago)

During the 1870s and '80s, when mineral exploration was just beginning, numerous dome-shaped mounds, clearly of human construction, were encountered.

"Indian mounds," as they were then called, were common all over the country and attracted only mild attention from people far more interested in seeking fortunes in iron, silver and gold.

Mining, lumbering and the clearing of land for towns and farms obliterated most of the mounds. However, a few can still be seen. There are several in the vicinity of Esquagama Lake south of Biwabik. One of these mounds must have been an impressive sight when first encountered by George Stuntz in the 1860s.

"It was about 20 feet in diameter and 7 feet high … on an open plain" and "so situated as to command the earliest rays of the rising sun above the Mesabi-Watchu" (the big man hills). In his 1885 paper to the Minnesota Academy of Natural Sciences, Stuntz concluded that a "semi-civilized people" lived in the area, "cultivated the soil, planted fruit trees and oak trees," cultivated the rice in the lakes, improved navigation on the rivers and "left lasting monuments of their engineering skill."[20]

Unfortunately no one will ever know all that Stuntz saw in those early years. However, today we know a whole lot about the people who made the mounds, thanks to the science and scholarship of archaeology. Until 1932, when anthropologists Albert Jenks and Lloyd Wilford established a field research program at the University of Minnesota, archaeology in the state amounted to little more than random collection and labeling of artifacts picked off the ground.

In 1940, Wilford carefully excavated a portion of a large mound at Lake Vermilion's Pike Bay and laid open a previously unknown version of prehistoric mound building.[21] A unique mound-building people once lived at the lake. Twenty-two years later, excavations by Gary Hume, Elden Johnson and Timothy Fisk expanded our understanding of these people. Extensive

archaeological work in northeast Minnesota during the last 10 or 15 years produced an even clearer picture of Iron Country's mound-building past.

Recent archaeology uncovered two phases to northeast Minnesota mound building: an early Woodland or Laurel phase that lasted from about 1,000 B.C. to A.D. 1,000 and a terminal woodland phase from 1,000 to A.D. 1,650. About 3,000 years ago, the very dry climate of Eastern Archaic times changed to the climate we have today. Our present forest, with its pines, balsam, aspen, maple and birch came into being. There were heavy rains, water levels rose and wild rice spread across the lakes.[22]

At some point, after this climate change, a new way of living – and possibly a new people – moved into the region. Small villages appeared at Lake Vermilion, Esquagama, Rainy River and other places. The term Woodland is often used to identify this village-living, which spread rapidly across the rivers and lakes of today's eastern United States and Canada. It is distinguished by two features: 1) the construction of earthen mounds for human burial; and 2) the invention and use of pottery. In order for these two cultural features to occur, a more settled lifestyle was necessary. Wild rice allowed this settled living.[23]

The Woodland Laurel people continued to hunt and fish as did the people before them and their tools and weapons show this. Like the Eastern Archaic miners, the Laurel people manufactured a wide assortment of scrapers, knives, gouges, axes, drills and punches. One thing was different. They seldom, if at all, made any of these tools out of copper. And one thing was the same. They continued to use the atl-atl as their main hunting weapon – we know this from studies of their projectile points.[24]

Probably their most outstanding accomplishment was the use of pottery. They made and used thousands of peculiar wide-mouthed pots with pointed bottoms. Broken pieces of pots like this have been found in many places throughout northern Minnesota. They were made by hand-coiling local clays that had a small amount of sand mixed in them for temper. Archaeologists can tell a lot about a people once they begin making pottery. Changes in style, methods

of production and decoration can be used to date sites and to determine cultural relationships within a given site.

The Laurel people were Iron Country's first mound builders. Their mounds were cemeteries for the dead. The largest mound in Minnesota is credited to the Laurel people and can be found near the Canadian border on the south bank of the Rainy River about 15 miles west of International Falls. Known as the Grand Mound, it is about 130 feet in diameter and almost 25 feet high. It's been estimated that the mound might contain the remains of as many as 5,000 individuals.[25]

The mound wasn't built in a day. Although estimates vary, the consensus seems to be that construction began around 200 B.C., about the time Rome was fighting Carthage in the Punic Wars. It was in use as a final resting place for a very long time – maybe as long as 1,500 years.

Lake Vermilion's Pike Bay Mound is thought to be even older and may well be the oldest excavated mound in northeast Minnesota.[26] It is located only a half mile below the Pike River Falls on the south shore of the bay and was excavated in 1940 by archaeologist Lloyd Wilford. Prior to excavation, the mound was about 65 feet in diameter and 7 feet high. Digging revealed more than 6,000 pieces of broken pottery, 12 projectile points, the remains of three fire hearths, some fragments of copper, the bones of a bison and 32 human bones arranged for primary and secondary burial.[27]

In primary burials the dead were interred at or below ground level, sometimes in a pit. Often the bodies were placed in a sitting position with the head resting on updrawn knees. In a secondary burial the dead appear to have been interred somewhere else first and later moved to the mound in the form of what we call "bundle burials." While artifacts often accompany primary burials, secondary or "bundle burials" have none and are, in fact, usually incomplete.

These "bundle burials" puzzled early investigators. What could possibly have caused these ancient people to exhume their dead and go through the trouble of carrying their bones to a second place of burial? After all, these were food gathering people and gathering food takes a whole lot of time.

The pigment for ancient pictographs at Lac la Croix is believed to be red ochre, a material found in abundance on Minnesota's iron ranges.
MARVIN LAMPPA

Why did they spend the precious little time they had left bringing the bones of their dead to these mounds? They must have been highly motivated.

Early theories about Minnesota mounds included such notions as, maybe the mound marked the site of a battle or a massacre. After it was over the dead were simply piled up and dirt thrown over them. Some people thought these mounds had to do with ancient cannibal rites. Certainly this would account for the way some of the bundles of bones were arranged and the fact that many of the bodies had parts missing.

An answer to this puzzling phenomenon is suggested by history. Early European accounts of the way the Huron and Algonquin Indians lived include descriptions of a practice referred to as the "Feast of the Dead."[28] They laid their dead out in the open, sometimes on wooden platforms or on scaffolds. Every 10 or 12 years, a gathering of tribal members took place at one of the villages. An elaborate ceremony followed and there was dancing, feasting and gift giving. As part of the ceremony, young men of the tribe would cut down the dead from their scaffolds. Some of the bones would be cooked. The rest would be tied together in bundles and eventually carried off to a place of mass burial. There they would be covered with a mound of dirt.

Sometimes when peace was reached between warring tribes or an alliance was made, members of the involved tribes gathered at a given place, carrying with them the bones of their dead ancestors. A "Feast of the Dead" ceremony followed and the bones of each tribe's dead were laid together in mass burial as a symbol of unity. The result was an earthen mound. Radisson and Groseilliers witnessed just such a feast in the 1650s. According to Radisson it was hosted by the Sioux and "18 Indian nations" participated.[29]

The fact that the ceremony occurred among many different tribes leads one to suspect the custom was ancient, leading back, possibly, to a time of common ancestors. To Europeans, the ritual seemed barbaric, but to native people it was sacred and confirmed a common belief. Placing the dead on a scaffold allowed the animals of the forest to reclaim the spirit and body of the hunter, who had lived by taking the lives and spirit of animals. The sharing of bones of tribal ancestors was more than a simple agreement among the living. The mound signified a common bond, the bringing together of different peoples as one. The practice faded quickly after contact with Europeans. Could the mounds of Iron Country be the remains of an ancient and long forgotten version of this practice?

The Laurel people are thought to have appeared first at Lake Vermilion, after which they migrated northward to Rainy Lake and eventually into Manitoba. Where they came from continues to be debated by scholars and their connection to other mound building peoples remains unclear.[30]

The Terminal Woodland Peoples
(1000-1650 A.D.)

Beginning about 1000 A.D. there seems to have been a rise in population.

Three new mound building peoples moved into the region and established numerous villages all across Iron Country. All displayed a continued preoccupation with the dead through mound building and all are thought to have been heavily dependent on harvests of wild rice. Because of their globular pots with constricted necks and flaring rims, archaeologists have little trouble identifying terminal woodland sites. No longer was clay coiled by hand. Instead an entire pot was formed in a basket. Because each of the new peoples decorated their pots differently, it is easy to tell one from the other.[31]

It has been suggested that the first of these new arrivals, the Blackduck people, might be culturally related to the forefathers of Ojibway people living in northeast Minnesota today. The second of these cultures, the Selkirk, are believed to be ancestors of the Cree and the third, the Sandy Lake people, are thought to be ancestors of the Assiniboin.[32]

During the terminal woodland period, two revolutionary innovations appeared in Iron Country: the bow and arrow and the birch-bark canoe. Archaeologists notice distinctly smaller projectile points – small unnotched triangles of chipped flint at most terminal sites – a good indication that the bow and arrow had come into use.[33] The birch-bark canoe soon proved to be the most practical water device ever invented. Light, portable and seaworthy, it carried heavy loads over long distances and, because it was made of materials of the forest, it was easily repaired or even replaced.

The canoe and bow changed woodland ways. With birch-bark canoes and armed with bows and arrows, hunters from Mille Lacs, Esquagama and Lake Vermilion were able to reach the western prairie for buffalo hunts. Bones of these animals have turned up among the mounds of Iron Country. The bow proved an extremely effective weapon for hunting big game and its continued use by Indian hunters even after firearms were brought in is well documented. But it was the birch-bark canoe that brought in competing Indian hunting parties and products of European trade, precipitating years of sporadic intertribal warfare and population change. The canoe also brought the keepers of journals and records, the writers of history, to Iron Country.

When first described in journals, the inheritors of woodland ways were already a changed people. The Ojibway and Cree were engaged in trapping and the Assiniboin, pushed out of the region by competing Dakota, were making their hunts for buffalo near Lake Winnipeg. There, fur trader Alexander Henry recorded their continued use of mounds for secondary burial.[34]

Spoken traditions of other tribes suggest that they too occupied portions of Iron Country at some time in the prehistoric past. The old speakers of the Cheyenne talked about a time when their ancestors lived among the lakes of a great eastern forest. The Blackfeet spoke the language of the tribes of the Great Lakes and the prairie Sioux once lit their fires on the shores of Iron Country's lakes.[35]

There was enough wild rice to keep people around for rather long periods of time. The Cheyenne, Assiniboin, Blackfeet, prairie Sioux and other tribes may all have called the region home at one time or another. They differed in their languages and the way they designed their pots, but they hunted, fished and gathered rice in much the same way, probably the way their woodland ancestors once did.

If there is an outstanding feature to any of these prehistoric cultures, it is the fact that they were highly successful. These ancient peoples didn't do much to change their ways because they didn't have to. Eastern Archaic culture lasted 4,000 years, Woodland another 2,000. By comparison it has been a mere 300 years since the first traders and missionaries introduced the people of Iron Country to European ways and changed their lives forever. ■

Fur trader Alexander Henry, who passed through the region in the 1760s, recorded use of mounds for secondary burial. NORTHEAST MINNESOTA HISTORICAL CENTER

CHAPTER 2

The Time of the Traders

When the first Europeans arrived in North America they found a vast network of trade already in place and a diverse people well schooled in the intricacies of barter. Along the waterways of the continent's interior from the Atlantic coast to the Rocky Mountains and beyond flowed the goods of pre-European America: pipestone, salt, flint fire striking stones, copper from Lake Superior, obsidian from the Rocky Mountains, tobacco from the fields of the Tionontati; and jaspelite, quartz and red ochre from the monadnocks (isolated rock masses rising above surrounding landscapes) of Iron Country.

The heavily forested region north and west of Lake Superior was far from an isolated backwater at the time of contact. The Winnipeg, Pigeon, St. Louis, Savanna, Vermilion, Mississippi, Little Fork and Rainy rivers were routes for travel and trade. For a thousand summers or more, artifacts of trade were carried across the Saganaga and down the Kawishiwi. Exotic stones and tools of hammered copper uncovered at Mille Lacs, Rainy, Vermilion and Pelican lakes bear witness to this trade. In 1865, explorer George Stuntz saw what he believed were stone dams and improved channels on the Embarrass River.[1] In 1936, 20 "arrowheads" of black obsidian were found on the north side of the Mesabi's Esquagama Lake. Obsidian is native to the Rocky Mountains more than a thousand miles away.[2]

The Beginning of the
Fur Trade (1550-1650)

Tribal tradition suggests that news traveled fast along the trade lanes and, by the time Quebec was established in 1608, news of thunder sticks and wonderful manufactured items had probably already reached many of the tribal peoples of the interior. Spoken traditions of the diverse tribes of the Great

Lakes describe the beginning of the fur trade in a variety of ways. They speak of "journeys to the villages of bearded men," "visits to the place of men wearing hats," trips to the lodges of "those who carry sticks." The consistent thing about these stories is that it was always the native trader who did the traveling, not the Frenchman.

Long before the founding of Quebec, Basque fishermen traders on the Gulf of St. Lawrence quickly learned that it was easier and more profitable to trade inexpensive European items for furs than to fish. When Samuel de Champlain arrived in North America in 1603 as part of a French government-backed fur trading expedition there were already fur posts along the gulf's shores and they had been carrying on trade with the nearby tribal peoples for 50 years.

Although Champlain is sometimes credited with organizing the trade, it's clear he had interests beyond furs. He explored everywhere he could and took notes on everything he saw – animals, plants, rocks, minerals and any native peoples he encountered. After traveling up the St. Lawrence River until he was stopped by three miles of rapids, he was told by natives that a vast sea lay to the west. Convinced China was not far away, he named the rapids Lachine (China Rapids), founded Quebec and laid the foundations for French colonization of North America.

He also made enemies of the Iroquois. In 1609, while exploring the country south of Lake Ontario, his Algonquin, Huron and Montagnai guides were attacked by an Iroquois war party. Although the attack was aimed only at the natives, Champlain took out his arquebus (an early matchlock firearm) and drove the Iroquois off, killing two of their chiefs and one of the warriors. The shots set a pattern of demographics that held for the next 150 years.

During the time of the fur trade, the Native American birch-bark canoe became the supersonic transports of their time, carrying trade goods from eastern Canada to the inland posts and returning with bales of furs that made merchants fabulous fortunes.
PHOTO BY AUTHOR

The Iroquois never forgot. They blocked every attempt by the French and their tribal allies to expand their trade and trap lines into the Ohio Valley. French traders, missionaries and settlers suffered torture and death, while pelts from the fur rich regions south of the Great Lakes flowed steadily to posts of the British and Dutch. The French, forced to confine their activities to regions north of the lakes, had to rely on Native American "middlemen" to expand their trade to the fur rich interior. These middlemen were probably the first representatives of New France to arrive in Iron Country.

The summer fur fairs of the St. Lawrence, transplanted from the market towns of France, combined festival with business and became the normal way of trade with the tribes. First there was the smoking of pipes followed by formal proclamations, then came the speeches and tables loaded with food, the entertainment, music and dance. Sometimes during, but more often after negotiations, trading brandy and wine appeared on the tables and the gathering ended in a wild free-for-all. There was "singing, shouting and whooping," as natives and Europeans alike "ran through the avenues of the commons."[3]

Pelts brought to these gatherings found ready markets in Europe and in 1627 Cardinal du Richelieu, chief minister of France, formed a "Company of 100 Associates," to take full control of the North American trade. The company was really a government-run partnership of aristocratic business investors formed to raise money for the crown and curb the trade of Huguenot merchants. Limits were placed on the number of people who could trade and licenses were required for anyone going into Indian territory.

However, during the 1640s the profit potential of fur was so great that hundreds of independent traders without licenses set out across the Great Lakes to find the inland native villages. These unlicensed traders were known as *couriers des bois*. They were often joined by Jesuit missionaries. The Jesuit order held great political power in Quebec and more than a mild interest in furs.[4]

The furs, of course, were obtained by the tribal people and the French did everything in their power to win their favor, for they were indispensable to the trade. They wanted the products of the French and were willing to go a long way to get them. But the French wanted good relations even more, for it gave them access to the interior, complete with canoes, guides and paddlers. This meant two things: more profits in furs and the opportunity to explore for a northwest passage through the continent.

At that time, many Europeans had the idea that China and India could be reached by sailing on some natural passage through the North American Continent. The French suspected that the passage lay at the far end of the Great Lakes that they were just discovering.

From 1740-1760, Lake Vermilion was a war zone, as the Ojibway people fought the Sioux for control of the rich hunting and wild rice grounds. ELY-WINTON HISTORICAL SOCIETY COLLECTION AT THE IRON RANGE RESEARCH CENTER

They found it hard to believe that the Great Lakes were really fresh-water lakes. They were sure the waters would lead them through the continent to the ocean beyond. They were constantly testing the waters for salt and checking for signs of a tide. Even after the uppermost of the Great Lakes, Lake Superior, had been crossed, many Frenchmen remained convinced that the "Vermilion Sea of the West" was not far away.

Tribal Peoples of the Upper Great Lakes (1640-1670)

When the first French explorers reached Lake Huron in 1640, the total native population of the upper Great Lakes region was probably no more than 100,000. There might have been 10 or 11 different tribes scattered across the 200,000-plus square miles of countryside surrounding Lake Huron, Lake Michigan and Lake Superior. They spoke dialects of three basic languages: Iroquoian, Algonkian and Siouan.

The Huron people spoke Iroquoian. They were close associates of the French, but bitter enemies of their close relatives, the Iroquois, who lived south of Lake Ontario

and traded with the Dutch and English. Huron villages were located across the lake from the Iroquois and along the northern shoreline of Lake Huron to the west. By the 1650s they were already serving as middlemen for the French trade on the two lakes. This meant that they were the transporters of trade goods and furs between remote tribes and French fur depots at Montreal, Three Rivers and Quebec.

Most of the upper lakes tribes – the Miami, Sauk, Fox, Menominee, Potawatomi, Ottawa, Cree and Ojibway – spoke dialects of the Algonkian tongue. The Ojibway are called "Chippewa" in later treaties made with the U.S. government and in Minnesota go by that name today.

The Ojibway were the most numerous of all the tribes on the Great Lakes. They were also the least organized. They had no formal tribal structure like the Huron and other tribal people. Instead they were divided and subdivided into numerous independent clans. Some of these clans sided with the Algonquins and Hurons in wars against the Iroquois. The clans of the Ojibway were constantly on the move and Ojibway wigwams could be found almost anywhere in the thickly forested countryside between Lake Nipissing and Lake Superior.

In 1640, a number of these clans were encamped at the Sault Ste. Marie (Saint Marys Rapids), most likely because it was easy to catch fish in the rapids. The French who first encountered them in that place named them Saulteurs (people of the rapids). By the 1670s, these Saulteurs were helping French merchants carry goods to native villages at the far end of Lake Superior, where they traded the goods for trapping rights and pelts.[5]

The Alliance (1660-1730)

The Siouan speaking tribes included the Winnebago of Lake Michigan and the legendary Seven Council Fires: the Yankton, Yanktonnai, Santee, Teton, Oglalla, Sisseton and Wahpeton tribes living south and west of Lake Superior. The land they occupied was vast and stretched from the shores of the lake all the way to the Great Plains and beyond. They referred to themselves as Dakota (or Lakota), "people of the alliance."[6] The first maps made of the region mark Lake Superior as the Lake of the Sioux. Sioux was a word the French learned from their Saulteur canoe men who were having mixed experiences with these people. When Saulteurs said the word it sounded more like nadouessioux and meant "like the snakes" (Iroquois) in the Ojibway language. There had been years of bad blood between the Ojibway and Iroquois. The Sioux were a force to be reckoned with and the French bent over backward trying to win their good will. The Ojibway didn't.

The Dakota still had villages at the far end of Lake Superior when the first Jesuit missionaries arrived. Father Claude Allouez noted "hostile Sioux" at the mouth of the St. Louis River in 1665, but a few years before, some had been visited by explorers Radisson and Groseilliers who described them as "the Nation of the Beefe."

According to Radisson's journal of 1660, the two explorers found themselves "in a town where there were great 'cabbans' covered with skins and other close matts. They told us that there were 7,000 men and this we believed…. In their country there are mines of copper, of pewter and of lead.…

The people stay not there, all the year; they retire in winter toward the woods of the North, where they kill a quantity of Castors (French for beaver).…"[7]

The Dakota wanted the guns, axes and kettles of the French and in the summer of 1660 Radisson and Groseilliers returned to Montreal with a large number of beaver pelts and a lot of enthusiasm. Instead of welcoming them and listening to their report, the French governor threw Groseilliers in jail for exploring without a license and confiscated their pelts. This alienated the two men and they went to England with their notes and maps. The result was the formation of a rival fur company, the British Hudson's Bay Company, chartered in 1670.

There are reliable descriptions of Dakota people living in Iron Country during the period 1670-1735. They are found in the journals of French traders, missionaries and military personnel who had dealings with them. The French used the Mississippi River to divide the Dakota into two groups, the Sioux of the West and Sioux of the East. The earliest French contacts were with the Sioux of the East – the Issanti (Santee Dakota). Maps drawn in 1697 and 1702 name 10 Eastern Sioux villages and locate seven of them in the vicinity of the Cuyuna Range.[8]

The largest of these villages, Izatys, was near the outlet of Mille Lacs Lake and, according to French trader Pierre-Charles Le Sueur, was composed of "about 300 cabanes (cabins)." The people of Izatys grew no corn and lived by hunting and harvesting wild rice. They called themselves Medewakanton, people of the lake of the spirits, their name for Mille Lacs. They called their hunting grounds Minnesota, or "Mini-sota," which Lakota speakers translate as "smoky water," so this was their land of smoky water.[9]

Although the French maps show no Santee villages on either the Mesabi or Vermilion ranges, tradition has it that both were once home to Dakota people. Their villages are reputed to have been located at Lake Vermilion and Esquagama. However, these Dakota might not have been Santee. The villages have been described as groupings of long narrow lodges made of poles and bark and lived in only during the summer months. After the ricing season was over, they were abandoned for the winter

hunts and during this time Dakota families lived in tepees made of animal skins.

In 1698 they had no horses or firearms and, armed with stone axes and bows, they hunted on foot and traveled the lakes and streams in tiny "two-man canoes." Le Sueur wrote, "their light birch-bark canoes are almost impossible for anyone to use who are not accustomed to them." The Dakota could take these craft deep into the marshes and small lakes where enemies in larger vessels could not follow. Their small size was an identifying mark, and Dakota fleets, when seen on area lakes, were easy to recognize.[10]

In the early 1660s, Sioux country was described by French explorer Nicolas Perrot as "nothing but lakes and marshes full of wild oats (wild rice); these are separated … by narrow tongues of land … not more than 30 or 40 paces at most, and sometimes five or six, or a little more." According to Perrot, a Huron war party invaded the country and 3,000 Sioux warriors were assembled to meet them. The Hurons hid themselves in the tall wild rice. Unable to see them, the Sioux attached "trade bells" to their fishing nets and stretched them across the narrow tongues of land. Every time a Huron warrior tried to crawl out of the thick rice, the bells would ring and he was promptly captured.[11]

The French were continually impressed with the bow and arrow skills of the Dakota. "They could hit a duck on the wing," said Le Sueur. It appears that Santee hunters joined their western cousins in buffalo hunts all the way to the western plains. Buffalo bones turned up in archaeological digs at Lake Vermilion suggest a long history of extended hunts to the open country of the West.[12]

Evidence of Dakota occupation of other parts of Iron Country is scant. Bois Forte spoken tradition tells of war roads leading westward from Lake Vermilion to the villages of the Sioux. The Sioux referred to in their legends might not have been Santee Dakota. Maps produced for French expeditions in the 1730s mark the upper region of the St. Louis River as "Sioux Country."[13] Duluth pioneer R.E. Carey, in an 1870 history of the region, said Bureau of Indian Affairs agent C.N. Webb was told by "an old Nett Lake Ojibway born on Esquagama Lake" that a large native village existed there at the time of his birth. The village, he said, dated back

to the time of Sioux occupation. Carey was convinced that mounds discovered near the lake were left by the Sioux. Esquagama is, however, a Chippewa word and means "the Last Water," referring to the last of five small lakes used by travelers to cross the Mesabi-Watchu, the Big Man Hills.[14]

War in the Woods (1655-1763)

To the north of the Dakota villages were the nations of the Cree and Assiniboin. The Cree spoke an Algonkian language closely related to Ojibway and the Assiniboin were a Siouan-speaking tribe believed to have splintered away from the Dakota of northern Minnesota in late prehistoric times. When first seen by Europeans in 1670, they were living near Lake Winnipeg, where they hunted for buffalo. Sometime prior to 1699, hostilities between the two tribes brought a combined eastern and western Dakota war party to the "edge of the sea" where "people with robes" sold them "metal knives."[15]

There is little doubt that the "sea" was Lake Winnipeg and the "people with robes" were Hudson's Bay traders. The Cree, who were trading with the company and receiving some firearms for their furs, could not have appreciated the arrival of these strangers. This and the fact that the war party raided not only Assiniboin encampments, but, apparently, some Cree hunting camps as well, gave the Dakota a formidable enemy. The result was a Cree-Assiniboin alliance and a long smoldering war against the Dakota. Armed with English "fusils," the alliance went on the offensive.

The Cree advanced southward to the shores of Lake Superior and Rainy Lake and the Assiniboin moved up the Rat River and occupied the Lake of the Woods. The region between their encampments and Dakota villages to the south became an extensive no man's land where few people dared travel. The Warroad, Big Fork, Little Fork and Vermilion rivers became travel routes for war parties on both sides, in other words "war roads." The Warroad River in northwestern Minnesota still retains the old label.[16]

In 1665, driven westward from Lake Huron by Iroquois raiders, French-supported Huron and Ottawa traders attempted to establish a fur post at Lake Superior's Chequamegon Bay and extend their trade to

the south and west, but were driven off by repeated Dakota raids. A mission established in the vicinity at about the same time was also closed. The French, frustrated in their attempt to establish good relations with the Dakota, placed a hold on all trade beyond the western tip of Lake Superior.[17]

Fifteen years later another trading village was established at this strategic place, this time by Saultier Ojibway who had been migrating westward following the south shore of the lake. At about the same time, small groups of northern Ojibway trappers began to be seen along the north shore of Lake Superior. These people probably had moved west along with the French traders who had set up posts at Nipigon and at the mouth of the Kaministiquia River.[18]

In 1852, William Warren, who collected the spoken history of some of the Ojibway elders of his time, said this about the northern Ojibway, "A considerable body of the northern Ojibway are denominated by their fellow-tribesmen … men of the thick fir woods, derived from the interminable forests … which cover their hunting grounds. Their early French discoverers named them 'Bois Fortes'…. Another section forming the most northern branch of this tribe are denominated … 'Swamp People.'" Warren noted eight generations of separation between northern Ojibway and the southern bands, "So great was the separation that subtle differences could be detected in their language."[19]

Some northern Ojibway warriors joined the Cree in their attacks on Dakota villages and hunting parties. The Dakota responded with furious raids against any Ojibway or Cree camp they could find. The threat of tribal warfare spreading eastward across Lake Superior brought a representative of the government in Quebec, Daniel Greysolon, Sieur Du Lhut, and four well-armed soldiers to the west end of the lake in 1679. During the summer of that year, they visited three Santee villages and proclaimed the Dakota subjects of the King of France, promising them French protection and trade.

Du Lhut then called the Assiniboin and Ojibway to the mouth of the St. Louis River for peace talks with the Santee Dakota. The city of Duluth gets its name from this French soldier and it has been suggested that

the peace council was held within, or very close to the present day city limits.[20] The talks didn't stop the Cree and Assiniboin war parties, but it did bring about a peace agreement between the Santee and the Lake Superior Ojibway. The agreement allowed Ojibway trappers access to the fur rich Santee hunting grounds north and west of the lake in return for a share of the trade goods received for the furs. The peace was to last until 1736, well more than 50 years.[21]

During this time, the Lake Superior Ojibway, like the Huron traders before them, became the main carriers of furs on the lake. Their large canoes, sometimes 40 feet long and manned by as many as 20 paddlers, could occasionally be seen as far east as Detroit. The French traders worked closely with them. Marriages took place between the Frenchmen and the daughters of the Ojibway and lucrative trade pacts were finalized with celebration and ceremony. Ojibway spoken tradition refers to prosperous times during the early years of the trade. These were probably the best years.[22]

Large numbers of Ojibway from Sault Ste. Marie moved to the western end of the Lake and the Chequamegon village grew large. It replaced the old village at Sault Ste. Marie as a center for Ojibway culture. It was located on Madeline Island, or La Pointe as the French called it. It is said that at its height it was 3 miles long and 2 miles wide with gardens of squash and corn scattered among its many wigwams. Grand medicine ceremonies were centered here and, after the winter hunts were over, a thousand Ojibway would gather in the village. Born here were the ancestors of the Ojibway of Mille Lacs, Leech Lake, Fond du Lac and other places in Minnesota.[23]

At this same time, Ojibway hunting and trapping parties gained access to the St. Croix, Snake, Kettle and St. Louis rivers. An Ojibway village was established at Fond du Lac and undoubtedly Ojibway hunters and trappers from Lake Superior reached the headwaters of the St. Louis River, the lower Embarrass River and Esquagama Lake. It's likely that both Ojibway and Dakota hunters could be seen at Lake Vermilion between 1680 and 1736. According to Warren, "the good feeling between the two tribes was such that intermarriages even took place."[24]

The good feeling was carried to a point where fusil-carrying Ojibway war parties from the south shore would join the Sioux in raids on northern tribal villages. William W. Warren, who collected spoken traditions of Ojibway peoples in the 1840s, wrote about a time when an Ojibway war party from Fond du Lac raided a small northern Ojibway encampment at the mouth of the Pigeon River. During the early 1700s Sioux and Ojibway raiding parties were able to penetrate deep into the heart of Cree country and were encountered as far east as the Kaministiquia River.[25]

At the same time some northern Ojibway warriors fought on the side of the Assiniboin and Cree and along with them were a band of natives known to the French as the "Monsoni." Not much is known about them. Some believe they were a small group of tribal people closely related to the Cree. Others say they were a remote northern Ojibway band that had moved into the area from Canada's Moose River country. Although described as a small band, French records show the Monsoni could put together a war party of almost 400 warriors when called upon.[26]

In 1688, French Canadian explorer Jacques de Noyon made a trip through Cree country hoping to negotiate some trade agreements with them and thus divert furs from going north to Hudson Bay, where English traders were at work. He wintered with the Assiniboin on Lake of the Woods and there he was told that the river at the far end of the lake emptied into a great western sea. The sea, of course, was Lake Winnipeg, but it was enough to get the French excited again about finding a northwest passage.

Before anything could be done about exploring the region to the west, the War of the Spanish Succession broke out and French interests in North America turned to driving the English out of Hudson Bay. For 12 years, from 1701 to 1713, the French did not supply their posts on Lake Superior. If there was going to be any trade at all, it would be up to the local tribes. Chequamegon Ojibway had to go all the way to Detroit or York Factory to find the goods they needed for trade.

The war went badly for France and, by the terms of the 1713 Treaty of Utrecht, France had to give up all claims to territory around Hudson Bay. The French returned to the Great Lakes and plans to explore to the western sea were revived.

But to explore to the west, the French would either have to pacify the Sioux or go around their territory. They tried both strategies. In 1717, they established Fort Tekamamiouen on Rainy Lake to win over the Cree and thus divert furs from English to French posts. The strategy worked and, in 1731, Pierre Gaultier de Varennes Sieur de la Verendrye, along with his nephew, three sons, 50 French troops and a priest, arrived at Fort Kaministiquia to extend a fortified route of trade all the way to the Pacific, if possible.

He had a map drawn for him by a Cree man showing a previously unknown water route to Rainy Lake and the regions beyond – a route that could be used to avoid Dakota war parties. The route began with a long rough portage to the upper region of the Pigeon River, today's Grand Portage. From there it was relatively easy going all the way to Rainy Lake, the site of Fort Tekamamiouen and the villages of the Cree and Monsoni.

Earlier, in 1727, the French built a fort and post on Lake Pepin as part of their plan to win the confidence of the Dakota and to gain access to their fur-rich region. The post bypassed the Ojibway middlemen and delivered trade goods directly to the Dakota.[27] Apparently the trade goods included some of the French "fusils" that the Dakota had been trying to get from the Lake Superior Ojibway.[28] Meanwhile, La Verendrye's men pushed westward along the present day border lakes, building Fort Saint Pierre on Rainy Lake in 1731, Fort St. Charles on Lake of the Woods in 1732 and Fort Maurepas on the Red River in 1734.

By this time tensions were mounting between the Santee Dakota and the Lake Superior Ojibway. No longer middlemen for the Dakota trade, the Ojibway knew that the only way they could survive was to take over the hunt for furs themselves. This couldn't be done without the Santee hunting grounds. They knew the Santee would never give them up without a fight and they knew some of them were now receiving French firearms.[29]

In 1736, the Ojibway struck. Joining forces with the Assiniboin, Monsoni and

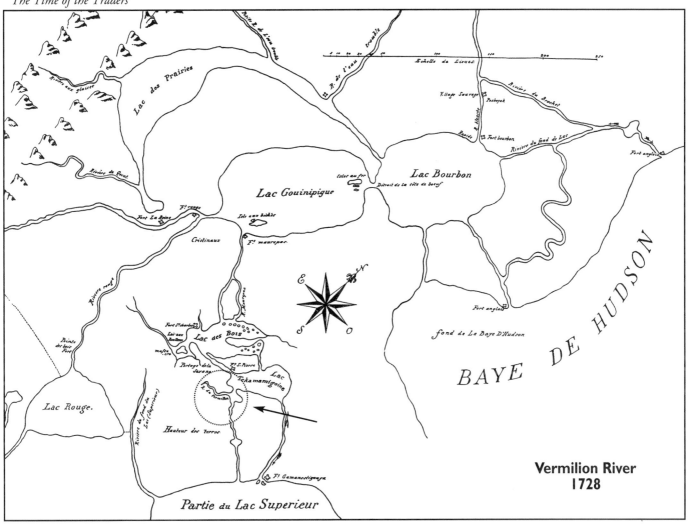

Vermilion River 1728

Cree, they launched a large scale offensive against the Dakota. The Dakota responded in kind. A war party killed and beheaded 21 Frenchmen on Lake of the Woods, presumably for trading on contested territory and providing arms to their enemy, the Assiniboin. The dead included La Verendrye's oldest son, Jean Baptiste.

The French bolstered their northern forts and evacuated the post at Lake Pepin. The northern portion of today's Minnesota became a war zone as the Ojibway and their allies waged relentless war against the Dakota. The fighting was bloody and widespread. At one place, an Assiniboin-Cree war party of 200 is said to have killed 70 Dakotas and taken numerous prisoners.[30] Ojibway historian Warren describes a surprise attack on a Sioux village and the taking of 335 scalps.[31]

The war caused wholesale relocation of tribal populations. Ojibway hunters living in Dakota villages had to leave quickly – sometimes leaving their families behind. On December 22, 1736, French traders Bourassa

and Eustache reported "a great number of Saultier" gathering on the Vermilion River to seek "refuge with them … through fear of the Sioux."

La Verendrye, commander of the forts at Rainy Lake and the Lake of the Woods, ordered the traders to construct "a little fort" there "so as to be less exposed to attack."[32] If the Vermilion River is the same one located and named on La Verendrye's maps, then this is the earliest documented account of Ojibway settlement in the vicinity of Iron Country. By 1741, the French were referring to Vermilion River Ojibway as the "people of the grease of the bear," probably because they sometimes marked their trap lines with symbols sketched into bear grease smeared on the trunks of trees and on rocks. The term "beargrease" has been associated with Lake Vermilion, Grand Portage and Fond du Lac Ojibway people until recent times. Early Duluthians talked of a John Beargrease who ran the mail between Duluth and Grand Portage by dog team in the formative years of the city.

The Vermilion River, which flows out of Lake Vermilion, was the site of the first documented account of an Ojibway encampment in the Iron Country vicinity.
FROM "CARTE DE LA VERENDRYE," OF 1728, AS PRINTED IN BURPEE, 1927, CHAMPLAIN SOCIETY, TORONTO, CANADA

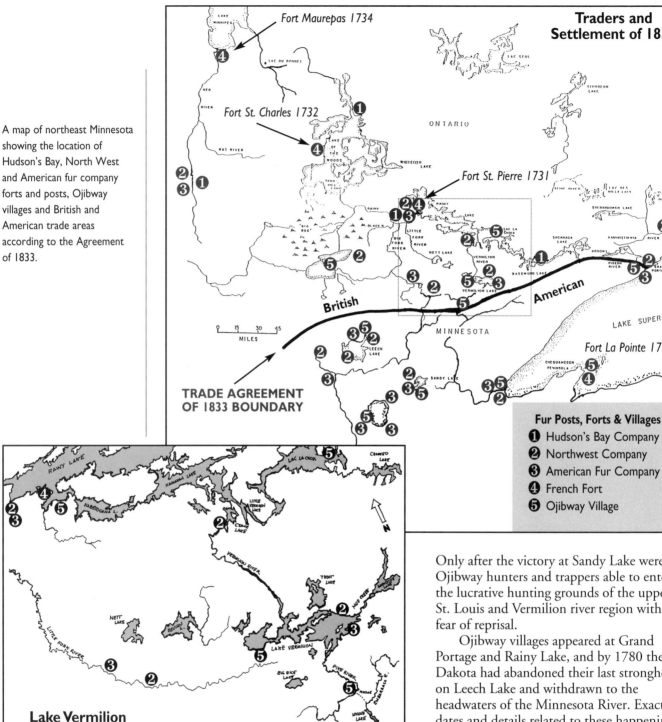

A map of northeast Minnesota showing the location of Hudson's Bay, North West and American fur company forts and posts, Ojibway villages and British and American trade areas according to the Agreement of 1833.

Traders and Settlement of 1833

Fort Maurepas 1734

Fort St. Charles 1732

Fort St. Pierre 1731

Fort La Pointe 1718

TRADE AGREEMENT OF 1833 BOUNDARY

Fur Posts, Forts & Villages
1. Hudson's Bay Company
2. Northwest Company
3. American Fur Company
4. French Fort
5. Ojibway Village

Lake Vermilion Region Close-up

Warfare among the tribes lasted a considerable time. Between the years 1740 and 1760, the Ojibway drove the Dakota from Mille Lacs Lake and Big Sandy Lake, took control of the main route of travel from the Mississippi River to Lake Superior and the northern iron ranges. Until the Battle of Sandy Lake in 1760, the entire length of the St. Louis River was a war road and the Mesabi and Vermilion ranges a war zone.

Only after the victory at Sandy Lake were Ojibway hunters and trappers able to enter the lucrative hunting grounds of the upper St. Louis and Vermilion river region without fear of reprisal.

Ojibway villages appeared at Grand Portage and Rainy Lake, and by 1780 the Dakota had abandoned their last stronghold on Leech Lake and withdrawn to the headwaters of the Minnesota River. Exact dates and details related to these happenings will probably never be known. The French, who might have documented some of it, had their own war to fight, the Seven Years War, known on this side of the Atlantic as the French and Indian War.

Most of the fighting occurred in the eastern portions of the continent and little attention was paid to events in this part of the world. One thing seems certain though. The French armed even more Ojibway men and in some places trained Ojibway recruits in European methods of warfare.[33] The fact that the Ojibway had the advantage in terms of amount and quality of firearms, contributed greatly to the wholesale realignment of tribes in this part of the world. The Cree withdrew to the north, the Assiniboin left the area forever and the Dakota abandoned all of their hunting grounds north of the Minnesota River. One thing didn't disappear. Animosity between the Sioux and Ojibway persisted until modern times.

In 1759, 5,000 British regulars led by James Wolfe floated down the St. Lawrence River in boats and took Quebec, defeating the previously invincible Louis Montcalm and his combined French and Indian army. On July 25, 1759, the French garrison at Niagara under Chevalier Pouchot surrendered to a British army under William Johnson, and by September 1761 British troops were in Detroit. Finally, in 1763 the French armies were defeated on the battlefields of Europe, leaving France with no bargaining position at all. In the treaty that followed, France ceded all of its holdings in North America to Great Britain.

After the French defeat, Ojibway people from settlements near French forts and some Lake Superior villages joined with the Ottawa and Wyandot in a war of resistance against the British. Led by the Ottawa Chief Pontiac, they attacked settlements on the frontier and laid siege to Detroit. Other tribes joined the fighting on the side of Pontiac, and three years of bloodshed and destruction of property followed. Finally in 1766, Pontiac negotiated a treaty with British General Sir William Johnson. The treaty called for the punishment of some natives but went easy on the rest, including Pontiac. This angered frontier farmers who were never repaid for their losses and there would be animosity toward both the British government and native people on the colonial frontier.

During this time, Iron Country became a fur rich region populated by people who understood the ways of the animals and understood the rules of the trade. They were, of course, the ancestors of northeastern Minnesota's Ojibway people of today. Some called them *Sug-waun-dug-ah-win-in-e-wug*, "people of the thick fir woods."[34] They would be known by the French translation of this name, Bois Forte. Fifty years or more of tribal warfare had left their region relatively

untrapped. It was inevitable that British merchants would want to locate trading posts here.

The Time of the Great Fur Companies (1763-1803)

Two large fur companies extended their influence into the region, the old Hudson's Bay Company chartered in 1670 and the North West Company organized in 1783.

The Hudson's Bay Company was not active south of Lake Winnipeg until just before the turn of the 18th century. During its first 100 years it was strictly a seaboard company. It didn't send its traders into the native villages as the French did. Instead the natives came to them. The men of the Hudson's Bay were proud, independent and powerful. "We know only two powers – God and Company," said John Rowand, chief factor of Edmonton House.[35] This approach worked well for a while – until the company found itself competing with a dynamic fur company from across the Great Lakes, the North West Company.

By 1800 most of the trade of Iron Country and all of the trade of the Great Lakes was being picked up by this partnership of enterprising Scotsmen from Montreal. The North West Company was little more than an agreement among a diverse group of independent operators to take over and profit from the well-developed network of trappers, traders and forts that the French left behind.

The company was unbelievably successful, partly due to the fact that the senior partners were so ready to cooperate and work for the common good. What made them so willing to work for the good of the company was not just that they all belonged to the company, but that they belonged to the same families. There were McTavishes, Camerons, MacKenzies, McGillivrays, Grants, Roys, Finleys and Frasers in numbers, all related. It is said that there were so many John McDonalds on company rolls that the town each was born in had to be written in after their names.[36] Members of the same family could be found at all levels of company activity. There were 14 Grants in the firm. They were partners, factors, clerks, interpreters and voyageurs. They were all aware of their family name and the prestige

Stephen Bonga, son of a Jamaican voyageur and an Ojibway mother, was born in 1799 in what would later become Superior, Wisconsin.
NORTHEAST MINNESOTA HISTORICAL CENTER

it held within company circles.[37] The company traded and followed the routes of the old French trade across the Great Lakes, up the rivers that drained into them, up the St. Louis, over portages to the Mississippi, over the Grand Portage to Rainy Lake and beyond. By 1790, they were in Athabasca country and in 1805 they were trading west of the Rocky Mountain's Great Divide.

They made Grand Portage their wilderness headquarters. Here, once a year in July, from about 1788 to 1803, was held the Great Rendezvous. Something like 350 voyageurs would arrive from Lachine with the year's supply of trade goods for the company's interior posts. Their huge Montreal canoes of birch bark, patterned after those of the Huron and Chippewa, were up to 40 feet long and 5 feet wide and carried up to three tons of trade goods. Sometimes there would be sailing ships from Sault Ste. Marie with even bigger cargo to unload. Then the "elite of the corps," the "Winterer" voyageurs from interior posts would arrive, some in canoes from down lake, most walking down the 9-mile long portage. The voyageurs who carried furs and trade goods along the Great Lakes between Montreal and Grand Portage were called "Pork Eaters" because often their daily meals included pork from the farms of eastern Canada.

During the rendezvous, months of drab living in far away posts were forgotten. Tables were filled with fresh bread, butter and special treats brought in from Montreal. There was singing, dancing, heavy drinking and carousing – and fighting. When it was over, the Winterers returned to their smaller and lighter "north canoes" for the long trip

back to interior posts, while Pork Eaters loaded their canoes with bales of fur.

In order to keep the furs flowing to depots in Montreal, the North West Company had to stay on good terms with the native peoples. The fact that many of the Winterers and other employees of the winter posts had native wives and were accepted by the various tribes helped. Old French ways prevailed at the fur posts and ceremony and gift-giving continued to be part of negotiations with the native fur hunters and trappers.

There were changes, too. No longer were Ojibway people serving as middlemen and transporters of furs. At the height of its activities, the North West Company had 1,100 voyageurs on its payroll. Most of their names were French, although company records show there were also Englishmen, Germans and Scots – and later, even a Jamaican by the name of Pierre Bonga (in some references Bunga).[38] Not one was a native.

The role of the tribes in the trade had changed profoundly. Before, European traders dealt with tribes as a group. Trade goods were distributed to individuals through the chief, headman or other spokesman for the band, who in turn told the trader how many furs he could expect in the spring. After 1800, trade goods were carried by voyageurs to posts close to the native settlements and individuals told the trader what materials they needed. The trader then assigned a value in furs for each item.

It became a common practice to outfit families and individuals for the winter fur hunts. Each outfit was based on a list of items such as a gun, powder and shot, percussion caps, ice chisel, steel traps, twine for nets, fish hooks, pain killers and provisions such as flour, lard, tea and tobacco. Each outfitted trapper could pick what he wanted from the list and credits would be assigned for each item decided upon. The articles were then delivered to the trapper and, at the end of the winter hunt, he would pay the credits in fur pelts. So many credits would be assigned to each pelt. For instance, mink would be worth one credit; a beaver, three; a martin, six.[39]

In remote posts, where trade goods and provisions had to be brought in over distances of thousands of miles, each item was precious and carefully counted. Hudson's Bay Company

records tell us that it took a full day to outfit six to eight families.[40] The Ojibway and Cree usually hunted in family groups – every fur-hunting family member had his or her task to perform. Not every family was directly involved in the hunts. Many occupied themselves in support activities such as canoe building, mending equipment, gathering and storing food, construction work, guiding, interpreting and providing a variety of services at the trading posts.

The system worked well, especially when the trading post was located close to where the people lived. If the natives moved to a better hunting ground, the old post was abandoned and a new one constructed closer to the new encampment. Once outfitted, trappers usually remained more or less obligated to the post, especially if it was nearby.

To deal with the natives, the North West Company divided its operations into 16 departments, each under the direction of a proprietor experienced in the trade. The proprietor usually had his own log house located along with other buildings inside a stockaded post. He sometimes had his family with him. A North West Company post was seldom without its flags. Below the Union

Jack was always the company flag with "NWC" on the fly of a red ensign. Sometimes flags were presented to tribal bands to symbolize trading pacts and other agreements.[41]

Three NWC departments located their activities within or close to Iron Country. One was the site of the yearly rendezvous, the company headquarters at Grand Portage. In 1799, a Doctor Munro was the proprietor at this post and six clerks were employed.[42] In 1803, the Grand Portage post was abandoned and the North West Company established a new rendezvous site farther to the north at Fort William, presumably to avoid problems with the United States.

A second department was at Fond du Lac. In 1799, a man by the name of John Sayer was in charge and seven clerks were employed there.[43] The Fond du Lac Department was center for a number of company posts located farther west. One was at Big Sandy Lake.

The third was the Lac La Pluie Department at Rainy Lake. In 1799, Peter Grant, a partner in the trade, was its proprietor and three clerks were employed. The Lac La Pluie Department also

Ruins of a fur trading post at Fond du Lac as seen in 1890. Unlike the earliest posts, which were located on the Wisconsin side of the bay at the head of the lakes, this post was in the Fond du Lac community of Duluth.
NORTHEAST MINNESOTA HISTORICAL CENTER

established the trading post of "Vermillion Lake," (Lake Vermilion), probably in about 1800, and it operated sporadically for almost 40 years. The post was manned by a single clerk only at certain times of the year, usually in the fall when outfits were delivered and in the spring when furs were collected. There were bad years when the rice crop failed and no company employee showed up at the lake. Everyone knew if there was no rice, the native peoples didn't hunt for furs.[44] Supplies to Vermilion Lake were transported by voyageurs along the Vermilion River and furs were shipped out the same way. Although company records make no mention of Ojibway actually living at the lake in 1800, the fact that a trading post was built there around that time suggests that they were in the vicinity.

The strategy of taking control of the supply lines and bringing the goods directly into the native villages paid off handsomely for the "Nor' Westers." By 1800, the North West Company was handling 78 percent of the Canadian fur sales and had net profits of well more than a million pounds sterling during its first 20 years of operation.[45]

The Hudson's Bay Company was shaken out of its complacency. It, too, began bringing trade goods to native villages. Hudson's Bay Company posts sprang up all over Canada. By 1793 one post was situated on the Rainy River downstream a mile or so from the North West Company post. Their records suggest that they may have outfitted Bois Forte trappers on Lake Vermilion even before the North West post was built.

Competition became heated and pitched battles were fought between the two companies. In 1803, the British Parliament passed the Canada Jurisdiction Act designed to bring the Hudson's Bay Company under closer government control and end the fighting. It didn't end the rivalry, and after 1810 the struggle between the two companies became so intense that it caused problems, not only for the British government, but for the companies themselves. In 1821 a solution was reached through merger. The name of the older company was retained.

Meanwhile, North West Company partners grew rich and influential. However, it would be the Winterers and lesser employees of the company who would pass the legacy of the trade to future generations. They often stayed on at the posts, even when their contracts expired. Some found wives among the tribal families with whom they traded. Their children, like them, became participants in the trade. The Roys, Roussains, Cadottes, Conners, Morrisons and McCraes – their families have lived in the region for years – even before they knew the land they lived in was the United States of America.

While the United States was expanding and becoming concerned about its western frontiers during the first decade of the 1800s, it was business as usual at Lake Vermilion. The British clerks were hardly aware of the existence of the new nation. This was not to last. ∎

CHAPTER 3

From Furs to Gold

It was 1804. Thomas Jefferson was president of the United States. Fifteen years had passed since George Washington had taken his oath of office to become the nation's first president. It would be another 44 years before a territory called Minnesota would appear on the map.

In that year, Peter Grant, chief factor of the British North West Company's Rainy Lake Department, writing his sketch of Sauteux natives, described the region that was to become Iron Country as a place of "rocky barren mountains and flat lands … covered by a forest of maple, poplar, pine, birch, oak and white fir."

"Some parts of the lowlands," he wrote, "abound in swamps which produce cedar and different species of willows which furnish the Natives with materials for their canoes. The willow serves also as a food for the moose deer, an animal which delights in those swamps."[1]

There were no white-tailed deer then. They wouldn't be seen north of Lake Superior in any numbers for another 100 years. There were other animals: caribou, bear, wolves, wolverines, fisher, "foxes of different colors," lynx, otter, marten, mink, rabbits, squirrels, "a sort of badger of the smallest kind" and, of course, beaver and moose.[2] According to Grant, "Moose may be reckoned the staff of life of the natives … a scarcity of moose in the winter season is sure to cause a very severe famine."[3]

The region was by then home to Ojibway people. Grant called them Sauteux and described the area that they populated as an immense territory extending "from Sault Ste. Marie, in a northwest course, to Lac Ouinipique (Lake Winnipeg), a distance of about 1,770 miles." However, "the frequent emigration of several of their tribes to the country of Assiniboines and Crees," he admitted, "makes it difficult to ascertain the real boundaries of their present possessions. Their population may be reckoned to be about 6,000 souls, spread over this vast tract of country."[4]

It's clear from their reports that British traders knew very little about the interior country away from the main fur posts. It was the domain of the tribes. Grant wrote:

"Though, as I have said, no country can boast of larger reservoirs of fresh water than the Sauteux country, yet, innumerable shoals and rapids greatly impede the navigation in the interior country, and, except on large lakes, it would be almost impractical with boats or any wooden craft. Their (Ojibway) birch canoes are, therefore, most ingeniously adapted for this purpose; being composed of light materials, they are easily carried over the portages and have sufficient strength to resist the greatest swell and carry as heavy loads as any wooden craft of the same dimensions.

"They have them of different sizes, from those to carry 12 men, generally used by the tribes that live on Lake Superior, to others which contain only two or three men and even only one, used by the tribes of the interior.… They carry their canoes through the bushes and over rocks with comparative ease, where it would be impossible for the traders to clear a track for the transportation of their large canoes and goods."[5]

Trader canoes needed crews of five, carried loads of up to 3,000 pounds and drew a good 18 inches of water. It took two men just to get one of them over a portage. As a result, fur companies tended to locate their main depots on larger waterways and depended on individual traders to set up subposts in the vicinity of more remote native encampments.

We don't know how many of these posts there were or where they were all located, but we do know that most of them belonged to the

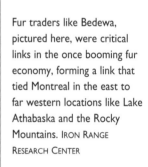

Fur traders like Bedewa, pictured here, were critical links in the once booming fur economy, forming a link that tied Montreal in the east to far western locations like Lake Athabaska and the Rocky Mountains. IRON RANGE RESEARCH CENTER

Bois Forte trapper in traditional dress. IRON RANGE RESEARCH CENTER

North West Company. North West traders often referred to their posts as "forts," probably because they surrounded almost any sort of cabin or lean-to they put up for a season's trading with a picket post fence or stockade. Stockades with heavy gates and locks were often needed to protect trade goods and liquor supplies from thieves, both animal and human. Without this protection there would be no trade.

Most of the posts were no more than small wintering stations. They operated maybe a season or two and then were abandoned for a more advantageous site. A wintering station was only profitable if the trapping was good. When the natives moved to a new hunting ground, the trader picked up his goods and followed.

Few nails were used in the construction of these forts. To hold up the walls, logs were grooved and set upright at each corner of a rectangular foundation. The ends of each log selected for the walls were carefully notched to fit exactly into the grooves on the corner posts and the logs were laid one above the other. Floors were made of split logs and roofs were often thatched with boughs held down with poles. Windows were covered with greased deer skin, but doors tended to have iron hinges and locks. Fireplaces and chimneys were made out of local clays and sticks.[6]

Company records mention wintering posts of this kind at Crane Lake, Basswood Lake and Saganaga Lake on the Canadian border and at Pokegama Falls across the river from the present site of Grand Rapids. There was also a post on Lake Vermilion. It was located just across the water from the Isle of Pines. Fur posts were usually staffed from September to May. A flag flying above the complex let people nearby know that company clerks were in residence and the store was open for business.[7]

In 1804, none of Iron Country's scattered Ojibway communities could go long without access to European products. Although they continued to get their goods and provisions in time-honored ways, through negotiation, gift giving and ceremony, it was the fur trade in the last analysis that determined where Ojibway people located their villages.[8] Records mention such villages at Sandy Lake, Lake Vermilion, Fond du Lac, Rainy Lake and Grand Portage.

Three "for real" heavily stockaded forts, complete with guns and cannon, helped regulate the flow of furs through the region. One was on the Rainy River just beyond the outlet of Rainy Lake. Another was at Sandy Lake in present day Aitkin County. The third, called "Fort St. Louis," was about three miles upstream from the mouth of the St. Louis River within the present city limits of Superior.[9]

Colonel Hiram Hayes, who arrived in Superior in 1855, wrote this about the St. Louis River fort:

"There was a stout palisade of posts, 20 feet high, sharpened at both ends and driven into the ground. There were thick double-ribbed gates in front and rear, a grim two-storied tower formed a bastion at one corner, bristling with port holes and cannon. Stores and magazines and workshops were ranged inside the enclosure, with an open court in the middle, where the Indians brought their game and peltries. Inside also were the dwellings of heavy timber, mortised – Canadian fashion – and painted white."[10]

There weren't many people in this part of the world, native or white, who felt any allegiance whatsoever to the United States of America. By right of conquest and exploration the land belonged to Britain. The nearest American Customs House was at Mackinac and Americans were seldom seen west of Sault Ste. Marie. As a matter of fact, they were not welcome in this part of the world. Ojibway people saw no reason to be friendly with the "long knives," as some called the Americans. Since the days of Pontiac's War, American frontier settlers were the enemy. British traders didn't like Americans either. Anything that limited tribal hunting grounds or encouraged settlement was seen as a threat to the trade.

In 1804, the North West Company's fur production was at its height, but the fur trade itself was in trouble. The U.S.'s westward expansion threatened native fur hunting grounds. War in Europe had closed two of England's best fur markets – Germany and Russia – and fur prices fell. At the same time competition increased. A North West offshoot calling itself the XY Company appeared on the scene. Competition became intense.

Agents of both companies brought outfits and plenty of whisky and rum to the region's Ojibway villages. "The effect was to get the Indians so consistently and persistently drunk that it nearly ruined the trade."[11] The Hudson's Bay Company set up a trading house on the Rainy River just downstream from the North West post and began outfitting Ojibway trappers.

The competing companies used every means available to corner the trade, including rum, brandy and whisky. Trader's rum (watered down liquor) was freely distributed to the natives at almost every occasion. It was often used to buy wild rice and other provisions for winter storage at the posts. People who sold their food supplies for rum would often run out of provisions early in the winter, leaving their families at the mercy of the post for survival. For a while, it was policy for traders to buy all the provisions they could with rum because it was a way to hold the loyalty of trappers.[12]

In the long run, the practice served to diminish the trade. Natives who sold their rice for liquor or didn't want to be beholden to the traders spent their winters hunting for food rather than furs. It was well-known among fur buyers that if tribal food supplies ran short or

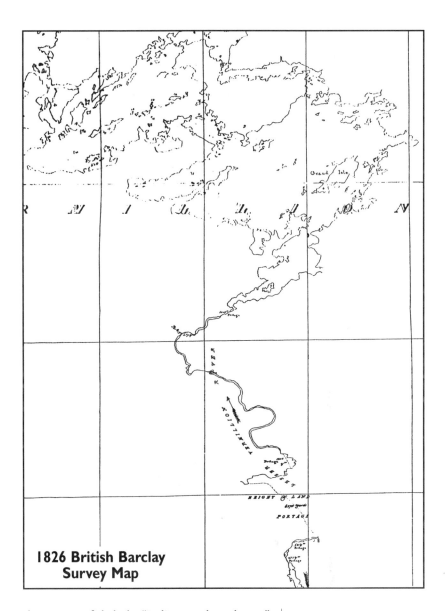

1826 British Barclay Survey Map

the rice crop failed, the "Indians made no hunts." The result was, of course, great hardships for natives and fewer pelts for the company. By the time the first Americans arrived on the scene, few British traders were meeting their credits at the summer rendezvous at Fort William.

Americans Arrive in Iron Country (1804-1816)

The 1783 Treaty of Paris officially ended the American Revolution and set boundaries for the new nation, but it was not at all clear about the region west of Lake Superior. According to the wording of the treaty, beginning at the St. Marys Rapids, the boundary separating American and British territories was to run, "through Lake Superior northward of the Isles Royal and Phillipeaux to the long lake and thence through the middle (of) said long lake and the main water communication between it and the Lake of the Woods...."

The 1826 Barclay Survey Map, showing British version of the American and British areas, identifies Pike River as "Lesser Vermillion River" and shows the Lake Vermilion area. FROM HOUSE EXECUTIVE DOCUMENT NO. 451 OF THE 25TH CONGRESS. DULUTH PUBLIC LIBRARY

The question was: Where was the "long lake" and what was the main water communication between it and Lake of the Woods? Even if these could be determined, the framers of the treaty shared a misconception common to their time. They thought that the Mississippi River began somewhere north and west of Lake of the Woods. A second treaty, the Jay Treaty of 1794, recommended a joint survey of the Mississippi River to its source in order to help determine exactly where the northwest corner of the United States was located. The survey was never made.

None of this really mattered much until March 10, 1804. On that day the northern portion of the Territory of Louisiana, purchased from France the year before, was officially handed over to the United States. It contained some 58,000 square miles of land west of the Mississippi that would one day be part of the state of Minnesota. Suddenly there was concern over the location of the northern boundary.

In the eyes of the British, all of what today is Minnesota was their domain. Their flags were the ones flying over the posts. President Thomas Jefferson saw it differently. He saw British traders smuggling liquor past the collector at Mackinac and selling it to Indians on American soil. This was not just illegal by American law, it perpetuated Indian war and discouraged settlement. It was in the national interest to clarify and secure the northern boundary.

The Pike Expedition of 1805-1806
The army was given the task of establishing a presence at the source of the Mississippi and securing the northern frontier. A detachment of 20 U.S. Army regulars under the command of Lieutenant Zebulon Pike left the Mississippi border town of St. Louis on August 9, 1805, and proceeded up the river toward its source. The trip upriver was plagued with difficulties. Before Pike and his troops could get to its upper regions, the river froze. They resorted to an overland march. They made sleds to carry their supplies and pulled them by hand. One of the sleds broke through the ice, the ammunition got wet and while trying to dry it in a steel pot, they almost blew up three of the men. Pike's tent burned, and then it got so cold that they had to stop every three miles to build fires to keep from freezing.[13]

Finally, on the night of January 8, 1806, Pike and one of his corporals stumbled half-frozen through the open gate of the North West Company fort at Sandy Lake. The rest of

the detachment, suffering from frostbite, followed five days later. Americans had arrived in Iron Country.

They were warmly welcomed and well-fed by company clerk James Grant but, after resting there for 12 days, they went on to Leech Lake, arriving on February 1. There, Pike wrote a letter to Fond du Lac Factor Hugh McGillis, telling him that duty must be paid on all goods coming into American territory, no political treaties are to be made with the Indians and under no circumstances are British flags to be raised above company posts. To make his point clear, he had the flag shot off the mast at Leech Lake.[14]

The Treaty of 1783 had been enforced for the first time west of Lake Superior.

The War of 1812
Pike's efforts were little more than symbolic. The Cross of St. George continued to fly over British posts on American territory for another 10 years.

Undoubtedly there was strong support in the region during these years for the Shawnee chief, Tecumseh, and his brother, the Prophet, in their attempt to establish a tribal confederacy to resist encroachment of American settlers and developers into their lands. According to Ojibway historian William Warren, "150 Chippewa war canoes" set out on Lake Superior to join the Prophet in his war against the frontier settlements, only to be turned back by fur trader Michael Cadotte who was on his way back with the annual supply of "outfits" for winter trapping. In 1811, the Prophet's army met defeat at the hands of U.S. General William Henry Harrison in the famous Battle of Tippecanoe. When the War of 1812 broke out, company agents received commissions in the British Army and recruited and armed tribal warriors to fight against the United States.

The participation of native armed forces on the side of the British was anything but blind obedience to company agents. They were given something to fight for. The British promised them a realignment of the northern and western boundaries of the United States and the formation of an all-tribal territory. This had been Tecumseh's dream: no settlers, no Americans. The British even came up with a map showing the Ohio River as the northern frontier of the United States.[15]

Missing from most of the history books is the fact that there were Ojibway volunteers who also fought for this dream – and fought

well. Although Warren claimed that the main body of Ojibway "occupying Lake Superior and the waters of the Mississippi firmly withstood every effort made by the British to induce them to enter into the war," he admitted that there were others who joined the native war parties then under the command of commissioned British agent Robert Dickson and won victories at Mackinac, Fort Dearborn and Prairie du Chien.[16] It seems reasonable that some of these volunteers came from villages at Rainy Lake, Lake Vermilion and Grand Portage. "Without these allies it is difficult to believe that the British could have retained Upper Canada."[17]

Despite the victories, when peace came in 1814, the treaty put together at Ghent was a disappointment to both native people and traders. The 1783 boundaries were reaffirmed. Although British flags began coming down at some North West posts, the location of the northern boundary remained at issue.

The American Fur Company (1816-1847)

At the time the North West Company began abandoning its posts, a fully organized and politically well-connected American Fur Company was ready to take them over. Chartered in New York in 1808, the company was put together by German-born John Jacob Astor, a man with friends in Congress.

Unlike the British, American Fur Company traders did not promote wilderness. Instead, they cooperated with territorial officials and federal commissioners anxious to get the land opened for settlement and development. Native people were encouraged to charge large amounts of goods against the company account, ensuring their indebtedness. Debts were assessed, not against individuals but against entire tribal nations. As a result, the only way American tribes could meet their growing debt was to sell their land. American Fur Company traders always had a place at the treaty table and collected debts owed them from the payments for the land being sold by the native tribes.[18]

Patriotism that was stirred up during the War of 1812 led to the passage of the Indian Trade Act in 1816. It provided that "licenses to trade with the Indians within the territorial limits of the United States shall not be granted to anyone but citizens of the United States."[19] The act made it easy for Astor to take control of the trade networks already in place on American soil.

He retained the *engages* and voyageurs of the British company, but replaced factors and clerks with ambitious young Americans. Voyageurs and others employed by Astor had no problem getting the necessary naturalization papers. In this way some of the very earliest white residents of Iron Country and Western Lake Superior became citizens of the United States. They didn't come to America. America came to them.

In most cases, the American Fur Company simply took over the facility that had been abandoned, but this was not true at Fond du Lac. The British fort was burned and a new post constructed about 18 miles up the St. Louis River from the old North West site. It consisted of "a range of log buildings enclosing three sides of a square open to the river and containing a warehouse, boat yard, dwelling house for the resident clerk and accommodations for voyageurs," when Henry Schoolcraft visited the post in 1820. It also had "three cows, four bulls, two oxen and three horses" grazing in a recently cleared field and four acres were under cultivation at the new site.[20]

The clerks of the American Fur Company were also well-situated at the old British post on Sandy Lake when Henry Schoolcraft passed through that same year. However, the company didn't get much of the trade on Lake Vermilion. In 1821, the Hudson's Bay Company was able to absorb the North West Company, bringing an end to a long era of bitter conflict and division. The new unification solidified British interests at Rainy Lake and allowed them to retain the Lake Vermilion trade as well.

The Fur Rebellion of 1821

An American Fur Company post did appear on Lake Vermilion, but it came from an unexpected direction. In 1821, shortly after the merger of the British companies, a former North West clerk from Rainy Lake, Joseph Cadotte, "disgruntled at being put out of work," moved his "men and merchandise" to Lake Vermilion. There he proclaimed allegiance to the United States, threatened to burn down the British post and promised to personally seize the goods of any Hudson's Bay trader he found on the lake.[21]

The fact that Cadotte had the support of other former Nor'westers and was popular with Sauteux trappers posed grave problems for the newly formed Hudson's Bay coalition. A traders' revolt supported by the native trappers could break the company's hold on the region.

When Cadotte, along with Paul and Brazil Beaulieu, paddled down the Vermilion River and seized the company post at Crane Lake, Hudson's Bay Factor Roderick McKenzie responded. Announcing his determination "to crush the rascal," he sent eight armed men to the post and "dislodged" the three traders.[22]

The next year Cadotte went to Fond du Lac and came back to Lake Vermilion with an American Fur Company force and a 15-year veteran of the trade, former North West factor and now-naturalized American citizen Pierre Cotté. In the name of the American company, the two men took over the British post at Lake Vermilion and built a second one – directly across the river from the Hudson's Bay fort at the outlet of Rainy Lake. They brought with them a U.S. customs inspector to discourage the British from trading on "American soil."[23]

That fall, Paul Beaulieu returned to Lake Vermilion from Sault Ste. Marie with voyageurs Charles LaRose, Baptiste Longpre, Jean Baptiste Joinville, David Dezilette, Francois Rochelo, Francois Picquet and the son of a Connecticut farmer turned trader, Youngs L. Morgan. Morgan was the first officially licensed American trader to reach Lake Vermilion. Not to be outdone, Hugh McLaughlin, McKenzie's replacement at Rainy Lake, sent Simon McGillivray and six men to reoccupy their post near Vermilion's Isle of Pines. This time it was a stand-off. Intense competition followed.[24]

The Bois Forte trappers were delighted. Being citizens of neither country, they had free access to both sides of the border and could play one company against the other. Besides, if things really got tough and they couldn't meet their credits, all they had to do was cross the border and they couldn't be pursued. In response, both companies tried to limit their credits to only reliable hunters, encouraging others to trade with the opposition. This led to a trade war between the two companies. It got so intense that the British placed armed men at the "crossing of the rapids" to try to stop native trappers from going to the American posts.[25]

The Intercompany Agreement (1833-1847)

The British tried every trick in the book to discourage the Americans from trading north of Lake Superior, which included lowering prices on trade goods and giving hunters gifts of rum and tobacco. McLaughlin was convinced

that the Americans "across the river" were losing money and would soon be forced to quit.[26] The Americans were losing money, but they continued to outfit trappers from both sides of the border. Licenses to trade at Lake Vermilion were awarded to Paul Baubien in 1825, Paul Beaulieu in 1826 and Ambrose Davenport in 1831.[27] The Americans arrived with expanded inventories and were consistently less than conservative with their credits. The number of Ojibway at Rainy Lake declined, while Lake Vermilion's population grew.[28]

It soon became clear that the trade war, which had spread west to the Red River, was doing neither company any good and an agreement was negotiated. In return for a payment of 300 pounds per annum, the American Fur Company promised to leave the region from the upper St. Louis River to Rainy Lake in the hands of the Hudson's Bay Company. The agreement lasted from 1833 to 1847. During this time and for many years after, Iron Country Bois Forte people considered themselves British subjects and traded almost exclusively with the Hudson's Bay Company at Rainy Lake.[29]

The Border is Established (1825-1842)

The intercompany agreement is quite understandable when one considers the fact that no one really knew for certain where the border lay. Although the Treaty of Ghent had left the question of the border unresolved, it did provide for a joint commission to determine its exact location. However, the commission didn't form until 1822. A joint survey was ordered, but when the report came back in 1824, it was so sketchy it only led to more controversy.[30]

John Hale, British agent to the commission, produced letters written by William McGillivray and David Thompson showing that at the time the treaty was framed, the St. Louis River was the best way to get to Lake of the Woods and "should have been fixed upon as the boundary line." "Along the whole circuit of Lake Superior, this river (the St. Louis) has no parallel for being navigable," said David Thompson, a highly reputable mapmaker of the time.[31]

The British commissioners called for a joint survey of the route as the intended and true border between the United States and Canada. The American commissioners led by Peter Porter refused. They were quite comfortable with the first survey, which apparently had

followed the old North West route beginning at Grand Portage. Anthony Barclay, who headed the British team, stuck to the 1783 treaty wording, "the border shall run through Lake Superior." To him, this meant the full length of the lake. So sure was he of the validity of his claim, that he ordered a complete survey of the St. Louis River route to Lake of the Woods – entirely at British expense.[32]

The survey was made in the summer of 1825 and apparently no expense was spared in the effort. Samuel Thompson, brother of David Thompson, and a large party of surveyors and mapmakers arrived at the mouth of the St. Louis and proceeded upstream to the Embarrass River. From there they crossed the Mesabi ridge via Wynne and Sabin lakes, portaged across the height of land and proceeded down the Pike River to Lake Vermilion and down the Vermilion River to Crane Lake, measuring, charting and recording everything they encountered.

According to Duluth historian W.E. Culkin: "They were equipped with every instrument known to science and the maps that they produced are the first accurate portrayals of any portion of Iron Country. Every rapid and portage on the St. Louis, Embarrass and Vermilion rivers and every island on Vermilion Lake was carefully delineated and numbered. No survey was made since that time with greater care or more conscientious fidelity than by this body of men, perhaps 50 in number."[33]

The survey report was flatly rejected by Peter Porter. He had consulted with his own experts and now presented a counterproposal. The border should run from Lake Superior up the Kaministiquia River from Thunder Bay to Dog Lake and along the old French route to Lake of the Woods. This would have placed much of today's Quetico Park in American hands.[34]

The British commissioners refused to consider the idea and separate border reports were filed in 1827. The northern border remained unclear until the Webster-Ashburton Treaty of 1842 and then only through compromise was the present boundary accepted by both sides – with the stipulation that "all the usual portages" remain "open and free for use by both countries." This includes the Grand Portage.

If American commissioner Peter Porter had accepted the survey of 1825 and given in to the British position, the entire Arrowhead region of Minnesota, thousands of acres of prime timber and billions of tons of iron ore would have been added to the Dominion of Canada.

Aurora, Hoyt Lakes, Tower, Soudan and Ely would today be in Canada; so would Duluth.

Only after the border controversy was settled did people in the United States get their first good look at Iron Country. Beginning in 1847, a series of geographical and geological surveys of Wisconsin, Minnesota and Iowa territories took place under the direction of David Dale Owen, U.S. geologist. In late August 1848, one of his surveyors, James Norwood, set up camp at the site of the old North West post on Lake Vermilion and wrote the following:

"The buildings erected here by the Northwest [sic] Fur Company about 35 years ago, have long since disappeared, nothing remaining of them now, except piles of fallen chimneys, to mark the spot where they stood. The rocky point is bare for a short distance in front of the old building spot and the rock slopes gradually down into the water. Back of where the houses stood are the remains of a garden, now overgrown with bushes and small saplings. Where the ground is yet open, the Indians have planted potatoes within the last two years. September 1st."[35]

Norwood's words describing the fading remains of the last days of the trade were quickly overshadowed by his discoveries of the next few days. Traces of gold were found in the quartz veins that bordered the Vermilion River. It was this gold that caught the eye of readers when the survey report came out in 1854. Lost in that glow of gold and the hundreds of pages that made up the report was the fact that Norwood also noted iron ore – near Gunflint Lake – on the northern border.

That same year, the Lake Superior Chippewa Tribe was called to a meeting at Madeline Island to discuss a treaty giving up all rights to the northeast portion of territorial Minnesota.

The Time of Treaties (1826-1869)
Tribal peoples within U.S. territories had lived as free and independent nations until 1790. From 1790 to 1800, congressional legislation was designed to do two things: keep the peace and control the activities of fur traders and whisky peddlers. In 1824, a Bureau of Indian Affairs (BIA) was created – under the Department of War.

The bureau was still part of the War Department when the Fond du Lac Treaty was negotiated on August 5, 1826. This treaty came about shortly after the discovery of copper along Lake Superior's north shore and

Through several treaties between the Ojibway and the United States, native people maintained their pride, but lost more and more land and sovereignty. The Treaty of La Pointe in 1854 left the Vermilion Lake band of Ojibway without a reservation.
IRON RANGE RESEARCH CENTER

contained a provision important to the future development of mining in Iron Country. It gave the United States the "right to search for and carry away any metals or minerals from any part of Chippewa country." However, the treaty made it clear that this would have no effect on Chippewa title to the land. Six hundred native people are said to have attended the treaty meeting and nine "chiefs" from "Vermilion Lake" put their mark on the document.[36]

In 1849, the BIA was transferred to the Department of Interior, and during the next 20 years some 400 treaties were made with tribes across the nation. The result was the loss of tribal title to a billion or more acres of land. In return, tribes received tax-exempt reservations, cash payments (much of which were used to pay off debts to fur traders), provisions and promises of educational programs, technical training and medical care.

Five of the treaties, the Ontonagon Treaty of 1836, the 1837 Treaty at Fort Snelling, the

Wisconsin Treaty of 1842 and the 1850 Treaty of Sault Ste. Marie, resulted in tribal loss of title to lands, trees and minerals on both sides of Lake Huron, Lake Superior and the St. Croix Valley. The reservations set aside for use by native people tended to be small and located on unproductive land. Many natives simply migrated west into Minnesota Territory and beyond.

The Treaty of La Pointe, finalized on September 30, 1854, probably did more than any other to open the lands of Iron Country to development and settlement. The signing came after two months of negotiation between representatives of the federal government and 11 Chippewa bands from Minnesota, Wisconsin and Michigan. Only three of these bands, the Fond du Lac, Grand Portage and Bois Forte, actually lived on the land being ceded. The parcel included all of Minnesota east of the Snake, St. Louis, East Swan and Vermilion rivers. Included in the cession were the iron ore deposits of the eastern Mesabi and Vermilion ranges.[37]

Reservations were established for the Fond du Lac and Grand Portage bands, but the Bois Forte, or "Vermilion" band as it was often called, was left without a clearly defined reservation. Article 12 of the treaty said this about them: "In consideration of the poverty of the Bois Forte Indians who are parties to this treaty … and of the great extent of that part of the ceded country owned exclusively by them … the United States will pay the sum of $10,000 …" to be used as their chiefs direct and "the further sum of $10,000, in five equal annual payments, in blankets, cloth, nets, guns, ammunition and such other articles of necessity as they may require.[38]

"They shall have the right to select their own reservation at any time hereafter, under the direction of the President." The reserved land was to be equal in size "as to their numbers," and was to receive the same services as did the other two reservations. This meant a blacksmith, blacksmith shop and instructions in farming.[39]

The Vermilion people simply stayed on the lake. They had no wish or need to sell their lands in the first place. Trappers were getting good prices for their furs. The ricing and fishing were good and their hunting grounds were far more productive than those closer to Lake Superior. In fact, only three of their people went to Madeline Island in 1854. They said later that they only went to watch the proceedings, but somehow they all got their names on the treaty.

At first, nothing seemed to change at Lake Vermilion. The Bois Forte version of the entire treaty affair was that, because the 1854 treaty was invalid, two years later the agent sent for them to make another treaty, but if the treaty was signed, they knew nothing about it. The agent gave them a paper and said they would get lots of provisions for it, but two or three years went by and nothing happened, so their chief threw the paper away.[40]

But big changes were taking place elsewhere. When ratified in 1855, the La Pointe Treaty laid the entire Minnesota shore of Lake Superior open to development and settlement. On the Wisconsin side of the lake, a town called Superior was booming. Its streets were filled with copper prospectors and land speculators from all parts of the country.

New townsites appeared overnight: Milford, Buchanen, Oneota and a cluster of buildings on Minnesota Point called Duluth. The sawmills of Oneota attracted millwrights, sawyers, lumberjacks and timber cruisers and, in Buchanan, a newly established U.S. Land Office signaled momentous change.

Along the north shore, other towns appeared – Portland, Endion, Montezuma, Beaver Bay. Within three years of ratification, the Minnesota side of the bay was a place of sawmills, brickyards, warehouses, tar paper shacks, log houses, stores, hotels and boardinghouses. Large commercial sailing vessels docked daily at the newly built Oneota pier, speculators arrived in droves and, across the bay, regular sidewheeler steamship service connected the bustling town of Superior to other port cities of the Great Lakes.

**The Lake Vermilion
Gold Rush (1865-1866)**

In 1858, Minnesota's political leaders were very much aware of the possibility of precious metals north of Duluth. In 1864, Governor Henry A. Swift established the office of state geologist and picked Augustus Hanchett for the job. Hanchett wasn't much of a geologist, but his assistant, Thomas Clark, was. During the summer of 1864, Clark led a field survey team into the area, but they had neither the time nor the equipment to do much more than camp.[41]

This didn't stop the Hanchett-Clark Report from coming out in early 1865. The report stated what many people already knew;

there was copper near Lake Superior and iron ore at Lake Vermilion. Although the report made no specific mention of gold, it did talk about ores of "abundant richness" and suggested that the region be looked at more closely.[42]

Many people were convinced that a closer look would reveal signs of gold. One of these was Stephen H. Miller. When he took over as governor of the state in 1865, Miller expanded the budget of the geological survey and appointed Henry H. Eames to the position of state geologist and Henry's brother, Richard, as assistant. They were given specific tasks: explore the north shore of Lake Superior for minerals, extend explorations north to the Vermilion region, where Norwood noted signs of gold, analyze any metal-bearing ores encountered, ascertain their commercial value and draw maps showing their locations.[43]

In the spring of 1865, the two brothers set up headquarters in the frontier town of Duluth. They sought and received the guiding services of Christian Wieland of Beaver Bay, who took them to Lake Vermilion.[44] After a month and a half on and about the lake, they came back with a canoe-load of specimens suspected to contain iron, copper, silver and gold.[45]

The St. Paul to which they returned that fall was bubbling with talk of gold. Excitement over what were being called the "Minnesota gold fields" had been growing steadily since publication of the Owen report of 1852.[46] These were gold-fever times and the precious metal bonanzas of Colorado, Nevada, Arizona, California, Idaho and Montana were fresh in the minds of many Americans.

When it was learned that the governor of Minnesota had sent a three-pound specimen of "Eames quartz" to the U.S. mint to be assayed and the report came back with a finding of "$25.63 in gold and $4.42 in silver per short ton," a rush to Lake Vermilion began.[47] Loans were taken out and properties mortgaged as hundreds of men said goodbye to their families and hurried off to what was now being called "Minnesota's golden land," despite the fact that winter was coming on and flakes of snow were already in the air.

The *St. Paul Pioneer* was soon reporting that some of the Eames samples had also been examined by Professor Edward Kent, an eminent New York chemist, and were found to

The popular "Park Point" was known as Minnesota Point when the region was opened to settlement in 1855. It attracted a mix of old and new cultures in those early days. NORTHEAST MINNESOTA HISTORICAL CENTER

contain gold at a rate of more than $40 a ton.[48] Newspapers in Chicago, New York and all across the country spread news of the discovery. The *Cleveland Herald* excitedly described Lake Vermilion gold as "not found in its native state, as in California, but in iron and copper pyrites, as in Idaho. It is in bright, sparkling quartz veins from 3 inches to 10 feet in width and extends for miles; the amount, in fact, being almost unlimited."[49] Newspapers in St. Paul and Superior reminded their readers that in California gold was being mined profitably at a rate of $10 a ton and "on Lake Vermilion – it's gold at $40 a ton!"[50]

But the flames of gold fever were fanned even more by the writings of a *St. Paul Pioneer* reporter, Ossean Euclid Dodge, a former itinerant singer, songwriter and poet sent north in early October to report on the rush. Under the pen name *Oro Fino*, Dodge wrote glowing descriptions of Lake Vermilion and the veins of gold-bearing quartz that he saw on its shores, all of which were published in the *Pioneer*. On October 25, he predicted that a new town to be called "Vermilion City at the falls of the South Vermilion River (Pike River) … will soon be populated by not less than 10,000 people." He also mentioned "immense beds of rich iron ore hundreds of feet in height" on the south shore of the lake.[51]

In the frantic rush that followed, iron ore would be ignored as prospectors and speculators staked out gold claims along the lake. Mining companies formed overnight. Within weeks of its November incorporation, a Vermilion Falls Gold Company was selling stock in what was said to be the "10-foot Vein" from which the Eames samples had been drawn. One of the men behind the venture was none other than Ossean Euclid Dodge. By March, the company had sold 6,000 shares of gold mining stock at a rate of $50 a share and shipped a steam boiler to the lake – not to mine gold, but to run a sawmill and sell lumber for buildings under construction at the lake.[52]

Incorporated on December 3, 1865, a Minnesota Gold Mining Company, headed by two well-known political figures, Governor Stephen H. Miller and former governor Henry Sibley, quickly laid claim to something like 1,000 acres of Vermilion shoreline on the basis of Sioux and Chippewa "half-breed scrip." The 1854 Treaty of La Pointe and a bill passed by Congress that same year had provided Sioux and Chippewa band members of mixed blood with certificates, or "scrip," allowing them to locate and file land claims within unsurveyed regions of what was then territorial Minnesota. Manipulated by shrewd attorneys working in the interest of timber dealers, "half-breed scrip" soon became a convenient way to access valuable pine land. In 1858, when Minnesota became a state, scrip was being bought and sold at a regular market rate. By 1865, much of it had fallen into the hands of developers and speculators.[53]

With the news of the discovery of gold at Lake Vermilion, Chippewa scrip rose in value from 85 cents an acre to $4 and Sioux scrip jumped from $2 to $12 an acre.[54] The use of this scrip by gold mining companies to lay claim to choice locations angered individual prospectors staking out claims at the lake. They saw no reason why Lake Vermilion should be any different from the mineral regions of California or Idaho, where miners could only lay claim to land they actually worked.

The Gazette of Superior, Wisconsin took up the cause against the "scrip layers." As early as November 1865, its editor warned that "a

monopoly of this territory by a horde of speculators would be a curse to the region." [55]

In December 1865, a Mutual Protection Gold Miners Company was organized to challenge absentee ownership of land at Lake Vermilion. It was made up of 25 members, mostly young men and Civil War veterans who had recently mustered out of the Union Army. Each member was required to kick in $150 along with a promise to go to Minnesota's gold fields and locate a claim. Their strategy was to scatter themselves about the region and, if one of them struck it rich, all would share in the profit. They also invited other prospectors to join their ranks, upon payment of $300 and a vote of acceptance from the original stockholders.[56]

Heading the "Mutuals" was Major Thomas M. Newson, who ran the company like he was

Map of Vermilion Lake, St. Louis County, Minnesota, by A.J. Hill, 1866, showing locations of gold mines, gold town, North West Company trading post, Roussain's post, silver vein, gold bearing quartz and original place names.
MINNESOTA HISTORICAL SOCIETY

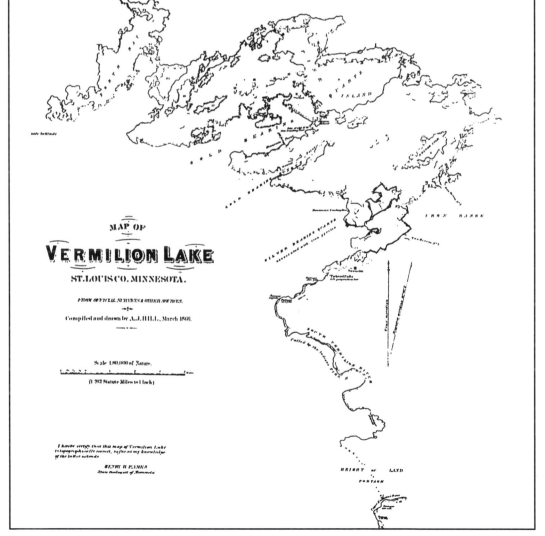

35

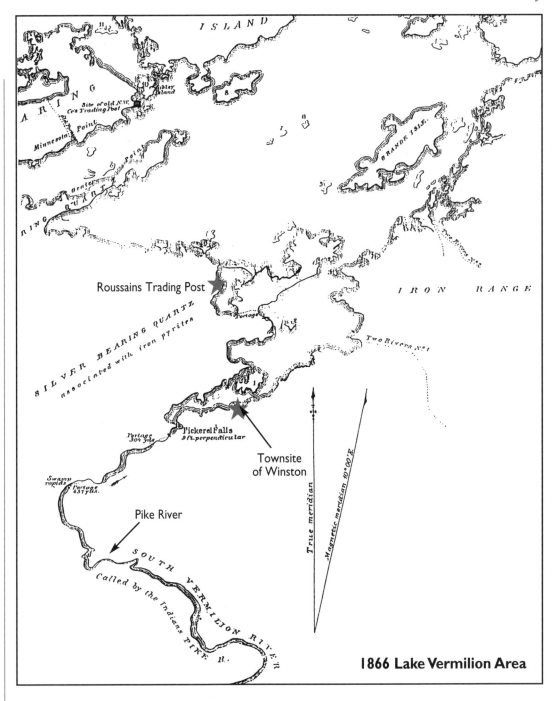

Roussains Trading Post

Townsite
of Winston

Pike River

1866 Lake Vermilion Area

This detail from the map on the preceding page more clearly shows the townsite of Winston, the Pike River entering the southeast shore of Lake Vermilion and correctly identifies the iron formation that would eventually lead to permanent settlement of the area.

commanding an army. In many ways it was a little army. When they left St. Paul on December 27, 1865, the Mutuals looked like a Civil War task force. They had a captain, engineer, quartermaster, commissary sergeant and a wagonmaster. They even had a chaplain. All were heavily armed. They arrived in Superior, Wisconsin, on January 13, 1866, and, according to the *Superior Gazette*, displayed an impressive array of equipment:

"The train consists of eight sleds: five of them drawn by two yoke of oxen each, one drawn by a single yoke, one by a span of Canadian ponies, and one fitted up as an ambulance, drawn by a single horse. On one of these sleds

is a cooking and eating car, 6 feet wide, 6 feet high and 18 feet long: the whole is covered with a canvas roof; it is fitted up with a cooking stove in the forward end and on the other side are narrow tables from which the party take their meals standing. The noon meal is prepared while the train is in motion, thus doing away with detention during the middle of the day."[57]

They were welcomed in Superior. Gold excitement had taken over the town and turned it into a place of prospectors and citizens turned gold seekers. Some, like George Stuntz, J.J. Hibbard and Thomas Clark, had been to Lake Vermilion the summer before and, although they didn't find any gold, most of

Superior's citizens were sure it was just a matter of time before it would be discovered.[58]

There was also talk in town of a plan by Governor Miller and a group of Minnesota politicians to take control of the gold fields through the laying of Sioux and Chippewa scrip. The Mutuals made it clear they had no intention of recognizing any property "not personally occupied and being developed." This is what people in Superior wanted to hear. The local newspaper proclaimed its approval:

"We have met and conversed with most if not all of the party, and find them as good a set of fellows as one would wish to fall in with, and were we about to start for Vermillion [sic], we should endeavor to cast our lot with them … they will settle on and take possession of such veins and leads as may look most favorable, without regard to the mythical proprietorship which is pretended to be held there by scrip land grabbers."[59]

Superior citizens held a banquet and ball for the Mutuals, speeches were given, toasts were made. Seven additional members were gained. *Gazette* editor Washington Ashton made this prediction:

"… the whole thing is destined to end in the defeat of these scrip layers, and the Vermilion gold fields are being peopled by the

right class of claimants, men who go there with the substantial means to open and work the ground; men who are making the road which the scrip-men falsely claim to have made through a wild and difficult country."[60]

The Mutuals did find a trail to Lake Vermilion. The route had been hacked out in the fall of 1865 by a crew of men led under the direction of Colonel Joshua Culver of Superior. Crews of Civil War veterans paid from Superior and St. Paul city treasuries had since been at work cutting brush and improving the road, but the last half was still too narrow for the Mutual's equipment. They had to widen it as they moved. Their progress slowed to less than two miles a day. Mutual leader Thomas Newson later remarked, "The road we have cut is much better than that we have passed over. I do not believe that any other party could do what this company is doing. Minnesota could well afford to donate $10,000 to this company as a token of what we are doing toward opening up this rich mineral area and surely inducing the tide of immigration."[61]

The Mutuals arrived at Lake Vermilion on March 5. By this time, a cluster of tents and hastily built shacks on the shore of Pike Bay was already beginning to take the shape of a town. At first referred to as Vermilion Falls, the town was later renamed Winston City in honor

By the 1860s, settlers were already clustering in several platted townsites that would eventually be incorporated into the city of Duluth. Northeast Minnesota Historical Center

37

of the Mutuals' general manager, Ralph R. Winston. By mid-May, a three-story hotel was in the making and a saloon, gambling hall, blacksmith shop, livery stable, general store, post office and 14 rough "cabins" gave the place the trimmings of a booming town.[62]

Resistance to absentee speculators holding scrip claims began with the arrival of the Mutuals. On March 10, 1866, led by Major Newson, 78 prospectors gathered in Winston to petition the state Legislature to regulate claims and recognize the right of Vermilion gold miners to organize a governing district.

The resulting Vermilion Lake Mining District limited individual claims to 900 yards by 450 yards and required claimants to post their names at each corner. No claimant could hold more than one claim at a time, one day's work had to be done on a claim each month in order to hold it and a position of test miner was established to inspect and certify all claims at the lake. The new governing body elected Thomas Newson as its first president.[63]

Members of the Mutual Protection Company, acting as test miner's deputies, began inspecting existing claims and locating their own. If they found a vein of possible gold-bearing quartz that had not been claimed, properly signed or recently worked, they marked it out for themselves, according to the laws of the district. There was resistance. In mid-May the *St. Paul Pioneer* reported:

"The Mutuals are located so promiscuously that some of them may be sure of doing well.... They have built a good home on crater point (Birch Point), but have been ordered to leave by Mr. Palmer of Duluth who personally surveyed and located the same in October last.... Others of the company are scattered about Ely's Island and in this city of Winston.... The hotel in which this is written is not yet finished but will accommodate the present run of custom."[64]

There were other gold companies at Lake Vermilion during these years. A New York Gold Company hauled in a steam boiler and sank a shaft at Pine Point. A boiler and a stamp mill were set up at Trout Lake portage by the Wabasha Gold Mining Company. A Superior Lands and Minerals Company made several excavations in the vicinity of Stuntz Bay and a heavily financed Chicago firm calling itself the Vermilion Lake Mineral Land Company sank shafts on Ely Island, Gold Island and at many other places on the lake. It has been estimated that at least a dozen different mining companies attempted to mine Vermilion gold at one time or another.[65]

Gold fever probably reached its height during the summer of 1866 when thousands of prospectors poured in from all parts of the country. Rumors of gold and silver nuggets and "gold in the washings of a gulch" circulating in Chicago, New York and most of the towns of Minnesota contributed to the excitement.[66] At Lake Vermilion there were arguments over scrip claims and disagreements on mine limits. There were threats of violence, there was tribal unrest. A federal law, passed on July 26, 1866, prohibiting a person from filing a claim at the local land office until he had occupied it and improved it did little to quiet things down. The nearest U.S. marshal was 90 miles away in Duluth and nothing would probably have stopped impending violence, had not gold fever begun to die.

At the height of the excitement, the *St. Paul Pioneer* published an article that carried a grim warning for all those who hoped to get rich overnight. "We have a number of experienced California miners here. All claim there is no gulch mining, such as in California, to be found."[67] This meant there was no hope of panning for gold or finding nuggets. The report suggested, if any gold was to be obtained at all, "much capital is needed to mine it." People should come to the area, not with the idea of staking personal claims, but as laborers willing to work for a wage."[68]

As the summer days of 1866 wore on, one by one the men began returning from their diggings. They congregated in Winston City with their piles of quartz. An expert was brought in to assay the ores. He made the necessary tests. The report was the same for everyone, "Not a trace of gold in any of it."

Thus, the first phase of the gold rush came to an end within a few months after it started. Picks, shovels, hand drills and other gold mining tools were left rusting on the shores of the lake, as prospectors abandoned their claims and began the long trek back to civilization. Mine offices were boarded up and Winston City's hotel would never be finished. Although a few diehards stayed on still hoping to strike it rich, no one will ever know how many men came to Iron Country during those first months, nor will anyone know how many suffered injury, lost their savings or even lost their lives during that wild rush for gold. ∎

CHAPTER 4

From Gold to Iron

The Bois Forte Treaty of 1866

When news of gold first rolled off the presses in St. Paul, Lake Vermilion was home to the Bois Forte Band of Chippewa. They were not yet reservation peoples and still roamed freely across the land, as their ancestors had done centuries before. Like their forefathers, the men of the tribe continued to rely on trapping and trading to meet their family needs. However, by 1865 Bois Forte trappers were no longer bringing all their furs to the British at Rainy Lake as they had in the past. Instead, members of the dozen or so scattered bands were often customers at a small trading post located in Lake Vermilion's Sucker Bay.[1]

The post was managed by two Fond du Lac fur buyers, Francis Roussain and his son, Eustace. The Roussains had taken over the trade at Lake Vermilion after the collapse of

the American Fur Company and employed both whites and native people in their business. They were constantly traveling back and forth between Vermilion and Fond du Lac, where they had their main post and were often joined by traders and merchants from the frontier settlements. Peter Bradshaw, John Rakowsky, Vincent Roy, Paul Beaulieu, Benjamin LaRose, Alex Paul, Charles Cadotte, D. George Morrison and George Nettleton all had dealings with the Roussains and the Lake Vermilion people. Undoubtedly, these fur buyers and peddlers were aware of prospectors at the lake and may have been at least partially responsible for a surprisingly strong Bois Forte reaction to so-called white intruders at the lake in the fall of 1865.[2]

At this time, most people assumed Lake Vermilion was the property of the Bois Forte

Native people gathered for the yearly payment made to Lake Superior Chippewa at Grand Portage. Because the payments were typically made during their wild ricing season and they lived so far from Lake Superior, the Bois Forte people were often unrepresented. NORTHEAST MINNESOTA HISTORICAL CENTER

bands. Even employees within the Bureau of Indian Affairs referred to the lake as the Vermilion Reservation. Agent Luther Webb explained:

"My immediate predecessor Agent Drew located a blacksmith shop near Vermilion Lake and since the location of the shop at that point, it has been called the Vermilion Lake Reservation. There are no Indians residing permanently on what is termed the Reservation. A number of years ago, a trading house was established on the banks of Vermilion Lake. Near the site is the smith shop. The Indians cultivate patches of land at this point in potatoes and come to the lake for blacksmith work, to trade their furs for supplies, to plant, hoe and harvest their potatoes and to fish in the lake. There are only three or four log houses at this point, which are occupied by the government employees and traders. The Indians have no houses, living all together in wigwams or lodges – they live almost exclusively by hunting and fishing. Game is much more abundant in that region than on the south shore of Lake Superior and the furs collected are among the finest in the North West.

"As a consequence the Bois Forte Indians are the most independent and self reliant of any Indians within this agency."[3]

The Bois Forte people also thought the lake belonged to them. As far as they were concerned they had never participated in any treaty with the American government and, although one of their nine chiefs did attend the council at La Pointe in 1854, he denied signing any treaty. Besides, payments for the ceded land were made long distances away at places like Grand Portage and Fond du Lac – and at the height of the wild ricing season. As a result, bands were often unrepresented at the payment table and only a small number of people actually benefitted from them.[4]

Strangers cutting clearings and exploring about the lake in the summer of 1865 were therefore looked upon as trespassers and in early September the Indians held council – presumably at the Roussain trading post – and agreed to contact the commissioner of Indian Affairs to obtain a statement reaffirming their right to the lake. This was done on October 5. In the meantime, they began ordering prospectors off the grounds.[5]

Minnesota was just three years removed from its last Indian War, the so-called Sioux Uprising of 1862, and state leaders were still a little shaky. They knew the Ojibway living at Lake Vermilion were armed, and it seemed just a matter of time before there would be a confrontation.

Reports of what seemed a "Bois Forte War Council" filtered back to the office of Minnesota Governor Stephen Miller. On November 13, in a strong letter to the commissioner of Indian Affairs, Miller made his position clear:

"By the treaty of Septr (sic) 30, 1854, in which the Bois Forte bands participated, all the lands in the vicinity of Vermillion (sic) Lake were ceded to the United States and no vestige of title thereto remains in any of the Chippewa bands.… Citizens of this and other states are making valuable mineral discoveries upon the territory in question and some of them have already been interrupted by the said Indians. And as thousands of whites will at an early day attempt the development of these lands, I ask that said bands be promptly instructed as to their duty and that they be removed from Lake Vermillion (sic) at as early a period as may be practical."[6]

Miller went on to suggest that a military post be located at the lake "as promptly as possible." He added, "Otherwise these badly advised savages may interfere with our enterprising citizens which, I am persuaded, would lead to unhappy results."[7]

It never came to armed conflict, but it did lead to another treaty, the Bois Forte Treaty of 1866. Alexander Ramsey, who was then serving in the U.S. Senate, arranged for nine Bois Forte chiefs to travel to Washington, D.C., in February 1866. Making the trip were Gabeshcodaway, Going through the Prairie; Sabawmadjeweshcang (Mountain Traveler); Adawawnequabenac (Twin Haired Bird); Sagwadachinegishcang (He Who Tries the Earth); Neoning (Four Fingers); Wabawgamawgan (Tomahawk); Ganawawbamins (He Who is Looked At); Gawhandawawinao (Berry Hunter); and Abetang (He Who Inhabits). Along with the chiefs were Nawgawnab, head chief of the Lake Superior Chippewas, traders Francis and Eustace Roussain, Vincent and Frank

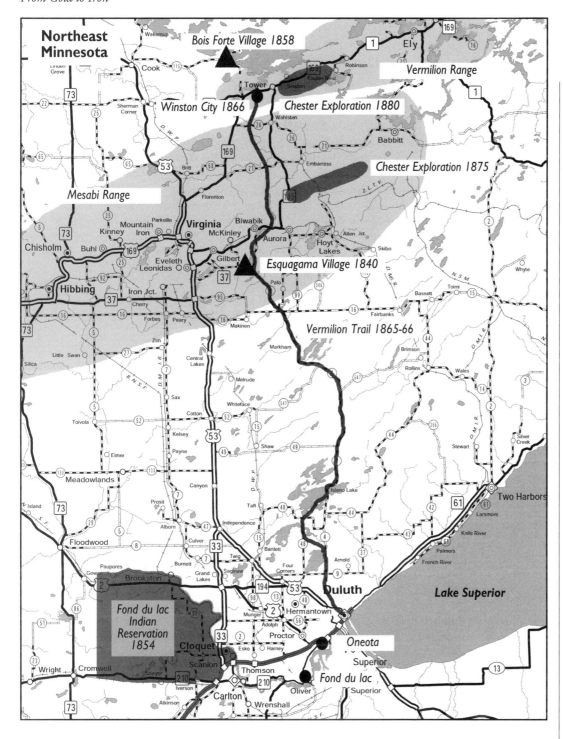

Northeast Minnesota

Bois Forte Village 1858

Vermilion Range

Winston City 1866

Chester Exploration 1880

Chester Exploration 1875

Mesabi Range

Esquagama Village 1840

Vermilion Trail 1865-66

Fond du lac Indian Reservation 1854

Lake Superior

The map of Northeast Minnesota shows the Vermilion Trail, Ojibway sites, Duluth and frontier settlements and Chester explorations of 1875 and 1880. MAP PROVIDED COURTESY OF THE STATE OF MINNESOTA

Roy, Superior register of deeds D. George Morrison and interpreter Joe Gurnoe. Ignatius Donnelly and Peter Roy did the negotiating on behalf of the tribes and the treaty was concluded on April 7, 1866.[8]

It provided that the Bois Forte give up all claims to Lake Vermilion and other places in northern Minnesota in return for a 100,000-acre reservation along with the usual amenities: a blacksmith shop, school, agency office, warehouse and, as a bonus, eight homes for the chiefs. For their services Francis Roussain, Frank Roussain, Eustace

Roussain, Peter Bradshaw, Joe Gurnoe, Frank Roy and Vincent Roy were given the right to select parcels of land at Lake Vermilion varying from 80 to 160 acres each. Because the treaty was concluded at a time of gold excitement, the parcels were without mineral rights.[9]

The Bois Forte people were now expected to leave the lake and the only pressing need was to survey out a 100,000-acre reservation for them. Treaty negotiators came up with Nett Lake as a likely site for the new reservation, and state leaders were

anxious to have someone check the area for precious metals before the site was finalized. Reservation selection commissioners Shubael P. Adams, J.C. Ramsey and John G. Webb, along with seven voyageurs and government surveyor George Riley Stuntz, set out for Nett Lake that same fall and arrived at Lake Vermilion late in the afternoon of October 17.[10]

A winter storm was brewing and freeze-up was only weeks away. They delayed two days at Winston City procuring additional supplies and a larger canoe. The name of the town had recently been changed to Vermilion City, and Commissioner Adams described it as "a place of 20-some log houses and a third that number of inhabitants."[11] Gold fever had cooled with the weather and prospectors anxious to get back to civilization before winter set in had tossed their tools aside and left their mining machinery scattered about the lake. Few would return.

Despite the lateness of the season and the threatening weather, the commissioners were determined to push on. They left Vermilion City on the evening of October 19 and made their way to the post in Sucker Bay, where they hired a guide. No one in the original party had any idea of how to get to Nett Lake. The next morning, the wind picked up and there was sleet in the air. By late afternoon, the sleet had turned to snow and it continued to snow for the next 17 days.[12]

This didn't stop the exploring party. They broke ice on the Ash River. By the time they reached Pelican Lake, it was completely frozen over. There, they exchanged their canoes for toboggans, waited for the ice to thicken and then pressed on, arriving at Nett Lake on November 5.[13]

Surveyor Stuntz in a letter to Indian Agent Luther Webb said this about the expedition:

"The early season at which winter set in and the unusual depth of the snow which fell in October came near defeating the object of the commission and added immensely to the labors of the party and the expenses necessary to carry it out. It was not practical to reach the small reservation at Deer Creek on the Big Fork River and we did not attempt it.… I was constantly bathed in ice water from the snow melting upon my cloths. We completed the survey and started upon the return on the 16th of December."[14]

They did their job. They made sure there were no outcroppings of gold, silver or other valuable minerals. They ran the lines, marked out corners for the reservation and headed back, the first of the party arriving in Superior on Christmas Eve, 1866. The new home for the Bois Forte Chippewa bands consisted of 100,000 acres of land. Most of it was swamp.

Gold Again at Lake Vermilion

Gold excitement, which had faded in the fall of 1866, was stirred up again in the spring of 1868 after a certain Colonel David Tindall of St. Paul announced the successful testing of a process he had developed to extract gold from the "sulphureated ores" of Lake Vermilion.

According to Tindall, during the winter of 1867, 2,000 pounds of pulverized quartz from a Vermilion Gold Mining Company claim had been processed by his method to produce 67^1/$_2$ ounces of gold bullion. Tindall announced he would go to Lake Vermilion that same spring and, using his process, would test the ores of all the mines at the lake. Articles appeared in the press, word spread and money was invested.

In March 1868, *The Gazette* of Superior reported: "On Wednesday last, Mr. Zachau started four teams to Vermilion, with the supplies of Col. Tindall's party. One of the loads was a reverberatory furnace for the roasting of ore, made of thin boiler iron, about 10 feet long, three feet wide and, on an average, about 30 inches high, weighing 540 pounds; the remainder of the freight was for the most part made up of provisions."[15]

By mid-May, Tindall assays were identifying traces of gold and silver in quartz samples from 15 different parts of the lake. The Superior newspaper reported, "The veins in question are situated on the shores and islands," but "the most remarkable of the results" are "from claims of the Wabashaw Company, which appear to be exclusively from the islands of the lake."[16]

In August, there were reports that the process had been used to successfully refine significant amounts of gold and silver from quartz taken from the Minnesota Gold Mining Company's shaft on Minnesota Point, the New York Company's shafts on Pine Island, the Chicago Company's veins on Ely Island and from other workings.[17]

However, before the process could be fully proven, Tindall's furnace broke down and apparently all gold and silver production at Lake Vermilion came to an end. In an article published in the Superior *Gazette*, William H. Nobles of St. Paul, a heavy investor in the Chicago Company, claimed to have witnessed some of the gold refining: "On account of the giving out of the furnace, with which the Colonel was operating, myself as well as others, did not have as full and satisfactory opportunities of witnessing the use of his process in all the different veins as was desired. The New York Gold Mining Company had quartz on hand (believed to be very rich) from Scott Island Shaft 72 feet deep which the Colonel could not work and some were very anxious to see the rock from the Tindall vein tested … but enough was ascertained from actual observation to satisfy all, that with Col. Tindall's or a similar process, the mines of Vermilion are second to none in point of value…."[18]

As briefly described in August 1868, Tindall's process subjected crushed Vermilion quartz to intense heat and then loaded it into a vat containing special chemicals. The chemicals supposedly freed tiny "precious metal particles" from where they were "concealed in the sulphurets" so that they could be dissolved in mercury to produce a gold or silver amalgam.[19] The thing was, Tindall didn't reveal the precise nature or the names of the chemicals that he used and apparently couldn't be reached at the time. It was reported that he had gone to Chicago to procure a better furnace and larger stampmill. In September, there were rumors of heavy machinery being shipped north and talk of plans to build a giant "ten stamp mill" at the lake.[20] However, in the midst of all the excitement, other rumors began to circulate. It was suggested that the quartz tested by the Tindall process might have been "salted."[21]

The truth of these rumors was never established, but it seems they were enough to discourage future investment in gold mining. The equipment didn't materialize, the big stamp mill was never built and interest faded quickly after 1868. Was there ever any gold at the lake? Highly respected geologists examining the Vermilion formations in the years that followed differed in their opinions as to the existence of gold. Duluth historian John R. Carey, in his narrative of 1898, probably summed it up accurately when he wrote "… there was not enough gold to pay at Vermilion Lake, yet thousands of dollars were expended in sending to the Vermilion wilderness men, supplies and even machinery to crush the rock and extract the gold."[22]

George Stuntz and the Mountain of Iron

A few gold seekers stayed on for a year or so, still hoping by some miracle to strike it rich, but by the summer of 1870, they, too, were gone. Except for a few clearings, some rubble and a scattering of tools, it seemed that nothing had changed. The Vermilion Bois Forte people saw no reason to move to the new reservation, and it was business as usual at the Roussain post. It remained this way for five years.

Then the prospectors were back. Two things had happened during the gold rush that made the return of mineral explorers inevitable. One was the opening of an overland road connecting Duluth to Lake Vermilion. The other was the fact that exposures of rich iron ore on the south side of the lake were seen by men who knew something about minerals and mining.

One such man was George Riley Stuntz. Born in Erie County, Pennsylvania, Stuntz, a highly educated man for his time, had studied science and engineering and mastered the skills of surveying. After teaching school in Illinois for a few years, he arrived in Superior in 1852 as a federal government surveyor. A year later – even before the Treaty of La Pointe was concluded – Stuntz had a cabin and trading post on the Minnesota side of the lake.[23] In 1865, while others were seeking gold, Stuntz was looking for iron. He described his activities of that year:

While others searched for gold, government surveyor George Riley Stuntz explored a "mountain of iron" near Lake Vermilion. Hibbing Historical Society collection at the Iron Range Research Center

"It was in October 1865 that Captain Pratt and myself left Superior with two months supplies and a resolution to search the Vermilion country for iron, my attention having been called to the matter by one Joe Posey, a half-breed Scotchman. In those days we ascended the St. Louis River, made the portage to Pike River and down that stream into Pike Bay on Lake Vermilion. At the time we came up, Henry Mayhew, now of Grand Marais, Richard Eames, a geologist, and J.J. Hibbard of Michigan were also en route, together with others, all of whom were attracted by gold."[24]

Stuntz and his partner learned about Bois Forte objections to prospectors at the lake upon their arrival at the Roussain Post: "One Francis Roussain had established a trading post with the Indians across Sucker Bay opposite from what now is the government reserve. Roussain was absent at the time of our arrival and the post was in charge of a Captain Simons, whose initials I have forgotten, and a half-breed who could interpret. We stopped there that night and were rather surprised when the half-breed told us that the Indian chiefs, of which there were several present, objected to our coming up here in their country. I did not suspect Captain Simons of being at the back of this and began to expostulate and through the interpreter to make my defense."[25]

Stuntz continued: "Fortunately, I discovered the interpreter was not telling the chiefs what I requested him to and at once suspected that Simons was at the bottom of the whole affair. It required but a few moments for me to express myself. I had the Indians informed that if they injured a hair of our heads, they would have United States troops after them, not neglecting to give the jealous Simons a little wholesome advice at the same time. Then with considerable ceremony, Capt. Pratt and myself laid ourselves on the floor to pass the night, first significantly placing a small United States flag on a stick at our heads."[26]

Stuntz and Pratt managed to get through the night unmolested and early the next morning quietly left the post to resume their search for the so-called "mountain of iron" from which Posey had taken his specimens. They found the place and on the same day also took specimens at a "great outcropping"

which later became the Breitung Mine – Minnesota's first commercial iron mine.[27] Stuntz later stated: "I saw the location, at the east end of the bluff, where it showed the richest, and where I got the specimens that finally called the attention of capitalists to that part of the country."[28]

After spending a few weeks at the east end of the lake, going as far east as what later became the Pete Armstrong claim (Armstrong Lake), the two men began their journey back to Superior.

According to Stuntz, "On our return to Roussain's post, Capt. Simons expressed great solicitude for our welfare and had thought us lost, but it isn't probable that he had worried much as to our safety, although he was fearful that we would discover something. In November, with 60 pounds of specimens, all iron, we ascended Pike River and began our return to Superior. The rivers froze and we were compelled to make 60 miles through the wilderness."[29]

Stuntz went on: "While I was making the explorations, I found afterwards that J.B. Culver and Vose Palmer were on my trail, very anxious to know what I had found. At a Sunday conference, when asked my opinion, I told the boys: 'When this country is developed, that big mountain of iron will do it. When they get to hauling that iron out, they will haul in its supplies cheap.'"[30]

Iron Country's Lands Are Opened to Entry and Sale

But the iron ore deposits of the Vermilion Range were destined to lie dormant for almost 20 years more. There were reasons. The deposits were too far from Lake Superior. The steel industry was then well-served by iron mines located closer to the eastern mills. Even if there had been interest in mining the Vermilion, it would have been difficult to obtain the land. By treaty, title lay with the federal government and pre-emption laws passed by Congress made it necessary that the land be surveyed before it could be put up for sale. No such survey had been made.

Even if the land could have been had, there remained the question of mineral rights. When the nation was first formed, the federal government looked at its mineral lands as a potential source of revenue and

protected them. But by the 1860s, Congress had changed the laws for acquiring mineral lands so many times that no one was quite sure as to what was legal or what was illegal. But in the case of Lake Vermilion, the government made its position clear. The 1866 treaty withheld the mineral rights from parcels awarded to the men who had negotiated in the name of the Bois Forte bands. Supposedly the mineral rights were being reserved for some sort of special sale or lease. If this was so, a procedure for doing this was never spelled out.

It wasn't until 1872 that a procedure was established under the law for opening federal land to mineral exploration and purchase. In that year, Congress set the price of federal mineral land at $2.50 an acre for placer deposits and $5 an acre for lode mining.[31] This would have made the Vermilion Range available to any mining concern willing to invest in it, except for the fact that the very next year Michigan Senator Zach Chandler had Congress remove "Minnesota, Wisconsin and Michigan mineral lands" from the mining codes established by the 1872 law.[32] According to Chandler the bill was "purely a local measure and will not affect the mines on the Pacific coast. However, the law is necessary to develop the copper and iron mines of the Lake Superior region."[33]

Chandler's bill sailed through Congress on February 18, 1873. From that time on, Minnesota's Iron Country was open to entry and sale under prevailing homestead and pre-emption laws. The mineral rights went with the land. But iron ore was not as attractive as copper when it came to mining ventures and there was copper – copper in its most pure form – on the south shore of Lake Superior. In 1844, the discovery of a rich lode of this "native copper" on Michigan's Keweenaw Peninsula led to a copper boom, and towns and mines appeared almost overnight.[34]

There was so much copper in Michigan that the Quincy Mine near the town of Hancock was able to meet all of the Union's copper needs during the Civil War. Until 1887, Michigan mines produced almost four-fifths of the nation's copper.[35] During these years the Keweenaw was seen as a place of opportunity and attracted people from all parts of the world.

Almost unnoticed in the midst of the copper excitement was the discovery of iron ore at the Jackson Mine near the present site of Negaunee. On February 10, 1848, a Jackson Company blacksmith working a tiny forge became the first person to turn ore from the Lake Superior region into iron.[36] But the Jackson project came to an unprofitable end in 1854. There had been transportation problems, smelting iron was a costly process and the market was at best uncertain.

Just two years after the Jackson Mine closed, a new process for making steel was developed by an English iron master named Henry Bessemer. Steel was the finest and most pure form of iron known to mankind. It had always been difficult to produce and was, therefore, rare and extremely expensive. Bessemer's process involved a pear-shaped receptacle designed to allow a stream of air to be blown through molten pig iron. The intense heat created by the process burned away the impurities from the iron, turning it into steel.

The new process made it possible to produce a large amount of steel quickly and inexpensively. However, the Bessemer Process was effective only when the phosphorus content of the iron ore was less than half of 1 percent. In 1856, there weren't many known bodies of iron ore with that low a content of phosphorus, including the ores of the Appalachians that were then the main source of iron ore in this country. Although no one knew it then, in the long run, the problem would give American steel manufacturers an incalculable advantage over steel makers in other countries. It led them to the ores of Michigan and Minnesota.

In 1861, two things happened that turned all eyes to Lake Superior and gave the industry its advantage. In the East all those old wooden bridges built during Colonial times began falling into disrepair and the Civil War broke out. The Civil War demonstrated the advantages of railroads and initiated a 60-year period of intense railroad building. Steel was needed for all those rails – and steel was needed to replace all those old bridges. Soon there were a thousand more uses for steel.

But in order to make more steel, the problem with the Bessemer process had to be solved. Ores from existing American iron

mines simply had too much phosphorous in them to make all the steel that was needed An all-out effort was made to find low phosphorous iron ore. The ores of Michigan's Marquette Range met this requirement and received all the attention of steel manufacturers until the low phosphorous ores of the Menominee Range were discovered in the 1870s and the Gogebic Range was opened in the 1880s.

Eventually, a way was found to remove phosphorous from iron ore right at the steel mill, but by that time the steel industry had grown to a point where all the iron mines in America weren't enough to meet its needs. By this time interest had switched to the already well-known iron deposits of northeast Minnesota.

The first attempt to mine iron in Minnesota, however, did not occur at Stuntz's mountain on the south shore of Lake Vermilion. It took place on the Mesabi Range and was the product of developers from Michigan.

The Ontonagon Syndicate Attempts to Mine the Mesabi

In the late 1840s, while the copper boom was sweeping across northern Michigan, the town of Ontonagon became a major shipping port for copper being mined in the Rockland and Victoria districts. By 1848, it had grown into the largest town on the south shore of Lake Superior.[37] Speculators and developers filled its hotels and boardinghouses.

It was during this time that a few immigrant families from Germany began arriving in Ontonagon. Known as "Forty-Eighters," these families were part of a large wave of Germans who migrated to America after a failed attempt to establish parliamentary government in Germany in 1848. Many of these highly skilled people were attracted to the country around Lake Superior where land could be had cheaply and opportunities seemed unlimited. Among the arrivals at Ontonagon in 1849 was Henry Wieland. He was followed over the next two years by four of his brothers, Christian, Ernst, Albert and August.[38] The arrival of the Wielands on the docks of Ontonagon marks the beginning of iron mining on northeast Minnesota's Mesabi Range.

By the time August, the youngest of the brothers, arrived in 1850, copper mining in nearby mines had declined sharply. Businesses were closing, people were moving out but, in the saloons and emporiums of Ontonagon, there was talk of great stands of white pine and rich veins of copper along Lake Superior's north shore. The problem was that the territory was Indian country and closed to development.

Christian, caught up in tales of white pine and treasure, soon convinced his brothers that they should move to the other side of the lake as soon as the territory was opened for settlement. Most people in town believed that it was just a matter of time before this would occur. It did occur and, two years after the Treaty of La Pointe, the brothers, along with a group of German and Swiss immigrants, chartered a steam sidewheeler, loaded it with all their belongings and set out for the north shore of the lake where they established a settlement at the mouth of the Beaver River. They called it Beaver Bay.[39]

There, the Wieland brothers set up a sawmill, logged out both sides of the Beaver River and became suppliers of lumber to the mining towns of Michigan and other settlements on the lake. They hired Native Americans, former voyageurs and unemployed Michigan miners to work in their mill and lumber camps. It is said that Christian learned to speak Ojibway and came to know the country north of the lake quite well. His reputation was enough for State Geologist Henry Eames to hire Christian to take him to Lake Vermilion in 1865.[40] He told Christian that he had been directed by the governor of the state to investigate rumors of gold discoveries in that vicinity. He said that he was also interested in investigating the possibility of minerals on the range of hills known to the Indians as Mesabi-Watchu, the Big Man Hills.

The route they followed took them to Greenwood Lake. From there they traveled by canoe to Birch Lake and camped at the mouth of the Dunka River. There, at the east end of the Mesabi Range, they noted a deflection of the compass needle and Christian Wieland became convinced that they had encountered a vast body of iron ore. However, the party pushed on to Lake

Vermilion, where Eames found the samples of quartz that set off the Gold Rush of 1865-66.

The Wielands were more impressed with the iron ore they had seen south of Birch Lake. They left Eames at Lake Vermilion and went back to the Mesabi heights to get a better look at the iron formation and pick up samples to take back to Beaver Bay.[41]

Christian Wieland is said to have carried these samples with him on visits to Lake Superior ports where he traded lumber for supplies. At Ontonagon they were inspected by some Michigan mining men who described them as "high-grade magnetic iron ore, similar to that of the Marquette Range."

While interest in Vermilion gold dwindled in Minnesota, interest in Mesabi iron grew in Michigan. Around 1869, a group calling itself the "Ontonagon Syndicate" began meeting at Ontonagon's Bigelow Hotel to try to figure out ways to gain title to the land where the samples were found. Attending were William Willard, Lewis Dickens, Louis Longpre and James Mercer, all Ontonagon businessmen; Linus Stannard, a telephone company owner from Rockland; W.W. Spalding, a well-known promoter; Thomas Hooper, operator of Michigan's Nonesuch and Victoria copper mines; and Peter Mitchell, an expert mineralogist and prospector. There were others.[42]

Also at the meetings were George C. Stone, Clinton Markell, Calvin Baily, Joshua Culver, Daniel Cash, John Hunter and J.D. Ensign, all Duluth people – all speculators and promoters – all destined to play their role in the opening of Iron Country. The group was not without political clout. Alexander Ramsey, former governor of Minnesota, then U.S. Senator, was also a member.[43]

Christian Wieland missed few of these meetings. It is said that for the information they provided, the Wielands were promised a quarter-interest in any property acquired by syndicate members.[44] The plan for acquisition was simple and not unlike others of the age. Members shared the expense of sending a competent explorer to examine the iron formation and determine exactly what land should be secured for future speculation and mining.

Peter Mitchell was picked for the job. During the summer of 1870, Mitchell, some of the Wielands and a party of miners set out for Birch Lake to explore the eastern Mesabi heights. There, they encountered a landscape of windfalls, boulders and vast areas of bare gray-banded, iron-laden rock. It seemed to stretch for miles. Mitchell was sure he had seen exactly the same kind of rock on the Marquette Range. He was also sure that rich ore lay below the exposed lean ore, as it did in Michigan.[45]

The five Wieland brothers set up a sawmill in Beaver Bay and became suppliers of lumber to the mining towns of Michigan and other Lake Superior settlements. This 1888 photo shows a boat waiting to load.
NEWTON COLLECTION AT THE NORTHEAST MINNESOTA HISTORICAL CENTER

He ordered the sinking of a test pit. The iron-laden rock was taconite and proved to be extremely hard to penetrate. The men, using heavy sledges, hand drills, chisels and black powder, took weeks to sink a single test pit 6 feet deep. However, several more test pits were sunk and toward the end of summer, Mitchell found ore to his liking. He described "an iron mountain … 12 miles long and 1¹/₂ miles wide."[46]

The Mitchell party did go to Lake Vermilion that same fall to look at Stuntz's "mountain of iron." At the time, neither mountain had been surveyed and Mitchell could just as easily have recommended to the Ontonagon partners that they acquire the Vermilion iron land. The question is why didn't he? It could be that Stuntz's outcroppings of hematite seemed small and scattered compared to the vast iron formation Mitchell had encountered on the Mesabi. More likely it was because Stuntz was promoting the Vermilion and, as official government surveyor, had the power to classify any land he surveyed as swamp, farm or mineral and thus control not only the method by which it could be acquired but also the price. In other words, the Ontonagons "would not be able to secure title to good mineral lands there except at prices they would consider exorbitant."[47]

All of this occurred before a legal way to obtain the minerals had been established. In 1870, no one in either Michigan or Minnesota was quite sure how to go about securing any of Minnesota's iron lands. But the Mining Act of 1872 and Chandler's bill of 1873 excluding Minnesota iron lands from the act's provisions changed all that. After February 18, 1873, iron land was in the same category as nonmineral land and could be had for as little as $1.25 an acre, but it had to be officially surveyed first.

There was more to it. Prevailing laws limited the amount to 160 acres and required the person buying the land to live on it. But the 1870s were speculative times and anyone wanting to acquire property in northeast Minnesota, mineral lands or not, could hire a professional homesteader to build a shack on the desired land and file a claim to it at the Duluth Land Office. As soon as the professional homesteader, or entryman, as they were sometimes called, received the deed, he signed it over to the person employing him and collected his fee.

Not legal, but in those days openly condoned by government land agents, elected officials and even the courts.[48]

Christian Wieland was appointed official government surveyor, undoubtedly the result of Ramsey's influence. Weiland appears to have begun his work in February 1872 and by September he had surveyed two Mesabi Range townships: Township 60, Range 12 and Township 60, Range 13. By that time, there were 24 so-called homesteaders in the surveyed region. The Duluth Land Office recorded deeds for something like 9,000 acres of land in those two townships. All of it eventually fell into the hands of syndicate members.[49]

The syndicate went so far as to incorporate a railroad to connect their holdings to Duluth. On December 21, 1874, the Duluth and Iron Range Railroad Company was formed and quickly secured a so-called "swampland" grant from the Minnesota Legislature amounting to 10 square miles of land for each mile of track constructed between Duluth and the Mesabi Range.[50]

Although no track was ever laid by the Ontonagons, they did go on to establish the Mesaba Iron Company, with Alexander Ramsey as president. It was the first mining company formed to mine on the Mesabi Range, although it never went beyond offering options on the property to promoters. However, the railroad company with its land grant was later to have important implications for actual iron mining in Minnesota.

At about the same time the railroad company received its grant, the first of Albert Chester's two reports came out. Chester, a reputable professor of mineralogy at New York state's Hamilton College, had been hired by Pennsylvania promoter Charlemagne Tower to determine the feasibility of commercial mining in Minnesota's Iron Country. The report condemned Mesabi ores as "too lean."[51] There is little doubt that the report put a damper on Ontonagon plans to build a railroad and mine the Mesabi. The Panic of 1873 left investors shaky, and there were few who were willing to put their money into railroad ventures. If there were any who might have been willing to invest in a railroad to the Mesabi, they lost their enthusiasm after reading the Chester Report of 1875.

Superior Street, Duluth, Minn., in 1871.

All eyes then turned to the Vermilion Range and Stuntz's mountain. A man who played a key role in turning attention to the Vermilion Range was Duluth's city treasurer, George C. Stone. Stone had been with the Ontonagons during their formation years, but quietly left the organization after his election to city office.

Stone fit his times. He was in every way a typical 19th century rugged individualist and promoter. He was a smooth talker – the kind of man who inspired confidence. Brought up near Boston, he moved west to Muscatine, Iowa, where he established a general store and, a few years later, a bank. He might have been overly aggressive in his bank investments because when the Civil War broke out and nervous depositors demanded to see their money, Stone filed bankruptcy.[52]

After a number of attempts to re-establish himself in Chicago, Philadelphia and other places, Stone ended up in Duluth as secretary to George B. Sargent, who was acting agent for one of the country's foremost bankers, Jay Cooke of Philadelphia. Cooke and a partner, William Moorhead, had acquired a vast acreage of pine land west of Lake Superior and were building a railroad to connect St. Paul with Lake Superior. Cooke decided that he needed a bank in Duluth to protect his interests and in 1869 sent Sargent to the area to establish it. Stone, then 47 years old, came with him.[53]

Cooke's greatest investment in railroad building followed – the Northern Pacific Railroad to connect Lake Superior with the Pacific Ocean. During the same year that Sargent arrived in Duluth, Cooke took control of the Lake Superior and Mississippi Railroad and connected it to the Northern Pacific system in a bold attempt to divert Red River wheat shipments from Chicago to Duluth. There was talk of a railroad to Lake Vermilion to bring iron ore to Duluth, where a steel mill designed to manufacture rails was under construction.[54] By 1872, Duluth was a boom town.

Three years later, Duluth was a ghost town. In 1873, the House of Jay Cooke collapsed as a result of over-extended investments and, during the next two years, Duluth's population shrank from nearly 3,000 to less than 500. "Grass was growing in the streets; there were many unoccupied houses and a general air of gloom pervaded the community," Albert H. Chester later remembered. [55]

The fall created a nationwide panic, along with six years of depression. It was during these years that George Stone, who had also lost most of his holdings, began a desperate search to find a way to rebuild his fortune. In early 1875, he took samples from Mitchell's Mesabi test pits along with a few chunks of Vermilion ore to Chicago, Detroit and Cleveland, hoping to find a person with wealth who might be interested in developing the region.[56]

Duluth boomed during Jay Cooke's time, but two years after this picture was taken, circa 1870, the town was in a state of rapid decline. VOSS COLLECTION AT THE IRON RANGE RESEARCH CENTER

In 1875, George Stone of Duluth brought samples of iron ore from George Stuntz's mountain to Charlemagne Tower Sr. in Philadelphia, setting in motion plans to develop the Vermilion Iron Range. Ely-Winton Historical Society collection at the Iron Range Research Center

Although he managed to meet with some wealthy people, including Eber Ward, the "steel king of Detroit," no one was willing to risk money on what seemed in every way to be a speculative railroad venture. These were depression years and everybody knew what had happened to Jay Cooke.

However, it was through his connection with Jay Cooke that Stone managed to get into the Philadelphia law office of Charlemagne Tower Sr. Tower, along with his partner Samuel Munson, had made a bundle on a speculative venture involving Pennsylvania coal lands. Tower was interested in reinvesting the money he had made. He had also been involved in some of Jay Cooke's ventures and had actually done legal work for him from time to time. He had heard of Cooke's plan to build a railroad to the iron region north of Lake Superior and was still interested in it.[57]

The timing was right. Tower and Munson immediately authorized Stone to arrange for an exploring party to go to Minnesota's Iron Country to examine not only Stuntz's mountain, but also Peter Michell's workings on the Mesabi Range. It was then that Albert Chester was hired to determine the feasibility of mining in Minnesota. Stone picked George Stuntz to guide the expedition. It took place during the summer of 1875.

The Chester Expedition of 1875

Chester, a geology professor at Hamilton College in Clinton, New York, arrived in Duluth on July 10, 1875. With him was Richard H. Lee, an engineer, surveyor and Charlemagne Tower's son-in-law. According to Chester, Tower expected his son-in-law to play a prominent role in future mining operations and, therefore, wanted him to be part of the preliminary exploration. In a paper presented to the Old Settlers Association of the Head of Lake Superior in 1914, Chester detailed his voyage into Iron Country:

"Mr. Lee and I started on July 13 with two explorers and four Indians, going by rail to Northern Pacific Junction and from there across the portage to Posey's on the St. Louis River. Our explorers were the veteran George Stuntz, who also acted as guide, and Benjamin F. Bishop. The Indians were John and Frank Houlle, Billy Church and Antoine Couneyer. At the river we found two large canoes in readiness and started at once up stream. As we left Joe Posey's house, we left behind us the last signs of civilization on the St. Louis River."[58]

The main purpose of the 1875 expedition was to investigate the Ontonagon Syndicate's mountain on the Mesabi Range. By the time Chester arrived in Duluth, members of the exploring party put together by George Stone were already on the Mesabi and had cut a trail to their camp "at Section 28, Town 59, Range 14 west," close to the Mitchell workings. The group included expedition manager Anson Northrup, explorer William Bassett, woodchoppers Charles Northrup, John Lightbody and Stewart Caley and miners Dennis Higgins, Martin Casey, John Lynch, Daniel Carr, Michael Sharkey, Charles Hoffenbecker, Nils Nelson, George Hull, Jacob Zimmerman and John Mallmann. With the group were James Northrup, teamster, camp cooks Edward Sterling and Burton Northrup and expedition blacksmith James Drogan.[59]

It took 10 days for Chester's party to reach Lake Vermilion by canoe. There they were entertained by the George Wheeler family at what Chester termed "the Indian Agency." He recounted:

"The Wheelers were most hospitable and did their best to treat us well and feed us while we stayed with them. As a special treat that night we were served with cove oysters. Think of it! An oyster stew in the middle of July and in the wilds of northern Minnesota. It was interesting to note the complete way in which the government positions at that post were filled by the Wheeler family. The father, George E. Wheeler, was Indian Agent and also blacksmith – whether he was paid salary for each I do not know – his wife was schoolmistress for the Indians of the reservation.... The elder son was a farmer ... the younger son was helper to his father, the blacksmith. Only the little daughter, perhaps

nine years old, failed of a government appointment."[60]

The Chester party spent only one day surveying the Vermilion hematite deposits and then retraced their steps to the Embarrass River and followed the trail that had been cut to their main camp near Birch Lake at the east end of the Mesabi. There, they located one of Peter Mitchell's pits, gathered "promising looking samples" and estimated the thickness of the vein to be about 3½ feet. Although indications of iron were all around and compasses spun wildly, most of the ore appeared to Chester to be "loose blocks, float-ore so-called, and there was none found in place." Although the party covered more ground than had been assigned, examined every favorable location and brought in samples of all rocks noticed from likely appearing sites, none assayed higher than 44.10 percent iron.[61]

Tower wanted weekly reports on Mesabi exploration, so an arrangement was made whereby Indians acted as mail carriers between the Chester camp and Stone's office in Duluth. From there, the messages were telegraphed to Tower. One of the native runners left camp every Monday morning,

arriving in Duluth on Wednesday and was back in camp the following Saturday. Apparently one of the runners, Billy Church, once made the 100-mile distance in record time. It is said that he left camp on Monday morning and was sitting in George Stone's office at 2 p.m. the following day.[62]

On July 31, George Stuntz and John Mallmann, along with two native interpreters, were sent back to Lake Vermilion where they set off a blast into Vermilion ore on the Lee Hill. In an 1890 letter to State Geologist Newton Winchell, Mallmann recalled this first blast:

"We started the stripping of ore … where Mr. Stuntz had first discovered the iron ore during the gold excitement in 1866. I was the only miner in the party and Mr. Stuntz asked me to put in a blast in the ore, which was the first blast ever put in the iron ore of the Vermilion Range. I had Indians striking the drills for me and bored a hole about five feet and threw out a mass of ore…."[63]

Meanwhile, Chester, satisfied that he had a good look at Mesabi ores, broke camp, sent most of his party back to Duluth along the overland road and returned to Lake

Iron exposures were immediately recognizable shortly after the first blast at the Lee Hill in 1875. Assays of rock samples from that blast proved that the iron content was rich and that the ore would be merchantable. IRON RANGE RESEARCH CENTER

51

Vermilion by way of Birch, Burntside and Mud lakes. Stuntz and Mallmann showed him their work and Chester was impressed.

"There was a natural break in the vertical bed of ore … so that it showed a solid cliff of pure hematite standing at least 30 feet out of the ground with large blocks of the same rich ore scattered in profusion … at the foot of the cliff. It was a magnificent site. Nature had done the mining, and it was only necessary to break up these large blocks to have the finest iron ore available when a railroad should come."[64]

Chester was back in Duluth on September 8, and his report to Tower came out that same fall, along with a copy that was submitted to Minnesota State Geologist Newton Winchell. It was long and detailed, but the findings were simple. Mesabi ore was too lean for commercial mining and the Vermilion Range was worthy of greater attention. The Ontonagon people would never build their railroad.

But a year went by, then another, then another. Nothing happened. No mining resulted on the Vermilion Range. The depression following the Panic of 1873 seemed to worsen. Prices on Bessemer ores sank to new lows. Stone penned letter after letter to Tower, urging him to grab the Vermilion iron land while he could. Tower agreed that it looked like good iron ore and there seemed to be lots of it on the Vermilion Range, but it was such a long way from the shipping lanes that even if the land could be had for next to nothing, it still wouldn't be an attractive investment.

Although George Stone did everything he could to get mining started in Minnesota, it was probably the rise in Bessemer ore prices in 1879, more than anything else, that convinced Tower he should act. At any rate, in that year Tower contacted Chester and asked him to lead a second expedition to Iron Country, this time to concentrate on the Vermilion Range.

The Chester Expedition of 1880

A large shipment of supplies was shipped to Lake Vermilion during the winter of 1879-80 and, the following July, Chester was again in Duluth. He again found a large crew of miners and explorers who had been assembled by Stone, with George Stuntz as guide. The party left Duluth on the 5th of July.

Of this second expedition Professor Chester's paper reads:

"The men engaged were all on hand, but most of them had been celebrating too much of the 'Glorious Fourth' and were not worth much for work. We made a start, however, and camped quite late that first night at the lower end of Grand Rapids in Section 34, Township 50, Range 17.

"Our party consisted of the following men: Albert Chester, professor in charge; Herbert M. Hill, assistant; Thomas Monoque, cook; Henry Eyre, James Wheeler and E. Dykeman, miners; John Houlle and Ben Cadotte, Indians. Mr. Stuntz was with us, partly as guide and explorer, as on the previous trip, but he also had charge of a surveying party, which was to survey for the government those towns which we expected to explore…. It was of great service to me to have Mr. Stuntz with us and his party and mine were never far apart the entire summer, though we did not camp together after we reached the scene of our work.[65]

"The trip up the St. Louis River was slow, there were frequent rains, the water was high, the current was strong and some member of the party brought a dog, which was forgotten on one of the portages and part of a day was lost in sending back for him. He was found and, as far as I remember, went with us to the end of the trip. We reached Embarrass bridge on July 14th and found there the rest of the party, which had arrived ahead of us."[66]

The group consisted of William Bassett, explorer in charge; Robert Whitford, Peter Armstrong, A. Sandell, Pitt Erickson, John Drohan, Angus McKinnon, James Cutter, F. Fristburg, A. Nelson, John Hogan, Pat Cudayhay, miners. George Wheeler, who was on the ground at Lake Vermilion, had been engaged as expedition blacksmith. The expedition arrived in good shape at Zack Brown's on Lake Vermilion on July 16. Zack J. Brown was the government farmer placed at Lake Vermilion in 1877 and supplies for the expedition were stored in his barn. A native runner system was again established to make weekly reports to Tower. John Houlle took the report of safe arrival back to Duluth the following day.[67]

Permanent camp was set up in the "green timber" in Stuntz Bay close to a log

cabin that had been built for storage the previous winter. A full month of trenching, drilling, blasting, measuring and sampling followed and, by August 21, Chester was satisfied with both the quality and quantity of the ore. Camp was broken and the men were sent home.

While most of the crew walked the Vermilion Trail back to Duluth, Chester, his laboratory assistant, Zack Brown, and four of the Ojibway men went back by canoe. A young Bois Forte youth named *Pashiguun* went back with Chester. He wanted to see what white man's civilization was like. In the next few years it would become all too real.

Stuntz and his crew stayed on. They had some surveying to do. Tower, who had received weekly reports on Chester's findings, was not waiting for his final report. He was ready to invest in Vermilion iron land, but before he could do so, existing law

required that the land be surveyed and thrown open for entry. By the end of December 1880, a total of 63 entries were made in the new township that Stuntz surveyed on the Vermilion Range. All were destined to fall into the hands of Charlemagne Tower.[68]

Chester was back in Duluth on August 25, where he spent two days sorting and packing his samples for analysis. The completed report sent to Munson and Tower was long and detailed, but it was clear. The Vermilion samples varied from just more than 50 percent to nearly 70 percent iron. It was rich ore, and the formations from which the samples were taken were massive. But the big thing was that most of the samples had hardly any phosphorous in them. It was true Bessemer! Every steel mill in the country would want to buy this kind of ore. ∎

Workers relax at a Vermilion Iron Range exploration camp in the 1880s. IRON RANGE RESEARCH CENTER

CHAPTER 5

A Wilderness Transformed

Carving a Slice from the Public Domain

Before Charlemagne Tower and Samuel Munson could even think of putting together a company to mine the region's iron deposits, they had to gain title to the land. In 1880, the Vermilion Range was still part of the unsurveyed public domain and its lands were as yet unavailable for public sale. Although prevailing law did provide a way for a private citizen to purchase property in the region, it was limited to 160 acres and only available for sale after it had been surveyed, improved and lived on. At any rate, prior to 1880, Vermilion country was too far removed from civilization to attract much attention from potential homesteaders. However, an attempt by a wealthy easterner like Charlemagne Tower to acquire land on which iron ore had been discovered was sure to attract attention – a lot of attention. George Stuntz put it this way, "Once news of iron on the Vermilion Range leaks out, homestead and pre-emption claimants will settle down there like grasshoppers in June."[1]

If Tower and Munson were going to acquire the land, it had to be done quickly and quietly. If any man could find a way to do this, it was George C. Stone. In early December 1879, Stone wrote a letter to Tower suggesting that the iron deposits could be had immediately, secretly – and for next to nothing. Instead of waiting for the public land sales which were sure to follow the federal survey then under way, Tower might want to secure ownership under the pre-emption law using fraudulent entrymen. The method was illegal, but had been used by lumber companies for years and was more or less publicly condoned.[2]

Apparently Tower saw sense in Stone's suggestion. In January he wrote Munson: "If we are obliged to secure any of the lands under pre-emption rights, I think you will understand, as I do, that it will be quite an economy for us to secure them through the aid of the workmen who will be employed by us in the survey and exploring the lands."

Tower did not want his name associated with any of the entries and urged that they be made as quietly as possible so all of the best mineral land could be picked up before Chester's findings were made public. This would remove any threat of competition. He reminded his partners, "We don't want anyone concerned in that ore property but ourselves."[3]

On February 26, 1880, Tower and Munson hired Stone to obtain the "choicest pieces" of mineland for them at the "lowest possible cost." Stone did his work effectively. With the blessings of the Duluth Land Office, he arranged for government surveyor George Stuntz to set aside all "forties" showing iron at the same time that he officially measured out the townships south and east of Lake Vermilion. He also convinced the 1881 State Legislature to establish a tax of one cent a ton on all iron ore mined in the state, to take the place of any and all other taxes on mining property.[4] This was the first tax on iron ore in the history of Minnesota and was obviously designed for one purpose – to encourage Tower to mine.

In the summer of 1880, while Albert Chester prospected for iron, Stuntz surveyed the land for purchase. Because the most promising exposures seemed to be in Township 62 North, Range 15 West, the vicinity of present-day Tower and Soudan, Stuntz surveyed this township first, setting aside more than 8,000 acres for Tower and Munson. When recording his survey, Stuntz made sure that his notes showed little or no swamp in any of the forties measured in this particular township. Long-standing federal law removed surveyed lands designated as

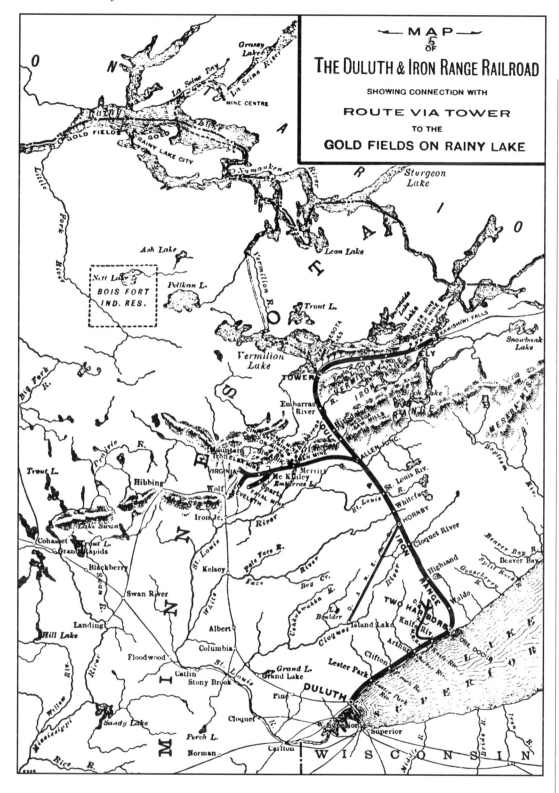

—MAP—
5
OF

THE DULUTH & IRON RANGE RAILROAD

SHOWING CONNECTION WITH

ROUTE VIA TOWER

TO THE

GOLD FIELDS ON RAINY LAKE

This 1890s map of northeast Minnesota shows the route of the Duluth and Iron Range Railroad from Duluth through Two Harbors, Mesaba Station, Tower, Soudan, the Minnesota Mines, the Chandler Spur, Ely and nearby mines, and spur to the eastern Mesabi Iron Range mining locations. COMPILED BY FRANK A. KING, IN *THE MISSABE ROAD*

"swampland" from public sale and instead granted them to states to be held in reserve.[5]

Some of the property Stuntz set aside for Tower had been scripped to the Roussains and their partners under the 1866 treaty and they were quite happy to part with 840 acres for what must have seemed a tidy sum – $3,360. The acres had no mineral rights, but in those days no one cared much about that.

For the rest, Tower used hand-picked entrymen who were paid a $1.25 an acre for a 160-acre parcel that did include mineral rights. Instead of developing their parcels into homesteads, the entrymen sold them to Tower for $500 a quarter section. Nobody cared about that, either.[6]

It amounted to a quick and easy $300 profit for George Wheeler, Benjamin

This surveying chain and compass were used by George Stuntz during his pioneering government surveys from 1852 through the 1882 completion of the government survey of the Vermilion Iron Range.
NORTHEAST MINNESOTA HISTORICAL CENTER

Cadotte, T.A. King, August Johnson, Robert Whitford, Henry Eyre, Thomas Englishby, Bernhardt Fitzaff, William Mathison, John Whelan and a host of others, including some who spent no more than a few days on their parcels piling logs and throwing brush over the piles so they could claim that they had made the improvements required by law.[7] Descendants of these men must have regretted the haste of their forebears. A number of these parcels turned out to be worth millions.

The death of Samuel Munson in 1881 left Tower without a partner, but it did not slow development. Tower bought out Munson's share of the Vermilion operation and with the help of Stone brought Edward N. Breitung into the venture. Breitung, an immigrant from Germany, was then serving as a legislator in the Michigan House of Representatives. He was an experienced mining man, having operated iron furnaces and invested in iron properties near Negaunee, Michigan. It was he who opened the Republic Mine, the largest and most profitable iron mine in the Upper Peninsula, and it was he who, on December 22, 1881, was holding a 40 percent interest in Tower's Vermilion properties.[8]

Tower now had the iron lands, but rich as they were, they were no sure thing. They were located in an almost inaccessible region. The country was densely wooded and broken by long stretches of muskeg swamp that made it almost impossible to get to the iron region in summer. Provisions, supplies and heavy equipment had to be hauled in during the dead of winter, frequently at subzero temperatures. All of the first equipment for Tower's mine, including heavy sawmill machinery and steam boilers weighing tons, were dragged to Lake Vermilion by oxen at the going rate of three cents a pound.[9]

Much of the operation was conducted under the name "George C. Stone and Company," but most of the money spent was Tower's money. Tower expected to use other people's money to develop his mine and railroad, but as the months passed he found himself putting in more and more of his own money just to keep the project alive. It has been estimated that he spent more than $3 million just getting ready to mine

the Vermilion range. It has also been said that he had barely $1 million left when George Stone wrote to him asking for a half million more. Tower replied, "You have ruined me!"[10]

Acquiring Vermilion mineland turned out to be the least of Tower's expenses. According to Duluth historian John S. Pardee, "It cost Tower $40,000 for 17,000 acres of land in 1881" and the following year, with very little additional expense, Tower added 3,000 more. He was now ready to form a company to mine the property.

On December 1, 1882, the Minnesota Iron Company was incorporated with headquarters in St. Paul and Charlemagne Tower as president. Edward Breitung was named vice president, George Stone, general manager, Charlemagne Tower Jr., treasurer, and Thomas L. Blood, Stone's son-in-law, secretary. On December 20, Tower transferred all of his holdings to the new company; these included certain forties bordering Lake Superior that he intended to

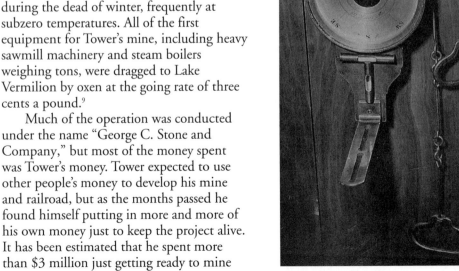

use for harbor purposes. Six-tenths of the company's capital stock of $10 million was kept by Tower and four-tenths went to Breitung. The bylaws, however, gave Tower "ironclad and steel-riveted control."[11]

Minnesota's First Commercial Iron Mine

In early September 1883, Franklin Prince, a mining engineer employed by Tower, arrived on the Vermilion Range complaining of sore feet from the long walk from Duluth. Prince was there to solve technical problems and make progress reports on the opening of what was already being touted nationally as Minnesota's first commercial iron ore mine.

Tower didn't simply want progress reports, he wanted positive progress reports. The reason he wanted positive reports was that he needed money to finish the railroad that he was building to his mine. To get the money, he needed to convince prospective investors that he had a market for his ore. In order to have a market for his ore, he needed to convince ore buyers that his mine and railroad were for real.

What Tower was really looking for was a partner willing to contribute money to the project, but not so much money as to endanger his control. He found two such men in brothers Samuel and George Ely, prosperous Marquette Range mine promoters who, in 1883, allowed themselves to be talked into buying several thousand shares of Minnesota Iron Company stock. Samuel, who had studied Prince's reports and personally inspected some of the ore,

was enthusiastic. "The most important thing is to get the line begun and finished at the earliest practical moment," he reasoned. "We shall not make much impression on the minds of consumers until we can say … when our ore is coming to market."[12]

Railroads were usually financed through the sale of bonds. But at a time when public confidence in railroad building was at best shaky, it was going to take a lot of convincing to get anyone to believe that there was profit in an expensive railroad to an unsettled wilderness. Tower played his cards carefully. After forming the Minnesota Iron Company, he gained majority control of the Ontonagon Syndicate's Duluth and Iron Range Railroad and its potential land grant of 600,000 acres. He made sure title to the railroad was transferred to his mining company. Next, he had his railroad directors issue for public sale, $2.5 million worth of bonds "running 20 years at six percent from May 1, 1883."

To secure these bonds Tower had all of the holdings mortgaged, including deeds to the railroad land grants, which would only be his *after* the track was completed to Duluth. He then made George Stone manager of the mine and replaced him as head of the railroad with his son, Charlemagne Tower Jr.[13]

If Tower needed to hear good things from Prince, he was not disappointed. In September 1883, Prince reported, "A large number of men are already at the mine site and approaches to the iron exposures are being cleared. The sawmill is turning out

In 1883, construction began on the first iron ore loading pockets at the Minnesota Mine ST. LOUIS COUNTY HISTORICAL SOCIETY COLLECTION AT THE IRON RANGE RESEARCH CENTER

Already in 1884 it was well known that the Vermilion Range was no poor man's country. It was going to take more than a rope and well bucket to mine it, and Charlemagne Tower Sr. provided the vision and much of the money to open the new iron lands. OLIVER IRON MINING COLLECTION AT THE IRON RANGE RESEARCH CENTER

lumber at a rate of 10,000 feet a day and land for a 10-acre company farm has been cleared near the lake."

In October, Prince announced, "The townsite of Tower is being developed. The site selected is a good one and although no work has yet been done on laying out the streets … one large boardinghouse, an office and a hospital have been erected on the townsite."[14]

Tower was the third town in the United States to be named after the Philadelphia financier. Even though he never set foot in the place, Charlemagne Tower Sr., more than anyone else, was responsible for its inception. Although it was necessary for his company to operate a store close to the mine workings, Tower was never a believer in company controlled towns.

What Tower wanted was to have a town platted on some of his less promising mineland so that he could profit from the sale of lots to businessmen eager to take advantage of the rising market created by the mine. As early as 1882, even before all of his land purchases were finalized, he had George Stuntz marking out corners for this town. Operating from his Philadelphia law office, he personally drew up company resolutions for approving purchases and setting aside lots for churches, public buildings and schools. He even donated a lot to William La Beau, the first white child born on the townsite.[15]

Two miles to the northeast at the mines, the work force grew steadily and the company was hard pressed to find housing for new arrivals. In the fall of 1883 Prince apprised Tower of the situation:

"Enough iron has been picked up from the old gold diggings to make nails at the company forge and we are completing 12 houses at the Breitung Location.… We will build 13 more houses on the Stone Location as soon as the supply of nails arrives. The building site is a fine one; the ground being high with a fine southern exposure and a ridge on the north for protection from the winds."[16]

Despite the difficulty and high cost of hauling in supplies, construction continued at a rapid pace. By January 1884, Prince was able to describe a brick factory, boiler houses, engine houses, smoke stacks and many other mine buildings.[17] These were the kind of reports that impressed buyers and opened the way to bank loans. Large scale construction also made it clear to men who were still prospecting for gold and iron on the Vermilion Range that "this was no poor man's country. It was going to take more than a rope and well bucket to mine it." By the time the Minnesota mines made their first shipment of iron ore, the Tower syndicate had spent close to $3.5 million.[18]

Building the Duluth and
Iron Range Railroad (1881-1884)

Plans for the railroad were laid out even before the iron deposits were surveyed and purchased. Tower wanted the shortest amount of track possible – and he wanted to know as soon as possible what that route might be. In fact, George Stuntz and Richard Lee were already laying out a rough survey for the line in August 1880. Stuntz later recalled:

"… in August he (Chester), had a sudden call to go home. I bought his supplies for use in my surveys. After Chester had left engineer Lee, a son-in-law of Charlemagne Tower, came up, missing Chester on the way. When he found me he had no supplies, but I fixed him out. We looked over the country for a railroad route."[19]

Stuntz and Lee did a lot of walking during the fall of 1880. In order for Tower to get the land grant from the State Legislature, the southern terminus for his railroad had to be in Duluth. The surveyors were forced again and again to retrace their steps and lay out a new direction for the line. It soon became clear that the distance and extremely rough terrain between Duluth and Lake Vermilion made a direct track impractical.

In November 1880, Richard Lee, in a preliminary report to Tower, outlined the problem and suggested an alternative. Instead of directly connecting the mine with Duluth, the railroad could run to Agate Bay, 26 miles up the shore, where there was an excellent harbor for ships.[20] Lee estimated that the distance in a straight line from the mine to Agate Bay couldn't be much more than 60 miles. True, it was 60 miles of rough terrain, but the distance was not nearly as long as the distance between Lake Vermilion and Duluth.

Tower was delighted with the report and was immediately convinced that Lee "was the 'select' man for building the iron range railroad." Lee left his job as "resident engineer" on the New Jersey Central Railroad and, in 1882, as the new chief engineer for the Duluth and Iron Range Railroad (D&IR Railroad), began the survey for the alternate route. Assisting him were George Stuntz and Colonel John B. Fish, an experienced civil engineer.[21]

In the end, an early George Stuntz suggestion that an ancient Indian trail to Agate Bay might be the shortest practical route to Lake Superior was accepted by both Lee and Fish as the proposed right of way for the line. The surveyors recommended a track approximately 68 miles long, pointing out that Agate Bay contained two natural harbors for ships. They further recommended that if a Duluth terminus was needed to meet the state's land grant requirement, a 26-mile spur could easily be built to connect the bay with that city.[22]

While Tower, Stone and others wrestled with the problem of getting the Minnesota Legislature to allow them to retain the much needed swamp land grant, final surveys for the line began. A team of engineers led by William McGonagle walked over the ice from Duluth to Agate Bay and, living in tents in below-zero weather, worked their way north toward Iron Country, completing their survey for grade and bridges in late summer of 1883.[23] By this time the Vermilion iron formations were clear for mining, Edward Breitung had paid Tower $110,000 for his 40 percent interest and Charlemagne Tower Jr. had arrived in Duluth to take control of the railroad.

Richard Lee moved his office to Agate Bay where he could direct full attention to construction. During this time, he and Tower Jr. were in constant communication by means of a newly completed telegraph line connecting Lee's office to Duluth. Although records show that the two men didn't always see things eye to eye, it is clear Tower Sr. relied on both equally. "Charlie and Lee … represent me and are, in fact, myself," he once wrote Stone.[24]

More important than the differences, was the excitement Tower Jr. and Lee shared over the unbounded possibilities that lay ahead. Shortly after their arrival in Duluth, the two young executives, Lee's wife, Deborah (Tower Jr.'s sister), and company secretary, Isaac P. Beck, dressed themselves in heavy furs to have their picture taken for friends back home in Philadelphia. The message was clear. They had come to the edge of civilization to face the unknown and seek their fortunes in iron.

There is little doubt that they were dealing with the unknown. A writer of the

time said that the Duluth and Iron Range Railroad was built "on the strength of an estimated ore body of 50,000 tons." This was an unbelievable gamble and most Duluthians were against it. No one lived there except the Ojibway and they had no money. "There was no incidental traffic and no hope of getting any," but the Towers pressed on.[25]

While Tower mortgaged his properties and looked for additional money, construction of the railroad began. On June 20,1883, John S. Wolf and Company of Ottumwa, Iowa, a well-known railroad builder, was awarded the construction contract on a low bid of $12,519 per mile. The company agreed to complete 68 miles of track from Lake Superior to Tower's mines by August 1, 1884. On August 29, 1883, the first stretch of track was put in place at Agate Bay.[26]

In September of that year, Franklin Prince assured Tower that there was least $1 million worth of ore on the surface at the mine site, enough – it seemed then – to pay the cost of the railroad, possibly even the 26-mile spur to Duluth. But construction proved far more difficult and expensive than anyone imagined. Before it was over, the cost was more like $2 million. But there was more iron ore in the Minnesota Mine than even the most optimistic had dared dream.[27]

Six hundred men went to work on the railroad that fall. Manpower was needed to clear right of way, grade road bed and lay ties and rails. A temporary narrow gauge track had to be laid first to allow mule drawn dump cars to bring in the fill needed for the grade.

During the time of construction, "Whisky Row," a collection of 22 saloons, brothels and

gambling halls, did a lively business at Agate Bay. By 1885, enough people had moved into the area to establish the Township of Two Harbors.[28] The Village of Two Harbors was incorporated three years later.

Meanwhile, another collection of saloons and questionable establishments formed at the foot of the Mesabi heights, 50 miles north of Two Harbors. In the spring of 1884, it was possible to ride the train to this place. "At tracks-end" was "a shack with MESABA lettered over the door. Around it tents and shanties huddled in the half-cut woods, with teams dragging pine logs toward the whine of a sawmill."[29] Anyone wanting to go on to Tower's mines had to walk the remaining 19 miles along a brushed-out right of way. Many did.

Between Mesaba and the mines stood the great granite ridge of the Mesabi. A tremendous amount of drilling, blasting and grading had to be done before the railroad could be brought through the heights to the Embarrass River valley beyond. During this time the hotels, brothels, saloons and gaming houses of Old Mesaba were filled to capacity.[30]

All construction materials had to be transported by boat from Duluth to the railroad's terminus at Two Harbors. From there it was shipped by rail to the work site. This was accomplished by three small steam locomotives, the first of which was shipped over from Duluth in 1883 on a scow pulled by the company tug *Ella G. Stone*. Known as the *Three Spot*, it is remembered as the Duluth and Iron Range Railroad Company's first locomotive.[31]

The muskeg swamps proved deep and the rock ridges wide and numerous. After

By 1885, there was more activity at the Minnesota Mine. The stock piles of ore are from the original open pits. Note the absence of head frames to support equipment to lift ore to the surface, indicating that the company had not yet begun the underground working that would mark the Vermilion Range through most of its active mining history. TOWER-SOUDAN HISTORICAL SOCIETY COLLECTION AT THE IRON RANGE RESEARCH CENTER

the first month of construction, everyone knew that the railroad was going to cost a whole lot more than estimated. The question was, would it be finished on time? Tower couldn't claim title to the land grant that he desperately needed until the railroad was finished. This made his property poor security for raising money. He had contractor Wolf post a $50,000 bond to be forfeited if the line was not completed on time.[32]

As a result, railroad workers were driven hard and forced to endure many hardships. Heavy snows and cold weather slowed construction and brought colds and flu to the camps. Bad water resulted in typhoid. Many died. There were desertions. In the spring of 1884, company stockholder Sam Ely, who knew something about railroad building, inspected the line and told Tower that the road could still be finished by the August 1 deadline. "It is a question of force. It will take 1,500 men to do it and there are not more than 400 men now."[33]

Excellent summer weather and 1,400 men laboring around the clock brought the line past the Embarrass River bridge in early July. Less than 12 miles of construction remained. But for contractor Wolf, with $50,000 riding on an August 1 deadline, time was getting short.

Production Begins at the Minnesota Mine (1883-84)

Meanwhile, the mine was brought to a full state of production. Tower was adamant that ore shipments begin as soon as the railroad was finished. To get the mine ready, an enormous amount of materials were shipped from Duluth to the site along the old Vermilion Trail. It took three days and two nights to cover the distance of 100 miles. Five roadhouses were built along the way: one at Cloquet River 18 miles north of Duluth, with others at White Face River, St. Louis River, Embarrass Lake and Wynne Lake Portage.[34]

At each of the road houses, one could expect a noon meal and, if necessary, a bed and breakfast, as well as water and forage for horses and oxen. The trail was open to teams all winter long, but in summer the only way it could be negotiated was on foot. From 1882 to 1884, hardly a day went by that didn't find at least 200 people en route between Duluth and Lake Vermilion. Weekly mail was carried to the mines by horse and wagon and so was the Minnesota Iron Company payroll. The pay was in gold and "nailed up in a box" protected by company agent John Mallmann. According to an early account, "'thousands of dollars were transported over that long winding trail through the pines,' yet Mallmann was never molested."[35]

Here is the Duluth and Iron Range Railroad station at Embarrass River Bridge in 1890. TOWER-SOUDAN HISTORICAL SOCIETY COLLECTION, IRON RANGE RESEARCH CENTER

THE D-I.R.STATION.EMBARRASS.MINN.

Elisha Morcom was the first captain of the Minnesota (Soudan) Mine. He would go on to pioneer exploration on the Mesabi Range, as well as establish a brick factory in Soudan that supplied the material for many of the later buildings on the Vermilion Range. ELY-WINTON HISTORICAL SOCIETY, IRON RANGE RESEARCH CENTER

In 1883, George Stone, acting for Tower, hired Elisha Morcom to put together a crew of available miners. Morcom was a well-known mining captain who had successfully opened a number of iron mines in northern Michigan. Born in Kenwyn, Cornwall, in 1835, Morcom came from a long established mining family. He left school at the age of 15 to work in a coal mine and came to Michigan's copper country in 1854 with an uncle. He found employment in the iron mines, which were developing not far away, and earned a reputation as a highly respected captain at the Vulcan and Iron Mountain mines on Upper Michigan's Menominee Range.[36]

Morcom recruited most of his crew in Quinnesec, Michigan, located between the towns of Iron Mountain and Norway, but because the Vermilion mines were in such a remote area, the only way he could attract top miners was to sign on whole families. By early 1884, 350 men, women and children had been registered to go to the Minnesota Mine.

Morcom's Vermilion miners were described in 1884 as "the finest crew of miners ever assembled in one place." The first of these miners, led by Morcom himself, left Quinnesec on March 10. They traveled by train to Superior and from there crossed the harbor ice in open sleighs and headed north along the Vermilion Trail. They arrived at the mine site on March 17 – St. Patrick's Day.[37]

Morcom's party was followed by daily arrivals from Quinnesec until April. That same month, Prince happily reported to Tower, "The population at the mines, including the carpenter force, are now nearly 200 souls!" In June, Prince described the construction of homes and buildings at three different building sites, which he referred to as Tower, Breitung and Stone. Most of the activity was taking place at the Tower site, where two general stores, a meat market, drugstore, restaurant, saloon and boardinghouse were already doing a lively business, even though part of the 100-acre site was uncleared and cordwood was still being cut on the south side of the main street.[38]

Under Morcom's direction, all surface material was stripped from five promising outcroppings of iron ore near the top of the 300-foot ridge south of Lake Vermilion's Stuntz Bay. Mining proceeded from the top down and at first amounted to little more than breaking up surface ore and stockpiling it for shipment. By June, Prince was reporting that an outcropping he referred to as the Stone Mine was being worked on a double shift and was producing 250 tons of ore a day. The other, which he called the Breitung, was producing 170 tons of ore a day and almost 6,000 tons were in stock. But Prince was also quick to note, "The vein does not present such a promising appearance as it did at the time of my last report.... " By mid-July, the stock pile at the Breitung was ready for shipment, several new pits were beginning to take shape and the work force had risen to much more than 500 men.[39]

There was plenty of work for all, but houses for only a few. According to Prince, "Building improvements are not being made very rapidly, owing to a difficulty in getting a supply of nails and building supplies, but as the railroad advances, this trouble is being overcome and it is practical now to have nails packed in from the end of the track at a reasonable expense."[40]

The First Shipment of Iron Ore (July 31, 1884)

The last week of July found Wolf himself working side by side with his men in a desperate effort to meet the deadline. It had been advanced one day to July 31, because August 1 fell on a Friday. There was an old superstition among miners that Friday was an unlucky day to open a mine and, apparently, Tower was taking no chances. Wolf and his crew were still at work on the morning of July 31. The train that was to take on the first shipment of ore had already left Two Harbors and was steaming north to the mines.[41] The final spike for the track was driven just hours before the train arrived. Wolf had met the deadline.

Mining at the Minnesota Mine's Breitung pit amounted to little more than breaking up the ore formation and stockpiling it for shipment.
NEWTON COLLECTION, NORTHEAST MINNESOTA HISTORICAL CENTER

The schedule called for the train to leave the mine at 2 that afternoon so it could get back to Two Harbors before dark. The locomotive was a recently purchased No. 8 Baldwin coal burner. It pulled 10 eight-wheeled 20-ton wooden ore cars, the first of their size in the Lake Superior region. In charge were Henry Black, conductor, and Thomas Owens, engineer. Charlemagne Tower Jr., Richard Lee, contractor Wolf and their guests were riding along in the caboose.[42]

The mine employees and their families greeted the train with cheers, the mine whistle blew and engineer Thomas Owens at the throttle of No. 8 responded with a series of loud blasts that drowned out all other sounds. Owens carefully backed his cars alongside the loading pocket and everyone lined up to toss in a chunk of ore for good luck.

"Chunks of ore rattled like hail into the cars as the people on the docks competed for the honor of loading the first piece. The official honor went to Wolf. At Tower Jr.'s request, he put in the first barrowful, smiling broadly as he wheeled it up to the edge of the platform and dumped it into car Number 406," Hal Bridges wrote in his book, *Iron Millionaire*.

"Cheers and applause. Captain Morcom hoisted the American flag and the loading crew went to work."[43]

At 11 a.m., a second train arrived from Two Harbors. It was a passenger train loaded with more railroad officials, wives and Deborah Lee, Charlemagne Tower Sr.'s daughter. A special ceremony had been planned for them. Tower Jr., who loved anything that pertained to American Indians, had sent out a special invitation

asking the Vermilion people to be part of the celebration. They did not disappoint him.

Tower Jr. reported to his father, "They came flocking in accordingly, men and women, painted and decked with beads and feathers, making altogether a very remarkable appearance and adding to the celebration of the opening of the road in such a way as to make an impression upon us which we should never forget. They formed a large circle, all sitting on the ground with their drum in the center, and I went close to them in order to distribute the presents.... We gave them pork enough and flour to content them and left them cooking and eating, promising to come to see us again, whenever we should send them word. I think there were more than a hundred of them."[44]

It was a beautiful summer day. There were speeches and handshakes. It was late afternoon by the time the train was ready to leave. As the loaded cars were pulled on to the main track for the journey back to Two Harbors, exuberant onlookers scrambled aboard for a short slow ride to the East Two River, where the engine took on water. A Cornish miner unveiled a cornet and the strains of "America" (or was it "God Save the King?") blended with the beat of an Indian drum.[45]

Engineer Owens was careful – very careful. He was not sure of the new roadbed, there were high officials on board and he had never pulled a train with such large ore cars. The 24-ton capacity cars that Tower had purchased for ore haulage were twice as large as any he had ever seen, they were without air brakes and he was sure they were all overloaded. His locomotive, a brand new Consolidation type (2-8-0) Baldwin coal

This is a tramming stockpile in 1884 at Minnesota Mine's Stone pit location. NEWTON COLLECTION, NORTHEAST MINNESOTA HISTORICAL CENTER

burner, had plenty of power, but he was afraid that the heavy ore cars might get away from him on the downgrades. The train moved slowly down the track, stopping at every river crossing to draw water – there were no water tanks along the way – and it was nearly midnight by the time it reached Two Harbors. According to the timetable Tower Jr. had drawn up, there were 12 stations along the line. Most had Indian names. Most didn't exist.[46]

The next morning the first iron ore from the state of Minnesota tumbled into loading pockets on the newly built 1,200-foot-long wooden ore dock. Meanwhile, the steamer *Hecla* and schooner *Ironton* sided up and took on about 1,400 tons each. By the end of the 1884 shipping season, 62,124 tons (one boatload today) of Minnesota Bessemer, averaging close to 68 percent iron, had been shipped to the Ely brothers in Cleveland.[47]

Ten years later, Minnesota Bessemer was the most sought after ore in the nation. In 1894, Minnesota State Geologist Newton H. Winchell was able to say, "The quality of Vermilion Range hematite has made it famous. 'Minnesota No. 1 Bessemer' is as well and favorably known to blast furnace operators as 'Minnesota No. 1 Hard' is to grain men."

The Towers Lose Control of the Mine and Railroad (1885-87)

Even though the ore was rich, Tower had trouble selling it. The first shipments were made at a time of a sluggish steel market.

Furnace men were overstocked and simply refused to buy any more iron ore. Minnesota Iron Company stockholders George and Samuel Ely, both experienced mine promoters, opened a company sales office in Cleveland. There, they bent arms trying to sell Tower's ore. But steel producers were reluctant to put an untried ore into their furnaces. Of the 62,124 tons of ore shipped to them in 1884, the Ely brothers were able to sell only 523.[48]

Meanwhile, Tower got a loan through the efforts of Edward Breitung, another from the widow of a former partner and a third from Lazarus Silverman, a prominent Chicago banker. They were enough to keep the company afloat until the market improved. But Tower paid a heavy price. He was forced to put his personal holdings up as collateral and write out hundreds of thousands of dollars worth of promissory notes, some collectible on demand at 12 percent interest. Worse yet for Tower was the fact that he accepted money from Lazarus Silverman. Silverman had connections with Illinois Steel Company and its director, Henry H. Porter.[49]

The steel market improved in 1885. The superb quality of Minnesota No. 1 Bessemer might have been a factor in a rather sudden interest in new ores on the part of some steel manufacturers. The Elys announced contracts with two Chicago steel mills and one with Carnegie Brothers and Company of Pittsburgh. The shipping seasons of 1885 and 1886 were so good that Tower was able to pay off his debts, complete the railroad link to Duluth and even raise the pay of his miners. However, his success was carefully monitored in Chicago. The list of watchers included some big names: Henry H. Porter, associate of Lazarus Silverman and head of Illinois Steel Company; Marshall Field, highly successful Chicago merchandiser; Cyrus McCormick, well-known manufacturer of farm machinery; J.C. Morse, owner of Chicago's Union Steel Company; and John D. Rockefeller, owner of Standard Oil Company.[50]

Led by Porter, the group formed a syndicate to buy up as much of the Vermilion Range as possible. They picked up something like 25,000 acres near the present site of Ely. Good ore had been noted on this land in the fall of 1884 and there was no doubt that the Porter syndicate could successfully mine it. When they announced plans to either buy the Duluth and Iron Range Railroad or build a competing line to Lake Superior, members of the Minnesota Iron Company became alarmed. A second railroad meant only one thing. The Porter group intended to squeeze the Tower people right out of the mining business.[51]

Charlemagne Tower Sr. and his son had never discouraged others from developing new mines. They were confident that the D&IR could haul other people's ore so cheaply that there would be no advantage in a second railroad. They were sure that the Porter group would see this. An arrangement could be negotiated. They agreed to meet with the Chicago people.[52]

The negotiations turned out to be about selling. Lazarus Silverman suggested that Tower sell everything to Porter. The Ely brothers, who had been dealing with Porter and Morse since 1884, thought Tower should take advantage of the good market and at least sell the railroad. The Towers didn't want to do either.[53]

There were more meetings. During the winter of 1886-87, Porter lawyers called young Tower in and laid their cards on the table. They had clear evidence that George Stone and Edward Breitung had gained ore properties through the use of fraudulent land entries. They told Tower that Porter didn't really want a court battle, but was convinced that the Tower land claims were invalid and open to legal challenge.[54]

The death of Edward Breitung on March 7, 1887, left George Stone as the only person named in Porter's charges. He got shaky and contacted Tower.

"We're up against a strong and unscrupulous crowd. We have got to make the best deal we can and get out."[55] Tower, then 78 years old, was not anxious to spend his last years in a transportation war or in

Ore was raised by means of a skip hoist during the last days of open pit mining at the Minnesota Mine. NEWTON COLLECTION, NORTHEAST MINNESOTA HISTORICAL CENTER

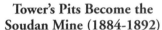

The No. 8 shaft next to the Tower pit in 1886, just as underground mining was replacing open pit mining at the Minnesota Mine. NEWTON COLLECTION AT THE NORTHEAST MINNESOTA HISTORICAL CENTER

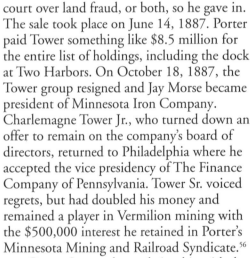

court over land fraud, or both, so he gave in. The sale took place on June 14, 1887. Porter paid Tower something like $8.5 million for the entire list of holdings, including the dock at Two Harbors. On October 18, 1887, the Tower group resigned and Jay Morse became president of Minnesota Iron Company. Charlemagne Tower Jr., who turned down an offer to remain on the company's board of directors, returned to Philadelphia where he accepted the vice presidency of The Finance Company of Pennsylvania. Tower Sr. voiced regrets, but had doubled his money and remained a player in Vermilion mining with the $500,000 interest he retained in Porter's Minnesota Mining and Railroad Syndicate.[56]

George Stone, whose relationship with the Towers had cooled because of disagreements over mine management and politics, received a half million dollars from the sale. Except for a very small interest in Porter's syndicate, his association with Vermilion mining ended in 1887. He remained in St. Paul and continued to involve himself in promotional enterprises until his life came to a sudden and tragic end on the night of October 25, 1900, when he accidentally left the gas valve on while turning out the lights in his room at Duluth's Kitchi Gammi Club.[57]

Tower's Pits Become the Soudan Mine (1884-1892)

The Soudan Mine wasn't called "Soudan" during the Tower-Morcom era, nor was there a town named "Soudan." Instead, the mine consisted of seven large pits bearing the names Stuntz, Stone, Ely, Tower, Armstrong, Breitung and Lee, all men associated with Tower's Minnesota Iron Company. The pits were often referred to as if they were separate mines, but all were part of a single complex, the "Minnesota Mine," described in 1887 as "one of the largest iron mines in the world." The mine that year had already set shipping records and employed a work force of 1,300 men, all housed in two nearby clusters of company cottages and boardinghouses known as Stone Location and Breitung Location.[58]

Donald H. Bacon replaced Captain Elisha Morcom as general manager of the Minnesota Mine in 1887, when his boss, Jay Morse, became president of the Porter controlled Minnesota Iron Company. Housing was scarce when Bacon and his family arrived in Tower. The local newspaper had this to say about their arrival, "Captain D.H. Bacon and family of the Minnesota Mine are enjoying a season of camping on the shores of beautiful Lake Vermilion. The family residence will be completed shortly and until that time, unless the weather grows stormy, they will occupy their canvas home."[59] When finally completed, the residence was nothing short of a mansion and was often described as the finest residence north of Duluth.

Bacon, a native New Yorker, moved to Ishpeming, Michigan, in the early 1870s where he was hired as a timekeeper at the Cleveland and McComber Mine. He was an ambitious man and in those days ambition and industry took a person a long way. By 1882, Bacon had risen to the position of superintendent of the mine. His success as a mining executive caught the attention of Union Steel Company owner Jay Morse, who hired him as company agent in 1885.[60]

When Bacon took over the Minnesota Mine, Morcom's pits were still being worked and underground mining was just beginning. Diamond drills had discovered lenses of extremely rich iron ore encased in an almost vertical formation of jasper that continued to drop downward deep into the earth's interior.[61] The sinking of shafts had begun, expensive equipment was being called for and it had become clear that although the ore was rich, it varied enough in both iron and phosphorus content to make it necessary to keep a close watch on all that was mined, so that it could be properly

classified for sale. Up to this time, the ore had been hand sampled at the mine into three grades: Red Lake, good ore; Minnesota, better ore; and Bessemer, the best ore.[62] However there were enough inaccuracies in the shipments to make it necessary to sample the ore again at Two Harbors and once or twice again at the steel mill. These were the days of Bessemer converters and no matter how rich the ore, phosphorous content was always an issue.

One of Bacon's first tasks at the Minnesota was to establish a more exact system for monitoring, sampling and grading the ore. Although Bacon is often credited with giving the mine and its residential area the name "Soudan," it was probably the ore that he named first. The system Bacon established for the mine in 1888 identified six grades of ore: Minnesota, Braddock, Nipigon – all Bessemer ores; Vermilion, Red Lake and Soudan – all high phosphorus ores.[63] The new names were drawn up at the time French and British exploits in the African Sudan were in the news and Bacon, a student of Napoleonic history, chose the French spelling, Soudan, for the name he gave to the ore being raised via the No. 8 shaft at the edge of the Tower pit. Although the ore had a little too much phosphorous in it to qualify as Bessemer, it was rich enough in iron for steel mills to take more than 30,000 tons of it during the 1888 shipping

The No. 8 (Soudan) shafthouse in 1889 indicates that the Vermilion Range had begun transition to underground mining. NUTE COLLECTION, NORTHEAST MINNESOTA HISTORICAL CENTER

Miners gear would change through the years. Note the soft hats and candles used by these underground miners at the Minnesota Mine. OLIVER MINING COMPANY COLLECTION, IRON RANGE RESEARCH CENTER

season.[64] From then on, "the No. 8," which eventually became the main shaft for the mine, was called the "Soudan shaft" and by 1890, the entire mine complex and its locations were referred to as "Soudan."[65]

During the first years of Bacon's management, the mine's biggest seller continued to be Minnesota Bessemer, a low phosphorous ore with an almost unbelievable 67 percent iron content. Over a 140,000 tons of it went down the rails to the docks at Two Harbors during the 1888 shipping season. Between December 1, 1888, and August 1, 1889, the Minnesota Mine shipped much more than 300,000 tons of iron ore. Nearly half of it averaged 65 percent iron, with a phosphorous content of less than six-hundredths of a percent. No other mining region in the world could claim such a showing.[66]

A real effort was made in 1890 to get the last pockets of ore out of the pits. The work was noisy and dangerous. The ore was extremely hard and could only be broken up by drilling and blasting, using combinations of dynamite and nitroglycerin. A hole about 3 inches in diameter and 3 to 4 feet deep had to be drilled and filled with explosives. Heavy duty compressed air drills were used for this

and they made so much noise that it was impossible to speak and be heard, even if a person was 100 yards from the drill and six inches away from the listener's ear.[67]

The blasts were unbelievably powerful. They occurred every three hours and could be heard 40 miles away. Heavy fragments of hematite were tossed high in the air and sometimes broke through the roofs and windows of miners' cottages in the nearby locations. A series of warning notes from the mine's steam whistle would send everybody running for cover.[68] Sometimes the sides of pits gave way, showering work sites with tons of falling rock. There were casualties. The exact number is unclear. According to the editor of Tower's weekly paper, the *Vermilion Iron Journal*:

"In last week's *Industrial Age* of Duluth, some jay who calls himself the 'explorer' says there is an average of two men killed in the mine every week. He then goes on to rant about the cost in human lives…. The records show that in the last 12 months only five men were killed."[69]

Underground stope mining eventually replaced all open pit workings. A steplike method of excavating ore from around a mine shaft, stope mining was less dangerous.

By the end of summer in 1890, many of the pits were more than 150 feet deep, underground shafts reached levels hundreds of feet below the pit floors and three new mine shafts, the Alaska, Montana and Butte, were bottomed into iron rich hematite.[70] In that year, the mine included 14 underground shafts, 10 open pits and about 20 other cuts and scrams (small exploratory pits). At the surface, eight engine houses were at work and miles of railway connected the shafts to huge stock piles of ore. In 1892, the mine employed 2,000 men and set a production record of 568,471 tons. It was a record that would be approached many times but never again equaled.[71]

Heavy investment in machinery followed the Porter take over. The best and latest designs in steam engines, drills, compressors, tram cars and ore crushers were brought to the mine during the 1890s. But below the ground, old ways persisted. Two 10-hour work shifts were maintained and ore was moved by human power to chutes and hand-trammed to shafts where it was raised to the surface. Water from the surface drained freely into the underground passages and miners worked under the light of candles carried Cornish-style in tin holders pinned to their soft broad brimmed hats.[72]

The men who worked in the mine were described as "mostly foreigners … a large number of Scandinavians" and "a good proportion of Cornish miners who are to be marked by their peculiar accent."[73] Mining was the Cornish heritage and the vocabulary of these men from England's "west country" became vocabulary of the mine. The terms they used were generations old and had the ring of the sea that surrounds the Cornish coast. They called their bosses "captain" and when they mined downward they called it "sinking." Mine shafts were never dug, only "sunk." When Cornishmen mined horizontally it was "drifting" and the resulting passage was a "drift." When they mined upward they called it "rising," but when Cornishmen said the word it sounded like "raising," and the resulting vertical tunnel at Soudan became a "raise."[74]

Work positions below the ground were clearly defined and based on a hierarchy of unquestioned command. Responsible to the superintendent for the practical direction of the mining work, was the "underground captain." He was usually a man of considerable experience who was easily distinguished by his symbol of authority, a somewhat formless cap, which resembled only slightly that of a ship's captain – but, like a ship's captain, his directives required prompt action. Refusal to obey an order meant immediate dismissal. Below the captain were the "shift foremen," hand-picked men who spoke the language of the miners and saw to it that the captain's orders were carried out. Next in line were the contract miners, the men who did the drilling, blasting, barring, scraping and timbering in assigned areas of the stope called "pitches." They were considered men of special skills and worked in partnerships of two to four, according to a contract based on the amount and selling price of the ore they mined. Below the contract miners were the "trammers," who moved the ore to the shaft, and gangs of unskilled laborers, the muckers and laborers, the men who did the heavy lifting, carrying and shoveling under the watchful eye of the shift foreman. Later, when mules and machines were brought into the mine, many new positions were added to the work force, but the total number declined.[75]

It is impossible to obtain exact figures as to what earnings all this boiled down to, but the Minnesota Bureau of Labor *Biennial Report* for 1901-1902, published a list of "company statistics" for 1892 and claimed that the average pay for "976 Vermilion underground miners" was between $1.96 to $2.55 per day for 257 days of work. This is slightly more than one would expect for the times and certainly more than some Michigan underground contract pay scales. However, the bulletin of the Bureau of Labor for 1909, *The Minnesota Iron Ranges,* shows that contract pay in underground mines on the Vermilion varied between $1.60 and $1.75 a day in 1896, $1.60 to $1.85 in 1897, $1.60 to $1.95 in 1898 and $1.85 to $2.00 a day in 1899. Trammers averaged $1.25 a day and laborers $1.20 a day, less than those in Michigan mines.[76]

The iron deposits being worked occurred "in lenses 200 to 1,000 feet long and 5 to 80 feet wide," standing "at an angle of from 65 degrees to 75 degrees with a

vertical height of 250 to 500 feet."[77] The cut and slice back stoping system was particularly suited to these formations. Horizontal slices of ore were removed in sequence parallel to the drift, giving a stepped appearance to the hanging wall at the top of the stope (the ever-expanding hollow created by this system of mining). Mining was always "overhand" or upward, allowing the ore to fall to the floor of the stope, where it could be pushed and scraped into chutes and dropped into ore cars lined up on a "hauling level" located below the floor of the stope. Hauling levels were constructed of trapezoidal timber frames called "drift sets" and connected to the shaft by "crosscuts," passages driven through the rock at vertical intervals of 75 feet. Once a stope began producing ore, the crosscut was referred to as a level. As mining proceeded upward, the floor of a developing stope was built up with fill dropped from above through raises called "mills." While all this was going on, diamond drills probing the depths hit new pockets of ore and the shafts deepened.[78]

By 1894, some of the shafts were 800 feet down and at the surface, with its engine houses, brick stacks, warehouses, change houses, heating houses, mule barns, blacksmith shops, drill houses, powder houses, crusher houses and offices, the mine took on the appearance of a small town. An electric light plant served all of the surface needs and the company even had its own surgeon and hospital. State Geologist Newton Winchell's assessment of the mine in that year was as follows:

"It is generally admitted that there is not a better planned, better kept and more complete and efficient mining plant in the Lake Superior District. It is in many respects a model of how mining operations ought to be conducted.... Ore is being hoisted in eight different shafts at the Minnesota mines. These shafts are between 400 and 800 feet deep and most have underground connections with each other. They are sunk in the footwall and communicate with the ore body by crosscuts at the various levels.... The present working force is between 600 and 700 men.... The compressor house is on the shore of Vermilion Lake, north of the mine. Ore is loaded from pockets and stockpiles on the railroad tracks, which are

laid along the south ridge in which the ore is mined. The mines are at present under the direction of Captain Edwin Ball."[79]

The Mystery of the Lee Mine

In 1891, the Lee Mine, located about a half mile northeast of Tower, was described as "nothing but iron ore." In that year, the Minnesota Iron Company was operating two shafts, the North Lee and the South Lee, and employed about 300 men. At the surface were two engine houses, an office building and a large amount of machinery, including a compressor, steam hoist and loading pocket complete with rails and ore cars. The ore coming out of the North Lee tested well above the 62 percent iron content requirement for marketable Red Lake-grade hematite and the formation was large. It appeared that a long future of mining lay ahead. Yet in one night the mine vanished.

"Miners who dropped their tools at 6 o'clock in the evening" and were back at the mine at 7 the next morning "had to do some hard blinking." There was nothing there. Nothing but the hill itself. "All trace of surface property was blotted out," even the railroad tracks were gone. For years, the people of Tower talked about this mysterious disappearance.[80]

Only later was the cause discovered. It seems that the Lee was part of property purchased in 1880 from fur trader Francis Roussain. Roussain and his sons had been awarded government patents on tracts of land near Lake Vermilion "for services rendered" according to the terms of the 1866 Bois Forte Treaty. In early 1892, Minnesota Iron Company ownership was challenged in a U.S. circuit court case known as *Winthrop Pond vs. Minnesota Iron Company.* The plaintiff claimed title to the same property under a deed alleged to have been made out to him by a Francis Roussain in 1866. As it turned out, the lands in question were without mineral rights, but the court action was enough for the Minnesota Iron Company to put an abrupt halt to its operations at the Lee. A special train was brought in during the night and all surface property removed. The company spent years tangled in litigation before finally, in 1909, it gained clear title to the property and access to its minerals. Although there was a lot of talk about resumption of activities, the mine was never reopened.[81]

Mining Expands Across the Vermilion Range

Winthrop Pond vs. Minnesota Iron Company was only one of many court cases that erupted during the rush for iron that followed the Porter takeover of the Minnesota Mine. More than 60 iron mining companies were incorporated under Minnesota law during the years 1887-1889. Most of them were formed to explore for iron on the Vermilion Range. At the center of the rush were the Porter syndicate lands near a lake the Ojibway people called Shagawa. Although some of the exploration there was conducted under the direction of the Minnesota Iron Company, the Illinois fee holders were not adverse to letting independents do most of the hard work of exploration. By 1888, the woods east of Tower were filled with log and tarpaper prospecting camps, with rude signs nailed above their doors bearing such names as Consolidated Vermilion Iron and Land Company, Union Iron Mining, North Star Iron Lands, Chandler Iron Company and Chippewa Mining.[82]

The first real mining lease at the east end of the Vermilion Range was recorded on June 24, 1886. It was taken out by the Pioneer Vermilion Iron Company, an independent exploration firm formed by William Conan, Martin and William Pattison and Robert B. Whiteside. The Pattison brothers were loggers from Superior, Wisconsin. In 1883, while searching for pine land northeast of Tower, they found fragments of hematite scattered along the south shore of Shagawa Lake. Making their way carefully up a high ridge south of the lake, they traced the source of the ore to an iron laden outcropping which later became the Pioneer Mine.[83]

The Pioneer Vermilion Iron Company was designed to do what other iron exploration companies did in those years. The procedure was simple. First find a patch of ground showing the unmistakable stain of iron ore, then dig a test pit, bottom it in ore and hurry back to civilization to take out a mining lease – not to mine, but to sell the lease to a well-funded company that could do the mining. At the time, the likely firm might have been the Towers' Minnesota Iron Company, but the Pattisons and their

Robert B. Whiteside was a Duluth iron ore speculator and co-founder of the Pioneer Vermilion Iron Company, which was formed after Martin and William Pattison of Superior discovered high grade ore on Shagawa Lake.
NORTHEAST MINNESOTA HISTORICAL CENTER

partners, knowing they had found high-grade Bessemer hematite, decided to mine it themselves. Two shafts were sunk, but the deposits were scattered and the mines remained unproductive until 1889.[84]

The Pattisons came back to Shagawa Lake in the summer of 1884 and made a second discovery. This one was located on land that was later purchased by the Porter Syndicate when it started its 1886-1887 takeover attempt of Tower's properties and was destined to become the premier mine of the Vermilion Range – the famous Chandler. Anxious to develop the property, the Porter people began building a branch railroad to the site shortly after their purchase of the Minnesota Iron Company in 1887. The railroad was completed to the Chandler in the summer of 1888.[85]

The Chandler Mine was already in a full state of production when the railroad arrived. This was due to the work of Captain John Pengilly, an experienced mining captain from the iron fields of Michigan. Pengilly immediately recognized four wonderful qualities in the Chandler deposit: 1. It was extremely low in phosphorous, making it some of the best Bessemer ore in

the Lake Superior District. There were always buyers for this kind of ore; 2. The ore body had been subjected to a massive folding of the earth's crust, breaking it into pieces, all just about the right size for the steel mills. It didn't have to be crushed before shipment; 3. It didn't need the skills of a hard rock miner to bring it to shipment. Drilling and blasting were hardly necessary. About all that had to be done was to cave it and let it fall into tram cars. Nowhere in the world could iron ore be mined so easily – and so cheaply; 4. Probably the most important quality of all was the fact that the deposit was close to the surface. The first ore was removed from an open pit using an inclined hoist, allowing Pengilly to have more than 54,000 tons of it ready for shipment the day the railroad arrived.[86]

It has been said that the Chandler paid its stockholders $100,000 a month net profit during its first 19 years of operation.[87] In 1889, with a crew of 650 men, it broke all records for ore production in the Lake Superior District.[88] There were those who said the mine would be worked out in two or three years. It was still shipping ore in 1940, more than five decades later.

Ely's quick rise to the position of premier city on the Vermilion Range was due almost entirely to the rich Chandler Mine. For a time it seemed that there was no limit to the ore formation's depth. Within a year, open pit mining was replaced with an

underground caving system. Underground levels 60 feet apart were developed and a system of drifts, raises and crosscuts divided the ore into large blocks that were allowed to cave gradually to floor level. From there, the ore was milled into tram cars, pushed to the shaft and raised to the surface. After the ore was removed, the supports were blasted out and the surface crumbled into the cavity, creating a deep steep-sided pit.[89]

A site for a mining town was platted in 1887 – the year the Porter Syndicate took over the Tower interests. Supplies for the new town were first hauled in by dog team during the winter, but by late spring there was such a demand for mining equipment that it became necessary to construct a road for horses, oxen and wagons. On May 31, 1888, even before there was a railroad to the place, a petition to incorporate the townsite as the Village of Ely was approved and notices of election were published in the *Ely Iron Home*, the town's first newspaper. The population of town at the time was less than 200. Ten years later, almost 4,000 people were calling Ely home.[90]

The Chandler excitement spurred the formation of new mining companies and an even more intensive search for similar bodies of ore. During the years 1887-1893 companies such as North Shore Mining, Vermilion and Grand Marais Iron, Vermilion Range Mining Syndicate and Grand Marais

Exploring for ore at the Pioneer Mine in 1886. Diamond drill exploration would not arrive in Iron Country until 1890. NUTE COLLECTION, NORTHEAST MINNESOTA HISTORICAL CENTER

and Vermilion Iron and Land Company sent teams of prospectors deep into the wilderness north and east of the burgeoning town of Ely.[91] The entire region from Basswood to Gunflint lakes was meticulously scoured for signs of iron ore.

During the early 1890s, mineral leases were filed on thousands of acres of Gunflint country, shafts were sunk and discoveries of ore running as high as 68 percent iron were reported in the Minnesota press. Excitement peaked in 1893, when John Paulson of Minneapolis-based Northeast Minnesota Mining Company announced that he had bottomed a shaft in some "very fine ore." At that time there weren't many who didn't believe "Gunflint Lake country was slated for the next boom in mining."[92]

"The properties are only a few miles from Port Arthur and also Grand Marais, so the expense of getting the ore to the lake will be but small.... Local iron men who have been asked regarding Gunflint country,

admit that there is plenty of ore to be found up there. It is of a very hard quality, being an extension of the Vermilion Range, which is a sufficient recommendation as to its worth."[93]

As it turned out, the ore wasn't nearly so hard as first reported, nor were the deposits very large. In fact, Gunflint country wasn't even on the Vermilion Range. Later geological investigation proved the Gunflint formation to be an extension of the Mesabi Range, but no commercial mining resulted.

On the Vermilion Range, it was iron all the way to Knife Lake on the Canadian border, but the kind of ore steel mills were willing to buy seemed to be found only in two places – at Soudan near Lake Vermilion and at Ely just south of Shagawa Lake. At Soudan, as the mine deepened, new and even larger lenses of hematite were encountered and Ely eventually became the center for seven successful mines. However, none would come close to matching the great Chandler in quality and scale. ■

Workers pose in 1890 at the Chandler Mine in what would become Ely. ELY-WINTON HISTORICAL SOCIETY COLLECTION, IRON RANGE RESEARCH CENTER

CHAPTER 6

Towns of the Vermilion Range Frontier

This map of the Ely vicinity showing the eastern Vermilion Range mine locations was taken from the 1891 Geological and Natural History Survey of Minnesota, Bulletin No. 6, Plate X, Winchell and Winchell, Minnesota Iron Ores, Minneapolis. DULUTH PUBLIC LIBRARY

Noted Evangelist Billy Sunday is reputed to have said this about frontier Ely: "The only difference between Ely and hell is that Ely has a railroad to it."

Similar comments have been made about many mining towns on America's mining frontier. Stories arising from such places as Tombstone, Deadwood, Cripple Creek and Leadville, with their hurdy-gurdy dance halls, all-night saloons, gamblers, gunfighters and town marshals, have thrilled generations of Americans and entertained people all over the world.

Although the appeal of these stories probably came more from the pens of writers than the real people who flocked to these places, there is little doubt that western mining camps and towns had their share of excitement, violence and vice. Along with its fortune

hunters, miners and turbulent politics, the mining frontier swept rapidly across the nation, pausing briefly on the Vermilion Range just before the turn of the century.

Like Deadwood and Leadville, Tower, Soudan and Ely were born in a climate of excitement and turbulence. Central to the excitement were the spectacular successes of the Minnesota and Chandler iron mines. Hastily organized mining companies, all hoping to find similar lodes of ore, rushed to the vicinity and sent teams of prospectors into the surrounding woods. The list of companies is long and includes such names as Zenith, Sibley, Savoy, Chippewa, Mutual, Section 30, Lucky Boy, Armstrong, Vermilion Iron Mining and Improvement, Vermilion Iron and Land, Fargo, White Iron and Vermilion Range Mining Syndicate.

The turbulence was caused by the arrival of land speculators, timber cruisers, financiers, business developers, promoters and investors, all seeking ways to get rich quick. Along with the developers and promoters came the usual mining camp crowd: saloon keepers, gamblers, card sharks, street fighters, hurdy-gurdy dance house operators, prostitutes, pimps and swindlers of all stripes.

Frontier Tower

"Call a meeting and organize a fire department! If Tower must have a fire, let us at least give it a few rounds of opposition," urged Will Harrington, former blacksmith turned newspaperman.

Within three years of its inception, Tower was a village of nearly 3,000 – a little metropolis in the woods complete with a school, bank, village hall, jail, railway station, sawmill, two churches, three barbershops and several stores, hotels and saloons. All, except the village hall, were made of wood. The town also had a newspaper – the *Vermilion Iron Journal*,

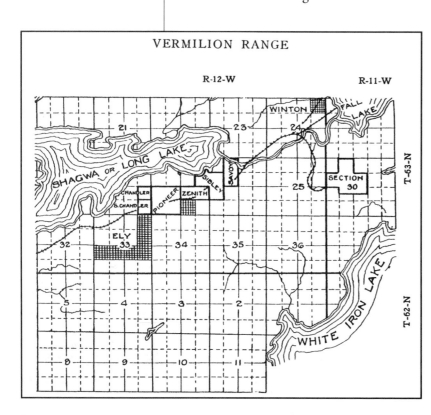

VERMILION RANGE

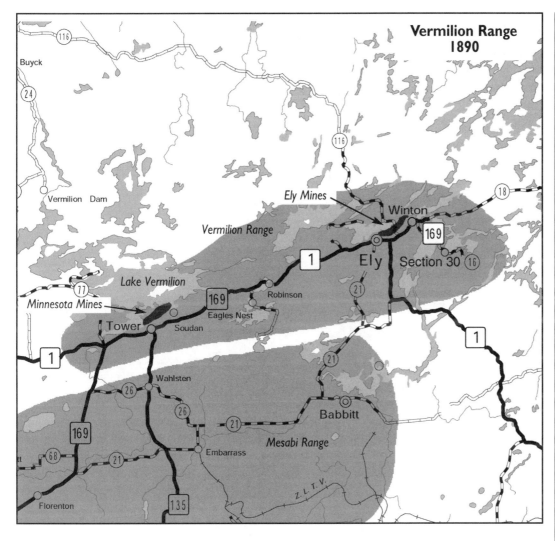

Vermilion Range 1890

Buyck

Vermilion Dam

Ely Mines

Vermilion Range

Winton

Lake Vermilion

Ely

Section 30

Minnesota Mines

Robinson

Eagles Nest

Tower

Soudan

Wahlsten

Babbitt

Mesabi Range

Embarrass

Z. L. T. V.

Florenton

Map of Northeast Minnesota showing Tower, Soudan, Ely, the Ely mines, Section 30 and Winton. MAP PROVIDED COURTESY OF THE STATE OF MINNESOTA

managed by Doctor Fred Barrett and edited by Will Harrington – but no fire department.[1]

Harrington saw danger in the closely built cluster of wood-frame buildings heated solely by wood-burning stoves. "Tower is sleeping the calm sleep of perfect safety from fire. So was Ironwood. It is now – ashes," warned the editor in the fall of 1887.[2] Although there were fires over the years and a few buildings did go up in smoke, the town, miraculously, never burned.

The *Journal* turned its attention to other threats, to the drunks and prostitutes who were steadily drifting in from Ashland, Hurley and towns of the Michigan ranges. A "clean up the town campaign" was launched and Harrington seldom missed an opportunity to rail against what he considered the town's "shady element."[3]

"Two drunken prostitutes were thrown from a buggy last Friday night in front of a

principal place of business. The beer singers and whisky soaks were not seriously hurt, although the fall was a bad one. Prostitutes are becoming a little too numerous on our streets. They, like the drunkards, are a nuisance in every sense of the word."[4]

He pointed out swindlers, called for better police protection and urged the village council to pass ordinances against the pimps, toughs and drunks who seemed to be taking over the town. His descriptions were vivid, and he wasn't afraid to use names:

"Ed Blake of Duluth, a notorious and lazy, filthy cur, was ordered out of town by police last Monday and left on the noon train. Blake is a miserable whelp and presented a disgraceful appearance on Main Street last Sunday, accompanied by a blear eyed, rum soaked prostitute from the Zenith city.... Blake can go back to Duluth and remain, for Tower has enough brutes like

Top: Railway to the Minnesota Mine's open pits and nearby Breitung location before underground mining began. TOWER-SOUDAN HISTORICAL SOCIETY COLLECTION, IRON RANGE RESEARCH CENTER

LOWER PHOTO: Tower's Vermilion Hotel opened its doors for business in the summer of 1892. LAKE COUNTY HISTORICAL SOCIETY COLLECTION AT THE IRON RANGE RESEARCH CENTER

him and his mud-bespattered drunken consort."[5]

Harrington was threatened constantly. Although notes appeared on his door ordering him to "Let up – or take the consequences," his efforts apparently did not go unrewarded.[6] As early as January 1889, the Tower paper was able to quote a *Duluth Daily News* article defending the town from what it claimed were "sensational articles" appearing in the *St. Paul Globe*, suggesting a "rawness of affairs" that simply "does not exist." The Duluth paper went on to say:

"Tower has 5,000 inhabitants. It has two day and two night policemen. It will compare with any town of its size in America, for law, order and morality. Its people are as intelligent and well-behaved as any of those in any ward in St. Paul, and more industrious."[7]

By this time Tower was large enough to be called a city and Fred Barrett had a second newspaper in nearby Ely, the *Ely Iron Home*.[8]

Neither of Barrett's papers could claim supremacy in terms of circulation. The most popular newspaper on the Vermilion Range during the 1880s and early '90s was *Bede's Budget*, "six solid pages" of land sales notices.

For a time, it was the official newspaper of Tower. J. Adam Bede, northeast Minnesota's premier politician, published his *Budget* until the Panic of 1893 closed the mines and sent land sales crashing. Bede moved his printing plant to Eveleth, where it was later used to print the *Eveleth Star*. Elected to Congress in 1902, Bede held that office until 1908, earning a reputation as an advocate for opening Minnesota's mineral and timber lands to development. It was once said, "J. Adam Bede did more to put Minnesota on the map than any Congressman before or since."[9]

With the arrival of the railroad, Tower became a gathering place for timber speculators, land buyers and entrepreneurs anxious to profit from the flood of arrivals in the new mining district. Incorporated as a village in 1884, Tower's first village president, John Owens, was the local sawmill operator. The town's first trustees – John G. Brown, John Sawbridge and James Bale – all ran businesses along Tower's stump-filled Main Street. Their first official act was to appoint Michael O'Keefe, a tough Ironwood, Michigan, lawman, to the position of town marshal at a salary of $50 a month. He was needed.[10]

During its initial years, the town was little more than a collection of saloons, gaming houses and brothels frequented mostly by transients and construction workers – much like "Whiskey Row" and "Mesaba Station" during railroad building days. Drunken brawls, knifings and shootings were almost daily occurrences and prostitution was rampant.

Village ordinances focused on protecting private property and curbing violence, but saloons were allowed to remain open 24 hours

a day. Their importance to the maintenance of the village is clearly seen in the town's first financial report "covering the period November 1884 to March 9, 1886. Out of a total revenue of $4,957.57, more than $4,000 came from holders of saloon licenses."[11]

Yet the violence, much of it initiated in saloons, continued. According to financial reports for Tower's first three years, the cost of lock-up and police protection nearly equalled that of town improvements.[12]

In 1887, the population approached 3,000, although it's hard to get an accurate count because people were coming and going every day. Hotels and rooming houses were packed and rooms were shared by strangers.

According to one new arrival: "Room No. 6 in the Hotel Sheridan has two beds. The obliging clerk told me I could occupy the one on the right, that the first one was pre-empted by a countryman of mine (I'm Irish) who would offer no objection if I kept real quiet…."[13]

That fall, eight people died in a fire that destroyed a three-story saloon and rooming house. Shortly after, a volunteer fire department was organized, a horse-drawn pumper was purchased and an all brick fire hall was built. The bricks were made in

former mine captain Elisha Morcom's brick factory, located in nearby Soudan. The factory used local clays which, when fired, turned a unique cream red. Fear of fire had Morcom & Company turning out bricks at a rate of 40,000 a day. The fire hall and other buildings of Morcom's bricks still stand on Tower's main street.[14]

In mid-1888, Tower was advertised as a village of 5,000 people. Brick buildings, hotels, restaurants, boardinghouses, clothing stores, department stores, furniture stores, jewelry stores, drug stores, millinery shops and dress-making establishments lined its main street. Located here were building contractors, tailors, blacksmiths, wagon makers, meat packers, bakers, barbers, doctors and lawyers. The town also had a fine school, three churches, a 60-member businessmen's association, a police force and a fire department. Daily passenger train service connected the town to all parts of the nation and two large sawmills busily supplied lumber for a growing number of nearby mining towns. Tower was not yet five years old.[15]

Three years later, a hydroelectric plant at Pike River Falls brought electricity and street lights to the town and construction began on

Pike River Hydroelectric Plant, completed in 1891, supplied electric power for Tower's first city lights, but it would be many years before electricity was a reliable enough power source for use in the mines. TOWER-SOUDAN HISTORICAL SOCIETY COLLECTION, IRON RANGE RESEARCH CENTER

The Tower Stage Line provided the only means of public transportation from Tower to the mines prior to 1891. **Bottom:** The Iron Range Brewing Association plant in Tower is pictured shortly after completion and shows the unique concrete icehouse where the brew was cooled. TOWER-SOUDAN HISTORICAL SOCIETY COLLECTION, IRON RANGE RESEARCH CENTER

what was promised to be "the best and most modern hotel in the state," the three-story, 40-room, Vermilion Hotel.

By the time the hotel opened its doors for business in the summer 1892, the town already had a brewery. In April of that year, the Iron Range Brewing Company established a plant near the East Two River. It could produce 12,000 barrels of beer a year and was managed by M. Fink, one of the foremost brewers in the Lake Superior region.[16] From 1892 to 1920, Fink's Iron Range Beer was popular in the bars and saloons of Tower, Ely, Winton, Two Harbors, Duluth and nearby Mesabi mining towns.

The brewery's cooling vat was described as "the largest and most ingenious construction north of Duluth." It stood three stories high and was built with double concrete walls. All winter long blocks of ice

cut from Lake Vermilion were hauled to the brewery, raised in a horse-drawn elevator and packed into the space between the walls. Even during the hottest days of summer the cooling vat functioned perfectly.[17]

In 1891, a streetcar line replaced the old Tower Stage, which since 1888 had provided the only means of public transportation between Tower and the mines. The streetcar was pulled by a small steam engine over three miles of narrow gauge track. It ran the full length of Tower's main street and regular stops were made on every street corner. The company was owned and operated by Charles Trengrove, a former copper miner from Anaconda, Montana. Trengrove's streetcar made 10 trips a day and ran seven days a week until the 1893 mine closing. It was not without its excitements:[18]

"Charlie Trengrove outsmarted a bunch of Italians in his streetcar Wednesday last. They wouldn't stop smoking, so he tried to throw one of them out of the car. A maccaronian friend of the swarthy Italian threw a mining boot at Trengrove. Charlie quickly put the train into reverse and backed the gang – right to the police station."[19]

Establishment of sawmills near Lake Vermilion did much to promote Tower's growth. Crews of choppers, swampers, barkers, sawyers, teamsters and drivers equipped with axes, saws, horses and oxen poured into the heavily forested lands north of the Mesabi Ridge and sent millions of feet of logs down the Sandy and Pike rivers into

Lake Vermilion. Beginning in 1886 and for 20 years thereafter, water was seldom seen in Pike Bay because of rafts of floating logs.

The first independently owned mill on the lake was that of two former Minnesota Iron Company employees, Charles Sellers and John Owens. Sellers was instantly killed on July 6, 1887, "by the bursting of a revolving saw." A few years later, the mill burned and Owens left Tower to establish a sawmill on the south side of the Mesabi Ridge near a small body of water named Silver Lake. A village was established there and Owens became its first president. They called it Virginia.[20]

The Owens Lumber Company mill was replaced by two much larger sawmills, both owned by the Howe Lumber Company, which in 1892 produced 24 million board feet of lumber and shipped most of it by rail to Two Harbors, from where it was carried downlake by barge to Chicago, Cleveland, Milwaukee and other eastern markets.[21] White pine stands along the shores of Lake Vermilion disappeared and a vast forest of prime timber near Trout Lake was removed. In January 1893, the company was able to announce that it had "experienced one of the

most profitable years in its history." In that year, the mills were consolidated and the plant was thoroughly overhauled. Equipped with new band, circular and gang saws, the mill's capacity was increased to 200,000 board feet of lumber a day. The local press of that year described the Howe Mill as "one of the largest in Minnesota."[22]

By maintaining a high water level with a dam at the Vermilion River and keeping logging operations close to shores of the lake, the company was able to post large profits year after year until the summer of 1899, when its mill was destroyed by fire. A few months later the Howe holdings were taken over by the Tower Lumber Company and a new mill was erected at the site.[23]

The Tower Lumber operation lasted for nine years, from 1900-1909. Trout Lake, Pine Lake and the countryside west of the Pike River furnished most of the timber. In order to get their logs from Pine Lake to the mill on Vermilion, the Tower Company saw fit to connect the two lakes with a short logging railroad.[24] The logs were cut in winter and hauled to landings on the lake. Each spring, after the ice melted, they were rafted by steam tug to Pike Bay to await the saw.

The Tower Lumber Company sawmill on Lake Vermilion's Pike Bay operated from 1900 to 1909. TOWER-SOUDAN HISTORICAL SOCIETY COLLECTION, IRON RANGE RESEARCH CENTER

Tower Lbr. Co. Saw Mill, Tower Minn.

This logging camp somewhere in Lake County is typical of the here-today, gone-next year nature of the times. LAKE COUNTY COLLECTION. IRON RANGE RESEARCH CENTER

Many of the logs floated to Tower in those years were dead and dying tamarack, victims of the blight of 1890-1895. Tamarack timbers were sold to the mines, where they were used to shore up underground workings. At its height, the Tower Company employed 500 men at the mill site and as many as 2,000 "jacks" went to work in its camps during winter.[25]

The Alger-Smith Lumber Company purchased the mill in 1909 and operated it until 1911, when they sold it to Cook and Ketchem, who ran the mill under that name until 1916, when they reorganized as the Trout Lake Lumber Company. By this time the easy to reach pinelands were gone and, although there were attempts to log some of the tall timber northeast of Trout Lake, hauling runs turned out to be long and difficult, profits declined and in 1918 the mill was closed and dismantled.[26] There would be other sawmills at the lake, but none would approach the record productions of earlier years.

The need for labor created by the expansion of the timber industry and

increased activity at the mine during the 1890s brought many European immigrants to Tower and Soudan. Some were Swedes, a few were Italians, but most were either Finns or Austrians. The Austrians were really Slovenian speaking people from Austria-Hungary's Carniola region. Their arrival was the result of the work of Father Joseph F. Buh, a Slovenian-speaking missionary to the Bois Forte people, whose dream was to establish a Catholic population and church in Tower. His efforts are said to have brought 300 Slovenian families to the Vermilion Range, enough for him to publish a successful newspaper in that language.[27] Coincidentally, he was also founder of the Catholic parish in Two Harbors and for a time served both parishes by commuting on the railroad.

Although there were Finnish-speaking people in Tower almost as soon as mining operations began, their numbers were small before 1890. Most of these early arrivals had previous experience in the iron and copper mines of Norway and Michigan. However,

heavy production at the Minnesota Mine during the years 1889-1892 brought a large number of young single Finns to Tower and Soudan, many in search of nothing more than adventure. They knew very little English, less about mining and, if they had a goal, it was to go back to their homeland with stories to tell and money in their pocket. The mine was a necessary evil – a way to stay alive until their luck improved. They sought escape from what must have seemed a drab and lonely existence – in Tower's 16 saloons.

A life of heavy drinking and lack of restraint, into which new arrivals were often drawn, destroyed many young men, not only Finns, but Swedes, Italians, Austrians, Americans and other nationalities as well. But because Finns made up a vast majority of the mine's work gangs, it seemed for a time that the entire nationality might be branded and the local paper did its best to help out in the branding:

"As Billy Williams was coming into town last evening, he was accosted by three Finns who immediately attempted to overpower him. Luckily Billy had a revolver and, rather than cultivate any further acquaintance, he pulled it and gave them notice to skip.… Many of these Finns, when met on the road, will not turn out at all and, if some night, some stout miner was to half kill a few of them, he would receive the thanks of many."[28]

Fortunately, there were Finnish-speaking families in both Tower and Soudan who recognized the problem and were prepared to fight against its cause. August Myllymaki, an early arrival in Soudan, is said to have paid the expenses of Scandinavian Good Templars organizer, Herman Helander of Republic, Michigan, to bring the message of the "evils of alcohol" to the Vermilion Range. The result was the birth of the Northern Flame Temperance Society, formed in the spring of 1886 at the home of Soudan miner William Erickson.

Dead and dying tamarack were victims of the 1890s blight and were cut for the market. TOWER-SOUDAN HISTORICAL SOCIETY COLLECTION, IRON RANGE RESEARCH CENTER **Bottom:** An 1898 view of the interior of the Northern Flame Temperance Hall in Soudan. IRON RANGE HISTORICAL SOCIETY

Steamboat *Mary Bell* docks at
McKinley Park in 1908.
HERMAN OLSON, IRON RANGE
RESEARCH CENTER

Not only did the society work to curb
heavy drinking in Tower's saloons, it had a
hall constructed in Soudan to serve as a
home-away-from-home for lonely young
men and helped needy members with funeral
and medical expenses. Membership soared
and the ideals of temperance quickly spread
to Ely, Virginia, Hibbing and other iron
range towns. For two decades or more, a
mostly Finnish temperance movement served
as a stabilizing force in the mining towns of
the Lake Superior District.[29]

The 1894 Gold Rush

In the spring of 1894, Tower was suddenly
a center for another gold rush, this time to
Rainy Lake on the Canadian border. Outfitting
stations sprang up overnight, hotels were
packed and each incoming train was filled with
excited gold seekers. Although there were other
ways to get to the gold fields, the route through
Tower was apparently the quickest and certainly
the most popular. It included a steamboat
trip across the lake to the Vermilion Dam,
where teams could be hired for an overland
ride through the woods to Crane Lake, "a
distance of 25 miles with one stop between."
From there the trip was "over the lakes" to
Rainy Lake City, which, in March 1894, was
described as having a population of "about
300, all living in tents and log cabins."

Although gold-bearing quartz was
reported and a number of shafts were sunk,
paying quantities did not materialize and the
excitement died out in late 1895.[30]

Tower Declines

For a few brief years, Tower was the
social and business center of the Vermilion
Range and seemed destined to become the
largest city north of Duluth. Businessmen,
entrepreneurs, politicians and the nation's
mining elite booked their meetings and
conventions at the city's luxury hotel located
on the corner of Main and Alder streets and
were entertained with concerts, recitals and
plays in the City Opera House. Here were
the homes of mine officials, lumber
company executives, professionals and
independent businessmen.

On the town's social calender were
baseball games, boxing matches, band
concerts, public dances, charity balls,
outings, picnics and moonlight excursions
on the lake. Steam yachts plied the waters of
Lake Vermilion, described as "the grandest
lake scenery in America," and a growing
resort business brought artists, naturalists,
hunters, fishermen and wealthy vacationers
to the city. There was reason and plenty of
talk about forming a new Vermilion County,
with a courthouse in Tower's public square.
It was even predicted that the city would
someday be home to 80,000 people.[31]

There would be no courthouse in the
city's public square, nor would there ever be
a Vermilion County – and the population of
the town never exceeded the 5,000 reported
in 1888. With the opening of new mining
fields at Shagawa Lake and on the Mesabi
Range, businesses were quick to relocate. By

1900, the booming city of Ely, surrounded by five active mines, had totally eclipsed Tower as the premier city of the Vermilion Range.[32]

Soudan (1887-1920)

Although almost 1,000 people were living in Soudan in 1887, it was not yet thought of as a single community, nor did anyone know it by the name "Soudan." It was, instead, Stone Location and Breitung Location – two parts of the mine set aside for employees' residences. Composed mostly of boardinghouses, miners cottages and mine buildings, the locations were off limits to independent businessmen and saloon keepers. They would remain off-limits until recent times.[33]

The *Vermilion Iron Journal* put it this way:

"The miners and their families all reside at the mines, where the Minnesota Iron Company has provided them with comfortable houses. In fact, nearly all of them own their own homes, owing to the liberal policy of this company, and the miners are not allowed to have any saloons or places where intoxicants are sold in their settlement."[34]

There were almost 2,000 people living at the mines in 1888, but it would be another year before the residential areas would be thought of as a single location named Soudan. It was then, as it would be for the next 50 years, a "company town" in every way. Miners rented or purchased company houses built on company land. Miners' wives drew water from company wells at stipulated times of the day. Streets were maintained by the company and the company supervised everything from house painting to garbage collection.

Simple frame cottages and two-story boardinghouses, painted gray with fenced-in yards, lined winding dirt streets. Cows wandered about at random. At night the town was dark, except for a few street corners where a dim light glowed, powered by electricity from the mine. Houses were heated with box stoves and rooms were lit at night with kerosene lamps. No home was without its outhouse. A boardwalk wound through the town and connected to a wooden stairway to the mine.

Almost everyone living in Soudan was associated with the mine. The status held by foremen, timekeepers and captains was reflected in the houses that the company built for them. Most were located closer to the mine and were often more substantial than cottages of ordinary miners.[35]

Live theater provided much of the entertainment in early Iron Range towns. ELY-WINTON HISTORICAL SOCIETY COLLECTION, IRON RANGE RESEARCH CENTER

The general store at the townsite of Section Thirty would grow from this early stage into a large enterprise that was popular not only with the miners there, but with sawmill workers and lumberjacks who made nearby Winton their home. NUTE COLLECTION AT NORTHEAST MINNESOTA HISTORICAL CENTER

Excellent work prospects after 1887 brought immigrant families and many young unmarried men to Soudan and the nearby village of Tower. Although some came by way of the Michigan mines, Swedish, Finnish, Slovenian and Italian could be heard as often as English in the streets of the location. To the English-speaking population, the foreign speakers were "Swedes," "Finlanders," "Dagos" or "Austrians." To everyone in the community, Cornish miners and their families were always "Cousin Jacks."[36]

The ethnic mix, particularly among the young, was not conducive to harmony. There were fights, there were burnings, there were angry feelings that lasted for years. Finnish, Slovenian and Italian miners – in their teens and twenties – frequented Tower's saloons and picked fights, not only with each other, but among themselves.

"A drunken brawl among a jolly party of Finlanders in Soudan Saturday evening resulted in one of the party receiving several cuts with a knife.… No arrests have been made."[37]

Young single men took advantage of recently arrived Slovenians by raiding their celebrations for beer and booze.

"It is a well-known fact that a crowd of Soudan boys inclined to be sporty, take every opportunity to participate in Austrian wedding festivities. It is reported that half a dozen of these young men lost their jobs in the mine because they participated in Sunday's brawl."[38]

It was the mine that did the disciplining in Soudan. Looming high above the town, with its tall stacks and engine houses, for years it remained the source of law and the symbol of unquestioned authority. Boiler fires burned day and night and its stacks poured out steady funnels of black smoke. Location children fell asleep to the rumble of the crushers which, on clear nights, could be heard at Mesaba, 30 miles away. The rumble of the mine and the sound of the mine whistle marking the changing of the shift became part of everyday life. But there were times when the whistle sounded unexpectedly with a long unbroken blast. This brought fear to every home in the location. One by one, wives, daughters and sons of miners would emerge from their cottages and make their way to the foot of the long stairway to the mine and await the

Sec. 30 – general store

NORTH. AMERICAN. MINE. TOWER. MINN.

announcement. Was it a breakdown of some sort? Had there been an accident? Would there be a reading of a list of the men who were injured – or dead?

As long as the whistle blew at expected times, as long as there was smoke in the air and the crushers rumbled, Soudan families were secure. There were times when the whistle didn't blow, when the air cleared and the crushers fell silent. These, too, were frightening times because they meant that there was no work. With no welfare or other form of compensation to tide them over, many miners and their families were forced to leave town in search of work elsewhere.[39]

The Soudan Mine experienced a closing like this as a result of the Panic of 1893. Headlines in Tower's *Vermilion Iron Journal* announced the shut down, "The Great Minnesota Suspends All Mining Operations and Its Machinery is Idle – Eleven Hundred Men Discharged." The mine retained 300.

The *Journal* continued: "The men retained at the mine are mostly men of families and it is an unusual sight to see experienced miners employed at sorting out ore on the stockpile as common laborers. Of the discharged men, the foreigners are many of them leaving the range. It is estimated

that 130 of them went south on Tuesday's train. Many of those remaining at Soudan are living economically, not a few salting down for winter's use kegs of fish caught in Lake Vermilion."[40]

The impact on the community was profound. Within a few months, its population dropped to a few hundred people. The local paper described the exodus:

"Every outgoing train carries a large number of miners and laborers. Capt. W.R. Hurd of the Minnesota stated Wednesday to the *Journal* that many of the unemployed are returning to Austria, a few have gone to the World's Fair and a great many have equipped themselves and gone out on Lake Vermilion to 'rough it' for a month or two. Not a few have gone west to the harvest fields."[41]

For months Soudan was almost abandoned. If it hadn't been for the company's announcement that they would keep "the best and most experienced men to have them on hand in September and October, when it is believed there will be a resumption of work," the town might have been completely evacuated. As promised, work was eventually resumed, but many who left never returned. The depression lasted well into 1894, ore production stagnated,

The North American Mine operating near Tower in the 1920s. VOSS COLLECTION, IRON RANGE RESEARCH CENTER

wages were cut and hundreds lost their jobs. Things did improve. By 1895, the work force at the Minnesota was back to 1,000, but it would never again be as large.

However, the population of the location continued to rise and, in 1901, surpassed the pre-1893 count. Soudan was hailed as "the largest iron mining location in the Lake Superior District."

In late 1903, another slump in the steel market caused the mine to be closed again – this time for 14 months. The population of Soudan dropped again, this time from almost 3,000 to less than 1,600, but in 1910, along with increased production at the mine, it was back to 2,000.[42] The mine closings and population fluctuations were almost always tied to the eastern steel market and continued to affect life in Soudan until well into the third decade of the 20th century.

The Corpus Christi Day Strike of 1892

There was a mine stoppage not tied to the eastern steel market. On June 16, 1892, a large contingent of recently hired Austrians and Italians, in an argument with the company over a religious holiday, seized control of the mine and held it for three days. It was not a strike of organized labor, but rather a disagreement with company officials, or possibly a misunderstanding over the need to work on Corpus Christi Day, the Thursday after Trinity Sunday – a day of celebration in some parts of Europe.

When that day came in June 1892, mine timekeepers noticed that a large number of men had taken the day off without advising management of their intentions. The next morning the company gave 315 of these men a 14-day suspension without pay.

The company's action drew a violent response. When the night shift came on at 7 p.m. that same Friday, the suspended men, armed with clubs, rocks and pieces of pipe, refused to let the workers pass. They then "drove the engineers, firemen and pumpmen from their posts" and occupied the No. 4 engine house. In the melee, it was reported, "a striker known as 'Calumet' drew a revolver on Captain Wallace." One by one, fires under the mine's boilers were extinguished, stopping the crushers and skip hoists and plunging the mine into darkness. That night,

the strikers, confident that they had control of the mine, paraded down the streets of Soudan, firing revolvers and calling out other miners to join them.

The next morning, with their numbers nearly doubled, the strikers marched to the company pay office and asked for their wages. Saturday was the scheduled pay day, but company President Donald Bacon met the strikers and announced that payment would be postponed until the disagreement was settled. The strikers responded with a demand for a 20 percent pay raise, fuel oil for their lamps and the immediate reinstatement of all those who had been suspended without pay. They made it clear that if their demands were not met, there would be no more production at the mine. Bacon refused all of their demands and dispatched a call for help to the St. Louis County Sheriff's Office in Duluth.

At 4:45 that afternoon, Sheriff Sharvey and 40 deputies armed with Springfield rifles arrived by special train and took positions at several approaches to the mine. Under this protection boiler fires were again started, but the first sign of smoke brought a large force of armed miners to the mine site. Realizing that he was outnumbered, the sheriff withdrew his men, but only after strike leaders promised they would do nothing more than put out the fires.

That night, while the strikers celebrated their victory, another call for help was telegraphed to the National Guard in Duluth, then under the command of Adjutant General J.B. Mullen. It received a quick response. At 4 a.m. Sunday morning, a troop train arrived bringing to Soudan three companies of federal militia. All day in a driving rain, company timekeepers Joe Jeffry, Thomas Edwards, Will Slogget, James Hooper and John Roberts, assisted by armed guardsmen, moved from house to house questioning residents and arresting strike leaders. By late afternoon, 21 suspected strike leaders were housed under guard in the company machine shop. By 8 p.m. Sunday, smoke rose again from the stacks of the mine and the electric lights were turned on, but troops continued to patrol the streets of Soudan for another day. At 7 p.m. Monday, the night shift went back to work and production resumed.[43]

From Company Location to Community

The various nationalities at Soudan eventually came together as a single community. Lessons of respect, tolerance, patience and cooperation were learned early underground. Working under the same contract, Austrians, Finns, Swedes and Cornishmen drilled, blasted, scraped and trammed the ore as partners. Under the light of the carbide lamp, old differences paled and were replaced with a new kind of identity, one that they all shared.

Issues of ethnicity blended with feelings of mutuality as miners came to know a new kind of bond, a special identity that others, even the owners and managers of the mine, could not share. No matter what their background, they were, before anything else, Soudan miners. This attitude was carried to the surface and became a contributing factor in the early transformation of the location into a community.

Mining camps and towns were often the antithesis of "community." Located in places far removed from established society and populated mostly by young restless men who had little intention of laying down roots, they often became centers for vice, violence and crime. If there was going to be any order it was up to the company to provide it. Soudan, during its initial years, was no exception. However, order created by imposition of restrictions backed by disciplinary action on company property and work sites was not conducive to community.

The arrival of women and families with the first mining crews in 1884 probably did more than anything else to bring about a sense of community. During the years that followed, they arrived by the hundreds – wives of company employees, sisters, sons, daughters, nieces and nephews. Women took jobs as school teachers, midwives, seamstresses, waitresses, boardinghouse cooks, maids and housekeepers. Some could not speak English, most were single and all were young.

There were weddings. It is well established that the insistence of women on standards of moral conduct for the town in

The people of the mining communities often gathered in parades, as demonstrated in this Memorial Day photo at Soudan location in the early 1900s. TOWER-SOUDAN HISTORICAL SOCIETY COLLECTION, IRON RANGE RESEARCH CENTER

The establishment of the townsite of Ely amounted to a small trading boom for the descendants of Hudson Bay Company trappers already living in the region. ELY-WINTON HISTORICAL SOCIETY COLLECTION, IRON RANGE RESEARCH CENTER

which they raised their children lay behind the early establishment of schools, restriction of saloons, removal of "elements of disturbance" and public health improvements within the location. Working through their husbands, they influenced company actions on everything from improved garbage collection to the establishment of a central water supply providing running water to the homes.

Identified often only by the name of the man they married or the name of their father, the women of the location instigated literary societies, organized church groups, participated in theatricals, gave piano lessons, taught in the schools, developed a temperance league and two even entered the world of business by moving over to Tower with the region's first millinery and women's clothing boutique.

Despite the move toward stability and community, control of the location remained in the hands of the company. Although most of the residents owned their own houses, the lots on which they stood were owned by the company and rented to the home owners for a nominal fee. However, the company reserved the right to break the contract should the property be needed for mining. This became the model for other company locations on the Vermilion and Mesabi ranges.

While Tower and Soudan moved toward order and community, the mining frontier

moved 21 miles up the track to Ely. Tower had its wild days, days of heavy drinking, violence and crime, but when it came to wild and lawless living, Tower was tame compared to Ely.

Frontier Ely (1887-1900)

Incorporated as a village in 1887, Ely was named after Samuel P. Ely, the man who helped the Porter syndicate of Chicago gain control of Charlemagne Tower's Minnesota Mining Company. The town was located and platted next to the Chandler property and eventually included several parcels of land totaling something like 360 acres. The boundaries of the town were carefully laid so as to exclude mine properties or any other land suspected to contain marketable iron ore. The town had little to base its taxes on.[44]

As a result, Ely began as a place of tents, log cabins and tar paper shacks. In 1888, a few rough frame buildings with plank platforms fronted a single dirt street. A steam-driven sawmill toted in from Tower Junction during the winter of 1885 produced lumber for the Chandler House, Pioneer Hotel, James A. Cormack's General Store and outfitters Fenske and Lawrence – the town's first places of business.[45]

Before the railroad was completed, supplies were hauled in during the winter of 1887 by sleigh over the old Mud Creek canoe route from Lake Vermilion or along a rough trail cut through the woods during the summer. It was enough to allow a daily stagecoach to bring in the mail and the miners' payroll.[46]

At the time Ely was platted, there was another townsite called Spalding about two miles to the northeast. It never amounted to more than a few log buildings, one of which, the Chandler House, was moved to the Ely site as soon the new town was platted. Some of Ely's earliest citizens, August Fenske, Asa Camp and Fred James, are said to have traded for furs at Spalding before they moved to Ely.[47]

At that time, the Ojibway people were scattered about the region in small family groups. They were descendants of Hudson's Bay Company trappers and traders and were living much as their ancestors had – hunting, fishing, trapping and selling furs to buyers on both sides of the international border. The arrival of prospectors and miners amounted to a small trading boom for them. An Ojibway village appeared at Sandy Point on nearby Shagawa Lake and native hunters walked the short distance to Ely, where they traded their furs and sold moose meat in the streets.[48]

Ely quickly became a place of mines. In 1889, the Pioneer joined the Chandler as a producing mine. It was followed by the Zenith in 1892, Savoy in 1898 and Sibley in 1899. These five mines became Ely's major employers. Not that there weren't other mines – the Sheridan, Chippewa-St.Clair, White Iron, McComber, Lucky Boy,

Howard, Section 30, Mud Creek, LaRue and Fargo all produced iron ore at one time or another.[49]

During their first years, Ely mines hired miners on an almost daily basis. There was no hourly rate of pay, nor were miners paid according to what they did or how hard they worked. Instead, they were organized into four-man crews and paid according to a "contract" based on the amount and market price of the ore their crew, or "gang," produced. If the vein being worked turned lean or the market price of ore fell, a miner could expect a reduction in pay.[50]

The underground mines were dangerous. The ores were cracked and broken, mine workings had to be shored with timbers. They were wet. Mine pumps ran day and night. But the ore was in demand and anyone who knew anything about iron mining knew that the demand for ore could drop without warning. The idea was to get as much out as possible, as quickly as possible. Captains, anxious to keep production high, drove their men hard. There were firings. Men walked off the job. There were accidents. It was easy for a new arrival to get a job in an Ely mine. The question was, how long would he last?

The Savoy took six lives in a cave-in. It was said that the lone Austrian survivor was trapped underground for eight days and survived on chewing tobacco – his own and that taken from a dead partner.[51] The body

In 1900, Ely was booming, with a lively business district with many churches and the usual assortment of saloons. ELY-WINTON HISTORICAL SOCIETY COLLECTION, IRON RANGE RESEARCH CENTER

Horses and drivers stop to have their pictures taken in front of Ely's Arcade Saloon in 1920. ELY-WINTON HISTORICAL SOCIETY COLLECTION, IRON RANGE RESEARCH CENTER

of another Austrian was taken up in a gunny sack after part of the hanging wall collapsed at the Pioneer. Six bodies were never found at the Consolidated Vermilion Extension, after the waters of Mud Creek poured into the mine. The Sibley took five more men as they were being lowered down a shaft. The Zenith took another in an explosion. Even the Chandler open pit was dangerous. In 1889, two Finnish miners eating lunch were hit with 50 tons of ore when a part of the pit wall collapsed.[52]

All of the mines had their share of accidents. Walls of stopes gave way without warning; blasts were set off prematurely; there were mine fires; miners were struck by falling ore; raw recruits fresh from the "old country" misunderstood directions and got in the way of machinery.

In December 1890 the *Ely Iron Home* reported: "Joseph Kreshman, an Austrian, got in front of a loaded car on the second level of Shaft No. 1 at the Chandler last week and sustained injuries that resulted fatally. The shift boss had repeatedly warned him against getting in front of mine cars. Nevertheless, either by carelessness or indifference, he, on Monday morning, got in front of a loaded car. He was buried Thursday from the Catholic Church."[53]

A week later the following news item appeared: "A fatal accident happened at No. 1 Shaft of the Pioneer mine this morning between the hours of 2 and 3 a.m. An Austrian 'lander' fell down the shaft a distance of about 200 feet and was killed instantly."[54]

It was hard to put together a crew of experienced miners. Most men lasted maybe a year or two underground. Their replacements were usually unskilled. To keep the mine producing and accidents to a minimum, mine captains were strict to the point of ruthlessness. Most were feared. Some were hated.

Replacements arrived by the hundreds – Swedes, Finns, Slovenian Austrians, Italians and Bulgarians – mostly young men, barely out of their teens. Some, still dressed in their mining clothes, were buried in rough pine boxes, their names not yet registered in the town's census rolls.

Ely's underground mines employed a method of mining known as "caving." Underground levels were made about 60 feet apart with floor drifts, connecting to the shaft. In the ground above, crosscuts and raises were made through the ore body in such a way as to leave great blocks of ore which were "milled," or allowed to cave through chutes into waiting ore cars in the drift below. The loaded ore cars were pushed, or "trammed," to the shaft and the ore dumped into waiting skips and raised to the surface. Large underground cavities formed as the blocks of ore were removed. Rocks, gravel and dirt from the surface were used to fill the cavity. As deeper levels were opened, a mined out "pit-like" area formed at the surface.[55]

Mine workers were hired on the spot. The only qualification required was a robust appearance. Once hired, a new worker was sent directly underground. There, he often became a "mucker," scraping spilled ore from around a chute and shoveling it into a car, or a "trammer," pushing loaded cars to waiting skips at the shaft. Twenty years later, if he hadn't quit or been fired, he was still scraping ore or pushing cars. There were few rungs on the ladder of promotion in the mines.

If the mines were dangerous, the town was even more so – especially at night. Drunks staggered down dimly lit streets. There were muggings, shootings and holdups. Saloons were hangouts for gamblers, bullies and prostitutes. A month's pay, or even one's life, could be quickly lost at such places as The Poker Chip, First and Last Chance Saloon, Maggie's, Dirty Bessie's, Faro Mike's, or The Bucket of Blood.

Men carried revolvers strapped to their sides. The crack of pistols was sometimes heard in the streets. Murders went unsolved. It is said that there was hardly a Sunday when the morning freight train didn't run over a man – a man who was probably already dead, the victim of an Ely Saturday night celebration.

There is a story told about pioneer Ely. It is reputed to have been told by Mary Hill, pioneer resident of Embarrass, who recounted her first impression of Ely when she arrived from Finland in the early 1900s thusly:

"The night freight to Ely always had a passenger car attached to it and this passenger car was often filled with immigrant families, usually from Austria or Finland, all anxious to begin a new life in America. In the 'Old Country,' they heard stories about what a wonderful place America was. 'Everything was beautiful in America. A person could get rich in America. There was gold in the streets in America!'

"On a particular morning, just as it was getting light, the night freight pulled into Ely, bringing with it a young family from Finland. The little daughter looking out of the train window saw Ely for the first time in the gray light of a Sunday dawn. She saw streets of mud, strewn with empty bottles, ugly frame buildings, board sidewalks on which drunken men slept.

"'Mother, mother,' she asked, 'Did we pass America in the night?'"

The Rise of Iron Range Town Politics (1888-1900)

If Ely's frontier years are to be remembered for anything, it should be the special kind of politics that arose in its streets. It arose with a boldness unprecedented in history of Lake Superior iron mining towns. It featured a colorful blending of direct action, loyalty to one's constituency, broad participation, "to the victor belongs the spoils" and an unfailing allegiance to a political leader who sometimes took on proportions larger than life. It became a totally understood and fully accepted part of everyday life in all iron range towns.

It began with a struggle between town promoters and mining company men over ways to finance the growing needs of the booming community. When Ely was incorporated, the Minnesota Exploration Company, which ran the Chandler Mine, took no responsibility for the town. It did take responsibility for the managers of the mine – the superintendent, captains, timekeepers and other officials. Houses were built for them on company property at a "location" close to the mine, and many ordinary miners and even a few laborers were housed there, as well.

The Chandler was planned in much the same way as other mines in the Lake Superior District and few were without their locations. As a result, assessed valuation of real and personal property in the incorporated village was low, too low to pay for all the improvements that were needed. In 1889, the village of Ely was able to raise only $6,838.20 to pay for water and lights, sewage disposal, street improvement, police and fire protection.[56]

In the town's first election, held May 31, 1888, John Pengilly, captain at the Chandler, defeated hardware store owner Asa Camp by one vote for the position of village president. Saloonkeepers, fearing Pengilly might try to close them down or at least attempt to regulate their businesses, immediately rose in opposition. Since some of the voters, including Pengilly himself, did not reside within the village limits, his election had to be illegal. After serving three months, Pengilly bowed to pressure and resigned. He was immediately replaced by a legal resident of the village, Edward Cram, who finished out Pengilly's term.[57]

There were only two more village presidents, Alexander Lawson, who lasted about six months, and Ely's first doctor, Charles Shipman, who finished out Lawson's term and was re-elected to office twice.[58] The politics were intense. The main issue was a plan for expanding the village limits to include all mining properties, thus making the mining companies responsible for paying most, if not all, of the town bills.[59]

Meanwhile, a unique system for raising money was established. An ordinance was passed making prostitution illegal within village limits and each month town marshal Joe Hopperton made his rounds of dance halls and saloons, fining prostitutes. Apparently there were enough of them around to improve the streets and establish a system of fire protection.[60]

All of this fining and regulation resulted in widespread criticism of the village system of government. Everyone in town knew the saloons and dance halls were contributing more to the town treasury than the mining company. When some of the more outspoken mine officials began suggesting that it might be a good idea to close the saloons on Sundays to reduce absenteeism in the mines, the saloon men struck back. A strong "tax the mining companies" movement was launched.

Petitions were dawn up to enlarge the townsite and establish Ely as a city. In 1890, new incorporation papers were drafted and on March 3, 1891, Ely became a city and its limits were expanded to include all of the Chandler, Zenith and Pioneer mining properties and part of the Sibley Location.[61]

But this placed the residence of John Pengilly within the town limits and made

him eligible to run for city mayor. He was a well-respected person and, besides, the mining company would have something to say about how its employees voted. If Pengilly won, he would have something to say about how the city spent its money.

The election was hard fought. Feelings ran high. There were public demonstrations. Pengilly gathered support "as the man who graded Ely's streets" and his supporters organized themselves as the "Pioneer Ticket." The day before the election, Ely's "Finn Band" and 200 Chandler employees carrying "Vote for Pengilly" banners paraded through the town's streets.[62]

The opposition, calling itself the "Citizens Party," was led by saloon operators and other businessmen who ran former mine employee Nick Cowling against Pengilly. Free drinks flowed in Ely's 22 saloons and many other favors were bestowed, but on election Tuesday, Pengilly and the entire mining company slate won in a landslide.

According to the local paper: "The results of the election surprised everybody. The Pioneer Ticket won in a clean sweep. One would be led to think that a great many followed the advice of the Chandler marchers. But although many were made happy, many were sad. The new city officers have been elected and we hope they will do their duty towards the city."[63]

Elections for city office were hard fought until well into the 1900s. Sometimes mining company candidates won, sometimes the "Citizens" ticket won, but all of the elections resulted in a clean sweep of city offices. Employees hired by the opposition were immediately fired.

Although the elections were often portrayed as "a struggle between the mines and the town," saloon regulation was a major issue. In the eyes of many of Ely's most respected citizens, saloon closings meant a rise in "blind pigs," unlicensed bars located in location houses where illegal whisky and home brew were sold.

According to the *Ely Miner*: "The saloon subject is a sore spot…. The illegal blind pigs must be broken up…. We have talked the matter over with several of our businessmen and saloon men and the consensus is that unless something is done with illegal liquor traffic, it would be injustice to rub it in on

those who pay for the privilege of selling liquors."[64]

On the other hand, an influential and vocal temperance movement, particularly among Ely's Finns, suggested that it might be time to close both licensed saloons and blind pigs.

The editor of *The Ely Miner* countered with the argument, "It is claimed on good authority that the 22 saloons in Ely do not sell as much beer as do the locations. For the privilege of selling liquor, the saloons pay $500 a year to the city. During my residence in Ely, I have not heard of a single entry in the books of the city where the location retailers have paid a single cent."[65]

Two of Ely's most powerful mayors, Grant McMahon and Louis Sletton, won landslide victories by opposing the restrictions on licensed saloons. Ely's bars remained centers of political activity and city improvement plans until well into the 20th century.

Mining company politicians had a platform based on what they saw as improvements for the town: expansion of churches, patriotism, building of schools, law and order and closing saloons on Sundays. Their candidates openly supported charitable causes and worked to promote service organizations.

Two of Ely's most noted politicians, John Pengilly and Charles Trezona, were both mining captains. Pengilly was born in the English mining town of Camborn in 1853. His father and grandfather had been tin miners in Cornwall. He gained his mining experience in the Pennsylvania coal fields and made a name for himself as a captain in the Michigan iron mines. He was hired by the Minnesota Iron Company in 1887 to bring the Chandler mine to production and served the mining company well as Ely's mayor for three consecutive terms.[66]

Charles Trezona was elected twice to the position of mayor. He was probably one of the most feared mining captains in the history of Iron Country. Born in Cornwall, England, in 1863, Trezona came to Michigan in 1885, where he rose to the position of captain at the Red Jacket copper mine. Donald Bacon hired him as one of his captains at the Minnesota in 1890. After a year, he returned to Michigan to become a

captain in a Wakefield iron mine. A few months later, he was back on the Vermilion Range, this time as superintendent of the Pioneer Mine. The people of Ely knew him as "Captain Charlie" and it is said "there wasn't a man under him who didn't do a good day's work." There wasn't a man hurt or killed in the Pioneer Mine whose family wasn't helped in some way by Captain Charlie, either.[67]

Section Thirty (1883-1923)

In 1883, almost two years before Ely became a town, iron ore was discovered about four miles to the east. When the land was surveyed a year later, everyone knew the iron existed and where it was located. "An iron exposure of high grade specular ore is located near the middle of Section 30 in Township 63 North, Range 11 West of the 4th Principal Meridian," wrote deputy surveyor James H. Hughs in his report of December 1884. Hughs also reported that there were already men claiming homestead rights near the exposure. By 1886, 25 homestead claims, five script claims and one pre-emption claim had been filed on 320 acres of this particular section of land.[68]

The original discovery is said to have been made by Edward Byrne, a prospector hired by Minnesota Iron Company manager George Stone. Instead of reporting the discovery to Stone, Byrne told Duluthians Frank Eaton and Leonidas Merritt about it. He knew that Eaton and Merritt had some Sioux scrip that could be used to place a claim on the iron exposure itself.

The two men paid Byrne $50 and promised him a third-interest in the property, if he went back, marked out the lines and made all the improvements required by law. On June 16, 1883, Eaton and Merritt filed their "scrip claim" with the Duluth Land Office.[69]

Byrne built a small shanty on the claim and put up the required sign. However because of the survey report, there were so many people "prowling around" that he had to walk the property lines carrying a revolver. Inevitably, two men, Thomas Hyde and Angus MacDonald, filed homestead claims on the same property and built shanties nearby claiming the land as their residence as of August 1884.[70]

Following a protracted lawsuit that was eventually settled in 1902 by the U.S. Supreme Court in favor of Leonidas Merritt and Frank Eaton, the Section Thirty iron ore property east of Ely was developed and shipped ore for nearly 14 years before closing in 1923. This photo shows a section of the townsite that developed adjacent to the mine. VOSS COLLECTION, IRON RANGE RESEARCH CENTER

A long and bitter court case resulted. It began on April 6, 1886, with a hearing at the Duluth Land Office and was not settled until the U.S. Supreme Court ruled on the matter on January 13, 1902. By then, more than $1 million had been spent on litigation. The court ruled in favor of Eaton and Merritt and, in 1909, George St. Clair and Alfred Merritt took a lease on the property from the now legal fee holders and organized the Section Thirty Mining Company.[71]

In 1910, a railroad spur was connected to the site, shafts were sunk, an engine house was built, and full scale mining began. During its first year of operation, mining crews working around the clock in eight hour shifts encountered "a large mass of hematite at a depth of 118 feet." It was as rich as any found on the Vermilion Range, the first assays showing an iron content of almost 70 percent – 10 to 15 percent above levels that steel mills considered acceptable.

From then on, except for a shutdown in 1921, the mine provided steady employment for a work force of almost 200. When high shipping rates forced its final closing in 1923, the mine had been in operation almost 14 years and had shipped 1,457,295 tons of ore.[72]

During these years, the town of Section Thirty flourished. It consisted of several boardinghouses, a hotel, dance hall, post office, hospital, school, numerous miners' residences and an active general store. Oppel's Store was, in a way, a forerunner of today's shopping malls. It consisted of several connected buildings and included a fur trading post, meat market, grocery store, clothing store, movie theater and a dance hall. During Section Thirty's heyday, business was so good that the place required eight clerks, a butcher and bookkeeper to keep it functioning.[73]

With closing of the mine, people left quickly. It took only a few months to turn Section Thirty into a place of vacant buildings and boarded up homes. Although most are now removed from the site, a few still remain and, along with the rubble of the engine house, they continue to remind the passerby that there once was an iron mine and mining town in Minnesota's Lake County.

Winton (1892-1915)
On March 2, 1889, a definite change in the land policy of the United States occurred when Congress acted to put an end to private entry on public lands. This was followed in 1891 by an even more sweeping change when the long-standing pre-emption law was repealed and the president was

authorized to set aside parts of the public domain as forest reserves.[74]

Eliminated too were the public land sales that had allowed sawmill owners such as Henry Wieland, R.S. Munger, Lewis H. Merritt, John S. Pillsbury and others to buy pineland for next to nothing.[75] There was now talk of conserving and protecting what forests were left, particularly those lying north and east of the Vermilion Range. Timber buyers, prospectors, land speculators and lumbermen saw this not only as a threat to future development in northeast Minnesota, but as the beginning of the end to their way of life. Veteran surveyor and prospector George Stuntz predicted imminent disaster:

"If these reserves are made it will take away or make unavailable for settlement 5,120,000 acres of land, a tract nearly as large as the three states of New Jersey, Rhode Island and Delaware, combined, and nearly as large as the state of Maryland. It will render 234,444 acres of school land unavailable for a long period. This land at five dollars an acre equals $1,422,220…. It will stop all settlements and improvements, cripple the mining industries and will damage the resources of the tributary country very greatly and immediately trammel every branch of business and travel over our local railroads, already built and to be built."[76]

However, even as untouched as parts of the region seemed, tens of thousands of acres had already passed into private hands. Pre-emptors, homesteaders and entrymen were holding claims to significant portions of it, but the biggest transfer came on August 1, 1882, when President Chester Arthur put most of Cook, Lake and St. Louis counties up for public sale. Although sections previously set aside for reservations, schools, railroads and iron mines were not included in the sale, vast acreages of pineland in the three counties were.

Buyers were numerous and among them were prominent men like John S. Pillsbury, Clinton Morrison, Samuel Simpson and David M. Clough of Minneapolis; William C. Yawkey and Marshall H. Alworth of Michigan; Thomas Bardon, David Miles and Anthony Hayward of Wisconsin. Also among the buyers was Daniel J. Knox, later of the Duluth sawmill firm of that name. More than 197,000 acres of federal wilderness passed into private hands at this sale and, despite all the conservation talk in 1892, much of the country east of Ely was already available for cutting. All that was needed was a mill.[77]

On August 11, 1893, the Knox Lumber Company was formed. Incorporators were Samuel G. Knox of Ironwood, Michigan, president; William C. Winton of Duluth, treasurer; Robert B. Whiteside of Duluth, secretary; and John Whiteside of Huntville, Ontario, director.[78] In the late summer of 1893, they sent cruisers into the woods east

Plank boardwalks and dirt streets were typical of towns like Winton in 1910. Unlike nearby towns, Winton was developed and sustained by logging and lumber mills that depended on Fall Lake and nearby rivers for log delivery to the mills. VOSS COLLECTION, IRON RANGE RESEARCH CENTER

ST. SCENE. WINTON. MINN.

Loggers for the Winton mills left behind miles and miles of clearcut countryside. ELY-WINTON HISTORICAL SOCIETY COLLECTION, IRON RANGE RESEARCH CENTER

of Ely. Camps were built, tote roads were constructed and in November a crew of lumberjacks began logging out the white pine around Fall Lake. In January 1894, Sam Knox, his son in law, A.L. Krenzen, an attorney from Wausau, Wisconsin, and William Winton visited the camps and located a site for their sawmill. It was important to have the mill next to the lake, not only for steam power, but so the logs could be rolled out on the ice to await the spring thaw, when they would be floated to the mill and turned into lumber. It was also important that the mill be located downstream from the area they eventually planned to log, some 300 square miles of pine country stretching from Birch Lake south of Ely all the way to Kekekabic Lake near the Canadian border. By mid-March they had their sawmill running, an electric light plant under way and almost 12 million feet of logs ready for the saw.[79]

The fate of the mill and the forest surrounding it were inextricably tied to national politics, relations with Canada and a certain amount of agitation for conservation in Minnesota. Sam Knox and the men who came to Fall Lake in the spring

of 1894 were mostly Michigan men who had been put out of work as a result of the depletion of that state's white pine industry.

At the time, Michigan lumbermen were either moving into Minnesota or investing in Canadian timber. Canadian investors were doing everything they could to get Washington to put an end to the existing tariff on rough lumber and logs. Although most lumbermen in Minnesota opposed them for fear Canadian timber would drive down prices, there were a few who saw that if duties were removed and a sawmill set up in Ontario, Minnesota logs could be floated across the border and turned into rough lumber there. This would open up vast tracts of previously inaccessible prime timber in the northern portions of the state.

The political wrangling resulted in the Wilson-Gorman Tariff, passed without President Cleveland's signature, in August 1894. All duties on rough lumber and logs were removed.

Logs could now flow freely into Canada and the pine forest of the border country became a subject of great interest and a certain amount of controversy. While speculators, timber cruisers and lumbermen swarmed to the Ely station and the Knox Lumber Company expanded its workforce, people like Christopher C. Andrews, former minister to Sweden, began talking about saving some of the forest still remaining in Minnesota.[80]

Meanwhile, in an attempt to tap into some of this forest, Knox and Winton incorporated the Northern Lumber Company and set up a second sawmill at Rat Portage on the north end of the Lake of the Woods. During the summers of 1895 and 1896, logs cut near the border waters – some, it appears, as far south as Itasca County – ended up at Rat Portage where they were turned into rough lumber and shipped by rail, duty free, to markets in the United States. The Northern Lumber Company's administrative and sales office, like that of the Knox Lumber Company, remained at 103 Paladio Building in Duluth.

It didn't last. In 1897, when the McKinley administration's Dingley Tariff restored the duty and Canada responded with a ban on the import of logs, Knox and Winton gave up the venture and returned to their mill at Fall Lake.[81] In its first year, the Knox Mill produced 15 million board feet of lumber, equaling the production of the Howe Company at Tower. Anxious to diversify shipments, the Duluth and Iron Range Railroad connected a spur to the mill and for the next six years sent a steady supply of white pine lumber to Minneapolis, Des Moines, St. Louis, Omaha and the shipping docks in Duluth.[82]

The mill was as well-equipped as any in its time. Described in 1895, it consisted of an engine house, fire room, electric light plant, band saw, two circular saws, edger, planing mill, lath mill and shingle mill, all "in excellent shape for turning out large quantities of dressed lumber." The entire yard was lit with electricity and the sawdust and other refuse conveyed by "means of endless chains" to a mammoth refuse burner near the mill leaving "the … surroundings … neat and clean and entirely devoid of the usual spattering of sawdust, chips, etc. that characterize saw mills."[83]

Next to the mill was an "embryo city of about 300 inhabitants … situated on a most beautiful spot." It was "located on a hill overlooking the saw and planing mill and the lumber yard with a good view of the lower end of Fall Lake filled to both edges with logs." The "embryo city" included a company store, boardinghouse, community stable for horses and 24 houses, all occupied by families of men employed at the mill. The development was named "Winton" in honor of the Knox Lumber Company co-founder.[84]

The Swallow and Hopkins Mill was near its peak production at Winton in 1920. VOSS COLLECTION, IRON RANGE RESEARCH CENTER

The men of Camp 8 on the Stoney River gathered, likely on a Sunday "washday," for this photo in 1907. ELY-WINTON HISTORICAL SOCIETY COLLECTION, IRON RANGE RESEARCH CENTER

The company employed 1,000 lumberjacks and, during the next six years, much of the forest around Ely was cut down and the logs floated to Winton via the Shagawa and Kawishiwi rivers. Each spring, lakes such as Shagawa, Garden, White Iron and Birch were covered with floating logs awaiting the drive down the rivers and sluiceways to the waters of Fall Lake and the mill.[85] Dams of timber and earth along the waterways, decaying remains of sluiceways and logs still lying at the bottom of lakes serve as reminders of this time.

In 1898, George Swallow of Minneapolis and Louis Hopkins of Duluth contracted Samuel Simpson and H.F. Brown of Minneapolis to saw at least 50 million feet of lumber from their holdings between Burntside and Ensign lakes. The Swallow and Hopkins Mill, as it was called, was equipped with the latest in saws and machinery and had 200 men on its payroll. The company was also responsible for a large hotel and 25 of the townsite homes, all complete with electricity and running water.[86]

The partnership of George Swallow and Louis Hopkins, however, had one central purpose and that was to log. By 1900, they had extended their operations north to

Basswood Lake and during the next 15 years logged out more than 200 square miles of border country from Crooked Lake to Knife Lake. The latest in logging machinery was brought in and logging railroads were constructed to connect Winton with loading docks at Pipestone Bay and Hoist Bay on Basswood Lake.

It has been estimated that Swallow and Hopkins established at least 50 lumber camps, each manned by 100 or more lumberjacks. Mature white and red pine were rafted to loading docks from areas previously impossible to log, such as those near Mud, Burntside, Fourtown, Moose, Newfound, Knife, Thomas, Ima, Snowbank and other lakes south of the international boundary. Swallow and Hopkins is said to have removed most of the original forest from the present Boundary Waters Canoe Area Wilderness (BWCAW).[87]

In 1900, Knox sold his mill to Martin, Earnest and Burt Torinus of Stillwater, Minnesota, who renamed it St. Croix Lumber Company. If the Torinus brothers could do anything, they could cut down trees. They left a good part of the south shoreline of Burntside Lake completely bare and clearcut the entire lower portion of Stoney River country. The workforce was expanded and both the planing mill and sawmill were enlarged. The brothers soon had so many logs floating around on Shagawa Lake that they polluted Ely's water supply.[88]

The St. Croix mill hired a large number of out-of-work "jacks" from Stillwater. Most were second generation Norwegians and Swedes and names like Johnson, Carlson, Gustafson, Westlund, Olson and Swenson filled the company's rolls. The St. Croix Store was expanded under the management of Ole Berg and a company hospital was established near the mill. Its doctor, Frank Metcalf, treated nearly 3,000 injuries during his first year in town.[89]

In 1901, Winton incorporated as the "Village of Fall Lake." It was the third corporate village to be formed on the Vermilion Range – and the last. "Fall Lake Village" appeared on legal documents until 1914, when the name was officially changed back to "Winton."[90]

The Torinus brothers ran into trouble in 1910 when low water put a stop to their log drives. Logs were left lying in dried-up river beds and floating on nearby lakes. The logs were still there when the brothers sold all of their holdings to Edward Hines of Chicago, who re-organized the company and renamed it St. Croix Lumber and Manufacturing Company.[91]

Under the management of Tom Whiten of Haywood, Wisconsin, a lath mill, box board factory and picket mill were added to the operation. The new company employed 450 men at the mill site and 1,200 lumberjacks in its 10 logging camps. Steam-driven half-track log haulers pulled trains of sleighs loaded with white pine logs to the shores of lakes, where they were rolled out onto the ice to await the spring drive to Fall Lake. There, they were rafted and towed to the mill by a 60-foot tug called *Bull of the Woods.* Spring log drives were yearly events on the Shagawa and Stoney rivers until 1913. The lumberjacks traded their winter footwear for hobnail boots and became "river pigs." Armed with spiked, hinged-hooked "peaveys" and aided by a rush of water when dammed reservoirs were opened, their job was to keep logs moving downstream.[92]

Winton grew accordingly, although census records suggest that the population was never large. The 1910 federal count had 423 people living in the village and, 10 years later, the census showed a population of 499.

For the inhabitants, however, the lumber era was a time of prosperity. "Most of the millworkers and even the men in the camps seemed to have money to spend in those days, the usual wage being $40 or $45 a month plus room and board."[93] Seventy-eight well-built houses stood on the site and

St. Croix location in Winton housed workers of the St. Croix Lumber Company, which went through several changes in name and ownership through the years on Fall Lake. ELY-WINTON HISTORICAL SOCIETY COLLECTION, IRON RANGE RESEARCH CENTER

Log drives featuring hobnail booted "river pigs" armed with peavey poles and floating "wanigans" were yearly events on the Shagawa and Stoney rivers until 1913. Ely-Winton Historical Society collection, Iron Range Research Center
Bottom: A Lake Vermilion fisherman shows off his catch in 1890. Tower-Soudan Historical Society collection, Iron Range Research Center

the St. Croix Boardinghouse was home to more than 200 mill workers. A passenger train arrived daily bringing salesmen, contractors, job seekers, artists and actors to the town. The main ballroom of the St. Croix Hall was the scene of lectures, theatricals and dances and the town had a five-acre baseball park complete with a grand stand – one that was always filled to capacity, especially when the Ely baseball team came to town.[94]

Twenty-four years after the first logs were cut, it was all over. Miles of barren stump land stretched out in all directions. Swallow and Hopkins began closing its camps in 1915 and St. Croix Company saws stopped operating in 1918. In 1922, Swallow and Hopkins sold its properties to the Cloquet Lumber Company and the mill was dismantled and shipped to that city.[95] For a few years, logs continued to flow into Winton, but like the mill, they went on by rail to Cloquet. Meanwhile, the great halls and boardinghouses of Winton's lumber era were abandoned, people moved away, businesses closed, houses were removed and Winton teetered at the edge of extinction.

The Superior National Forest
It was only after most of the prime timber was gone that conservation became a reality. On June 30, 1902, in the first year of Theodore Roosevelt's presidency, 477,440 acres of cut-over land east of Winton was withdrawn from public entry. U.S.

geological surveyor Edward Branniff, who studied the lands, said this about them, "The lands contain no timber, they are unfit for farming and there is no settlement on them. No one cares much what becomes of them."[96] The original forest with its magnificent stands of pine – trees 300 years old and 100 feet tall, a common sight to the pioneers of the Vermilion Range, would never return.

The Superior National Forest was proclaimed on February 13, 1909, but the forest that its rangers eventually came to protect bore little resemblance to the one lumbermen found at Winton.

The town, too, was changed. Its few remaining citizens, J.C. Russell, Leo Chosa, the Johnson Brothers, George Wegen and Son and others, established resorts and outfitting stations. They turned abandoned logging camps into fishing camps and guided naturalists and mineral explorers to remote places, often using the logging roads of the old Swallow and Hopkins and St. Croix companies. ■

The forest that the lumbermen found at Winton in the early 1900s bore no resemblance to the massive acreage of dead falls, slashings and stumps that federal rangers found after they were assigned to protect the newly proclaimed Superior National Forest in 1909. SUPERIOR NATIONAL FOREST COLLECTION, IRON RANGE RESEARCH CENTER

CHAPTER 7

Unlocking the Secrets of the Big Man Hills

The Legend

At some unknown time near the end of the 19th century a great storm passed over Minnesota's Mesabi Iron Range. Close to Embarrass Lake where the old canoe route of Ojibway trappers and traders crossed Mesabi-Watchu, the Big Man Hills, it swept through a stand of pines leaving in its wake a path of upturned trees. In the fall of 1889, while estimating pine values in the vicinity, Canadian timber cruiser John McCaskill saw what he thought was iron ore in the roots of one of the fallen trees. "Unaided, he dug a test pit, bottomed it in ore … covered it with brush" and hurried back to Duluth to start a mining company.[1]

So began the legend of the discovery of the greatest iron ore district that the world has ever known. Several versions of the legend eventually emerged. In one, the storm occurred in 1891 and McCaskill was there when the tree fell. A few days later he met up with a member of Duluth's Merritt family and told him where the tree was located. In another, buck scrapings near the fallen tree exposed the hematite and McCaskill's partner, Jim Hale of Duluth, was the first to see it. A third version has the tree almost crushing one of the Merritt family's exploration camps in 1890. Leonidas Merritt is said to have made a cane out of one of its roots "with a ferrule smelted out of the tell-tale ore."[2] And there is a fourth that tells of timbers from a fallen tree used to shore up the walls of a mine shaft near the Prairie River during the Civil War and plans to produce iron ingots on the spot and ship them to Mississippi River markets. The old timbers are said to have been used to build the first hotel in Grand Rapids after the mine was abandoned.[3]

It's difficult to separate facts from fiction in stories told about the Mesabi's iron prospecting days prior to 1892. The Mesabi

was then a mysterious place, a 90-mile expanse of forest, fallen trees and difficult terrain – an unlikely place to look for iron. But iron there was and experienced miners like Peter Mitchell, John Mallmann and Elisha Morcom tried to mine it. They failed. Geologists made studies of its rocks and reported iron, but no marketable ore. Yet, the search continued. There were stubborn men who would not stop believing that somewhere among those hills was a body of iron ore so rich, so vast, it would make all the other deposits in the Lake Superior District seem small.

The stories are accurate about some things. There was a family named Merritt, there was a Canadian named McCaskill and he did cover a test pit with brush. He had a simple reason for doing this. The countryside was filled with timber cruisers and he didn't want any of them to see what he had discovered. The great public land sale of 1882 brought scores of prominent timber buyers to Duluth and for the next seven or eight years their representatives tramped back and forth across the range, eyes fixed on towering stands of white and red pine, feet separated from even richer treasure by a yard or two of glacial drift. Most were local people – people from Tower, Ely and Duluth – some of whom had been living in the woods for years. They knew the Mesabi and they knew the value of good pineland. That's what most people thought the Mesabi was good for. Pineland. All walked over rich iron ore. Few recognized it. Fewer still would profit from it.

John Stone Pardee remembered: "When W.D. Duggan, a woodsman holding a (Mesabi) claim, got an offer of $5 an acre on his land, he thought that was good profit. The land had cost him $25 and the trouble of holding it down. They found the Biwabik Mountain (Mine) on the property; it was leased to John McKinley in 1892 and that

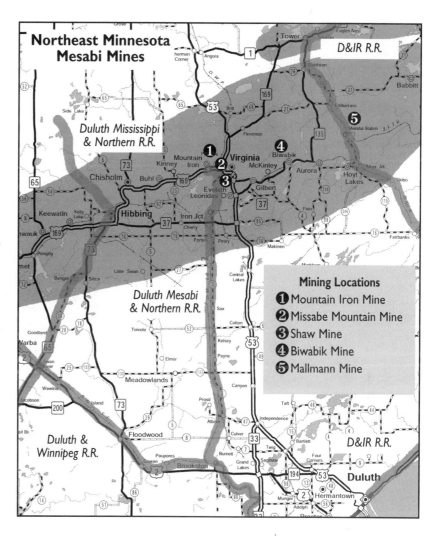

lease, renewed in 1911 for 30 years, is now paying John M. Williams of Chicago 20 cents a ton on not less than 300,000 tons a year."[4]

Often it was some uninterested party, a person who never set foot on the range, who, by chance, came to own and profit from Mesabi iron land. Many times these lucky people did everything they could to not claim title to it.

"Morris Thomas of Duluth bought for pine timber the lands which now comprise the Fayal, Spruce and Adams mines. He sold the timber rights to Murphy, Dorr and Flynn of Michigan, insisting that they take the land also. The lumbermen objected; like Thomas they were averse to taxes. The deal hung fire while Thomas looked for other buyers. Finally, the Michigan men took the timber and the land – land which would have made Thomas one of the most wealthy men in America."[5]

Story after story is told of fortunes won and lost on the Mesabi. Stories of timber cruisers, prospectors and land speculators blundering their way into wealth or, more often, out of it. The stories are usually about ordinary people locating homesteads among the pines, sinking wells and root cellars into iron ore and becoming rich – or, more likely, losing everything to wealthy individuals and well-organized syndicates.

Mesabi Land Falls Into Private Hands

Just beyond Mesaba Station, where the railroad began its cut through the Mesabi heights, construction crews laid open an ordinary looking hill exposing broad bands of rusting iron-stained rock which could be seen from every passing train. For those less interested in timber, this "Red Pan Cut," as it came to be called, became a place to begin a search for marketable iron ore.[6] At first, only a few got off the train but, by 1889, the trickle had turned into a torrent and Mesaba Station was teeming with hotels and outfitting stations.

But, even as the first prospectors entered the woods, much of the Mesabi was already in the hands of wealthy, socially prominent and influential individuals who had taken advantage of the liberal land laws of the time.

Years of *laissez-faire* government land policies and the prevailing myth of forest inexhaustibility made it hard for most people to see anything wrong with prosperous men increasing their wealth by removing trees and, if lucky, minerals from unsettled land acquired for next to nothing. It wasn't until 1891 that pre-emption and federal land auctions came to an end, and it would be two more years before Minnesota's Legislature was ready to look seriously at how its administrative officials were disposing of state lands.

By this time, using "soldiers additional scrip," the Pillsburys of St. Anthony, Minnesota's famous flour millers, were holding thousands of acres of Mesabi land, some of it located as early as 1875.[7] The Soldiers' Additional Act of March 3, 1873, was intended to help Civil War veterans who had not received their full allotment of 160 acres when they filed for homestead. The act allowed them to complete their quota by locating land anywhere in the United States that was subject to homestead. The right was issued as "scrip" and within a year it was circulating at a market rate of something like 40 cents an acre. Lumbermen became alert

Map of Northeast Minnesota showing the Mesabi Iron Range; Duluth and Winnipeg Railroad to Deer River; Duluth, Mississippi River and Northern Railroad; Dewey Lake; Diamond Mine; Shaw Mine, Mallmann Mine; Duluth and Iron Range Railroad; Duluth, Missabe and Northern Railroad; Mesaba Station; Biwabik Mountain Mine; Mt. Iron Mine; Missabe Mountain Mine; Franklin Mine; Lone Jack Mine.

Mesaba Station in its boom time, circa 1890. IRON RANGE RESEARCH CENTER

to this and often used soldiers' scrip to gain access to prime timber.[8]

The Pillsburys, with their long history of lumber dealings, were no exception and obviously bought the property for its timber. However, 20 years later, explorer Russell M. Bennett found iron ore on it. He talked John Pillsbury into a half-interest in the mineral rights, "provided he could show up 100,000 tons of marketable ore." Bennett then contacted John M. Longyear of Marquette, Michigan, an experienced iron prospector, and offered him a half-interest in his half "for all the ore he could uncover." Ten years later, iron mines on the property were shipping ore at a rate of a million tons a year and paying immense royalties to the Pillsbury estate and Longyear-Bennett partnership.[9]

During the public land sales of 1875 and 1882, Michigan lumbermen Ammi Wright, Charles Davis and C.W. Wells gained title to a vast tract of white pine in the heart of Mesabi country, some of it standing on top of rich iron ore. Unaware of what lay below the ground, they began working with Roger Munger, William Spalding, Andrus Miller, James Bardon and other Duluth developers on a grandiose plan to tap the timber resources of the western Mesabi and beyond by running a line to Canada and tying it to a network of logging spurs. Two railroads eventually resulted. After several false starts and a change of owners, the Duluth and Winnipeg Railroad

completed 100 miles of track from Duluth to the wilderness outpost of Deer River in 1892. Connected to it at Swan River was the Duluth, Mississippi River and Northern Railroad, about 50 miles of logging rail running to the Wright-Davis holdings at Dewey Lake, not far from the future site of Hibbing.[10]

The Panic of 1893 and depression that followed sent the Duluth and Winnipeg tumbling into receivership. In 1887, after an attempt to revive it as the Duluth, Superior and Western Railway, "empire builder" James J. Hill, acting through the Chase Bank of New York, purchased it "at receivers' sale" for about $2.5 million. Included in the sale was an ore dock in Superior, Wisconsin, along with several warehouses and elevators – and 10,000 acres of potential mineland.[11]

Wright and Davis tried to sell their holdings to German-born lumberman Frederick Weyerhaeuser with the understanding that the railroad would be used for Weyerhaeuser's log shipments. Weyerhaeuser took the trees but not the land and, in 1894, Wright and Davis found themselves paying taxes on 25,000 acres of cutover land they couldn't get rid of. Then came the discovery of iron ore. In 1899, Hill offered to buy both the land and railroad for a bit more than $4 million. Wright and Davis accepted. Included in the deal was one of most prolific iron ore mines of all time, the great Mahoning.[12]

Although it took his sons to get him interested, James J. Hill probably ended up owning more of the Mesabi than any other single individual. The railroads became part of his Great Northern Railway system but, in order to ensure a profit from the roads, he formed a second company, Lake Superior Limited, to hold the land that went with them for future mining. In return for guaranteed shipping contracts and royalties, he allowed small independent mining companies to explore for iron on the property and develop mines. It was a lucrative arrangement and enough to convince Hill and his sons to purchase potential mineland elsewhere on the Mesabi. According to a 1923 report, Hill holdings, by then known as Great Northern Iron Ore Properties, totaled more than 65,000 acres.[13]

People from outside the state also bought land on the Mesabi – again, mainly for its timber. During the land sale of 1882, Orrin T. Higgins of Cattaraugus County, New York, and his son, Frank, who later became governor of New York, bought more than 11,000 acres of land in Township 58-17 for $1.25 an acre. A town called Hibbing arose nearby and the first 50,000 tons mined from the Higgins property paid off the entire investment.[14] Similar purchases were made by such non-Minnesotans as Wellington Burt, Ezra T. Rust, Elbridge Fowler, Clarence M. Hill, Morton B. Hull, William Boeing, Hiram Sibley and George Robinson.[15] Although most of these people never set foot on the range, all would profit from it and all would have mines named after them.

The Mineral Lease Law

While Mesabi iron and timber lands were passing into private hands, the state of Minnesota was also coming into possession of valuable properties. Public surveys taking place during the 1880s were required by act of Congress to classify sections 16 and 36 in each township as *school lands*, wet marshy areas as *swamp lands* and the rest as *agricultural lands*. While so-called agricultural lands were "declared free and open to exploration and purchase," swamp lands and school lands were deemed state property.

Although it was policy in Minnesota to grant swamp lands to railroad companies, much of the Mesabi's swamp land was still in state hands in 1889. Added to the holdings were lands originally surveyed as agricultural that congress either granted for special purposes or returned as indemnity lands.[16] When all the iron excitement broke out in 1889, the State of Minnesota found itself owning more than 40,000 acres situated squarely on the Mesabi iron formation.[17]

That spring, experienced Vermilion Range prospector James B. Geggie and former Minnesota Mine captain Elisha Morcom sank test pits in townships 59-14 and 59-15, not far from the Duluth and Iron Range Railroad. While Morcom found the iron-bearing rock not to his liking and returned to Tower, Geggie was sure there was marketable ore in almost every pit that he dug.[18]

When it was learned that Geggie's explorations had "followed the trend of the ore onto state property," Minnesota leaders began looking for a way to "protect" the state's "prospective revenue interests in these lands," and at the same time establish some regulations for their sale or lease. Amid a clamor for iron leases, a bill "regulating the sale and lease of mineral and other lands belonging to the state" was drawn up and passed during the legislative session of 1889.[19] Often referred to as the Braden Act, the law authorized the state land commissioner to negotiate leases and contracts for "the mining and shipping of iron ore from any lands … belonging to the state … or from any lands to which the state may acquire title."[20]

Individual leases of 160 acres could be taken by any individual for a price of $25. A person could prospect on the land for one year and, if he struck iron ore, he could sign a binding contract with the state to mine it. The contract called for payment to the state of $100 a year until the first 1,000 tons of ore was shipped, after which the leaseholder was required to mine a minimum of 5,000 tons a year and pay the state a royalty of 25 cents on each ton mined. Before the law was repealed in 1907, some 872 contracts and leases were issued.[21]

Newton H. Winchell and Early Attempts to Mine the Mesabi

State geologist Newton Horace Winchell was convinced that the Mesabi Range contained numerous undiscovered bodies of

marketable iron ore. Winchell, a mineralogist and professor of geology with experience in Michigan and Ohio geological surveys, was selected in 1872 to direct the continuing geological study of the state of Minnesota. Beginning in 1878, he made several trips to Iron Country and was soon reporting exposures of high grade hematite on the Vermilion Range and scattered signs of iron on the Mesabi.

In 1881, Winchell recommended that the University of Minnesota establish some experimental mines on the Mesabi with the stipulation that money received from the sale of ore be used to pay for experiments to find ways to process the lean magnetic ore located by Peter Mitchell and Albert Chester in the 1870s. He called the lean ore "*taconite*."[22]

In 1885, while examining the iron-bearing formation on the south side of the Mesabi heights in the vicinity of Mesaba Station, Winchell noticed that the irony rock presented characteristics similar to formations he had seen on the Gogebic Range in both Michigan and Wisconsin. He persuaded John Mallmann to make an attempt at mining the formation – as it turned out, in the same place Chester had made his examinations 10 years before. Mallmann was the man who in 1875 set off the first blast for iron ore on the Vermilion Range. In 1888, with a crew of 25 hard rock miners and supplies drawn from the Minnesota Mine at Soudan, Mallmann established two mines not far from the railroad at Mesaba Station.[23]

The first, known as the Stone Mine, was opened by Michigan captain John Bice in the early summer of 1888. It was located about 300 yards west of the railroad, close to the famous red pan cut. A shaft was sunk to a depth of 125 feet into a "lens of jaspery hematite" which Bice decided was similar to outcroppings seen in Michigan, but of questionable value.[24]

The second mine, the Mallmann Mine in the northwest quarter of Section 11 in Township 59-14, was opened that same year. Under Mallmann's direction, a shallow shaft was bottomed into a "bed of hematite." It was enough to encourage plans for a town and a spur track to the mine. However, the deposit turned out to be smaller than first thought and the mine failed to generate

much interest among potential investors. The railroad was never built.[25]

During the summer of 1888, a third attempt was made to mine the Mesabi. It took place at the west end of the range in Township 56-24 near the present site of Marble, where three shallow shafts were sunk into soft hematite at a place called the Diamond Mine. That same year, Winchell visited the site and noted that the mine appeared to be "in the same formation and stratigraphic position, as the Mallmann Mine."[26] Although the mine did generate a certain amount of excitement among settlers at Grand Rapids, its ore was extremely high in silica and located too far from the Duluth and Winnipeg Railroad, which was then under construction, to attract investment.

David T. Adams

At the east end of the range, mining fever was raging. Prospectors filled the lobbies of hotels at Mesaba Station and every passenger train brought new arrivals anxious to try their luck in the wild country beyond the stumpland surrounding the crowded station on the Duluth and Iron Range track.

Among the arrivals in 1888 was a young prospector from Michigan who had been on the range before and was now well on his way to discovering the incredible secret of the Mesabi's special kind of ore. His name was David Tugaw Adams.[27]

Born in Illinois on September 5, 1859, Adams was the son of Canadians Moses and Jane (Castoney) Adams, who emigrated to the United States in 1840 and settled on a farm just outside of Rockford. In the fall of 1867, when David was 8 years old, his father died and his mother, unable to support her seven children, was forced to abandon them to strangers.[28]

Although extremely bright, David was unable to advance his education and became a miner in Michigan's Upper Peninsula at the age of 20. Michigan mining companies were always ready to sign contracts with bright, healthy young miners to explore for new bodies of ore, so Adams, able and anxious to make good, became an iron prospector. He found a deposit near Iron River, Michigan, and, although his company profited, David didn't.[29]

Drawn to northeast Minnesota by the iron excitement of the early '80s, Adams and

partner James Lane were cruising timber and looking for hematite near the site of Mesaba Station as early as 1883 – even before there was a railroad to the place. About a mile southeast of what later became known as the Mesabi Gap, in Section 20, Township 59-14, they noticed "fragments of quartz and clean pieces of hematite strewn over the surface." After spending a few days "exploring the country as far east as the magnetic cropping," they retraced their steps and headed west, following the "footlands along the slope of the Mesabi Heights for some distance."[30]

In place after place, Adams and Lane came across fragments of hematite and the unmistakable red stain of iron ore. Adams' curiosity was aroused by the fact that these signs were only in the low country south of the height of land. At first Adams, like most of the iron prospectors, presumed that the stains were caused by fragments of "drift ore" pushed down by the glacier from places farther north, possibly the Vermilion Range.

He later wrote, "I ascended the hills to the north of the places where I found the drift in the bottom lands to be the thickest and, in each ascent I made, I found that the drift ore of the character found in the low lands at the foot of the height disappeared completely, which was conclusive evidence that the … ore found in the low lands to the south of the Heights did not come from its summit, nor from the Vermilion Range to the north, but must have come from an iron formation under the surface of the low lands, immediately south of the Heights."[31]

Adams loaded his packsack with samples from the low lands and left the Mesabi the same way he went in. It would be three years before he returned. During this time, while studying the samples, he noticed a puzzling thing about them. They showed no signs of glacial wear. Could it be that they had been pressed up to the surface by frost from a horizontal bed of hematite that had formed long before the time of the glaciers? If so, the flat-looking bottom land stretching for miles all along the southeasterly slope of the Mesabi heights might actually be a giant bed of iron ore formed by "floods or torrents" from "ancient water courses." He had to go back.[32]

The chance came in the spring of 1887, when he was offered a contract to appraise

timber in the vicinity of the Prairie River at the west end of the range. Accompanied at the time by A.J. Harding of Duluth, he again encountered the red stain of iron ore. After exploring the western Mesabi for "a considerable distance" and examining what appeared to be "a ledge of quartz and iron" in Section 34, Township 56-25 and what seemed like a vast bed of sandy hematite in Section 20, Township 56-24, the men returned to the Prairie River and "pitched camp on the south side between the upper and lower rapids."

Adams later recalled, "That same night, Captain LeDuc, then of Duluth but a veteran explorer and mining man of the Michigan ranges, and his son, Ernest, who had come through the country from 59-14, on the eastern end of the range, pitched their tent alongside mine and we all spent a delightful evening around the campfire, talking of former exploring trips and of the possibilities of the new range. In the course of the conversation, the captain told me of many places where he had found drift ore and quartz on the surface, also that it was his opinion that some of the largest bodies of hematite ore in the world would be found … between Township 59-14 and where we camped."[33]

Adams spent the next few years exploring the region between Mesaba Station and the Prairie River and found plenty of hematite fragments and iron-stained ground, but all seemed to lie within a broad undulating belt that stretched the length of the range as if it were the shoreline of a great body of water. He was probably "the first" iron prospector "to promulgate the theory that this range was at one time the shore line of an extinct sea."[34]

According to Adams, "The theory I formed at that time on the possible merchantable deposits of ore in the low lands along the southeasterly slope of the Mesabi Heights was never changed and followed by me in all my explorations."[35] He spent months carefully charting out the phenomenon. The resulting map, published in 1893, turned out to be so accurate that mining companies were able to use it to locate potential bodies of iron ore.[36]

In 1893, Adams joined Pennsylvania furnaceman Peter Kimberly and John T.

Jones, a mining engineer from Iron Mountain, Michigan, to incorporate the Adams Mining Company, one of the more active mining firms on the Mesabi during its early years. Using knowledge gained from years of prospecting, Adams was able to pinpoint numerous hematite deposits. He was also involved in the establishment of several townsites, including Eveleth and Virginia.

Frank Hibbing

Another iron prospector arriving on the Mesabi Range before 1890 was a German immigrant named Frank Hibbing. He arrived in Beaver Dam, Wisconsin, in 1856 at the age of 18 and took a job, first as a farmhand and later at a shingle mill – a job which changed his life forever. He lost three fingers from his right hand in an accident and couldn't work at the mill any longer, so the company made him a timber cruiser.

During the 1880s, Michigan mining companies trained timber cruisers to prospect for iron and copper. These men were always in the woods and were the most likely people to run across potential bodies of mineable ore.[37]

Hibbing went to Bessemer, Michigan, where he learned how to prospect for iron and, in 1888, the Minnesota Iron Company offered him an exploring contract. The work was usually well-paid because in those days it was hard for mining companies to find and keep competent iron ore prospectors. Most were interested in exploring only for themselves. Hibbing might have been inclined to do the same, but had just lost his shirt on a Duluth property deal and the job would tide him over until things got better. He took the train to Tower.[38]

When he arrived, he discovered that everyone was talking about the Mesabi Range. Hibbing listened to stories of copper, silver and iron ore by the square mile – all on the Mesabi Range. A good prospector could make a fortune there. In the spring of 1889 he decided to go for broke. He skipped out on the company, took the train to Mesaba Station and set out into the woods to look for iron exposures.

It was during this time that Hibbing formed a lasting partnership with Alexander J. Trimble, a seasoned iron prospector and well-to-do iron mine operator on Michigan's

Gogebic Range. Trimble had earlier been part of John Mallmann's attempt to establish a mine and town at the east end of the Mesabi in 1888. They had just named their new town Trimble when their luck went bad. The Duluth and Iron Range Railroad refused to run a track to their mine and experts brought in from Michigan to evaluate their ore judged it unmarketable. No one came to live in their town.[39]

Hibbing became the explorer and Trimble the financier for what they called the Lake Superior Iron Company. While others continued to prospect for iron on the east end of the range, Hibbing headed an exploring party west, beyond the camps of the Merritt brothers, deep into white pine country where, in January 1892, while completing a root cellar for their camp, his men struck ore just below the surface in Section 22, Township 58 North, Range 20 West. This time they named their town Hibbing.[40]

In 1893, Hibbing and Trimble took leases on as many nearby parcels of pineland as they could and found ore just below the surface on almost every one. They had encountered the largest body of soft hematite in the world and really didn't know what to do with it. They were not even sure they could interest steel producers in buying this kind of ore. Their finds barely made the news, mainly because of the publicity surrounding the discovery of ore by Duluth's Merritt family at a place they called Mountain Iron.

Meanwhile other prospectors, unable to find marketable hematite, kicked at the the red dust that was everywhere and left the region in disgust. Little did they know that the red dust they were kicking around was the very iron ore for which they were looking.

The Discovery of Iron Ore: The Merritt Story (1889-1892)

When John McCaskill applied for his mining lease in 1891, he learned that the upturned trees were on property already leased to John McKinley of Duluth. Disappointed, he told John E. Merritt, a member of Duluth's Merritt family, about his find. The Merritts, already owners of the Mt. Iron Mine, were in the market for any

other potential mine land they could get their hands on. In a bold move, they paid McKinley $30,000 for a "10-day option" to open a mine on the property.[41]

Immortalized by author Paul De Kruif as the legendary "Seven Iron Men," the family of Oneota pioneers Lewis Howell and Hephzibah Merritt is usually credited with the discovery of the first commercial bodies of iron ore on the Mesabi.

"More than any other individuals, members of the Merritt family were responsible for the successful discovery and initial development of the Mesabi Range," wrote David Walker in his study of the discovery and early development of Minnesota's three iron ranges. Duluth historian Walter Van Brunt said this in a 1921 publication: "The Merritt brothers were, undoubtedly, the first of the exploring expeditions to carry their explorations to the point where they had a pit bottomed in ore," and according to Minnesota historian Theodore Blegen: "Discovery was bound to come with time. That it came when it did is the achievement of the Merritt brothers, the "Seven Iron Men."[42]

Yet in 1880 Oneota, the brothers were known only as "expert timber cruisers," not prospectors. Their father, Lewis Howell, a millwright and carpenter by trade, came to Oneota, West Duluth today, in July 1855 to supervise construction of a sawmill for Henry M. Wheeler, the first on the site of present-day Duluth. His wife, Hephzibah, and eight sons – Andrus, Cassius, Lewis J., Alfred, Leonidas, Lucien, Napoleon and Jerome, ranging in age from 2 to 22 – arrived in October, a year later.

They found a land that had only recently been opened to settlement, a land full of promise and opportunity. Whole forties could be had for next to nothing, there was talk of copper and, beyond the hardwoods on the hillside, were seemingly endless stretches of prime timber. "What a beautiful sight it was … no axe having marred nature … there being hardly a tree cut, from Minnesota Point to Fond-du-Lac," recalled Alfred many years later.[43]

The family moved into a house in a "small clearing, of perhaps one-half acre … on block 29 in Oneota," and during the years that followed, Lewis invested in

Members of Duluth's Merritt family in front of their hotel in Oneota, circa 1890. MERRITT FAMILY COLLECTION, NORTHEAST MINNESOTA HISTORICAL CENTER

Leonidas Merritt in 1890.
MERRITT FAMILY COLLECTION,
NORTHEAST MINNESOTA
HISTORICAL CENTER

pineland. When the gold rush came along, he went to Lake Vermilion and, like others, came back talking about mountains of iron ore. He was sure that someday the iron in those mountains "would be worth all the gold in California."

In fact, Jay Cooke talked about mining one of those mountains. Duluth boomed during Cooke's time, so, instead of looking for ore, the Merritts built a hotel. It was a two-story affair with a long porch overlooking the bay and river. The hotel served wonderful meals, but no alcohol. The Merritts were strict Methodists.[44]

After the collapse of Jay Cooke in 1873, Duluth took on the appearance of a ghost town and the elder Merritts moved to a farm in Missouri to join their son Napoleon. Jerome, Lewis J. and Andrus went with them. Lucien remained in Ohio, where he was studying for the Methodist ministry. In 1887, after serving several eastern pastorates, he would rejoin the family, most of whom had drifted back to Duluth during the mid-1880s. But Leonidas, Alfred and Cassius stuck it out in Duluth, making their living cruising timber for a growing number of lumber companies and speculating on pineland, some of it as far north as the Mesabi Range. It was said, "When Leonidas Merritt took up his first government claim in 1880, he was all over this northern country 'til he knew every foot of it." Then came the Vermilion Range iron excitement.[45]

In 1885, the three Merritts set out for Vermilion country to look for iron ore, but quickly became discouraged when they discovered "all the good iron land" had been picked up by others. However, Leonidas, with the help of Frank Eaton, did manage to get a scrip claim filed on some promising iron land east of Ely. This later became the controversial Section 30 Mine.[46]

It may have been the elder Merritt's talk of mountains of iron that inspired the

brothers to turn their search to the Mesabi heights. More likely, it was the job Cassius took in 1887 to help run a survey for a railroad from Duluth to the Canadian border, the Duluth and Winnipeg Railroad.[47]

That year, while in charge of a railroad survey team near the future site of the Mt. Iron Mine, Cassius saw what looked to him like a chunk of "good iron ore." He threw it into his packsack, said nothing and, as soon as he had a chance, he took it back to show his brothers. They had it assayed. It was quality Bessemer.[48]

According to Leonidas, "That year, I made an agreement with the Wisconsin Minnesota and Pacific, a railroad company having a land-grant in that vicinity, to prospect the whole country." Experts hired by the company explored the Mesabi and "because we were not supposed to know as much, we were to go over the Vermilion. Their experts reported that there was nothing there. The experts were in good company; nearly all the men who should know were of the same opinion."[49]

Leonidas Merritt continued: "The next year, which must have been 1889, we went over the Mesabi ourselves, from Embarrass Lake on the east to the Mississippi on the west … running diagonals across the formation and mapping the lines of attraction."

Four of the brothers, Leonidas, Cassius, Alfred and Andrus (who had returned to Duluth from Missouri) were involved, along with three nephews, Wilbur, John E. and Burt. Leonidas was the leader. They worked in pairs, using a "dip needle," a compass-like device invented in Sweden, in which a magnetic needle "dips" or swings downward if iron is in the ground.[50]

Both the Vermilion and Mesabi ranges had been officially surveyed during the years 1872-1882 and every corner was clearly marked. This made it easy for the Merritts to carry out a systematic search. Each team picked out a "forty" and walked in about 10 rods along the north line and from there carefully counted their paces south across an entire forty. The needle was observed every few paces and a notation made on a map whenever any kind of attraction was shown. By going back and forth in this way they hoped to get a fair idea of where there might be a deposit of iron ore.

But hematite does not often respond to a magnetic needle, so experts scoffed at their method of exploration. Leonidas, the leader of the Merritt teams, said afterward:

"Folks may say we were crazy, looking for non-magnetic ore with a magnetic needle, but the maps we made then showed the approximate location of every large body of ore known today and at that time I developed the same theory which was afterwards put forth by Van Hise and accepted as scientific. Only I wasn't a scientist and I called it a basin instead of a trough."[51]

Against all conventional wisdom, the Merritts' needles dipped. The brothers came to believe it was good ore attracting their dip needles and it must lie flat under the ground in "basins" shaped something like lakes. The Merritts weren't the only ones thinking along these lines. So was David Adams and he was well on his way to making public his theory that there were flat beds of hematite on the Mesabi that were created by an ancient sea. And Hibbing and his crew were out there in the woods digging root cellars for their camps. If the Merritts were going to be the ones to prove that these "basins of ore" were for real, they would have to move fast.

On March 17, 1889, after picking up supplies in Tower, Alfred and a crew of six men pulling toboggans made their way along the ice of the Pike River to where it is joined by the Sandy. From there they made their way south toward the Mesabi heights, to the place where Cassius found his hematite. Meanwhile, Leonidas went to work to finance the search. After selling some Merritt pineland, he went to Kelsey D. Chase, a wealthy Rochester, Minnesota, banker, and convinced him to invest in the project. The Merritt-Chase Mountain Range Iron Company was incorporated on May 31, 1889, and $20,000 was raised.[52]

Financial support from Chase and some other southern Minnesota investors allowed the Merritts to gain an advantage over other iron explorers. With access to skilled miners and good equipment, they were able to launch a full-scale search for their elusive basins of ore. During the summer of 1889, their crews dug test pits all over Section 34, Township 59-18. After a week or two of digging, most of the pits hit hard-banded taconite, ore too lean to mine.

Experienced miners among the crews thought there might be good ore underneath the taconite. Using hand drills and dynamite, they got some of the test pits down to almost 100 feet, but the formation was the same – taconite. A diamond drill and crew were brought in and, by the time the first snow fell, they had drilled right through the taconite and hit granite. There was no ore.[53]

Summer of 1890 found the Merritts still drilling and test pitting. They had moved even farther south to the next tier of sections. However, they were running short of cash. Money raised for exploration was spent cutting a 27-mile-long tote road to Mesaba Station, bringing in the diamond drill and hiring more help.[54] In late summer, they began finding a red powdery substance in their pits. It had the color and weight of iron ore, but it was so loose it could easily be shoveled out of the pit. Iron ore was hard and couldn't be shoveled. Merritt crews were again disappointed.

Diamond drilling exploration for iron ore near Mountain Iron in the 1890s. MOUNTAIN IRON COLLECTION, IRON RANGE RESEARCH CENTER

Duluth's Spalding Hotel was a beehive and the center for speculation on Mesabi iron land in 1892-93. Voss COLLECTION, IRON RANGE RESEARCH CENTER

Earlier, Leonidas was so sure of striking iron ore that he brought in two new investors from Duluth and formed a second company to mine it. Incorporated on July 10, 1890, the Mountain Iron Company issued 20,000 shares of stock at $100 par value. Its officers were Leonidas Merritt, president; R.H. Palmer, vice president; J.T. Hale, secretary; and Alfred Merritt, treasurer – all Duluth people. By transferring ownership of the lands being explored into mining stock, the Merritts managed to retain majority control of the company, while raising cash by selling shares at less than par value to such people as K.D. Chase, M.B. Harrison, W.K. Rogers and others.[55]

Heading the test pit crews was James A. Nichols, an experienced mining captain from Michigan. Nichols concluded that the red powdery substance in the test pits was some kind of rusty iron stain and this might mean a vein of hematite was nearby. Test pitting continued on into fall. The dense dark earth was everywhere. There were places where it was just below the surface. Using windlasses and buckets, the crews sank shafts into it, some as deep as 50 feet – or until they hit water. It was still the same dark earth. On November 16 came the realization. It was already cold – snow was in the air. In one of

the test pits, about 14 feet down, the dark earthy material took on a familiar blue luster. Hematite.[56]

The soft earthy material that was everywhere was the ore for which they were searching! Nichols filled a shot bag with it and took it to Duluth to have it assayed. The result – 64 percent iron, phosphorus content .016 percent – Bessemer!

Years later, Leonidas Merritt is reported to have said: "If we had gotten mad and kicked the ground right where we stood, we would have thrown out 64-percent ore, if we had kicked it hard enough to kick off the pine needles."[57]

The official account of the discovery was somewhat more dignified:

"On the sixteenth day of November, 1890, workmen under the direction of Captain J.A. Nichols of Duluth, Minnesota, encountered soft hematite in a test pit on the northwest quarter of Section 3, Township 58, Range 18, west of the fourth principle meridian. The mine, now called the Mt. Iron, was the first body of soft ore discovered on the Mesabi Iron Range."[58]

After the assay report was in, Nichols suggested caution. It might be a good idea to cover up the pit and stop digging until spring. In the meantime, the Merritts might want to pick up more potential ore property. But the Merritts had been scoffed at by geologists and mining men long enough. They would show the so-called experts that there really were great basins of pure hematite on the Mesabi. The problem was, it was different from any other iron ore in the world. They would strip away as much of the surface as possible so that their ore might be inspected.

In the spring of 1891, the experts arrived – mining engineers, mining captains from Michigan, men who knew iron ore – sent to inspect the Merritt mine. They saw log buildings, a clearing in the woods and what looked like a rough badly plowed field of dark purple soil. "Where was the mine?" "Where was the footwall?" There was no way you could sink a shaft in that soft damp earth. "No, the Merritts aren't miners, they're farmers!"[59]

Meanwhile, Merritt test-pit crews struck soft blue hematite again, this time on the property leased from John McKinley west of Embarrass Lake. Again, it was ore by the acre. Then others began finding the same kind of ore. David Adams, working for A.E. Humphreys and George Atkins, struck "soft hematite" a week later and a mile away. Two weeks later, Benjamin Hale found another pocket of soft hematite close by – another potential mine! Then explorers from the Minnesota Iron Company struck soft ore at the Canton.[60]

The frenzy that followed was like nothing ever seen in Iron Country, before or after. The Mesabi was hailed as a "poor man's iron range."

"Hundreds of prospectors are scattered along the range and, as soon as the snow is gone, the number will be increased to thousands.… Forty miles of this range are known to carry ore deposits. Exploring and developing on the Missabe [sic] means the outlay of a few hundred dollars for picks and shovels, buckets and windlass and a camp outfit; while on the other ranges, to show up a property … requires an outlay of thousands of dollars."[61]

When spring came in 1892, John Jones, a mine captain from Iron Mountain, Michigan, working for Pennsylvania steel mill owner Peter Kimberly and his newly formed Biwabik Ore Company, took one look at the Merritts' Biwabik Mine, leased it and brought in a steam shovel to mine it. Because there was no railroad to the mine, Jones had the shovel shipped in parts to Mesaba Station and, from there, the parts were carried on the backs of horses and men to the mine. "It was a monstrous undertaking, owing to the almost impassable character of the road for 12 miles."[62]

All through 1892 and well into 1893, new mining companies organized almost daily and Mesabi land changed hands at a rate of $1 million to $5 million a day. Speculators filled the lobby of Duluth's

The Merritts and their supporters gather at the Mt. Iron Mine, October 15, 1892, to celebrate completion of the Duluth, Missabe and Northern Railroad link between the mine and Stony Brook (now Brookston). MERRITT COLLECTION, NORTHEAST MINNESOTA HISTORICAL CENTER

Three explorers of the Mesabi Range post to have their pictures taken: T.H. Merritt at the bow, Lon Merritt in the middle and John Merritt at the stern. MERRITT FAMILY COLLECTION, NORTHEAST MINNESOTA HISTORICAL CENTER

Spalding Hotel, and there were times, according to Walter Van Brunt, when "it was impossible to elbow one's way through the throng." One hundred forty-one mining companies came into being during these years. Most were merely speculative companies, poorly organized and thinly financed.[63]

But the Merritts were organized and well ahead of the rest. They were holding 141 mining leases by the time the rush began.[64] They had incorporated numerous mining companies and were showing some of the most mineable ore in the world. They didn't need expensive equipment. They didn't need skilled miners. All they needed was a railroad.

Leonidas Merritt went straight to the president of Carnegie Steel, Henry Clay Frick, to tell him about the great potential of the Merritt holdings. He was sure Frick would build a railroad to the Merritt mines, if he had a chance to get a continual supply of cheap ore. Frick had used a railroad before to cut costs for Carnegie. Leonidas Merritt was enthusiastic. Frick was not. He had sent a man to look over the Biwabik Mine and was told what the Merritts had in their mine wasn't even real iron ore. "I had an interview with Frick.... Frick did not use me like a

gentleman and cut me off short and bulldozed me," recalled Leonidas at congressional hearings held in 1895.[65]

After trying unsuccessfully to convince several railroad companies to build a line to their ore properties, the Merritts and their partners decided to build their own. They bought out the defunct charter of the Lake Superior and Northwestern Railroad on June 23, 1891, and reorganized it into the Duluth, Missabe and Northern Railroad (DM&N). Kelsey Chase, who put up much of the cash for the venture, was elected president. Leonidas Merritt became vice president; S.R. Payne, secretary; Cassius Merritt, treasurer; and State Senator Moses Clapp, counsel.[66]

A 10-year agreement was made with the Duluth and Winnipeg Railroad (D&W), then operating the 100 miles of track from Lake Superior to Deer River. The DM&N would build a line from the mines to Stony Brook on the St. Louis River. From there, Duluth and Winnipeg tracks would be used to bring Merritt ore to a D&W ore dock at Allouez Bay in Superior, Wisconsin. An equitable shipping rate was established and it was agreed that each company would furnish 750 railroad cars to carry the ore to the lake.[67]

The Duluth, Missabe and Northern raised $1.5 million through the sale of bonds, three-fifths of which were purchased by K.D. Chase and the man who was awarded the contract to build the line, Donald Grant. The construction contract was signed on March 2, 1892, and the road was completed in mid-October of that same year. The railroad was a beauty. It was described as "48½ miles of track, sloping gently so that all one had to do was to give a loaded car a good shove at Mountain Iron and it would roll all the way to the Stony Brook Junction."[68]

With Pennsylvania furnaceman Peter Kimberly mining ore at the Biwabik with a steam shovel, things couldn't have looked better for the Merritts.

An 18.6-mile spur to the Kimberly operation was made part of the contract and built that same summer. It met the main line at Iron Junction and this became the operating headquarters for the railroad company. An engine house and rip track for handling repairs were located there and houses, stores, saloons and a 30-room hotel appeared, where a year before there had been wilderness.[69]

On October 15, 1892, 55 members of the Merritt family boarded a special train bound for Mountain Iron. There was cause for celebration. The Merritts had a railroad to their mines and it was Hephzibah Merritt's 80th birthday. Among the Merritts were 200 friends and well-wishers. While standing on the first mine dump on the Mesabi Range, the Reverend Doctor Forbes, a Methodist minister, commended the

Merritts for their imagination and exploring genius. It was a day of triumph! There was no champagne, but 25 gallons of milk were served.[70]

The Merritt Era Ends (1892-1894)

On November 1, 1892, the first shipment of ore from the Mesabi Range rumbled down the tracks to Allouez Dock and was loaded into a waiting whaleback steel barge and consigned for shipment to the Oglebay Norton Company of Cleveland, Ohio. It was followed by a steady procession of Merritt trains until cold weather froze the loading pockets and brought an end to the shipping season. That first season, 4,245 tons of ore from the Mt. Iron Mine went down the lake, all sold to Oglebay Norton. The Merritts left one loaded ore car in Duluth for public inspection.[71]

Duluth was jubilant. It looked like the Jay Cooke boom all over again, only better. City leaders began calling for an ore dock and an "all Minnesota line."

This should have been the happy ending to the Merritt story. It wasn't. In fact, their troubles were only beginning. Mesabi ore froze in cold weather and plugged up the chutes in the loading pockets. Special crews had to be hired to bang on the sides of the chutes with steel bars to keep the ore flowing. At the steel mill, the blast furnaces blew Mesabi ore right out of the stacks and covered half of Cleveland with fine red dust. There were lawsuits. Attempts to confine it caused a furnace to blow up. The ore was unlike any that furnacemen had ever seen before. New furnaces would have to be designed before Mesabi ore could

Whaleback ore carrier, *John Erickson* of the Pittsburgh Steamship Company. The first ore from the Mesabi Range was loaded into a ship of this design. VISUAL PERCEPTIONS INC., IRON RANGE RESEARCH CENTER

The Shaw Mine near Virginia in 1893 was one of many Merritt properties that passed to John D. Rockefeller's ownership in that year.
OKLOBZIJA COLLECTION, IRON RANGE RESEARCH CENTER

be smelted in any great quantity. The Merritts would have to be patient.[72]

"From the first, experts warned the Merritts of all this. But the Merritts saw in these counsels of prudence only a conspiracy of capitalists to destroy their credit and get their properties for nothing."[73]

As if things weren't bad enough, the rival Duluth and Iron Range Railroad began building a branch to Biwabik, where Kimberly and others were opening mines. Traffic contracts on which the Merritts were counting to pay bills could easily be lost. On top of that, the Duluth and Winnipeg failed to live up to its part of the agreement. The promised 750 ore cars were not delivered. In fact they weren't even built.[74]

The final blow came when a piece of paper drifted onto the floor from the desk of Merritt railroad president, Kelsey Chase. It was a letter. The letter was picked up and read by one of the Merritts. Chase was secretly negotiating with Don Bacon to sell 51 percent of the stock of the railroad and mine to the Minnesota Iron Company for $7.5 million![75]

Five years earlier, Charlemagne Tower was facing a similar situation. He sold. But Tower was a majority stockholder. The Merritts weren't. At the time of the discovery, Merritt family members held only 30.8 percent of the railroad stock.[76] But Chase and Grant, who did hold most of the railroad stock, didn't hold a majority of the mining stock. Then again, the mine was no good if there wasn't a railroad to it.

There were enough independent stockholders out there to make a difference either way, so the Merritts decided to make a fight of it. What they needed was an alternative that was more attractive than the $7.5 million. Things might have looked pretty bleak for them had not a certain Henry W. Oliver appeared on the scene.

The son of Scottish immigrant parents from Ireland, Oliver and his brothers had managed to transform a small Pittsburgh "nuts and bolts shop" into a full-scale steel manufacturing firm, the Oliver Iron and Steel Company. Oliver was also owner of the Edith Furnace Company and knew Andrew Carnegie personally.[77]

116

While attending the Republican National Convention held in Minneapolis in June 1892, he heard talk about the Mesabi Range. He decided to go there to see the boom for himself. Accompanying him were his secretary, George T. Tenner, and one of his trusted lieutenants, C.D. Fraser.

It was a strange trio that got off the train at Mesaba Station in 1892. Most people in the area were grubstaked prospectors with little or no money. They hired a horse and buckboard to take them to the Cincinnati Mine. The Mesabi Trail, the only road to the ore fields, was so rough and the countryside so wild that when they got to the Cincinnati, Tenner and Fraser put their foot down and refused to go any farther.[78]

Oliver left them there, mounted a horse and rode the remaining 15 miles to the Merritt camp. Merritt company captain John Cohoe, the man who opened the Biwabik Mine, had just uncovered another large body of soft rich ore at a place the Merritts were calling "Missabe Mountain." When Oliver saw the ore, he offered them $75,000 cash on the spot and a royalty of 65 cents a ton if they would let him mine it. The usual royalty at the time was 25 cents a ton. While the Merritts were thinking it over, Oliver hurried back to Duluth. On June 20, he negotiated a 19-year lease on the Cincinnati Mine. He agreed to pay its Duluth stockholders $25,000 and to mine at least 150,000 tons of ore a year at a royalty of 55 cents a ton.[79]

On August 3, as the railroad neared completion, Oliver again contacted the Merritts and promised them that he would mine 200,000 tons of ore in 1893 and 400,000 tons in 1894, if they would just accept his offer. In addition, he would pay the going railroad shipping rate.

At a time when immediate cash was desperately needed, an advance of $75,000, a royalty of 65 cents a ton on a minimum of 600,000 tons and a two-year traffic contract were impossible for the Merritts to refuse. The deal was made and the Oliver Mining Company was organized on September 30, 1892. The new company sent Captain Edward Florada and a steam shovel to mine the Missabe Mountain and Oliver went to Henry Frick to tell him about the ore he had seen.[80]

"When you talk to practical iron men on the other ranges who have not visited the Missabe they think that you have been telling them fairy tales, but after a personal inspection they become as enthusiastic as any and are anxious to invest," said Mesabi iron prospector J.H. James in the early spring of 1892. Oliver was enthusiastic. Frick, still recovering from a wound received from the gun of anarchist Alexander Berkman, forgot his pain. Here was a man Frick could believe. Oliver knew the steel business and its need for a cheap supply of iron ore. Carnegie Steel took 50 percent of Oliver Mining Company stock in return for a loan of a half-million dollars and thus established a steady supply of cheap iron ore for their mills.[81]

With the promise of Oliver and Kimberly royalties and prospects of guaranteed shipments, the Merritts had their alternative for the stockholders. They would build a branch into Duluth and construct an ore dock on the Minnesota side of the bay. To do this, it would be necessary to lay 29

Steam barge *John Fritz* of the Pittsburgh Steamship Company was early iron ore carrier on the Great Lakes. Note the masts for sails.
VISUAL PERCEPTIONS INC., IRON RANGE RESEARCH CENTER

The Franklin Mine near Virginia in 1894. Originally a Merritt property, the mine was named after Franklin Rockefeller and operated by the Oliver Iron Mining Company. OKLOBZIJA COLLECTION, IRON RANGE RESEARCH CENTER

additional miles of track. The Merritts knew that this was going to cost them money that they didn't have. They went to an old and trusted friend who had been living in Duluth since 1871, Alexander McDougall, designer of the "whaleback" ore carrier. It was his *Whaleback 102* that carried the first 2,000 tons of Mesabi iron ore down the lake in the fall of 1892.[82]

McDougall referred them to Charles W. Wetmore, one of the vice presidents of the American Steel Barge Company, a John D. Rockefeller-controlled concern, then under the presidency of Colgate Hoyt. The Steel Barge Company had earlier paid McDougall $25,000 for his whaleback patent and he obviously had a lot of confidence in the firm. Wetmore said he could raise $1.6 million – the amount needed to build the railroad and ore dock – provided that the American Steel Barge Company be given the lake shipping contract for Merritt ore.

The agreement, signed by Merritt and Wetmore on December 24, 1892, was popular with Duluth, Missabe and Northern stockholders. With Wetmore's help, the Merritts were able to block the sale of the railroad and mine to the Minnesota Iron Company.[83]

However, Chase and Grant, who owned three-fifths of the Duluth, Missabe and Northern Railroad stock, also had

investments in the Duluth and Winnipeg Railroad and didn't want to lose the D&W shipping revenues for Merritt ore. They wanted no part of a spur to Duluth. The Merritts would have to buy them out – and it was now 1893.

Wetmore planned to raise the promised $1.6 million through the sale of $2 million worth of bonds at 80 percent par value. In January 1893, John D. Rockefeller bought $400,000 worth. Wetmore tried to sell the rest to various banks, but no one wanted to invest money in a railroad, especially one to "undeveloped mines containing ore of questionable value." Financial markets were beginning to tighten.[84]

On February 26, 1893, the Philadelphia and Reading Railroad failed. Banks called in their loans and businesses failed. The stock market crashed and European creditors dumped their American securities and drained the nation of its gold. In July, the Erie Railroad failed and after that the Union Pacific, Northern Pacific and Santa Fe lines fell into receiverships. Production of pig iron dropped sharply. No businessman in his right mind would invest in a railroad, especially one that was connected to an iron mine – and the Merritts were building one.

Despite the hard times, Leonidas remained optimistic.

"The (Duluth, Missabe and Northern) Company expects to cover the entire Mesabi Range with branches and spurs. Extensions to some of the new mines are already under way. The important timber interests will not be neglected. The Company has $400,000 in its treasury and not a cent of debt."[85]

On April 6, 1893, the Wetmore-Merritt alliance was formalized into the New York and Missabe Company. The company tried to consolidate well-known producing mines in Michigan and Minnesota with the new Mesabi mines to make their railroad bonds more attractive to investors. The effort failed and, after the first $400,000 from Rockefeller, Wetmore's money-raising ability also failed. On top of this, unknown to any of the Merritts, Wetmore's personal finances were on the rocks.[86]

Meanwhile, the Merritts, believing that the American Steel Barge Company, Wetmore and John D. Rockefeller all stood behind them, let contracts to build both the railroad and dock. Hundreds of men went to work and soon a construction debt was piling up at a rate of something like $10,000 a day.

The Merritts were forced to sell some of their mining stock and put up railroad shares as collateral for loans to raise enough money to keep things going. Wetmore couldn't raise a dime. In fact, Leonidas Merritt bailed him out a few times – with Missabe stock. The only person who seemed to have money for investment anymore was John D. Rockefeller and he made it clear that he wasn't going to buy any more railroad bonds.[87]

Alfred Merritt, acting as Duluth, Missabe and Northern president, sent Leonidas to New York to see if he could get a direct loan from Rockefeller. Representing Rockefeller was a native New Yorker, Frederick Taylor Gates, an ordained Baptist minister who left the pulpit in 1891 to become a Rockefeller advisor.[88]

There were meetings. There were proposals. There were counter proposals. There were more meetings. Wetmore was present at most of them and sometimes George Murray, Rockefeller's attorney, was there. Rockefeller never was. There were informal discussions, formal conferences, readings of lists of intricate legal details. Papers were signed. Leonidas Merritt walked away with a Rockefeller check for $350,000. "I shoved [the check] in my vest pocket, the same as a southern gentleman would a roll of bills.… I remember their reprimanding me by saying this was a large amount of money and I ought to take care of it."[89]

Because of the mounting construction debt, the money didn't last long. Leonidas Merritt went back to borrow some more. Gates was always cordial, sometimes enthusiastic. More Merritt railroad and mine stock went up as collateral. The money came in dribbles, enough to keep the Merritts going – and borrowing. But Rockefeller and Gates knew exactly what a tight situation the Merritts were in:

"It was impossible to get money for the railroad, for the mines or for themselves, any where, at any price. May and June went by with conditions worse every hour … the

The Lone Jack Mine in 1893, another Merritt property that became part of John D. Rockefeller's Lake Superior Consolidated Iron Mines that year. NUTE COLLECTION, NORTHEAST MINNESOTA HISTORICAL CENTER

Lone Jack

mines were idle and no money was forthcoming from the East … the railroad was trembling on the brink of receivership. Interest was not paid. Suits were actually begun. There were riots on the Missabe [sic] Range. Contractors were knocked down by their enraged men. Knives were drawn. Men actually entered the railroad offices in Duluth and demanded their paychecks at the ends of drawn revolvers."[90]

The Great Mergers (1894-1901)

On August 28, 1893, Lake Superior Consolidated Mines was born. It was the result of all of the months of meetings, conferences and agreements. It was a single contract that bound together every point that had been agreed upon. It was also the first of many consolidations that would soon take place in the iron and steel industry.

Consolidated Mines took full control of the New York and Missabe Company, as well as the Merritt ore dock and railroad. Duluth, Missabe and Northern Railroad stock was converted into Consolidated stock at 50 percent par value and Consolidated Mines quickly acquired 70 percent of the stock of the Mt. Iron Mine. Along with this, it gained control of 51 percent of Missabe Mountain, Biwabik and Adams mining stock and 75 percent of the stock of the McKinley Mine. Consolidated was also able to take full ownership of the Great Northern, Great Western, Lone Jack, Rathbun and Shaw mines. Everything went into one single pot.[91]

The pot turned out to be a Rockefeller pot. The oil millionaire now proceeded to transfer his holdings into Consolidated: the Penokee and Gogebic mines, the Aurora Mining Company of Michigan, the Spanish American Iron Company and the West Superior Iron and Steel Company.[92]

The enormity and complexity of the new corporate arrangement were beyond anything the Merritts could have imagined. Family members were reluctant to place their holdings into this pot. Alfred suggested not signing and putting the railroad into receivership. Their attorney told them they could lose everything. Gates, however, assured them that Rockefeller still respected their knowledge and wanted to put Leonidas in control of the whole operation. Gates said Rockefeller told him he would very much

like to make the Merritts a personal loan of $150,000, so that they could pay off past debts and get back some of the stock they had put up for collateral. He was even willing to let them secure the loan with some of their Consolidated stock. They signed.[93]

Leonidas Merritt did become president, but Merritt shares in Consolidated Mines were now part of collateral used for expanded Consolidated investments and as payments to a growing number of creditors. They were in the financial fast track. Some members of the Merritt family began to see that their participation in Consolidated would in the long run drain them of their holdings. With creditors pressing at all sides, the Merritts decided to put all of their 90,000 shares in Consolidated on the market. The asking price was $5 million. They couldn't find a buyer. They offered them to Rockefeller for $3.6 million. He turned them down. In January 1894, they made a second and obviously desperate offer to Rockefeller. They would sell him 90,000 shares of Consolidated stock for $10 a share, $900,000. Rockefeller snapped it up. The Merritts were out.[94]

Headlines in the *Duluth Daily News* on February 4, 1894, said it all: "Merritts Step Out – John D. Rockefeller in full control of Consolidated Mines … Alfred Merritt declines Missabe's Presidency … will devote full time to straightening out his private affairs."

Frederick Gates replaced Leonidas Merritt as president of the Lake Superior Consolidated Mines and the following fall Gates took over the presidency of the Duluth, Missabe and Northern Railroad. It was said of him:

"Gates was essentially a businessman, cold, hard, skeptical and adroit in business, albeit a fervent exhorter and expert money raiser for church movements, as shown by his 'List of Ten Commandments' prepared for solicitors: Let your victim talk freely. Never argue or contradict. If he is talkative, let him talk, talk, talk. Give your fish the reel and listen with deep interest."[95]

A storm of controversy and litigation followed. There were years of claims and counterclaims. There were Senate hearings; Rockefeller paid the Merritts some more money and they signed a paper. But none of

it changed the fact that, after 1894, it was Rockefeller, not the Merritts, who controlled some of the best mines on the Mesabi. Even more important, he had the railroad.

Yet it would be Henry Oliver who would do most of the Mesabi's mining. After accepting Oliver's offer of a half-interest in his mining company in exchange for a loan of $500,000, Henry Frick found himself unable to convince Andrew Carnegie that the company should take Oliver's offer. But when Carnegie heard that Rockefeller had taken over the Merritt mines and owned the railroad, he changed his mind.

"Oliver hasn't much of a bargain in his Mesabi, as I see it … still I cannot but recognize we are right in flanking the (Rockefeller) combination as far as possible." In the spring of 1894, 6,000 shares of Oliver Mining Company stock were transferred to Carnegie Steel.[96]

During the shipping seasons of 1895 and 1896, there were three competing mining coalitions controlling the flow of ore from Iron Country. Rockefeller's Consolidated Mines and Missabe Railroad, the Oliver-Carnegie mining and steel producing combination and the Vermilion Range's Porter-controlled Minnesota Iron Company with its railroad and docks in Two Harbors. By charging high shipping rates, the Minnesota Iron Company quickly put independents out of business and gained almost total control of the Vermilion iron trade.

In 1896, Rockefeller, who controlled the Duluth, Missabe and Northern Railroad, seemed to be in position to do the same on the Mesabi. But the fact that he had no steel mills and had to sell his ore to Carnegie made this impossible. A compromise was inevitable. On December 9, 1896, the arrangement was made. Oliver would mine the ore, Rockefeller would ship it and Carnegie would turn it into steel.[97]

The merger demoralized independents on the Mesabi Range. Oliver-mined ore had priority on the Rockefeller railroad and the only way that small independent companies could profit from their ore holdings was to lease them to the combination. The profits for Oliver, Rockefeller and Carnegie were enormous. More mergers followed after 1896. The Oliver-Carnegie-Rockefeller combination merged with Porter's Federal Steel Company, which included the Minnesota Mine at Soudan, the Chandler and other mines at Ely, the Duluth and Iron Range Railroad and a number of Chicago steel plants.[98]

In the midst of all of this expansion, Carnegie decided to retire and sold all of his holdings to banker J.P. Morgan for $492 million. With its guaranteed supply of cheap iron ore, the conglomerate, now controlled by Morgan, was able to swallow up the American Tin Plate Company, American Steel Wire Company, National Tube Steel Company, American Steel Hoop Company, American Sheet Steel Company and National Steel Company.

The final amalgamation occurred on February 23, 1901. Rockefeller's Consolidated Mines, Bessemer Steamship Company and Duluth, Missabe and Northern Railroad were added to the conglomerate and the United States Steel Corporation was born. It was the world's first multi-billion dollar corporation – a trust in every sense of the word. Its subsidiary, Oliver Mining Company, was soon doing 70 percent of Iron Country's mining. ■

The Giant Mining Frontier

A typical Mesabi drill camp of the 1890s shows the number of workers needed to keep the steam engine and drill equipment operating. RUTH MASSENGER MOORE COLLECTION, IRON RANGE RESEARCH CENTER

Edmund J. Longyear and the Diamond Drill

There were thousands of explorers on the range during the Mesabi iron boom. Most, if not all, saw indications of ore, many noted signs of great bodies of ore and some even found ore. The problem was, nobody was sure they had marketable ore when they found it. The reason was that geologists, mining men and steel makers had fixed ideas about what marketable iron ore was. Good ore ran deep and was dense and compacted, like the ores of the Michigan ranges, or was heavy and hard, like the ores of the Vermilion Range.

On May 27, 1890, a man who was sure he could locate the kind of ore that steelmakers would buy got off the train at Mesaba Station. His name was Edmund J. Longyear and he brought a diamond drill to

the range. The steam-driven diamond drill, conceived and developed by Swiss engineer Rudolph Leschot, saw its first use in 1864 when it was used to drill blast holes for tunnel construction in the French Alps.

The drill quickly became a valuable tool for mineral exploration and several were already in use at the Minnesota Mine when Longyear arrived in 1890. Using diamonds set into the face of a hollow rotating tube, the drill collected a running sample of the rock through which it was passing. It was able to cut through the hardest of mineral formations and core samples from 1,000 feet or more below the ground could be raised to the surface for inspection.[1]

Longyear came to the Mesabi Range expecting to find the same kind of high-grade iron ore that had been found in Michigan. He had come at the request of his

122

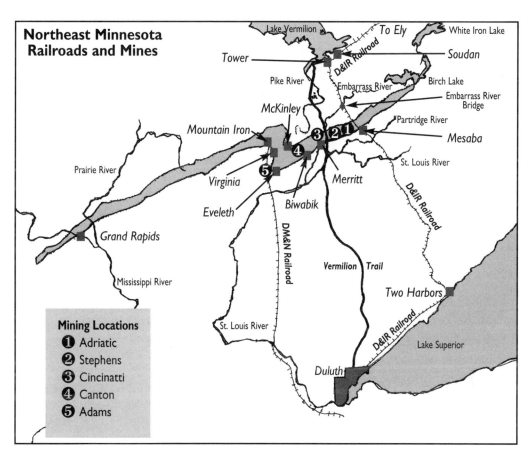

Northeast Minnesota Railroads and Mines

Mining Locations
❶ Adriatic
❷ Stephens
❸ Cincinatti
❹ Canton
❺ Adams

cousin, John Monro Longyear of Marquette, Michigan, who like other men of his time noticed that Mesabi rocks were similar to those on the Gogebic Range and theorized that the two ranges might be joined in a continuous sheet of iron ore that dipped below Lake Superior and surfaced in the irony outcrops on both sides of the lake. He knew that the Michigan iron formation, composed of quartzite overlain by good ore, lean ore and slate, consistently dipped north, while outcrops of quartzite, slate and lean ore being discovered on the Mesabi dipped south. This suggested a syncline. If so, the question was, where was the good ore on the Mesabi?

John Longyear was not only sure it existed, but was convinced that if it was like the soft compacted ore of the Gogebic, it couldn't be expected to outcrop. Instead, it would be found south of the exposures just below the lean ore and deep under the ground. The only way it could be located was with a diamond drill.[2]

In 1887, the Longyear Mesaba Land and Iron Company of Jackson, Michigan, was formed and a parcel of land purchased at the east end of the Mesabi in Section 34, Township 59, Range 14, directly above what John hoped would be high-grade iron ore. On June 3, 1890, under the direction of Edmund J. Longyear, diamond drilling began. By mid-December, the Longyear drill had reached a depth of 1,293 feet and, although no marketable ore was found, this first drill hole marks the beginning of a process that eventually led to a complete understanding of the Mesabi's geology and its strange flat-lying bodies of soft rich hematite.[3]

Exploratory Drilling Replaces Test Pitting

In the years that followed, drilling became the way to locate and determine the extent of Mesabi iron ore deposits.

Longyear's diamond drill functioned well in taconite and where the formation was hard, but when he moved his drill to the central Mesabi, where many of the deposits of soft hematite were located, he discovered that he was unable to bring up a solid core for analysis.[4]

Another kind of drill, the churn drill, was more successful when exploring an ore body in this part of the range. John Mallmann is sometimes credited with inventing this type of drill which, like the old hand drill, operated on the principle of percussion and used water pressure to send the cuttings through a casing pipe to the surface where they were collected in barrels and allowed to settle and dry before they were analyzed. Although the churn drill cut swiftly through surface overburden and soft hematite, it often broke down, was expensive to operate and was of little use in harder formations or when large boulders were encountered.[5]

Pick and shovel test pit crews, windlasses, buckets and 300 years of prospecting tradition continued in use, as witnessed by the Merritt family's success at Mountain Iron in 1892 and several other later ore discoveries, but such exploration quickly diminished after Longyear's arrival.

Map of Northeast Minnesota showing D&IR Railroad, Mesaba Village, Merritt, Biwabik, McKinley, Virginia, Mountain Iron, Grand Rapids, DM&N Railroad, early mining locations, Embarrass River Bridge, Embarrass River, Vermilion Trail, the road from Mesaba Village to Merritt and the towns of the Vermilion Range.

Constantly on the move, drill crews spent leisure time in meager quarters, as shown in this 1912 Oliver Iron Mining Company drill camp interior.
MILKOVICH COLLECTION, IRON RANGE RESEARCH CENTER

By 1895, steam-powered drills with their coal-burning vertical boilers and wooden tripods were a common site on the range. Log bunkhouses and cook shanties of drill camps appeared where before there had been only wilderness and became home, sometimes, to hundreds of drillers.

Drills exploring the range were not all Longyear drills. As early as 1890, Nute records that the Minnesota Iron Company shipped a "Bullock drill, complete with rods, boiler and pump" from Ely to the Mallmann exploration near Mesaba. By 1900, other private contractors, such as Reien Brothers, Cole and McDonald and Nelson Exploration Company also had diamond drills at work on the Mesabi and, in 1908, Oliver Iron Mining Company launched an immense drilling effort on Great Northern Ore Properties west of Hibbing.[6]

A drill rig was usually manned by a crew of three men, who were also responsible for building the road over which the drill was moved, clearing away trees and brush, bridging rivers and streams and laying "corduroy" across muskeg swamps.[7] Drills were constantly on the move – three weeks

drilling for the first hole on a 40-acre site – move – four weeks to bore to quartzite on the second hole – move the drill – two weeks to drill to taconite on the third – move the drill – two weeks for the fourth – move the drill – three more weeks drilling – move to the next forty. If ore was found, the forty was divided into 100-foot sections and drilled every 300 feet.[8] Each time the drill was moved, the entire process of tearing down the rig, building road, hauling coal and equipment, extending water lines and moving and setting up the rig in a new place was repeated – all accomplished with hand tools and a few teams of horses.

"Horses were used to move the drills through the woods. Roads were cut only wide enough to get the load through. Even so, they had to cut miles of roads. All the coal burned in the boilers was hauled by horses. One drill might work in one spot for two weeks before it was moved to another site. It took five or six teams to haul all the coal and move the drills. In summer, corduroy roads were built through the muskeg swamps. These were made by cutting poles about 8 feet long and placing them side by side so the horse would not sink into the muskeg."[9]

Within two decades, tens of thousands of drill holes dotted the Mesabi iron formation. Edmund Longyear claimed that he was responsible for 7,133 of them. Most were produced by a combination of churn drilling and diamond drilling. Drill crews were seldom without either and they were often interchanged during the drilling process, using the same steam engine, same boiler, same tripod and same water system.[10]

The Mesabi Iron Boom Turns Contract Drilling Into Big Business

From January to May 1891, using his Sullivan B drill, Edmund bored hole after hole into Longyear land, but was disappointed every time. He might have been discouraged, except that it was now summer and the Mesabi iron excitement had reached a state of frenzy.

"America had become accustomed to land booms, gold rushes and mass movements of population. She had seldom seen anything quite like the frenzied descent upon the Mesabi in 1891 and 1892 following the discoveries by the Merritts. Duluth was the port of entry. People poured into it – eastern millionaires, prospectors and explorers, miners, laborers and lumberjacks."[11]

Longyear put it this way: "Everyone from the elevator boy to the banker was investing in Mesabi land." Because he had the only available diamond drill on the Mesabi at the time, Longyear was besieged with requests for drilling. "I began to think that diamond-drill contracting might not be a bad line for me to consider," said Longyear in his *Reminiscences*, published in 1951.[12]

On June 15, 1891, after boring five holes for the Mesaba Syndicate at Iron Lake near the future site of Babbitt, Longyear began a 90-mile walk across the Mesabi in search of drilling contracts. With him were two associates, Robert Murray and Jacob Lehman. They were particularly interested in more than 32,000 acres of Pillsbury and Wright-Davis pineland located about 40 miles west of Mesaba Station. John Monro Longyear and Minneapolis iron explorer Russell Bennett had just made a deal for a half-interest in any iron deposits that might be found on these acres.

During the trip, which took them from Mesaba on the Duluth and Iron Range Railroad to Grand Rapids on the Mississippi River, Longyear witnessed the opening moments of Minnesota's giant range. "I knew that I was pioneering, even though at that time I could have no adequate conception of the tremendous development that would occur in a matter of months."[13]

Grand Rapids and Mesaba were then the only towns on the Mesabi and the logging roads that Longyear followed had not yet been connected to form the notorious overland supply route known later as the Mesabi Trail.

"Although there were so-called roads over part of the range, they were so execrable that we walked the entire distance, occasionally, however, availing ourselves of an opportunity to let a supply team carry our packs," said Longyear in 1951.

The path the Longyear party took passed through a magnificent and seemingly endless forest. Ten years later the forest was gone. In its place was a land of stumps, rocks and mines.

"I am glad that I saw those beautiful trees before they vanished," said Longyear in 1951. "For anyone who knows only the modern appearance of the Mesabi Range, it would be impossible to form a true mental picture of the original sites of Hibbing, Buhl, Chisholm, Eveleth and Virginia. Few areas in the United States have been so completely altered by man."[14]

The iron boom left many people holding properties they wanted explored and Longyear's drilling business prospered. Edmund J. Longyear exploratory drill camps near the future sites of Babbitt, Biwabik, Chisholm, Hibbing, Keewatin and Nashwauk were homes for the Longyear family until 1896, when they moved into a "real house" in Lake Superior Location, a cluster of residences for miners employed in the opening of the Lake Superior Consolidated Mine at Hibbing. In 1901, after establishing an office and living for a time in Hibbing, the Longyear family moved to Minneapolis. Ten years later the office followed.

In addition to contract drilling, Longyear successfully speculated in iron land, platted a number of townsites across the range and in 1903 partnered in a second firm, Longyear and Hodge, which drilled

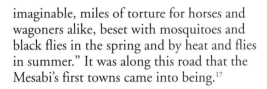

The Duluth and Iron Range Railroad Station at Mesaba would become the major jumping off point for exploration of the Mesabi Range. This photo in 1890 coincides with the start of that boom. NUTE COLLECTION, NORTHEAST MINNESOTA HISTORICAL CENTER

outside of Minnesota and manufactured and repaired diamond drill equipment. In 1911, the two firms merged into the corporation known worldwide as E.J. Longyear Company – after 1970, simply Longyear Company.[15]

The Mesabi Trail

It was a daunting task to move drills and transport heavy equipment to exploration sites during those early days. Until a road could be built, professional packers had to be hired to carry picks, shovels and other necessary equipment over rough terrain and across muskeg swamps to the properties being explored. At first, the only way to explore for iron was by digging test pits. Longyear resorted to test pits on Wright-Davis holdings before he was able to move in his diamond drill. To get the rig and all necessary equipment to the property, he had to hire 18 men to build "15 miles of road" and wait until winter.[16]

So that the Merritts could move a diamond drill to their properties west of the station in 1890, the St. Louis County Board of Commissioners authorized construction of a road. The first segment ran from Birch Lake to the bridge over the Embarrass River, east of the Biwabik Mine. The existing bridge was part of the old Vermilion Trail from Duluth to Tower and 20 years old. From there, the Merritts paid crews to cut a tote road to their Mt. Iron Mine, completing the second segment of what became known as the Mesabi Trail.

Longyear described it as "… first a packers' trail," then "a bridle path …" and finally "the most execrable tote road

imaginable, miles of torture for horses and wagoners alike, beset with mosquitoes and black flies in the spring and by heat and flies in summer." It was along this road that the Mesabi's first towns came into being.[17]

The Village of Mesaba

Mesaba Station was incorporated as the "Village of Mesaba" on May 29, 1891. The town was just 17 days old when Longyear and his two companions began their walk across the range. Its incorporation papers were signed 10 days before those of Grand Rapids, officially making Mesaba the first town on the range. At the time, it was little more than a collection of tiny mining offices. The Stone Mining Company, Moss Mining Company, Eureka Mining Company, Minnesota Iron Company, Mallmann Iron Mining Company and John Monro Longyear's Mesaba Land and Iron Company were all located at Mesaba by 1890.[18]

None of the companies found marketable ore, but this didn't stop prospectors and speculators from coming. The search simply shifted to the west and Mesaba Village became a place of packers, guides and outfitters. It was the time of Trimble, Hibbing, McCaskill, Adams and the Merritts. Edmund Longyear, who was in Mesaba when the Merritts struck iron ore, said this about them:

"I heard they were finding good soft hematite on the site of the Mountain Iron Mine. I saw a good deal of some of those sturdy, fun-loving brothers and nephews, for they attended the Sunday services in Mesaba, where I played the little organ. They were much given to dramatics and had great fun acting out of a certain book, directed by the young schoolteacher LaVerne Richardson, who also served as Methodist minister at Mesaba. I was told that the Merritts were expecting a diamond drill to be shipped to their diggings in July."[19]

Mesaba's boom came shortly after the Merritt iron strike. Within six months it was impossible to find a room in any of the town's 15 hotels.[20] There are no accurate population figures for the time, but it is clear that large numbers of people were arriving and leaving every day. It is also clear that most of the people were men. The opportunity was not overlooked. Saloons

were active and it was said that the hotels of Mesaba were equipped to "satisfy every need of roistering lumberjacks, dignified capitalists and wary gamblers."[21]

By the time the snow melted in the spring of 1892, there were iron exploration camps all the way to Mountain Iron and beyond and Mesaba Village was the chief supplier for every one. On March 17, the region's first stagecoach bumped along the Mesabi Trail, which now connected Mesaba to a new town called Merritt located on a hill near Embarrass Lake overlooking a cluster of nearby camps. The stage was run by Hiram J. Eaton, Civil War veteran from the Second Wisconsin Volunteer Infantry who had come to Mesaba two days before with high hopes and a team of horses. In October, the newly completed Merritt railroad to Biwabik put Eaton out of business, so he took his horses to another new town called Virginia. It was there that Eaton established one of the more successful dray line and delivery services on the range.[22]

Many early iron range businessmen had their start in Mesaba and for a time it seemed as if the place had all the advantages of a growing city. Iron had been found at its doorstep, the pine forest seemed inexhaustible, the demands for lumber insatiable and the town's location on a railroad had already made it the supply center of the Mesabi.

In 1891, the Mesaba Lumber Company, one of the more promising logging and milling firms on the range, established its main distribution center in Mesaba and appointed Frank Colvin general manager.[23] In 1892, Mesaba's future seemed secure.

A year later, it was well on its way to becoming a ghost town. Buildings were vacant, hotels were empty, outfitting stations and mine offices were closed. The much heralded Merritt railroad had turned all eyes to the west. Mesaba was bypassed. The panic of 1893 and the depression that followed made things worse. Frank Colvin relocated to Biwabik and other businessmen followed. By 1895, there were fewer than 200 people in town – and those who remained were talking about moving on. Over the next 10 years, Mesaba's population dwindled away to a low of 46. By 1905, the town teetered at the brink of extinction.[24]

Then in 1906, mining companies began running out of the easy to mine ores. Again there was interest in iron deposits near Mesaba. Most were hard to reach and underground mines were necessary.

By 1910, the Graham, Spring, Adriatic, Vivian and Stephens mines were all shipping iron ore.[25] Once again, Mesaba's population grew. New homes were built, stores reopened on Broadway, an all-brick town hall complete with jail was built and a water and electric lighting system installed.[26] It became a place for families – a place to bring up children. There were churches. A school was built. There were ice cream socials and Saturday night dances at the great pavilion near the edge of town.[27]

It didn't last. The large sandy ore bodies of the western Mesabi's Canisteo District were opened and they could be mined by steam shovel and conveyor belt. Along with this, completion of a double-tracked Hull-Rust Short Line allowed ore trains to run directly from the bottom of Hibbing's Hull-Rust pit to ore docks in Duluth.[28] Steam shovels began loading ore directly into waiting trains. Iron ore had never been mined so cheaply, so quickly and in such large quantities.

The underground mines near Mesaba Village couldn't compete. They closed. People left and the town again dwindled away. Election counts tell the story. In 1918, 184 votes were cast in Mesaba Village; in 1919, 84 votes were cast; in 1920, 54 were cast. In 1947, 3 votes were cast. All favored dissolution of the village.

Mesaba was a ghost town. All that remained of the old village were two houses,

The Mesabl Trail in the winter of 1890 graphically illustrates the rugged conditions encountered by travelers on that road. NUTE COLLECTION, NORTHEAST MINNESOTA HISTORICAL CENTER

GRAHAM.MINE.
MESABA.MINN.

The Graham Mine near Mesaba Village in 1914 was one of several iron mines in that area, but none could successfully compete with the easier-to-mine open pit mines of the western Mesabi. By 1920, Mesaba's heyday as a mining center was finished.
AUTHOR'S COLLECTION

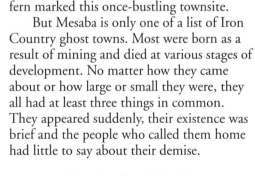

an empty city hall, an abandoned store and one "old timer" who refused to leave. His name was Charles Walberg. Some called him "the mayor of Mesaba."[29]

Today, not a sign of the old town remains. The townsite became part of the property of Erie Mining Company (later LTV Steel Mining Company) when modern-day taconite mining began on the eastern Mesabi in the mid-1950s. Twenty years later, only a small trackside railroad building with "Mesaba" on the side and the stray asparagus fern marked this once-bustling townsite.

But Mesaba is only one of a list of Iron Country ghost towns. Most were born as a result of mining and died at various stages of development. No matter how they came about or how large or small they were, they all had at least three things in common. They appeared suddenly, their existence was brief and the people who called them home had little to say about their demise.

Frontier Grand Rapids

On July 6, 1891, Edmund J. Longyear and his companions arrived at the frontier town of Grand Rapids on the Mississippi River. Grand Rapids was the second Mesabi Range town to incorporate as a village. It was different from Mesaba. It was not a mining

town. It would never be a ghost town. Although slightly younger than Mesaba in corporate organization, the place had been in existence for almost 20 years by the time Longyear arrived.

The town grew around a fur trading post established by Warren Potter of Aitkin in the early 1870s. A small village composed of native families of trappers was established nearby. When large-scale logging began, the site became a lumber mill town. In 1881, Grand Rapids was described as "a hotel, two stores, a saloon and three or four private homes, all built of logs."[30]

Itasca County logging had reached a grand scale by this time. To the region arrived some of the great loggers of Minnesota's past: men like Lenny Day, who had his start in the logging camps of Maine, and Al Nason, "reputed to be the strongest man ever to come to Itasca." It was said he could throw a 330-pound barrel of salt pork on his shoulder and walk away with no effort at all. "Saturday Wash Day" Hale of Pennsylvania came to Itasca County in 1872, along with Nate and Bill Tibbets, who spent their lives logging out the last of the pine forests in northern Minnesota.[31]

Minneapolis lumber companies with sawmills down river – firms such as Dorilus

MISSISSIPPI RIVER BRIDGE & COURT HOUSE.

The earliest Itasca County Courthouse in Grand Rapids dominated its treeless surroundings in 1908. **Bottom:** La Prairie had high hopes of becoming the county seat when this picture was taken in 1890, but those hopes were dashed by voters in 1891. ITASCA COUNTY HISTORICAL SOCIETY

Morrison, Joel Bassett, Akeny and Company and Eastman, Bovey and Company – set up logging camps above the great rapids on the Mississippi River. Seventeen lumber camps were operating within a few miles of Pokegama Falls in 1872 and well more than 400 men were employed. The camps required supplies and provisions, most of which were shipped upriver and unloaded at the dock below the rapids.[32]

Grand Rapids has always been closely tied to the river. Since Civil War times, Mississippi riverboats made their way upriver to the foot of the "long thundering rapids" from which the town gets its name. Each summer, such river steamers as the *Anson Northrup, Pokegama, White Swan* and *Andy Gibson* carried people and freight between Aitkin and Grand Rapids. There were docks and warehouses in the vicinity even before there was a town.[33]

Like other places on the logging frontier, Grand Rapids formed before the arrival of law and government. Itasca County itself, although established when Minnesota was still a territory, had no government until March 7, 1891.

At the time the county organized, the voting population was so sparse that the governor of the state had to appoint the county commissioners. In the first election, Grand Rapids competed with the logging town of La Prairie for designation as the county seat.[34]

The two settlements were just two miles apart and, although the Duluth and Winnipeg Railroad made La Prairie its

western terminus, Grand Rapids had the advantage of the river. It also had more scheming town promoters. Grand Rapids won the designation, but the total number of votes cast exceeded the number of legal resident voters. According to local lore, the clerk of a more remote Itasca precinct brought in an unexpectedly large number of ballots and was asked, "Who voted up there to account for your total?" The clerk replied, "Everything with hair on it." No one challenged him.[35]

It was in this atmosphere of free and undisciplined living that Grand Rapids incorporated as a village on June 8, 1891. The *La Prairie Magnet*, the only newspaper in the area, immediately moved its printing office to the new county seat. By the end of the year, Grand Rapids had the railroad as well and boasted a sawmill, church and school. But it remained a place of trappers, riverboat men, lumberjacks and saloon keepers.[36]

The Mesabi Range became world famous as a mining district, but Grand Rapids remained primarily a lumber mill town, with only a few scattered mines in the vicinity.
Bottom: There appears to be little that would have recommended the Kearney and Nason Hotel in Grand Rapids in 1889, but it was apparently adequate for the needs of the people who frequented it. ITASCA COUNTY HISTORICAL SOCIETY

Most of the town's saloons served meals. Some even offered overnight accommodations. Usually it was on the floor, but if there was a spare bed in the place, the saloon keeper was quick to call his establishment a hotel.[37] Saloon keepers in early Grand Rapids were much like those in other range towns. They tended to be active politicians and always knew what lumber camps were hiring or what company was going to be exploring for iron ore.

Even though most of the Mesabi became a mining district, Grand Rapids remained a logging town. The great pines of the Prairie River and western Mesabi fell by the thousands. At the turn of the century, there were well more than 300 lumber camps in St. Louis, Itasca and Beltrami counties and the timber products workforce numbered close to 16,000.[38] The town teemed with 'jacks, the saloon business was equal to any on the range and village government was largely supported by returns from liquor permits.

During their 1891 walk, the Longyear party found the entire west end of the range logged out. They followed 20 miles of well-used logging trail to La Prairie, visiting the vacated site of the Diamond Mine along the way. "The shafts were full of water and the dumps looked very silicious [sic]," Longyear noted.

At La Prairie's Wells, Stone Mercantile Company store, Longyear purchased a team, wagon, harness and sleigh to build his drill road to the Wright-Davis property.[39]

La Prairie and Grand Rapids served as supply stations for iron exploration on the western Mesabi until well into the 20th century. There were some mining excitements – the one in 1890 over activities at the Diamond Mine, another in 1891 at the Buckeye and another in 1895 when a shaft was sunk at the Arcturus Mine – but no real mining boom was generated. There was reason for this.

The ores of the west Mesabi were laden with sand and constantly tested well-below the 60 percent iron content then considered minimum for profitable mining. The sandy ore bodies of the western range would lie dormant, while mines to the east made the Mesabi Range famous.

The Mesabi's First Mining Towns

Mining advanced rapidly across the Mesabi. There was one mine in 1892, 20 in 1900, but by 1910, 111 mines were in operation on the range. Next to every mine appeared a small community. Most lasted only briefly, disappearing almost as soon as the mining situation changed. Mines opened and closed without warning, underground mines were expanded into open pits, ore was discovered beneath the streets, and the little towns lived and died accordingly.

Because the first mines were developed in an unsettled region and large work forces were needed to operate them, companies had to find ways to house and accommodate workers. The easiest was to allow employees to locate on company land and create their own accommodations. The result was often a shack town, a hodgepodge of "tar paper homes" set on blocks with plain board floors and homemade furnishings. As one resident recalled: "In the kitchen is a wood stove, some firewood, a barrel of water in one corner. Empty wooden dynamite boxes piled in the other [corner] serve as a cupboard.... As many as six to eight children sleep on two large beds...."[40]

To put up a house on land held by a mining company, employees were sometimes required to purchase a "squatters' license" at a nominal fee. This was probably done to protect potential mineland, much of it then under lease, from possible squatters' claims.[41]

Another type of housing retained by some companies at their mining sites until well into the 20th century was quite accurately labeled "the camp."

"The sides of a typical camp are usually built of two thicknesses of rough boards with tarred building paper between. A partition usually separates the cook-room from the sleeping room. Double-deck bunks are arranged along the sides of the sleeping room, which serves also as the dining room unless, as is sometimes the case, a separate eating camp is provided. Most of the bunks are of wood, but in some cases iron double-deck bed frames

In squatters' locations homes were often no more than tar paper shacks set on blocks and surrounded by stick fences. IRON RANGE RESEARCH CENTER

When wives and families arrived, the step from drill camp to mining camp or "location" was made. RUTH MASSENGER MOORE COLLECTION, IRON RANGE RESEARCH CENTER

are being substituted. Sometimes the camps are built of logs, as about Coleraine. Little or no provision is made for their ventilation. In a camp, 28 or 30 or even more men will frequently live on the cooperative plan. The cooking may be done by one of the men or a woman. Such numbers could not be accommodated but for the fact that some of the men work on night shift and others on day shift. Thus the camp dwellers often keep the bunks in continuous use."[42]

As their mines expanded, some companies set aside land, built cottages and developed townsites for the families of employees. Laid out in rows and grids, the little towns became the most common settlement pattern on the Mesabi during its first 30 years. Most were without stores or other places of business and the closest thing to public improvement was a raised boardwalk to the mine. On the range, they called these places "locations," as mentioned earlier.

The name is said to have come about in the 1840s in Michigan's Upper Peninsula, when mine companies were authorized by the federal government to "locate" copper

explorations on designated parcels of land.[43] But to people living in a location, how the name came about didn't matter. The important thing about a location was that the company always controlled the land on which miners' homes were located.

Edmund Longyear, who witnessed the evolution of some of these places, said this about them: "All these communities were first of all exploration camps; later, they became drill camps, in many instances at least; then they grew into mining camps.... As the mine expanded, more houses were required. The wives and families arrived and the step from drill camp to mining camp or 'location' was made when separate houses for the men's families appeared."[44]

The term "location" carries the same meaning in both Michigan and Minnesota. It refers to all buildings located on a parcel of land held by a mining company – everything from the mine office to employees' dwellings. Michigan copper mines, like Mesabi iron mines, were established in remote unpopulated areas where accommodation had to be made for employees. As a result, more locations were formed in Michigan's copper country and Minnesota's Mesabi Range than in all other Lake Superior mining districts combined. Between 1892 and 1925, the Mesabi Range alone spawned more than 175 of these little towns.[45]

In a location, miners usually rented the land they squatted on or the house they lived in. The rent was usually low and often deducted from a miner's pay. In some cases, miners and their families were allowed to buy location houses. In all cases, the company quickly disposed of the town when its usefulness came to an end. Houses were either torn down or moved to another place. Old location houses are still in use in iron range towns today.

After 1905, it became clear to mining company officials that they were running out of the easy-to-mine ores. Rich ore bodies still remained, but more sophisticated methods were needed to mine them. Miners had to be trained to do the specialized work required and mining companies, anxious to keep these trained employees on the payroll, began improving existing locations and developing new ones. By 1913, the Mesabi Range had some fairly attractive locations. Some were described as "models of comfortable living." Homes were well-built and equipped with electricity and running water. Large fenced-in lots provided room

for children to play. There were gardens. Streets were graded and lined with sidewalks. Almost every location had a school.[46]

The Incorporated Villages of 1892

Among the "locations" were some townsites that were planned and platted by independent entrepreneurs. The townsites were designed for the purpose of selling lots to merchants, saloon keepers and other businessmen who hoped to profit by providing goods and services to the mines and people living in the locations. Merritt was one of these towns.

The Town of Merritt

In the spring of 1892, the town of Merritt, located on a hill overlooking Embarrass Lake, was the fastest growing town on the Mesabi Range. Surrounded by the Biwabik, Cincinnati, Hale, Canton, Shaw and Kanawha mines, with two railroads building to nearby ore fields, it was easy for developers to advertise Merritt as "the future metropolis of the Mesabi Iron Range."[47]

The townsite was platted by Joseph Sellwood of Ely and James Hale and O.D. Kinney of Duluth. All three men were holding mining fees and parcels of land in the vicinity. The town was named Merritt, probably as part of the developers' strategy to

With Embarrass Lake in its front yard, the village of Merritt seemed a good bet to become one of the metropolitan centers of the Mesabi Iron Range in 1892. Lack of a railroad connection and a catastrophic fire that destroyed the town on June 18, 1893, put an end to that future. Unlike some other range towns that burned, Merritt was never rebuilt and the nearby townsite of Biwabik inherited the early promise that Merritt enjoyed. MITCHELL COLLECTION, IRON RANGE HISTORICAL SOCIETY

get the Duluth family to build a railroad to the place.

But the town developers were also doing everything they could to get the Merritts' rival, the Duluth and Iron Range Railroad, to build to their town. The Merritts, on the other hand, were counting on the ore traffic from nearby mines and undoubtedly knew what the developers were doing. They often avoided the town.[48]

Despite this, "Merritt developed like magic" and by spring 1892 had all the earmarks of a thriving town.

"Beside the Embarrass Lake there has sprung up with Alladin-like cerility [sic], the town of Merritt, which is already incorporated, has elected its municipal officers and boasts a good hotel, a newspaper and other appointments of a mining center."[49]

Incorporated as a village on May 10, 1892, the town boasted several good hotels, rooming houses and general stores. Along with these were two restaurants, a bank, post office, sawmill, clothing store, drugstore, barbershop, cigar store and "plenty of saloons."[50]

Because there was no railroad into town, saloon keepers resorted to another method of supply. Kegs of beer were transported by train from Tower to the Embarrass River bridge, where they were dumped into the water and floated 40 miles downstream to Embarrass Lake. Log drivers from nearby

camps were hired to make sure that the "ordered cargo" arrived safely. It was reported that a "beer drive" from Embarrass to Merritt took four days to complete.[51]

The first newspaper in the mining district was printed in Merritt. It was appropriately named *The Mesaba Range*. The first copy came out in May 1892, published by Doctor Fred Barrett, the same man who founded Tower's first newspaper, the *Vermilion Iron Journal*.[52] On July 14, Editor Ransom Metcalfe proudly proclaimed Merritt's right to be called a thriving prosperous mining town thusly:

"Mining towns are generally of spontaneous origin – built in a day, as it were. One day a wilderness, the next a thriving, prosperous community. Merritt is a fair example of the mining town. Hardly six months have elapsed since the first tree was cut on the townsite – now there is a village of about 300 people, with many good substantial buildings, streets being graded and sidewalks being laid."[53]

To Mesabi Range pioneer Fred M. Seely, who saw the place for the first time in April 1892, it had all the appearances of a wild west town.

"Other than there being no log houses, it was a typical mining town of the old West.… The buildings were constructed in traditional western fashion, all well set back

Because there was no railroad to the town, kegs of beer for Merritt's saloons were dumped into the water at Embarrass River bridge and floated 40 miles downstream to Merritt (Embarrass) Lake.
IRON RANGE RESEARCH CENTER

from the board sidewalk with hitching posts for horses in front. These included a greasy spoon restaurant, the town bank and, of all things in a wild mining town, a millinery shop run by a woman, called the Chicago Belle."[54]

Young Seely and his mother came to join Fred's father, H.G. Seely, who was then managing the Pratt and Company general store on Merritt's Main Street.

"Father and mother slept in father's bunk in a rear corner of the store while I slept on a shakedown of flour sacks. Sometimes, we ate breakfast and dinner either at the Mills House or the Svea House. Generally, we ate our evening meal at the store. Mother made tea on the alcohol stove and heated peas, tomatoes or corn on the same. Then there were soda and graham crackers, as well as cheese and kegs of sweet and sour pickles."[55]

Merritt wasn't just hat shops, greasy spoon restaurants, hotels, stores and saloons. Construction of a Congregational church began in September 1892, after the Reverend G.E. Northrup, an agent for the American Home Missionary Society, walked over from Mesaba Station with an offer of $500 to cover building costs.[56] There were also plans to build a school. On September 15, *The Mesaba Range* reported:

"There is now every probability that Merritt will have a good school this winter. When P.H. McGarry was in Duluth this week, he had a talk with O.D. Kinney and the latter authorized him to employ Attorney Sullivan to prepare papers petitioning the board of county commissioners for organization of a school district. Mrs. H.T. Rogers recently circulated a petition here and secured the signatures of nearly all the residents....

"The citizens of Merritt will probably be compelled to raise sufficient funds for a teacher this year as no public funds are yet available, but it is thought that there will be no difficulty in raising the amount."[57]

Although many were sure Merritt was destined to become the commercial center of the range, it still needed a railroad and, for this, there were plenty of competitors. On July 14, Editor Metcalfe noted one:

"The woods are full of newly platted townsites in this vicinity. The most of them are also full of woods. The latest addition to the list is located just south and west of the Biwabik Mine and it is being platted by the Merritts of Duluth. A force of about 30 men is now at work surveying and clearing the land."[58]

Biwabik Location, as it came to be called, was just west of the village on the road to the Sharon Mine. The east boundary line of the location was only a half-mile from

The site for the Village of Biwabik was cleared in 1892. Closer to area mines, Biwabik was also blessed with a rail connection to the outside world. Once Merritt was destroyed by fire, businesses previously located there moved their enterprises to Biwabik. NEWTON COLLECTION, NORTHEAST MINNESOTA HISTORICAL CENTER

The Elba Mine was one of the earliest of several mines near the McKinley townsite in 1900. IRON RANGE RESEARCH CENTER

the Merritt village limits. There was some talk that the two places might grow together as a single town, once the railroad arrived. But it was already clear in the spring of 1892 that the Merritts weren't going to extend their railroad beyond Biwabik. A roundhouse was under construction at the location. Promoters of the village now pinned all their hopes on the Minnesota Iron Company's Duluth and Iron Range Railroad.

In July, the company began building a branch line from Allen Junction toward Merritt and the nearby mines. Everyone was sure that trains would be running into town by fall. In October, Merritt's newspaper quoted a *Duluth Daily News* interview with railroad President J.L. Greatsinger.

"(President Greatsinger) expects to reach the Embarrass River with the rails by Friday or Saturday of this week.... From the river to Merritt is about a mile. The branch leading to Merritt will probably be constructed first, because no mine on the range will be ready to ship ore for some time."[59]

But there were delays – months went by. The 1893 Panic broke out and mining properties began changing hands. The branch was extended, but not to Merritt. The town began to die. Businesses closed. Shopkeepers began relocating to Biwabik. It is said H.G. Seeley walked over to Biwabik with a sack of flour on his shoulder the day after he heard there would be no trains to Merritt.[60]

Although lack of a railroad was a major cause of Merritt's decline, what really put the

town away were the Mesabi fires of 1893. It had been a dry spring and a lot of tree cutting had taken place to make way for roads, townsites and mines. The debris left on the ground became dry as tinder. There had been brush fires near some of the mines and locations that spring, but they were quickly put out. Apparently, some continued to smolder.

On the morning of June 18, high winds suddenly blew in from the north. Flames fanned by the wind swept across the Mesabi. Fires broke out in McKinley. Buildings at Cincinnati Location and Mountain Iron caught fire. Virginia burned. Biwabik was threatened and Merritt was engulfed in flames. When evening came it rained. Biwabik was saved, but Merritt was gone. It would never be rebuilt.[61]

The McKinley Camp Becomes a Village

During the years 1892-1895, a pattern developed in the way Mesabi mining towns were forming. Exploration camps became drill camps, drill camps became mining camps, successful mining camps became locations and some locations were incorporated into villages. But there was one mining camp that became a corporate village even before its mine was fully developed.

After selling their Biwabik option to the Merritts, John, William and Duncan McKinley established their own exploration camp about six miles to the west. In December 1891, one of their test pits bottomed into

ELBA MINE 1900, McKINLEY, MINN.

ELBA.McKINLEY.PUBLIC.SCHOOL.

soft hematite about 20 feet down. The McKinley Iron Company was formed, the Merritts were contacted and plans were made to bring a railroad to the mine. The following summer, the McKinleys had 80 acres of their camp platted as the townsite of McKinley. On October 12, 1892, 127 votes were cast to establish corporate government. The village of McKinley was born.[62]

Elisha Morcom of Tower was named captain of the mine. He developed a way to sink a shaft through the soft ore and mine it from underneath. Morcom was able to develop a main level beneath the bed of ore. A heavily timbered sub-level was developed above, pumps were installed and it was planned that the ore from these levels would be dropped through chutes into ore cars waiting on a track at the main level. From there it could be trammed to the shaft and raised to a loading pocket at the surface. It was described as a brilliant piece of work and a model for mines to come, but not a ton of ore came out of Morcom's mine.[63]

The fire of 1893 wiped out the camp buildings and burned part of the shaft house. The Panic of 1893 followed and, along with other Merritt holdings, the McKinley property passed into the hands of John D. Rockefeller and the Lake Superior

Consolidated Mines. No ore would be shipped from the McKinley Mine until 1907, when the Oliver Mining Company began mining the deposit with two steam shovels.[64]

McKinley might have dwindled away like Old Mesaba, had it not been for the opening of the Minnesota Iron Company's Elba Mine in 1898.[65] The mine spawned a large location about a mile west of town and it was not long before a boardwalk connected the two places. In 1899, a school was built on the boardwalk halfway between the two communities.

Elba resident Alex Sipola recalled: "The school was built half-way between Elba and McKinley. The boys in the two towns were always at war. We had many a tough scrap…. It was many years after the school was built that they finally put in a fire escape…. After some sort of dispute, my dad left the mining company and bought a team of horses. He hauled the children from Pettit (the railway station at what is now called Gilbert was Pettit) to the McKinley-Elba school in a surrey…. Mrs. Chinn, the [mine] superintendent's wife, was instrumental in starting a Methodist Sunday School, my first Sunday School."[66]

The period from 1898 to 1918 were active business years for McKinley Village.

The Elba-McKinley Public School was a considerable structure in 1900, serving children from both the Elba mining location and the town of McKinley. VOSS COLLECTION, IRON RANGE RESEARCH CENTER

North of Biwabik Mine on the Canton Iron Company's land was a squatters' location composed mostly of "Austrians." OKLOBZIJA COLLECTION, IRON RANGE RESEARCH CENTER

H.J. Millbrock, later of Biwabik, opened a bank and a town hall with courtroom and brick jail was built. L.N. Keeler served as judge in that building and Doctor J.C. Farmer, who arrived in 1900, turned a mining company building into a private hospital, which he maintained until his death in 1921.

In 1908, a water and light plant was established and a volunteer fire department and firehall were added under the able administration of Village President Ed Olson. Although McKinley's two stores and one saloon were very active during these years, most of the business came from Elba, Corsica, Pettit and other nearby locations.[67]

After the McKinley Mine re-opened in 1907, the town was advertised as the "future hub of the iron range," and there was a heavy campaign to sell lots. It didn't happen. Although a town hall was built and a bank opened, the town neither grew nor prospered. In 1910, there were 411 people living within the townsite.[68] This was probably McKinley's largest population.

Biwabik Location Becomes a Village

Biwabik is an Ojibway word that means iron ore. The town was named after a nearby spring where a hematite exposure could be seen. At the spring was a camping ground that had been used by native travelers for centuries. After 1890, it became an overnight stop on the Mesabi Trail.[69]

On November 10, 1892, when Biwabik location incorporated as a village, the population was already 247.[70] The town had advantages. After Merritt burned, it was the lone commercial center for mining crews at work at the the nearby Biwabik, Canton, Cincinnati, Duluth and Hale mines. The town already had a railroad and another was on the way. The only wagon road on the range, the Mesabi Trail, ran just north of town – and iron ore seemed to be everywhere. But unlike many other range towns, Biwabik didn't boom – at least not at first.

There was a reason for this. It was iron ore. There was so much of it around that promoters, suspecting some of it was under the town, hesitated to build. *The Mesaba Range*, which had moved to Biwabik after Merritt burned, publishing at a time of panic and depression, saw the slow growth as a positive factor in town development.

"One thing greatly in (the town's) favor is that it has never experienced a real estate boom and consequently its people have never been called upon to see the bottom drop out," argued the paper in 1893.[71]

But nearby, mines and locations were developing and would soon be desperate for building supplies and provisions. Good money could be made by anyone willing to go through the trouble of delivering these materials. Suppliers were happy to locate in Biwabik, where main street property could be bought for as little as $200 a lot.

A.P. Dodge was one of these men. He had a store on the site even before Biwabik was incorporated as a village. When it did become a village, he served as its first president. Frank Colvin and Jim Robb came over from Mesaba in the fall of 1892 and established a retail lumber yard.

"There was an enormous demand for camping and building supplies, as well as other accommodations.... Prices of all kinds went soaring and the services of a man and team were worth $15 a day," Colvin later recalled. The first shipment of freight over the Duluth and Iron Range Railroad in 1893 consisted of 17 carloads of lumber billed to the firm of "D.W. Freeman, Colvin and Robb."[72]

The depressed iron ore market in 1893 and 1894 led to layoffs and mine closings. The little ore that was shipped was sold at a loss. Biwabik's growth slowed. Most people living on the range were acutely aware of the depression, but few knew about the tremendous property changes taking place behind the scenes.

Edmund Longyear, in *Mesabi Pioneer*, explains, "During the period from 1893 to about 1898 many Mesabi properties changed hands. The outstanding example, of course, was the Merritt properties, which passed into John D. Rockefeller's hands in early 1894.

But there were many, many others. Nor did we on the range always know the ultimate purchaser, for he was often represented by someone else, who actually appeared on the range and bought in his own name."[73]

In 1894, a new company, Biwabik Bessemer, took over the Biwabik Mine and brought in steam shovels to strip away the surface, exposing a vast bed of rich hematite.

"The ore is unsurpassed in quality by any on the range.... The ore body is half a mile long ... nearly one-quarter of a mile wide, with a thickness of over 100 feet," wrote state geologist Horace Winchell in 1895.[74]

Other mines began shipping iron ore. The Canton underground lifted more than 200,000 tons to the surface in 1894, a "clam-shell grab" mining machine was installed at the Hale in 1895 and the iron rich Duluth Mine re-opened in 1898.[75] By then, miners were in short supply and Mesabi iron mines were recruiting workers wherever they could be located. Thousands were found in Europe.

Biwabik became a place of immigrants. Stores, restaurants and saloons tailored their services to meet the needs of the various ethnic groups. Matt Baudek's Slovenski Dom, Crooked Neck Pete's Scandinavian Saloon and Timo and Simo's Suomalainen Salonki became gathering places for hard-drinking, foreign-speaking miners.[76]

Places like these served a purpose. They helped bring an end to illicit sale of alcohol in squatters' locations just beyond the city limits. Two, Finn Location, a mile west of

Biwabik's main street was still a bit rugged when this photo was taken in about 1910, but the town did boast electricity, a number of significant businesses and amenities equal to most on the iron range.
VOSS COLLECTION, IRON RANGE RESEARCH CENTER

Biwabik's ethnic saloons were often gathering places for hard drinking foreign speaking miners, but also served as social and political centers for the many ethnic groups in the town. Photo taken in 1908.
JACK ERICKSON COLLECTION AT THE IRON RANGE RESEARCH CENTER

town, and Austrian Location, a mile and a half north of town, were particularly notorious. According to *The Mesaba Range:*

"North of the Biwabik Mine on the Canton Iron Company's land is a large settlement of squatters, mostly Austrians, who live there by virtue of the patience of the officers of the Canton Iron Company.... In at least six of the houses beer is constantly sold at (less than) 10 cents a bottle. Those people have no license whatsoever and can undersell and injure any man who pays a license.... If there was no beer sold at Canton Location more would be sold in town (by legitimate saloon men) and consequently there would be more revenue for the town."[77]

And revenue there was. Biwabik was the first town on the Mesabi to have its main street lit by electricity. The town had street lights in 1893. Steam from boilers at the Biwabik Mine turned a small generator, which produced enough electricity to light a string of dim lights hung from buildings along the main street. By 1906, 600 "eight-candle power" city lights made nighttime Biwabik the brightest town on the range.[78]

Just eight years after the town was platted, Biwabik had two railroads, its streets

were graded and its business section was one of the most prosperous on the range. Few homes were without electricity and indoor plumbing and the town had three churches and two schools. It also had a hospital, one of the first on the Mesabi Range.[79]

In 1899, a husband and wife medical team took over the hospital. Doctor Charles Bray and Doctor Mary Bassett Bray practiced medicine in Biwabik for 38 years. There are people still living today who feel a special kind of distinction in having been brought into the world by one of these two doctors.[80]

From 1895-1912, Biwabik was considered one of the more urban places on the Mesabi. Two motion picture houses, a hotel, opera house, brewery, lumberyard, bank, tailor shop, cigar store, confectionery, hardware and furniture store, roller-skating arena, six grocery stores and 18 saloons lined the town's main street.[81]

Virginia Becomes the Commercial Center of the Range

Virginia was the sixth Mesabi village to vote for incorporation. The vote took place at E.C. Burke's store on November 12, 1892. Sixty-five ballots were cast. All but one favored incorporation.[82]

Developments at the Missabe Mountain Mine and at least a dozen nearby exploration camps during the summer of 1892 prompted David Adams, A.E. Humphreys, George Milligan and others active in the area to organize the Virginia Improvement Company. The company picked up parcels of land from various fee holders. The parcels were surveyed, a townsite was cleared and lots auctioned off in Duluth.

"We rented a vacant storeroom in Duluth, hung up a large plat on the wall with maps showing the deposits of ore which had been developed," Adams later recalled.[83] The response was enthusiastic.

Adams named the town Virginia because the townsite was in "virgin country" and its most enthusiastic promoter, A.E. Humphreys was from the state of Virginia. By September, there were enough people on the townsite to circulate a petition for incorporation. The first election for village officials took place on December 6, 1892, and John Owens, former sawmill operator from Tower, became Virginia's first village president.[84]

Ransom Metcalfe, editor of *The Mesaba Range,* made a trip to the new town during the summer of 1892 and liked what he saw:

"A visit to the new townsite of Virginia City is sure to impress one favorably. It is handsome and well-located. Lake Humphreys lies to the west and Lake Adams to the north. Both are charming sheets of water. A range of hills to the west looking across the lake adds beauty to the scene. The only drawback to the place is that the land is rather low."[85]

A small portable sawmill, hauled to the site from a nearby mining camp, was put into operation by John Owens to produce lumber for Virginia's first buildings. His partner, Robert McGruer, was in charge of crews clearing the townsite and grading its first streets. Ransom Metcalfe noted only one woman living on the townsite – Robert McGruer's wife.[86]

Eight months later, 5,000 people were living in Virginia. It would be an understatement to say the town grew quickly. Nowhere in Iron Country was there a boom quite like that first rush to Virginia. Construction of buildings lagged far behind the population growth, although this was greatly speeded up by the extension of a branch railroad from Wolf Junction on the Duluth, Missabe and Northern track. By spring, there were 18 potential mines in the vicinity and boardinghouses, halls, stores and backyard sheds were packed with people.[87]

By then the village had a bank, newspaper and hotel. It didn't have a church, but it did have Crockett's Opera House and Hayes Hall. During the winter of 1892-

The Jackson and Company Store in Virginia as it appeared after the town's first fire. On the second floor was the office of Doctor Stuart Bates, pioneer physician and early village president. OKLOBZIJA COLLECTION, IRON RANGE RESEARCH CENTER

1893, they were centers for public meetings, socials, minstrel shows, dog fights, beer drinking, gambling – and church services. On June 18, 1893, Virginia burned. The two halls went with it.[88]

Although most of the nearby mining locations survived the fire, there was nothing left in Virginia. The fire was followed by severe depression. Many left, never to return. Money was in short supply and not even the mighty Oliver Mining Company could pay its bills. Doctor Stuart Bates, Virginia's first physician, accepted bushels of potatoes and piles of chopped wood for his services.[89]

Those who remained began rebuilding. By 1895, the Missabe Mountain, Commodore, Franklin, Victoria, Bessemer, Lone Jack and Norman mines were shipping ore and Virginia was again a place of hotels, rooming houses, restaurants and stores. It also became a place of saloons, gambling halls and houses of ill repute. The town swarmed with lumberjacks and miners – most young and single, many fresh from the "old country." In 1895, Virginia was possibly the most prosperous – and certainly the most wide open – town on the Mesabi.[90]

That same year, Dr. Bates and M.C. Palmer led a successful effort to obtain a city charter for the town. City status was achieved on February 7, 1895, but in the first city election, a "Citizens-Democratic Party" led by saloon keepers and hotel men, took over all of the city offices. Not many miners voted. Most were foreigners and living in locations outside the city limits. Robert McGruer became Virginia's first mayor, defeating Dr. Bates by a margin of 163 votes.[91]

In 1899, Virginia had a population of 3,000, eight mines were shipping ore, two sawmills were in operation, the city had two railroad terminals and its business section was described as the busiest place north of Duluth.[92] On June 7, 1900, Virginia burned again.

"Through carelessness in handling the shavings burner at the Moon and Kerr mill, a blaze was started, which in a short time had the whole sawmill in flames. The day was very hot and everything was as dry as it could be. This, together with a strong west wind, carried the flames directly towards the town and, when one of the many flying

sparks fell on the dry shingles of a building in the very center of the city, the work of destruction had begun. At sunset, there was nothing left of it but one vast space of smoldering ruins."[93]

The rebuilding of Virginia began almost before the smoke of the fire had cleared away.[94] This time it was resolved that nothing flammable would be built on Chestnut Street, all structures were to be of brick, stone or concrete. A new Virginia rose from the ashes. This time, it became the largest town north of Duluth and one of the most substantially built cities in the state.

The Mountain Iron Camp Becomes a Location and Then a Village

After the Merritts discovered ore in 1890, their camp quickly lost its temporary appearance and a more permanent mining location developed. Like all locations on the range, Mountain Iron was a place to house mine employees. Mesaba, Grand Rapids, Merritt, McKinley, Biwabik and Virginia were all incorporated before Mountain Iron – but not long before. Mountain Iron's vote on the question of village status took place on November 28, 1892, 18 days after Biwabik and 16 days after Virginia. George S. Brown became its first president; A.L. Culbertson, recorder; John Brennick and H.L. Chapin, trustees; Al Free, town marshal.[95]

When the town first began, there were few who doubted the prediction that it would soon be "the metropolis of the Mesabi." When a railroad was connected to it in 1892 and the mine began shipping iron ore, there were none who doubted it. Van Brunt noted, "Settlers, prospectors and others who contemplated engaging in various lines of business" flocked to Mountain Iron.[96]

When the Merritt family came to see their mine in October 1892, there were six frame buildings on the townsite. Lumber for these buildings had been hauled in from the closest sawmill at Mesaba Station, 27 miles away. But there were plenty of tents, log shacks and people.[97]

In January 1893, a portable sawmill was set up on the townsite and many new buildings were constructed. On June 17, Mountain Iron consisted of 16 private dwellings, five hotels,

three boardinghouses, four restaurants, a church, school, real estate office, bank, post office, blacksmith shop, livery stable and a few other places of business. On June 20, the church and school were gone, destroyed by the Mesabi fires of '93.[98]

By mid-summer the structures were already being replaced. The fact that the nearby mines passed into John D. Rockefeller's hands did much to encourage expansion of the business district. Many were sure the town would now live up to early expectations. It didn't.

There were only 443 people living in Mountain Iron in 1895.[99] At the same time, the town's mines were setting records for ore production. The Mt. Iron and Rathbun mines sent well more than a half-million tons of ore down the tracks, while other Mesabi mines were idle. By 1900, almost 4 million tons of ore had been taken from the Mt. Iron Mine alone and it continued to ship immense amounts of ore until well into the 20th century.[100]

The influence of the mining company was strong in Mountain Iron during its first 20 years. John D. Gilchrist, superintendent of the Rathbun Mine, served as village president from 1895-1898. His successors and many village council members were also connected with the mines. Mining company influence may have played a role in Mountain Iron becoming one of the more orderly towns on the range. A jail, fire hall, four churches and a "commodious public school building" were all added to the townsite. Only three saloons were allowed. Nearby Virginia had 52.[101]

But other community improvements seemed to come about more slowly. As late as 1910, Mountain Iron residents were still carrying water to their homes from mine pumping stations. The town didn't have a sewage disposal system or an electric light plant until 1912. When a plant was finally built, it provided not only water and lights, but steam heat for businesses and homes.[102]

After 1912, public improvements came quickly. A substantial all-brick two-story city hall complete with a jail and fire department was built. This was followed by an elegantly finished Carnegie public library, paved streets, a nine-acre public park and a public lighting system equal to any on the range.[103]

The Passing of the Mining Frontier

On October 6, 1892, Ransom Metcalfe, editor of *The Mesaba Range,* announced the end of uncertainty about his town and predicted a rapid pace of mine development with Merritt and Mountain Iron emerging as the leading towns of the range.[104] A year later, mining was at a standstill, Merritt was gone, Mountain Iron had fallen behind fast-growing Virginia and there was uncertainty about the Mesabi.

The standstill and uncertainty lasted only long enough for properties to change hands and in 1894 mining began again. This time, mine development and ore production accelerated to levels far beyond anything that could have been imagined on that October day in 1892.

Heavily financed mining companies, either in partnership or holding contracts with corporate steel-making giants, took over the iron deposits, expanded railroads, brought in thousands of miners and put the latest and best machines into the mines.

The result was profound. Within a decade more than 30 million tons of ore had been removed and the Mesabi was a 60-mile expanse of stumps, rubble, gaping open pits and rude mining camps and towns. By the end of the second decade, camps had been turned into towns, towns into cities and the giant mining frontier appeared all but closed. The era of explorers, prospectors and entrepreneurs seemed to be waning. However, there were surprises ahead. ■

Heavily financed mining companies took over the iron deposits, brought in thousands of workers and put the latest and best machines into the mines. OLIVER IRON MINING COLLECTION, IRON RANGE RESEARCH CENTER

CHAPTER 9

Mines and Mining Centers on the Mesabi 1892-1925

The prevalence of steam power in early mining is obvious in this scene of stripping operations for an open pit mine near Hibbing in the late 1890s. Notice the side arms needed to keep the shovel from tipping over and the dinkey locomotives at work on the narrow gauge track. LYONS COLLECTION, IRON RANGE RESEARCH CENTER

"North of Duluth there is a region where … wastes of land stretch for miles covered only with the charred, blackened stumps of a once magnificent pine forest. Yawning chasms, in all their ugly nakedness, mark the spots where man has discovered and removed or is now at work removing the treasures of the hills which Nature so carefully stored away.…

"Embedded in these rock strewn hills lie the wealth and the power of the American steel industry. Here is the home of 30 great iron mining companies. Man can lay back a few feet of top soil and load, with steam-driven shovels, an almost pure ore into cars of waiting trains. It is an Eldorado where iron takes the place of gold!"[1]

LeRoy Hodges, Special Agent,
U.S. Immigration Commission, 1912

"Mesabi" is an Ojibway word for giant and the range lived up to its name. In 1895,

it was already producing more ore than any of the Michigan ranges and 10 years later it was out-shipping all of the other ranges combined. The Mesabi produced more than 12 million tons of iron ore in 1902, 20 million in 1905, 29 million in 1910 and 32 million tons in 1912. Two million came from underground mines. The rest was dug by steam shovel with no more difficulty than if it were common beach sand.[2]

Enormous ore shipments like these couldn't have been made without the steel industry mergers prior to 1903. Because the consolidations involved people like Rockefeller, Carnegie and Morgan, fears were aroused that the nation would soon be dominated by big business. President Grover Cleveland, in an 1888 message to Congress, voiced some of these fears:

"As we view the achievements of aggregated capital, we discover the existence of trusts, combinations and monopolies, while the citizen

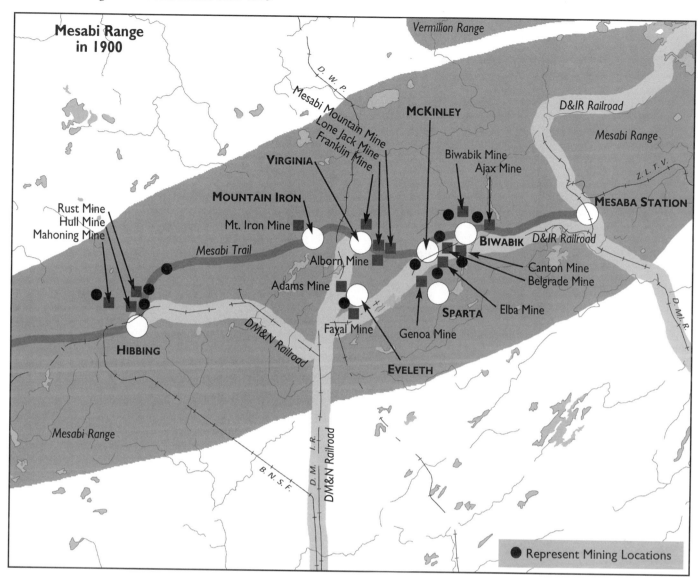

Mesabi Range in 1900

Vermilion Range

D. W. P.

Mesabi Mountain Mine
Lone Jack Mine
Franklin Mine

McKINLEY

D&IR Railroad

Mesabi Range

Z. L. T. V.

Biwabik Mine
Ajax Mine

MESABA STATION

VIRGINIA

MOUNTAIN IRON

Mt. Iron Mine

BIWABIK

D&IR Railroad

Rust Mine
Hull Mine
Mahoning Mine

Mesabi Trail

Alborn Mine

Canton Mine
Belgrade Mine

Adams Mine

Elba Mine

SPARTA

Fayal Mine

Genoa Mine

D. MI. R.

HIBBING

DM&N Railroad

EVELETH

Mesabi Range

D. M. I. R.

DM&N Railroad

B. N. S. F.

● Represent Mining Locations

---

is struggling far in the rear or is trampled to death beneath an iron heel. Corporations, which should be the carefully restrained creatures of the law and servants of the people, are fast becoming the people's masters."[3]

Government regulation of trusts and monopolies might have prevented the worst from happening, but didn't stop Mesabi mining from becoming big business. By 1903, United States Steel Corporation's iron mining-ore transporting-steel manufacturing interest was more or less in charge of the range. Although there were other companies, this was the interest that did two-thirds of the mining and employed three-fourths of the men. On the range they called it "the Oliver."

Such firms as Pickands Mather and Company, Republic Iron and Steel, Hanna Mining, Cleveland Cliffs and Inter-State Iron also operated mines on the Mesabi, but unlike "the Oliver," they were not owned by

a parent steel maker. They specialized in mining and shipped their ores to independent steel makers like Youngstown Sheet and Tube, Sharon Steel Company, Inland Steel Company and other Great Lakes blast furnace operators. Subsidiary companies mining for the Jones and Laughlin Steel Corporation and Republic Steel were also on the range. All of these companies had one thing in common. They were financially strong and could afford to mine and ship the enormous tonnages called for by steel producers after 1901.

Furnace men of the 20th century needed two things; lots of ore and a guaranteed supply of it. The Mesabi provided this supply. "In 1907 there were only 11 iron mines in the world that produced over a million tons. Of this number nine were on the Mesabi Range."[4]

Steam-powered shovels were the only practical tools for mining ore on this scale,

This map of the Mesabi Range in 1900 shows the important mines, the Mesabi Trail, all railroads, incorporated towns and major mining locations.
MAP PROVIDED COURTESY OF THE STATE OF MINNESOTA

but they were expensive to buy and costly to operate. Powerful locomotives, thousands of ore cars and miles and miles of track were also required. They, too, were expensive. For a mining company to show a profit, it needed several mines and a large supply of cheap labor.

Problems of labor supply were met with aggressive hiring campaigns – campaigns that brought thousands of unskilled foreign workers into the mines. On the Mesabi, with its soft, easy-to-reach ore and all those machines, a man didn't need mining skills to be a miner.

In his report, Hodges stated, "The babel of more than 30 different alien tongues mingles with the crash and clank of machinery. Here, side by side, work Finns, Swedes, Montenegrins, South Italians, English, Irish, Bohemians, Frenchmen, Hollanders, Syrians, Belgians, Danes, Russians, Magyars, Bulgarians, Germans, Greeks, Scots, Welsh, Dalmations, Norwegians and Servians [sic]."[5]

Open Pit Mining

Although open pit mining did not originate on the Mesabi, nowhere in the world was it used on such a grand scale. The range became famous for its open pits. Children studying geography in schools all over the world learned that more than 70 percent of the iron ore used by America's steel industry came from the Mesabi Iron Range.

Power Shovels

Nothing was more important to early Mesabi open pit mining than the steam-powered shovel. The first of these shovels was installed at the Biwabik Mine in the spring of 1892.

"To John T. Jones is due the credit of conceiving the idea of stripping the overburden from the ore and mining the ore with a steam shovel…. No railroad had reached the district when these men took hold and they conceived the idea of bringing a steam shovel overland from Mesaba Station, which job was accomplished under

An Oliver Iron Mining Company shovel crew poses for a photograph next to their 35-ton railroad steam shovel at a Virginia area mine in the early 1900s. Note the steel chain hoisting mechanism on the shovel and the side arms to stabilize the shovel during heavy lifting. MOORE COLLECTION, IRON RANGE RESEARCH CENTER

the direction of Captain Arthur Stevens.… It was a monstrous undertaking, owing to the almost impassable character of the road for 12 miles, but it was successfully accomplished."[6]

Despite frequent breakdowns, it took the shovel less than a month to dig out an approach to the Biwabik ore deposit. The firm of Fitzgerald and Sisk was then contracted to strip away the remainder of the overburden with teams of horses and scrapers, so the shovel could be moved in to begin loading ore. The horses and scrapers soon proved useless and Fitzgerald and Sisk, "not being practical shovel men, threw up the contract."

In 1893, the Drake and Stratton Company brought in a second steam shovel and, within a few months, had removed 100,000 yards of dirt, rocks and gravel covering the Biwabik's rich bed of hematite. "It was the success of their operations at the Biwabik that led to the adoption of the steam-shovel method at many range properties."[7]

The steam shovels weighed 27 tons each and had to be set up on railroad tracks before they could function. Equipped with upright boilers and single two-cylinder steam-driven engines, the shovels needed a constant supply of coal and water and a large workforce to keep them operating. An 1893 steam-shovel crew consisted of a fireman to fire the boiler, an engineer to operate the swinging and hoisting mechanisms, a craneman stationed on the boom to control the thrust of the dipper and trip the latch opening the dipper door, a track cleaner and five to eight pitmen to lay track needed for each forward move of the shovel. A spotter was also needed to keep the stripping train moving along a track parallel to the one on which the shovel was operating.

When a shovel was at work, the engineer and craneman had to coordinate their efforts with near perfect timing to get it to function effectively. During the loading period, pitmen prepared the needed roadbed and carried ties and rails forward for the next move. Because it was usual for a shovel to be moved a distance of five or six feet every hour, it was continuous hard work for the pit crew. When a long move was required, as many as 30 or 40 men were sometimes involved.[8]

After 1895, a heavier version of the railroad steam shovel, the first specifically designed to load iron ore, was introduced. It

A standard 100-ton railroad steam shovel loading rock at the Spruce Mine near Eveleth in 1925. Note the rails and ties on which the shovel operates. NORTHEAST MINNESOTA HISTORICAL CENTER

147

Twenty-four full-revolving shovels were put to work in Lake Superior mines during the 1920s, but because of their large size, they could only be used in the largest open pits. **Bottom:** In 1920 a 350-ton full-revolving shovel was installed at the Hull-Rust Mine near Hibbing. IRON RANGE RESEARCH CENTER

weighed 35 tons and, although its engine was larger, it needed a minimum of 10 men to keep it operating. To keep the long narrow shovels from tipping over, they were equipped with side-arms and jack-screws which had to be taken up and readjusted each time the shovel was moved.

Despite their shortcomings, railroad steam shovels proved far superior to hand-loading methods and were an important factor in the rapid growth of open pit mining. Nine years after they were introduced, 321 of these shovels were at work in American mines. A majority were on the Mesabi.[9]

Steel cables replaced chains on hoisting mechanisms in 1910, giving shovels a smoother, more easily controlled motion that made them more effective and paved the way for engines that used other sources of power. In 1916, single engine steam shovels were replaced by 100-ton "tri-engine steam shovels." The old upright boiler was replaced with a locomotive boiler and there was a separate engine for each of the shovel's three motions. This eliminated the need for friction clutches, the main cause of breakdowns, and made it possible to increase the size of the dipper.[10]

By 1912, most of the ore being mined was too compacted to be simply dug from a pit and loaded into a car with a steam shovel. It needed to be loosened. This was accomplished by a method known as gopher holing. A gang of miners using picks and shovels bored small tunnels – gopher holes – into the face of a bank of ore at its base, "the men lying flat within the excavation to take out the last portions of dirt." Several kegs of black powder were placed in each excavation, the hole refilled and a series of blasts set off, loosening the ore and making it more workable for the steam shovel.[11]

In 1920, a full revolving steam shovel was installed at the Hull-Rust Mine. Hailed as "a long forward step in shovel design," it could dig and load equally in all directions, didn't need a crane man and was so wide and

sturdy that jack-arm supports were no longer needed. Weighing well more than 350 tons with its long boom, dipper stick and six-cubic-yard capacity dipper, the giant shovel had to be set up on two sets of railroad tracks. Twenty-four of these shovels were put to work in Lake Superior mines during the 1920s, but, because of their size, they could be used only in the largest open pits.[12]

Until 1925, all power shovels moved on railroad tracks. The success of the military tank, with its crawler track, in World War I led to the development of a similar system for power shovels. The new system eliminated the need for pit crews and allowed the shovel to move freely about the pit. After 1928, all of the Mesabi's open pit mines were using power shovels with crawler tracks. Although much smaller than revolving shovels, they could load ore as fast as any revolving shovel and were less expensive to operate.[13]

M.A. Hanna was the first company on the Mesabi to use electric power shovels. The company put a 300-ton Marion electric to work at their Wabigon Mine near Buhl in the spring of 1924 and a somewhat smaller Bucyrus electric to work at their LaRue Mine near Nashwauk. The new shovels didn't need firemen, boiler cleaners or support labor. Three men on an electric shovel could do the work of 30 with three steam shovels. By 1938, electric shovels were a common sight in Mesabi open pits.[14]

In addition to electric shovels, powerful gasoline, diesel and diesel-electric shovels were also being used in Mesabi open pit mines by 1935. They had great flexibility and, during World War II, were particularly useful in removing small bodies of ore located in hard-to-reach places. No matter what the source of power, after 1940 the trend in shovel design was to increase engine power relative to the size of the dipper. As a result, loading time was shortened and the number of power shovels needed in a mine steadily declined.[15]

Moving the Ore

Iron ore is heavy. On the Mesabi, it is also soft and crumbly. A special kind of mechanical technology had to be developed to move large amounts of it from the bottom of pits to trains waiting at the surface. The first carloads of ore were pulled to railroad

After 1928 Mesabi mines were using steam shovels mounted on caterpillar tracks. NORTHEAST MINNESOTA HISTORICAL CENTER **Bottom:** An electric power shovel at work loading 75-ton capacity hopper bottom cars at the Hull-Rust Mine in 1946. OLIVER IRON MINING COMPANY COLLECTION, IRON RANGE RESEARCH CENTER

Steam-powered dinkey engines with cabs were used in most Mesabi open pit mines from 1895 to 1903. IRON RANGE RESEARCH CENTER

loading pockets by teams of horses, but "horse power" didn't last long. By 1895, tiny steam-driven locomotives were doing the job in a much more efficient way.

Miners called the little locomotives dinkeys. The first dinkeys weighed about six tons and pulled trains of 20 small wooden hand-dump cars along a narrow-gauge, 36-inch track laid with lightweight rails. They had neither cabs nor pilot wheels, but engineers had good visibility and the dinkey's small size allowed it to negotiate sharp turns with ease.

A slightly heavier version, complete with cab, was used in most Mesabi open pit stripping operations after 1895. The engines had water tanks above their boilers so that the greatest possible weight was placed over the drive wheels. This allowed a very tiny engine to pull a surprisingly long string of loaded cars. It was an ideal system for the time. In stripping operations, track had to be changed constantly and the lighter rails were more easily handled by work crews.[16]

However, improved steam shovels with larger dippers brought an end to the old dinkey trains. A dinkey ore car held just under two cubic yards of material. New shovel dippers had capacities of two or more cubic yards. Larger ore cars and more powerful locomotives were needed and 0-4-0 "saddle tank" engines, called "forty-fives,"

were in most Mesabi pits by 1903. Forty-fives had no pilot wheels, ran on standard gauge tracks and, although they were used for both stripping and hauling ore, they could negotiate only very shallow grades. Distances from steam shovels to loading pockets had to be measured in miles. Mesabi mines soon took on a terraced appearance, with railroads winding gradually upward along pit walls.[17]

As the open pits grew deeper, even more powerful locomotives were needed. By 1924, 60-ton "0-6-0" locomotives had replaced the old "forty-fives." The new locomotives were larger, more powerful and had six drive wheels instead of four. Although slower than the old "forty-fives," they could climb the steeper grades created by the ever-deepening pits.[18]

In the mid-1920s, some mines were using 127-ton "0-8-0" switch engines. Nicknamed "steamers," the locomotives were capable of pulling trains loaded with 1,000 tons of ore to the surface. The trains moved at speeds up to 15 miles an hour – provided the grade wasn't too steep. Only the very largest of open pits could provide the miles and miles of track needed by a steamer to bring the ore to the surface. Steamers were used almost exclusively at Hibbing's Hull-Rust Mine during the years 1925 to 1934.[19]

In 1925, electric locomotives began to replace steam locomotives in some Mesabi mines. They were more powerful and could more easily negotiate the steeper grades and sharper turns created by the ever deepening pits. "Electrics," as they were called, did not require coaling, watering and boiler cleaning and they more than made up for their purchase price with low maintenance costs. Two men could operate an electric. A steamer required a crew of three.

The first electrics weighed 65 tons and needed a trolley to draw their power from overhead lines. Hanna officials are said to have set up tug-of-war contests pitting electrics against 0-8-0 steam locomotives. The smaller lighter electrics won every time.[20] The Hill-Annex Mine in the Mesabi's Canisteo District was one of the first to replace all of its steamers with electric locomotives.

"The steamers could only haul five 75-ton cars up a two percent grade against six cars of the same size for the electrics. Even with five cars the steamers had to have a running start to negotiate the two percent grade and for perhaps 30 percent of the time had to back up for a fresh start. The situation was aggravated when the rails were wet or slippery. The maximum speed of the steamers while hauling five cars up a two percent grade was 8 miles per hour and the

electrics can easily haul six cars from a standstill and attain a speed of better than 10 miles per hour...."[21] reported Bill Beck in his history of Minnesota Power.

Many Mesabi mines were reluctant to buy electric locomotives. They were expensive and the installation of power lines, trolley systems and third rails needed to supply them with electricity called for a commitment that sometimes seemed beyond the scope of the projected mine. More so, it was the inconsistency and high cost of the electricity that deterred most companies.[22] A new kind of infrastructure had to be created.

Before World War I, all electricity generated on the Mesabi Range came from small steam plants set up at mines or in nearby towns. Grand Rapids, Hibbing and Virginia all had municipal electric utility systems by 1913 and other towns were served by such privately owned electric companies as Home Electric and Heating Company of Eveleth, Range Power and Western Mesaba Electric.[23]

However, none of the range electric systems were efficient enough to be of much interest to mining companies. Biwabik lights went out at 8 p.m. and Chisholm's electric power was shut off at 10.[24] Mines operated around the clock and mine captains, along

Mesabi open pit mines took on a terraced appearance with railroads winding gradually upward along pit walls. MUSEUM OF MINING COLLECTION, IRON RANGE RESEARCH CENTER

This four-ton electrically powered locomotive is tramming ore at the Leonidas underground mine near Eveleth in 1928. Oliver Iron Mining Company collection, Northeast Minnesota Historical Center

with their reliance on men, mules and steam power, put their faith in candles, kerosene and carbide lights.

Change came in 1917. Under the leadership of Chicago entrepreneur Rolland Heskett, some of the independent electric companies were merged to form a new company known as Minnesota Utilities. Heskett could see that it was just a matter of time before electric power would be used everywhere in the mines. He was determined to be ready with a reliable and cheap source of power when that time came.

Minnesota Utilities established coal-burning steam generators at Eveleth and Chisholm and in 1917 ran a power line across the Mesabi to Grand Rapids. America's entry into World War I increased the demand for iron ore, miners became soldiers, machines went into the mines, large amounts

of electricity were purchased, Minnesota Utilities prospered and Eveleth and Chisholm were covered with a dusting of soot.

By war's end, it was clear that Heskett's steam generators couldn't meet the needs of the expanding mines. Many sources of power were required so that if one source failed, power could be provided by the others. Minnesota Utilities didn't have them.

In 1923, the company was absorbed into a new and much larger consolidation known as Minnesota Power and Light. The new company inherited access to numerous sources of water power on the Mississippi, St. Louis and Kawishiwi rivers. It wasn't long before an intricate network of transmission lines replaced the Mesabi's coal-burning steam plants. The mines electrified rapidly.

Electric locomotives were in most mines by 1930, but by then some open pits were so

deep that no locomotive, electric or otherwise, could pull a train of ore to the surface. At the Shenango and Susquehanna mines, rail lines to the surface were replaced with electric-powered skip hoists. Railroad dump cars powered by electric motors carried the ore to the hoists. With the ore load placed directly over their drive wheels, motorized dump cars became surprisingly powerful. Once loaded down with ore, an electric dump car could pull a dozen or more fully loaded non-motorized ore cars anywhere in the pit. Trains of ore cars – seemingly without locomotives – became a common site in some of the deeper open pits.

Belt conveyors were introduced at the Hill-Annex, Spruce, St. Paul, Hale, Canisteo and Judd mines during the 1940s.[25] They worked well west of Hibbing, where the ore was soft and crumbly. They used a minimum of power and raised large amounts of ore up incredibly steep grades. They didn't work so well in the dense ore deposits east of Virginia, but rubber-tired diesel-powered trucks did.[26] In fact, diesel-powered trucks worked well everywhere. They could go

almost anywhere. By 1940, good ore was found mostly in scattered and difficult to reach places. Trucks such as the Mack and Euclid could easily drive to these places and carry out 4 or 5 cubic yards at a time.

During World War II, Lake Mining Company's Embarrass Mine near Biwabik became the first to use only diesel trucks to move its ore.[27] The Embarrass deposit was unusually deep, and trucks were the only vehicles able to climb the mine's unusually steep grades and make all the sharp turns that were necessary. Their use spread quickly across the range/ In 1944, the Mesaba-Cliffs

Minnesota Power and Light transformers were standard construction in most Mesabi mines by 1928. **Bottom:** Although trucks could be seen in some Mesabi mines during the 1920s, their use spread slowly and they were not used for ore haulage until the late 1930s. OLIVER IRON MINING COMPANY COLLECTION, NORTHEAST MINNESOTA HISTORICAL CENTER

In the photo annotations:
"3" Plank Floor 12' Long
12" Cap 12" Thick "D"
Post 6" Minimum 8" Top
Knee Brace
Pole Brace
Batter 2" to 1'

OLIVER IRON MINING CO.
STANDARD SINGLE TRACK WOOD
STOCKPILE TRESTLE.
ENGINEERING DEPT. LEONIDAS MINE
EVELETH MINN. OCT 25-23.
END VIEW.

With thousands of tons of ore being mined each day, attention to detail was an engineering necessity, as shown in this annotated photo of the stockpile trestle (head frame in background) at the Leonidas Mine near Eveleth in 1923. OLIVER IRON MINING COMPANY COLLECTION, NORTHEAST MINNESOTA HISTORICAL CENTER

Mining Company constructed a building exclusively for the repair of diesel trucks at their Holman Mine, near the town of Taconite. Soon most mines had similar repair facilities and even larger and more powerful trucks went into the pits.[28]

Underground Mining

Not all Mesabi mines were open pits. Serious underground mining began in 1895 and by 1907 one out of every three mines was operated as an underground. Forty years later, six of the Mesabi's greatest mines – the Agnew, Bennett, Fraser, Godfrey, Fayal and Sargent – were underground workings.

Despite advances in open pit technology, underground mining persisted on the Mesabi until most of the hematite deposits were gone. There was a reason for this. It was usually less costly to develop and equip an underground mine than it was an open pit mine.[29]

The Mesabi's special kind of iron ore provided mine developers with unprecedented challenges and several methods of underground mining resulted.[30] Much of the hematite was soft, softer than on other ranges, but its softness varied. In some places it could be dug with a shovel, in others it had to be blasted loose before it could be moved.

The depth and thickness of the ore body also varied. In some places the top of the body was 200 feet below the surface, in others only 10 or 12 feet down. Its thickness also varied. In places the deposit was 300 or 400 feet thick, in other places the thickness was only a foot.

Underground mining was most successful in thick bodies of dense ore located deep under the ground. The first underground mines, such as the early Canton, Elba, Adams, Spruce, Fayal and Kellogg, were room-and-pillar square-set mines. The method was imported from the Pennsylvania coal fields and, at the time, was considered the most inexpensive way to get ore out of the ground.

From heavily timbered chambers begun just above main level located beneath the ore deposit, untimbered drifts were extended in either direction to the mining limit and the ore stoped out overhand. As soon as a block of ore was removed, the open space was replaced with a square set timber frame with one wall remaining open to the ore. Miners worked with picks and shovels by the light of candles, the broken ore falling on heavily planked platforms, where it was shoveled into chutes to the main level below. From there it was trammed to the shaft and raised to the surface.[31]

Mesabi square-set mines earned a reputation for being terrible places in which to work – dusty, dark, sometimes wet, unpredictable, downright dangerous – and from the point of view of operators, totally wasteful. Although there are no reliable statistics related to accidents prior to June 30, 1906, when St. Louis County mine inspection began, many of the stories of bad working conditions and danger below the ground that have been passed on through the generations can be traced back to these underground workings.

The ore went hard and had to be blasted loose, charges were set off prematurely,

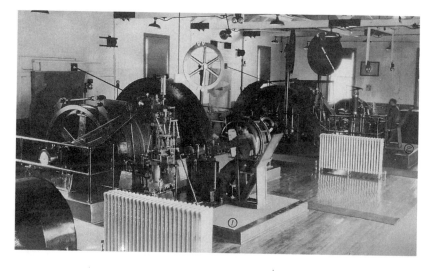

hanging walls gave way without warning, water poured into the mine, chambers receiving the ore did not always fill well. Sometimes they filled too well. There were no safeguards, there were deaths; the method was abandoned. Other ways were tried – room-and-pillar with saddle-back stulls, square sets using underhand stoping methods – the results were worse.[32]

In 1903, mines began to abandon all square-set methods in favor of top slicing, a method brought to the Mesabi from the iron mines of Lancashire, England. Mining began at the top of a bed of ore where a slice of ore was removed and dropped through chutes to waiting mine cars set on a track on the mine's main level beneath the ore body. From there trammers pushed the cars to the shaft located at the edge of the ore body, where it was dumped into a skip and raised to the surface. The ore was mined in slices beginning at the top and continuing downward through the ore body. Each level was shored with timbers, which were usually blasted out after the slice was removed.[33]

By 1912, variations of this method were in use in a majority of Mesabi underground mines. An exception might have been the Adams Mine near Eveleth, where the old

square-set system remained in places until 1930. Slicing and caving undoubtedly eliminated many of the old dangers, mainly because a great amount of the work was done on top of the ore body and often above ground.[34] The last of these underground mines, the Godfrey near Chisholm, closed in 1961.[35]

Mill Mines

Some mines, such as the Forest near Hibbing, the Duluth near Biwabik and the Auburn and Higgins near Virginia, were mill mines. In a mill mine, surface material covering the ore body was stripped away by steam shovels in the same way that open pits were stripped. A shaft was sunk at the edge of the ore body as in an underground mine

By 1928, mines were adopting electrical power sources, as shown by this electrically powered skip and cage hoist at the Leonidas underground mine. **Bottom:** In earlier days, trammers provided the power to move wooden hand-dump cars like this one at an Oliver Iron Mining Company underground mine. Note the carbide lamp pinned on the hat of one of the trammers. Carbide lamps began to be seen in Mesabi underground mines after 1912. OLIVER IRON MINING COMPANY COLLECTION, IRON RANGE RESEARCH CENTER

Mill mining involved both underground and open pit techniques. The southwest corner of the Leonidas Mine shows funnel-like craters at the mill openings. OLIVER IRON MINING COMPANY COLLECTION, NORTHEAST MINNESOTA HISTORICAL CENTER

and a drift driven from the shaft into the ore body about 60 feet below the top.

From the drift, raises were made through the deposit to the surface and the ore was milled down through the openings into chutes, then loaded into cars waiting in the drift below. Heavy steel chute gates operated by compressed air regulated the flow of ore through the chutes. Trains of loaded cars pulled by mules or electric engines brought the ore to the mine shaft where it loaded into a skip and raised to the surface.[36]

In many cases steam shovels were used to load ore into a mill, but sometimes the ore was so soft it could be milled by gangs of laborers using only picks. However, most deposits were so densely packed that the ore had to be blasted loose before it could be moved into the mill.

As mining proceeded, the mill grew larger and took on a crater-like appearance. Sometimes called "glory holes" by miners, these craters often became dangerous places in which to work. Miners working on their steep sides were supplied with ropes for safety, but many refused to use them and accidents were frequent. Men fell into the chute and were crushed by the ore. There were fatalities – many of them. In most mines of this type the mill eventually became too large to be mined safely and the method had to be abandoned.[37]

Mill mining occurred most often as an initial operation in the opening of an ore deposit or when it was no longer practical to continue a strictly open pit operation. "In 1904 about 7 percent of the output on the Mesabi was won by milling."[38]

Although a comparatively small amount of Mesabi ore was removed by milling, the system was used on and off in range mines until the early 1940s.

In some cases, a mine was opened as an underground working and later converted into a mill mine – usually when it was determined that this would be the cheapest way to get the most ore out of the ground. However, in most situations, as milling proceeded, it became increasingly expensive and the mine either closed or was worked by another method. Some Mesabi iron mines were worked by all three methods: underground, milling and open pit. There were some mines in which all three methods were in use at the same time.[39]

A New Wave of Mining Towns

For a company to profit from any of the three systems, many mines had to be opened and a large number of workers hired. This resulted in a new wave of mining towns. At least 60 new locations and nine incorporated villages came into being during the eight-year period from 1893 to 1905. Hibbing became a functioning village in 1893, followed by Eveleth in 1894, Sparta in 1896, Chisholm, Buhl and Kinney in 1901, Nashwauk and Aurora in 1903, Keewatin in 1905 and Gilbert in 1908.

Clustered around the villages were the locations, large numbers of them – Leonidas, Mississippi, Hawkins, Stevenson, Webb, Mahoning, Pillsbury, Susquehanna, Jordan,

Canton, Adriatic, Belgrade, Syracuse, Adams, Cincinnati, Lone Jack, Gilbert – almost every new mine spawned a location. The Mesabi became a place of little towns with muddy streets and miles and miles of boardwalk.

The new villages were, in every respect, boom towns. After a slow start, it took Eveleth five years to reach a population of 6,000. There were 10-times as many people living in Aurora in 1910 as there were in 1903. Buhl was little more than a logging camp in 1901, but 10 years later it was a bustling mining town with prosperous hotels, places of business, schools and public buildings. It even had a municipal heating plant. Two and a half miles of pipeline delivered steam heat to every home in Buhl. Nowhere in Minnesota have so many substantial towns come into being in such a short time.

Town populations fluctuated. There was a time in 1900 when it seemed that Eveleth was destined to be the largest town on the Mesabi – population just under 3,000. Virginia had suffered a disastrous fire and Eveleth was already bigger than Hibbing. Following close behind were the booming towns of Biwabik and Sparta. In 1900, Sparta was the fifth largest town on the range. Five years later, Eveleth had fallen behind Hibbing and Virginia, Sparta was larger than Biwabik and Chisholm was on its way to becoming the third largest town on the range – population just more than 4,000.[40]

Early town populations consisted mostly of men. Gambling, heavy drinking, prostitution and fighting were more or less the order of the day. During Mesaba Village's mining boom, the town is said to have been so wild that women refused to work in the town's boardinghouses – some turned down wage offers of as much as $5 a day.[41]

Saloon licenses often paid the expenses of village governments. In 1912, other than Mountain Iron, the only town on the Mesabi that did not have an abnormally large number of saloons was Coleraine – Oliver Iron Mining's "model community." There were two saloons in Coleraine. Nearby Bovey had 25; Eveleth, 40; Chisholm, 48; Virginia, 52; Hibbing, 60. Even McKinley, with a population of less than 300, had 10 licensed saloons, from which the village drew a yearly income of $5,000, "leaving but $2,000 to be raised by general taxation."

A 1909 estimate suggests that well more than 350 licensed saloons were in operation

In early iron range towns, saloon licenses often paid for most of the expenses of village governments. IRON RANGE RESEARCH CENTER

on the Vermilion and Mesabi ranges. The number of unlicensed saloons (blind pigs) may have been even higher.[42]

There were more sudden deaths per capita on the Mesabi than in other parts of the state, but mine accidents were not the major cause. In 1904, the *Virginia Enterprise* listed 160 unexpected deaths on the Mesabi during the previous year. Thirty-five were caused by mine accidents; nine by gunshot wounds; 22 were alcohol related and the rest lumped together with the suicides, of which there were many. In the vicinity of Virginia, eight deaths were caused by railroad accidents, 11 occurred in the mines, one from gunshot wounds, one from opium poisoning, two were alcohol related, one death occurred from exposure to the cold and six were suicides.[43]

The suicide rate was higher in Mesabi towns than in most other places.[44] The thing about Mesabi suicides is that a significant number seem to have taken place in the back rooms of bars. It is easy to suspect ineffectiveness of law enforcement as a reason for some of these so-called "suicides." Happenings within Mesabi Range saloons were seldom reported because most were off limits to local law enforcement. After all, they were often a chief source of revenue for the town.

In 1905, after an unusual number of complaints of "noise and rowdiness," Bovey saloon keepers did receive a summons from the village council, but there were no investigations, finings or closings. Instead, the council accepted a promise to "run things in a better and quieter way."[45]

In some Mesabi communities, bartenders were looked at as the only trustworthy source of law and order in town. During the first decade of mining, saloons performed a vital social function. People arrived as strangers, there were few opportunities to socialize, entertainments were scant, churches were few, family life was almost nonexistent and bars were the town's gathering places – places to make new friends, places to hear the latest news and, in some cases, saloons were looked at as "home away from home" – especially by single miners, many fresh from the "old country."

According to a description written in 1912: "The majority of the saloons are well-fitted-up and it is not unusual to find card rooms, dancing halls and lodging quarters in connection with the establishments. Lodging rooms in connection with saloons are most often found among the Finns. The Montenegrin and South Italian saloons are nearly all low class places and many of those of the Slovenians are little better. Those run by Americans are elaborately fixed up and cater to the better classes. When out of work, or on the 'off shifts,' the loafing places of the miners are the saloons conducted by members of their respective races."[46]

After 1900, the Mesabi was swarming with immigrants. There were Finns, Swedes, Norwegians, Slovenians, Italians, Poles, Croatians, Montenegrins, Serbs, Bohemians, French, Irish, Cornish, Dutch, Syrians, Belgians, Greeks, Bulgarians, Hungarians, Russians, Magyars, Danes and Dalmatians – even a few Arabs and Chinese. However, according to a tally based on 1905 census figures, "populations born in Finland, Austria, Sweden, Canada, Italy and Norway accounted for 88.5 percent of the total foreign-born population in the 12 towns and villages" of the Mesabi.[47]

In 1907, the U.S. Department of Commerce and Labor reported that, out of 12,018 men employed by the Oliver Iron Mining Company, only 1,879 were born in the United States. The rest – 84.4 percent of the work force – were foreign born, almost half having arrived in the United States within the previous two years. Only 48.6 percent of Oliver's foreign-born employees could speak English.[48]

By 1905, a unique kind of social structure prevailed. Recent arrivals from foreign countries often made their homes in the locations close by the mines that employed them and where inexpensive housing could be found. A significant number of earlier arrivals – usually those who could speak English – left the locations and moved into the incorporated towns and villages, where they went into business, often catering to the needs of their recently arrived countrymen. Italian bakeries, Finnish restaurants, Slovenian meat markets, Croatian saloons, Swedish hotels, Irish pubs and Serbian boardinghouses were common sights in Mesabi towns. Foreign language newspapers were read in the streets and

Sixteen-year-old Charles Latvala (holding pick) and his "brother" pose for a photograph at the Genoa underground mine in 1898. Note the soft hats, water resistant gear, rubber boots and candles. IRON RANGE HISTORICAL SOCIETY COLLECTION, IRON RANGE RESEARCH CENTER

restaurant menus were often printed in two or three different languages.

There is little evidence of prejudice occurring among foreign-speaking peoples during the first years of town development. According to one pioneer resident, "At first, there was no difference between the nationalities. All were interested in making a living and building up the community. A man was accepted for his contribution to the community, not his nationality."[49]

It is difficult to believe that this attitude lasted very long. By 1900, a pattern of

supplanting older miners by immigrant unskilled labor was well established in most Lake Superior mines and continued into the second decade of the 20th century. Although this same pattern of replacement existed in other mining districts, the easy-to-mine Mesabi ores made it possible for companies to hire an unusually large proportion of unskilled labor. Cornish and Scandinavian miners from the Vermilion and Michigan ranges were moved to the Mesabi as captains and foremen, while experienced Finnish, Austrian and Italian miners became

159

trammers, trackmen, pitmen, contract miners and laborers and, because these positions required few special skills, found themselves subject to possible replacement. Newly arrived Croatians, Bulgarians, Montenegrins, Slovaks and Serbians – along with more Italians, Austrians and Finns – were often seen by employed workers as threats to their jobs. Language barriers, church affiliation and cultural differences tended to combine with growing job insecurity to breed suspicion and mistrust. By 1930, it seemed that "every nationality was conscious of its superiority."[50]

Range style "get the mining company to pay" politics first seen in Ely spread swiftly into Mesabi towns after 1900. The hiring of large numbers of unskilled workers resulted in sharp increases in population and caused heavy strains on municipal budgets. New city halls, jails, police stations and firehalls were often needed. The police force had to be expanded, new and improved firefighting gear had to be purchased, additions developed, streets added, water and light plants improved, sidewalks constructed, sewage disposal plants developed and town limits expanded.

Town officials contended that mining companies, although never part of the towns, were responsible for problems caused by the sudden rise in population and should therefore take responsibility for needed improvements. If so, the question was who should determine what improvements were necessary? There were conflicting points of view.

Ever since the Legislature of 1897 repealed the 1881 production tax of one cent a ton, mining companies had been subject to taxation on an ad valorem basis, the same as any other property owner in the state. The problem with taxing ore properties as real estate was that, unlike most property in the state, they were located beneath the surface, making it difficult, if not impossible, to determine their worth. Companies themselves often did not know how much ore they were holding. Moreover, from a mining point of view, the value of the iron ore in the ground was subject to sharp fluctuations in the iron and steel market, adding an element of risk to a very expensive undertaking. It was not always profitable to

mine and there were times when it was necessary for a mining firm to let the ore deposit lie dormant. Therefore, any tax levied against ore in the ground that had to be paid year after year until the ore was finally removed would undoubtedly be objectionable to both mine and fee owners.

However the Minnesota ad valorem tax, based on 50 percent of an estimated value of the ore and assessed yearly until the ore was gone, became a problem for mine owners when the region's taxing districts – counties, schools, villages and cities – began levying their mill rates against the ore deposits. In fact, prior to 1909 the state Legislature often heard complaints that mining companies were not taxed as heavily as their peculiar nature warranted and demands were frequently heard for heavier imposition.

State representatives John Saari of Eveleth and Joseph Austin of Chisholm took the problems of town needs and iron ore taxation to St. Paul, and in 1907, after studying several proposals, a joint committee of both houses of the Legislature recommended that the best method of taxation would be a well administered property tax on an ad valorem basis. The recommendation was not entirely the result of iron range politics. There was at the time a strong feeling among many Minnesotans that the ore in the ground, being a natural deposit, belonged to the state as a whole and private companies had no right to remove it without leaving something behind for future generations.[51]

In 1909, municipalities were given the right to expand their limits to include mine properties and thus subject them to taxation. This launched a bitter legal and political battle over taxation that lasted for years. While company attorneys sought ways to limit steadily increasing taxes, ambitious politicians, mayors and village councils saw no end to the public improvements that should be made in their towns. Within a few years, city halls and courthouses that looked like palaces stood next to the humble homes of mine workers, while schools of the region gained nationwide attention for swimming pools, gymnasiums, auditoriums, bowling alleys, model kitchens and apartments. Schools in the nation's largest cities didn't have facilities like these.[52]

By 1910, the four most rapidly growing towns on the Mesabi were Hibbing, Eveleth, Chisholm and Gilbert. Hibbing had already surpassed Virginia in size and was on its way to becoming the "Iron Ore Capital of the World."

Hibbing Emerges as the Iron Ore Capital of the World

In 1893, Frank Hibbing told his partner, Alexander Trimble, "Hibbing will be the main town of the Mesabi Range." He was right. Hibbing, Trimble and their associates in the Lake Superior Iron Company were on their way to becoming millionaires when they platted the townsite of Hibbing. They were holding mining rights to the Burt, Sellers, Hull, Rust and Mahoning timber properties – properties containing the richest and easiest to mine ores in all of Iron County. The two men had a pretty good idea of what they had when they located Hibbing.

The problem was that other people knew it too, so when Hibbing and Trimble tried to lay out their townsite, they discovered that they couldn't buy the land they needed. They had to be content with an 80-acre leasehold

right in the middle of a sea of exploration camps, shacks, tents and test pits.

"Hibbing (in 1893) was a mere handful of buildings on the townsite proper, but there were all kinds of shacks … in all directions. They were occupied for the most part by men who did not know where the next meal was coming from."[53]

In fact, the occupiers of the shacks were seasoned prospectors – men who knew they were sitting on good iron ore, but didn't know what to do about it. It was 1893 and there were still many who thought that the Mesabi was a place where a poor man could get rich. Hibbing and his partners might have followed these poor men into oblivion, had they not, in April 1893, been talked into selling a half-interest in the potential profits from their mines to the Wetmore-Merritt syndicate.

The agreement paid Hibbing and his partners $100,000 in cash and $150,000 in deferred payments for the right to mine Lake Superior Iron Company land. The right passed into the hands of John Rockefeller when he took over the Merritt holdings and the Oliver mined it. The owners of the Lake Superior Iron Company still held their half-

In 1893, Hibbing consisted of a number of rude buildings to house the men of exploratory parties seeking iron ore deposits. HIBBING HISTORICAL SOCIETY COLLECTION, IRON RANGE RESEARCH CENTER

THIRD AVE NORTH HIBBING MINN

By 1920, Hibbing had grown into the "iron ore capital of the world," with more three- and four-story buildings than Chisholm and Virginia combined. Most were constructed of wood. HIBBING HISTORICAL SOCIETY COLLECTION, IRON RANGE RESEARCH CENTER

interest and became millionaires. Hibbing, however, didn't live long enough to enjoy his wealth. He died in Duluth on July 30, 1897, at the age of 40 from an attack of appendicitis.[54]

The village incorporated on August 15, 1893. It was the eighth town on the Mesabi to begin functioning. The first village president was J.F. Twitchell, a railroad construction timekeeper. The remainder of village officers was drawn from a body of prospectors and speculators who had drifted into the area following Hibbing and Trimble's discovery. Although Hibbing himself built and ran the town's first hotel and bank and even paid for streets and water, the place didn't prosper. There were three hotels and a restaurant in town during the winter of 1893-94, but by spring their doors were closed. There were also eight saloons. Their doors never closed.[55]

Only after a railroad was connected to the town in the fall of 1894 did things begin to improve. A thousand people were in town in the spring of 1895 when the Burt-Pool Mine began shipping ore. After that Hibbing grew rapidly. Its population jumped to 6,000 in a year. Mines opened everywhere: the Burt-Pool, Sellers and Mahoning in 1895,

the Hull-Rust and Penobscott in 1896 and the Pillsbury in 1898. Along with these, the Albany, Cyprus, Agnew, Laura, Longyear, Morris, Stevenson, Susquehanna, Utica and Webb were all shipping ore by 1906.[56]

In that year, Hibbing was described as "a town of 15,000 living in a space for 7,000." The town's population might have been closer to 12,000, but it was scarcely 100-acres in size.[57] Biwabik was larger. So was Mountain Iron. Hibbing, with its crowded conditions, became the most closely built town north of Duluth. The only direction it could go was up. The town ended up with more three- and four-story buildings than Virginia and Chisholm combined. It also had fewer brick and concrete structures than either town. Almost every building in Hibbing was constructed of wood, except, of course, the city hall. It was a magnificent structure – three stories of polished stone and brick – paid for, entirely, by the mining companies.[58]

The main employer was, of course, "the Oliver." The company constructed for its employees one of the more lavish buildings in the village, the Oliver Club. Its interior was paneled in oak and included a sitting room, reading room, card rooms, billiard tables, bowling alley, gymnasium and showers.[59]

Hibbing businessmen prospered. The Central Hotel, Hotel Hibbing, Mike's Cafe, Carlson's Mercantile and 50 other businesses were virtual "gold mines" during the years 1905-1918. But unlike Virginia, Hibbing remained strictly a mining town. Every aspect of life was dominated by the mines. In fact, the town was surrounded by mines. Its buildings perched precariously at the edge of encroaching mine pits – the Sellers from the north and east, the Rust from the west – and ore lay beneath Hibbing's streets.[60]

In 1918, the Oliver began buying surface rights from lot owners. The company spent something like $2.5 million for eight city blocks, including buildings. The result was wholesale removal of the town to make way for mining. During the years from 1918-1921, 185 dwellings, 12 frame buildings and eight brick buildings were moved to the company's "Central Addition," the site of present day Hibbing.[61]

Hibbing wasn't the only Mesabi town to be moved. Eveleth underwent a similar relocation.

Eveleth

When the year 1892 came to an end, there were seven incorporated villages on the Mesabi. On July 25, 1893, Eveleth might have become the eighth, just earlier than Hibbing.

At least there was a vote for incorporation on that date and the result must have been positive because the St. Louis County Board of Commissioners gave notice to Eveleth

voters that they could elect village officers on August 11, 1893.

No such election occurred. A year later, the commissioners again ordered a vote and this time, on October 18, 1894, Eveleth's first village officers were elected. As an incorporated village, Eveleth can be said to be 21 days older than Hibbing, but it wasn't a functioning village until the fall of 1894.[62]

David Adams located the townsite and, along with Peter Kimberly, John Jones and lumberman Fred Robinson, had it platted and cleared in early 1893. It was four miles south of where the good ore was thought to lie and this might have puzzled some people. But Adams knew what he was doing.

Just east of Virginia, the iron formation bends sharply and unexpectedly to the south. The hills directly between Virginia and Biwabik contain no ore. But to the south, at what was later called "the hook," Adams found hematite. The Adams, Troy, Fayal and Spruce mines resulted and, by 1903, all were producing quality ore.[63]

Eveleth had three big problems. The first was that no one knew what to name the place. Some thought it should be called "Iron Point." Others thought it should be "Iron City." David Adams wanted to name the town "Robinson," after the fee owner of the Adams Mine, but the man objected.[64]

"I never knew why, but I always surmised he (Robinson) thought the town would never amount to much and didn't

Said to be the first building in Eveleth, the mine office of David T. Adams shows a certain rough charm, as well as the size of timber growing in the area at that time. IRON RANGE RESEARCH CENTER

Beginning to take shape in 1895, Eveleth was moved in 1896 to make way for the Adams and Spruce mines to reach ore located under the original townsite. OKLOBZIJA COLLECTION, IRON RANGE RESEARCH CENTER

want his name attached to it. I then asked the name of the cruiser who estimated the timber on the land when Robinson bought it. They told me it was Erwin Eveleth…. The more I thought the name Eveleth over, the more I liked it…. It seemed to be an easy name for the Scandinavian element to pronounce."[65]

The second problem was that no one really wanted to move there. Virginia was only a few miles away and booming. It was hard to convince anyone that they should locate on a lonely windy hillside four miles away. Promoted heavily in the *The Mesaba Pioneer* in summer of 1893 as "the new townsite of the Mesaba [sic[Range surrounded by nine huge iron mines," Eveleth failed to draw much attention from investors and lot buyers. However, in late 1893, "a small start was made to establish the town…. Hank Hookwith came in to open a saloon. Archie McComb had a hotel … and Jerry Sullivan … a boardinghouse…." The population was so small that, when they tried to elect town officers, no one showed up to vote.[66]

When summer came in 1894, there were still only five buildings on the site, one of them a mine office and another a doctor's office. Doctor C.W. More had arrived from Ely in the spring of that year to treat a breakout of typhoid in one of the exploration camps. A year later, he established one of the Mesabi's first hospitals – a frame building with two beds.

Pioneer mining man John Hearding, who came to Eveleth in November 1894, recalled a "primeval forest" covering what was later the Adams Mine. According to Hearding, "On the south side of Section 31 there was a considerable clearing of the timber and about four buildings had been erected on the old townsite of Eveleth. There was a small sawmill operated by a man named Toll."[67]

According to pioneer resident Neil McInnis, "The whole of the manpower of Eveleth, namely, Hank Hookwith, Archie McComb and Jerry Sullivan, were too busy digging for their bread … to have much inclination to pursue matters of town planning and corporate government."[68]

A second try at an election that October was more successful. Ninety-one votes were cast and Marvin Van Buskirk was elected village president. A year later, Eveleth had a population of 764. The new arrivals were immigrants, mostly Finns.[69]

164

In 1896, Eveleth encountered its third problem. There was ore under the town. A new site was needed. It was found only a quarter-mile away. People were reluctant to move their buildings. Developers of the new townsite had to give businessmen free lots to get them to relocate. It took almost four years to get all of Eveleth's 100 buildings over to the new site.[70]

Heavy mining followed. Eveleth boomed and, for a few brief years, was a wild and dangerous place. Its streets swarmed with people from all parts of the world, mostly young single men looking for work and adventure. With them came transients, gamblers, forgers, bullies, thieves, dance hall operators, pimps and "back room beauties" from the red light districts of Chicago, Hurley, Superior and St. Paul. There were fraud and corruption, there were assaults and muggings – robberies went unpunished. Things got so bad in 1905 that the Civic League, a sort of vigilante committee, had to be organized to deal with some of the lawlessness.

"Hill's Place, otherwise the local sporting place, is no more and there is rejoicing by some and regrets by others. It ceased to exist with the last day of March in accordance with orders given by Mayor Smith at the behest of citizens and the Civic League."[71]

By 1915, Eveleth had re-incorporated as a city. Although 40-some saloons still lined its streets, much of the turbulence that plagued earlier years was gone. Its streets were paved and a population of 7,032 made it the third largest town on the Mesabi. Within the city limits were six churches, a high school, three grade schools, five hotels, two banks, two newspapers and a business district equal to any on the range. The city was served by two railroads and plans were in the making for electric street car service.[72]

The city also had two well-equipped hospitals, the Fabiola and the More, offering prepaid clinic services to area mines.

The More Hospital became a model for other hospitals across the range. It had a capacity for 40 patients, a "thoroughly equipped operating room," an X-ray machine which was in constant use and "a device … by which X-ray photographs may be taken in the wards on the floor above the operating room," according to a *Skillings Mining Journal* article.

The hospital, a frame building constructed with "extraordinary precautions against fire," was particularly equipped to meet emergencies arising in the mines. Its director, Doctor More, held the title of "mine physician" and clinic services were prepaid with regular deductions from the

Shortly after the original townsite was moved, Eveleth's Grant Avenue shows that the town was prosperous and well developed by the early 1900s.
EVELETH CENTENNIAL COLLECTION, IRON RANGE RESEARCH CENTER

Unlike some other mining locations, Monroe Location near Chisholm had a look of permanence and prosperity in 1909. IRON RANGE RESEARCH CENTER

wages of those employed by participating mining companies. In 1909, single men and men with families paid the same fee of $1 a month, which entitled them "to hospital service not only in the case of accidents, but of sickness, contagious diseases excepted." The plan also included medical attention for families of employees, but always in their homes, "except in cases of venereal diseases and confinement." For these, there was a charge, "though in confinement cases the charge is nominal."[73]

Beginning in 1908, the More Hospital developed "first responder" teams at every mine served by the hospital. Emergency stations equipped with splints, bandages, stretchers and other medical supplies were established close to work areas and superintendents, captains, foremen and "the more intelligent workmen" were trained to provide injured employees with immediate medical attention.[74]

Like Hibbing, Eveleth remained strictly a mining town. To its mines came the early elite of mining: John Hearding to the Adams, Richard Trezona and George Dormer to the Fayle, Tom Davey and Dick Mitchell to the Spruce. The mines were some of the most productive on the range and the homes of Eveleth's captains were large and elaborate. Mining company influence over the town was far-reaching but, like Ely, it was met with vibrant progressive politics that arose among the townspeople,

sent energetic politicians to high places of government and provided numerous public improvements for the city – most at mining company expense.

Chisholm Rises, Burns and Rises Again

When Chisholm incorporated as a village on July 23, 1901, there were already 250 people living on the site. Four years later, the town's population approached 4,000. Most of the new arrivals were immigrant miners and their families. During Chisholm's first years, there were jobs in the mines for anyone willing to work. The Chisholm, Clark, Pierce, Leonard, Monroe and Shenango were all desperately in need of mine workers.

"Mining officials are complaining of the lack of miners and other laborers and there are fears that production may be cut down for that reason. Several hundred could get steady work around here and at good wages. Miners are making as high as $4 a day and common laborers are receiving about $2 a day."[75]

The ore field around Chisholm was a bonanza. Something like 48 ore producing properties were eventually identified. Thirty-two of them were developed and operated by United States Steel's Oliver Iron Mining Company. Locations blossomed everywhere.[76]

If there was ever a good place to profit from a townsite, it was Chisholm. Quick to take advantage of the fact was the Chisholm

Improvement Company, consisting of Hibbing attorney William Power, Canadian-born mining man and banker Archibald Chisholm, Mountain Iron townsite developer John Costin and Captain J.H. Pearce. In early 1901, they purchased the land on which stood the Clark and Chisholm locations and platted "a new and better townsite." Lots sold fast.[77]

Chisholm became the business center for eight nearby mining locations. Each location was filled to capacity with families of immigrant mine workers, mostly Finns and Austrians. Out of Chisholm's total population of 4,231 in 1905, 2,705, or 63.9 percent were born outside of the United States – the highest percentage of foreign-born on the range.[78] Chisholm was described in 1907 as "beautifully located on a charming body of water known as Longyear Lake," its city hall was said to be "the finest and largest on the range" and its business section "compactly built for a distance of five blocks with businessmen enjoying a fair share of the general prosperity."[79]

In 1908, Chisholm burned.

The fire struck at 4:30 p.m. on Saturday, September 5. The weather had been dry for a month and there had been some brush fires. They were put out. There was a wind. Suddenly the grandstand at the ball park caught fire. Within three hours the entire business section was wiped out. The fire spread so quickly that all people could do was run for their lives.

"The buildings fell before it like corn before the sickle. So great was the heat that the brick buildings crumbled and fell, lasting but little longer than the wooden ones."

More than 4,000 people were driven from their homes. Somehow, no lives were lost.[80]

But there were lootings. Luckily, a state militia was stationed in nearby Hibbing. Martial law was declared and the militia occupied what was left of the town. By midnight, 100 suspected looters had been arrested and thrown into a makeshift jail located at the Monroe Location. Most were recently arrived Montenegrins who couldn't speak a word of English, and they were there probably more as spectators than looters. But in those days, all foreigners were more or less suspect. Two were shot.[81]

Like Virginia, Chisholm arose from its ashes as a city of stone, brick and concrete. Ten days after the fire, the *Chisholm Herald* was able to report "50 buildings erected or in the process of erection."[82] On the new buildings were carved the names of some of Balkan Township's immigrant pioneers, people who endured the fire. Once again Chisholm's streets were lined with fine restaurants, hotels and other places of business.

Sparta and Gilbert

There was another fast growing town on the Mesabi. It was called Sparta and in 1900 its population was already nearly equal to that of Biwabik, then considered one of the

Very little was standing in Chisholm after the fire of 1908, but the town would soon be rebuilt of non-flammable stone, brick and concrete to avoid any similar catastrophe in the future.
CONSTANZI COLLECTION, IRON RANGE RESEARCH CENTER

GENOA LOC
SPARTA. MINN.

As new mines opened across the Mesabi Iron Range, new locations like the Genoa Location near Gilbert (in about 1910) also arose. Some would go on to become villages, others declined or died when the nearby mine closed. VOSS COLLECTION, IRON RANGE RESEARCH CENTER

Mesabi's more urban centers. The village came about as a direct result of the opening of the Genoa Mine in 1896. Operating around the clock with its many mills and great double shaft, the mine became a major producer and employer.

George Hartley of Duluth saw immediate opportunity in all this and had 61.7 acres near the shore of Ely Lake platted as the business center of Sparta. Lots sold quickly, a petition for incorporation was circulated and, on September 26, 1896, Sparta became the 10th village to be formed on the Mesabi.

It seemed, too, for a time, that Sparta would become one of the more important mining villages. The opening of the Sparta Mine in 1897, the Malta Mine in 1898, the Pettit Mine in 1902 and expansions at the Genoa brought in hundreds of miners and spawned new locations, all within walking distance of the town. In 1905, almost 1,000 people were living within the village limits and another 1,000 were not far away. Along Sparta's main street could be found a department store, butcher shop, confectionery, blacksmith shop, barbershop, livery and several boardinghouses and saloons. The town had a hotel, city hall, public steam bath, water and electric light plant, two churches and a school. There were few in that year who would have doubted its permanency.[83]

But iron ore, which had given Sparta life, also caused its death. In 1907, Oliver drills tapped into hematite directly below Sparta's streets and to company officials this meant only one thing – the town would have to go. Negotiations to purchase the property of townsite residents began immediately and prompted a movement to relocate the town to one of the nearby mining locations.

The effort to move the town was not without conflict. There were disagreements over the price of properties, there was indecision, there were rumors. Some thought the town should be moved to the outskirts of Eveleth, others thought it might be better to relocate it closer to the newly opened Gilbert Mine, where a location was developing – and there were those who couldn't see any reason to move at all.

In 1908, the *Biwabik Times* reported, "The businessmen and citizens of Sparta are not worrying over the matter of the town moving as much as are others who really have no interest in the matter. A majority of the population have come to the conclusion that the situation will solve itself. The only complaint made is to the effect that no definite statement has been made as to the fate of the town....

"As heretofore stated, the village officers are proceeding on the theory that certain improvements must be made.... Something must be done, as sidewalks are gone and the light and water plant is inadequate."[84]

Meanwhile, stripping operations at the Gilbert Mine and discovery of marketable ore in several places nearby convinced four Eveleth men – W.J. Smith, J.A. Robb, C.E. Baily and D.W. Freeman – that a mining boom of major proportions was about to take place. They formed the Gilbert Townsite Company, platted 80 acres of "mainly cut-over land" next to the growing Gilbert location and in August 1907 offered lots to Sparta businessmen.

The location, mine and townsite were named after one of the mine's fee owners, Giles Gilbert. The response was enthusiastic enough for the developers to construct "Baily's Block," an all-concrete building with a "300-foot frontage" on a still-to-be developed "Broadway Street."[85]

On May 29, 1908, the *Biwabik Times* reported that the entire Village of Sparta would be moved to the Gilbert site. Many thought the village would eventually add the location to its new boundaries and re-incorporate as "the new village of Sparta," but it didn't happen. It was, instead, "the new village of Gilbert" that swallowed up Sparta.

In 1908, the exodus began. Sparta High School "was split into two parts" and shipped by sled in winter to Genoa Location, where it became a school for first through eighth grades. "All during 1909 up until 1910, resident and business buildings of Sparta were moved to the new town." Sparta's last town meeting took place on February 20, 1911. The three people in attendance voted unanimously to dissolve the village.[86]

Sparta businessmen were not the only ones to buy lots in the new townsite. Main street lots were rapidly picked up by entrepreneurs and businessmen from other places as well, and there were already enough people in town on March 4, 1908, for John Siegel and 29 other residents to sign a petition to incorporate 2,240 acres of land as the Village of Gilbert. The petition included hundreds of acres of unsettled territory, some of it active mine property.

No town on the range had ever attempted such an ambitious incorporation. Clarence Moore, general superintendent of the Pitt Iron Mining Company, owner of the

included La Belle Mine, objected strenuously and on March 6 filed a protest with county authorities. The politics were intense.[87]

The county board met that same day and immediately approved the petition, ordering a vote on incorporation to take place on April 7, 1908.

The vote favored incorporation and an election for village officers held on April 25, 1908, brought John Siegel, Joe Brula and C.H. Matthews to office as trustees, Frank Vertin as clerk and Captain D.T. Caine as village president. Captain Caine, an experienced mining man from Great Britain's Isle of Man, was then acting superintendent of Republic Iron and Steel Company's Pettit and Schley mines.

Once described as "an almost bottomless bog," the Pettit was already notorious for its lack of production and floodings when Republic took it over. The Schley Mine was still in its development stage. Both became producing properties under the direction of Captain Caine.[88]

Under Captain Caine's presidency, the village, too, began to function. Frank Vertin went to work as village clerk, John W. Carroll was appointed Gilbert's street commissioner, Charles Murphy became town marshal and a saloon license was granted to Victor Steh after he paid a fee of $500. The Gilbert Townsite Company donated two lots and sold another to the municipality for a village hall and jail. Several lots were also offered to religious organizations and an entire block was set aside for the building of a school.[89]

Meanwhile, the challenge of Gilbert's legality made by Captain Moore of Pitt Iron Company found its way through the courts. Company attorneys arguing that, while the La Belle Mine located a mile to the east of the platted townsite, was included in the village limits, the adjoining Gilbert location with 45 homes and a population of 500 was not.

The case ended up in Minnesota's Supreme Court, which ruled in October that the incorporation was "illegal and void." The village officers were ousted from office and, for a few months, Gilbert was little more than a collection of unregulated saloons, gaming houses, boardinghouses and general stores serving a few nearby mines and locations.[90]

GILBERT. LOG— GILBERT. MINN.

The effort to extend Gilbert city limits to include Gilbert Location (shown here in about 1910) and other nearby mining properties was opposed by mining companies, but passed on a 60 to 33 vote by citizens in 1914. Voss collection, Iron Range Research Center

On April 29, 1909, a second petition, this time asking for incorporation of only the platted townsite – 143.29 acres – was placed before the voters and approved without protest. A second election held on May 17, 1909, brought M.A. Masterson to office as village president, L.L. Sutton as clerk and Harry Silver, George Ratenbury and P.R. Cosgrove became village trustees.

The federal census of 1910 is said to have credited Gilbert with a population of 1,700. During the next 10 years, the town grew, not only in terms of population, but in size.[91] It was the last of the Mesabi hematite mining centers to be incorporated by developers independent of the mines. Like the other range municipalities, it was created to fill an economic niche for a growing population created by an expanding mining economy. The motivation for the town, like the merchants, jobbers and small businessmen who located there, was economic and in this sense it was no different from the mines. Although the interests of the town did not always parallel that of the mines, the interests of Gilbert's merchants and retailers did, at least at first. Prior to 1920, most of their customers' wages were drawn from the mines, and as mines opened and closed, local fortunes rose and fell.

Although the merchants, bankers, hotel operators and saloon keepers of Gilbert tended to be the town's investors and property owners, most of the voters living within the village limits in 1909 were less than 30 years old and owned little or no property at all. Some, single and thinking of moving on, felt little loyalty to either the

town or the mines, while others, married, raising families and often in debt, were far more interested in town improvements and good schools for their children – particularly if the town's elected leaders could find the money to pay for them. The situation was not much different in other range towns. When the Legislature in that year changed the law to give "legal voters," instead of property owners, the power to institute proceedings to extend village limits and thus increase the tax base, Gilbert became part of the change that swept across the range and ushered in a 30-year period of civic improvement, school construction and conflict.

The village's already strained relationship with nearby mining companies was exacerbated in 1914 when an expansion was proposed to include the adjoining Gilbert location and several other nearby mine properties – an annexation that would raise the tax base of the village from less than a million dollars to more than $5 million. A vote on the matter was ordered to take place "on February 21 at Malta School House." What some have called the "hottest political fight in Gilbert's history" followed.[92]

The involved companies responded with every means of persuasion possible to convince voters to oppose the expansion. According to an article published later in the *Gilbert Herald*, "Mining company police at times did all in their power to scare people away from the land in question and, on the day of the election, mining company police were in evidence everywhere. The fight was won by the village. The village revenue from taxes was greatly increased."[93] The annexation passed by a vote of 60 to 33 and three years later the village expanded again, adding more mining property to its tax base.

Civic improvements came quickly. The village soon had "the best equipped and most modern water plant, for its size, in the state of Minnesota, a new town hall was built, the fire department expanded, the town's streets paved and a beautiful high school was completed in 1911." Three rooms had been rented for the educational needs of Gilbert children in 1908, but 12 years later, "The schools had grown so fast that it was decided to erect a structure which is now known as the Technical Building. This houses a gymnasium each for boys and girls, a modern swimming pool, an automobile repair shop, mechanical drawing room, forge shop, print shop, agricultural laboratory, science laboratories and an atypical department for special courses." Ninety-six teachers were employed and 2,000 students were in attendance.[94]

Then came the closings. During the 1920s, one by one, Gilbert's mines began shutting down. Everyone knew there was plenty of ore in the ground, but still the companies left – it was said, "to work other deposits on which they had short-term leases" – and there came a time when Gilbert had no working mines at all. Labor left the community, and although the village was still to draw income from the tax on ore still in the ground, businessmen, particularly those operating saloons, restaurants, boardinghouses and hotels, were forced to seek out new ways to make a living.

Some left, while others turned their buildings into casinos or rented them out to demimonde organizations from Hurley, Superior, Chicago and elsewhere. Gilbert was an attractive place to establish a business of

this type. It was centrally located and could easily be reached from all parts of the range by inter-urban streetcar. It wasn't long before the village was once again a very busy place. This time in a much different way.[95]

Customers in Gilbert's business district during the 1920s and '30s were seldom Gilbert people. It was said at the time, "If Gilbert's resorts depended on local patronage they would have closed long ago." It was also said that, during the days of national prohibition, the village streets were well-patrolled by teams of fully uniformed policeman, but they never entered the town's "soft drink parlors." Everyone knew what was going on behind their doors.[96]

Although Gilbert of the 1920s was a far different place from the incorporated business center that resulted from the expansion of mining and the need to relocate the village of Sparta, it wasn't the only town on the Mesabi that had changed. An entire 90-mile expanse of lumber camps and rough mining towns, populated by a predominantly male work force, either single or separated from wives and families, had been converted into a belt of industrious towns and residential locations with most of the conveniences of any large city and populated by young families interested in bettering their lives and the lives of their children.

There are few places in the world that had been changed so profoundly in such a short time. In what 30 years before had been mostly a pristine wilderness, there were in 1925 almost 300 hematite mines, some already pronounced exhausted. By this time, mining had expanded into the Canisteo District of the Mesabi and the already settled Cuyuna Range was spawning even more camps, locations and mining towns. ■

CHAPTER 10

Giant Corporations, New Towns, New Districts

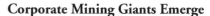

The great ironmaster Abram Stevens Hewitt once wrote, "Consumption of iron is the social barometer by which to estimate the relative height of civilization." If his statement is true, the progress of American civilization during the years following the discovery of Iron Country's ores was nothing less than extraordinary.

In 1865, when word of iron ore in Minnesota first hit the news, the main materials for construction were wood and stone. There weren't many people who even knew what steel was. Fifty years later the United States was producing steel at a rate of 30 million tons a year – more than any other nation in the world and by 1910 almost every manufactured item in this country was in some way dependent on steel – and steel was dependent on iron ore.

Mesabi hematite was in no small way responsible for the change – and for the birth of the nation's corporate giant, the United States Steel Corporation. The company was unbelievably successful. In 1903, two years after its birth, the great corporation had more money in its coffers than it knew what to do with. To rectify the situation, it created more steel plants.[1]

Each new steel plant needed a supply of iron ore and a frantic search for new deposits followed. United States Steel sent its experts into the woods west of Mesaba Station. They joined geologists, engineers and drill crews hired by other firms specializing in the mining of ore or the making of steel – firms like Inter-State Iron, Union Steel Company, Pickands Mather and Company, Cleveland Cliffs and M.A. Hanna.

The entire Mesabi Range was scoured for every new source of hematite that could be found. Deposits that were once thought to be too small, too lean or too difficult to work were marked as potential mines and there was talk of finding ways to make low grade ores marketable.

Corporate Mining Giants Emerge

Exploration soon proved there was still plenty of ore in the ground and, although much of it was lean, all sorts of companies were organized to mine it. Most were too small and thinly financed to mine at the rate now required by the steel industry. They fell by the wayside and were replaced by a few well-financed corporate mining giants. United States Steel's Oliver Iron Mining Company, already operating 65 mines in 1901, expanded the number to 128 in 1920. In that year, Pickands-Mather had 29 mines; Hanna, 33; Jones and Laughlin, 15; Republic Iron and Steel, 10; Cleveland-Cliffs, 9.[2]

Small independents did not disappear completely but, like the larger concerns, needed both capital backing and a guaranteed market for their ores. A few small operators like Perkins Mining, Bowe and Burke, Coates and Tweed, Tesora Mining and Liberty Mining managed to find buyers for their ore, but needed at least two or three mines just to stay in business.[3]

Stripping contracts for open pit mines brought in companies that specialized in the use of heavy equipment – firms like the well-known Butler Brothers Construction Company of Minneapolis. Butler Brothers had its headquarters in the burgeoning town of Nashwauk and concentrated most of its activities on the western Mesabi, where it was known not only for its stripping contracts but as an operator of mines.[4]

The Incorporated Villages of Buhl, Kinney and Spina

West of Mountain Iron, logging operations were still in full swing and as the new century dawned, Chisholm and Hibbing, with all their mines and locations, were little more than clearings in a still-vast forest of pine that cruised as much as "7 million feet a forty" in places. Thousands of

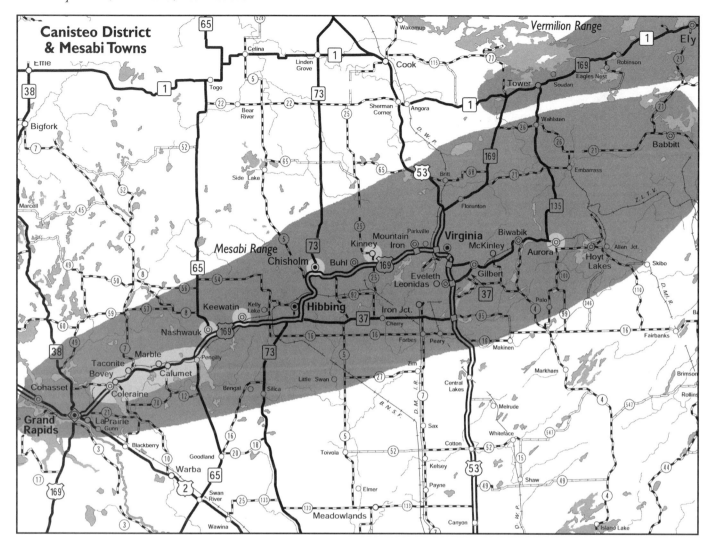

Canisteo District
& Mesabi Towns

woodsmen were at work in a string of
lumber camps that stretched from the Mt.
Iron Mine to the clear-cut countryside
beyond the old Nashwauk West operation in
Township 57-23. Lumberjacks were joined
by drill crews, logging camps doubled as
bases for iron exploration and iron strikes
became almost daily occurrences. In some
places the discoveries resulted in new mines
and the camps were turned into towns.[5]

The Buhl camp incorporated as a village
on February 15, 1901, just 10 days before
the United States Steel Corporation was
formed under the laws of New Jersey.
Already connected to the Great Northern
Railroad, Buhl had been an active supply
center for the lumber industry for almost
three years at the time it was platted. The
town was named after Pennsylvania
steelmaster Frank Buhl, president of the
Sharon Ore Company, owner of the town's
first iron mine.

Worked exclusively by the milling
process, the Sharon Mine shipped ore for

only three years, from 1901-1903, before it
passed to the Oliver Iron Mining Company
and was closed for stripping operations.
However, it was enough to give impetus to
the town and initiate a mining boom equal
to any in Iron Country.[6]

The Croxton and Grant mines began
shipping ore in 1902, the Kinney in 1903,
the Frantz and Yates in 1904 and the
Jennings in 1906. More mines followed. The
Shiras, Thorne, Culver, Wabigon,
Woodbridge, Whiteside, Cavour, Dean,
Itasca, Wanless and Margaret were all
brought to production by 1920. Mineral
lands explored by individual prospectors and
small independent mining companies
became the mines of corporate mining giants
or iron and steel combinations. Companies
large enough to have a market for their ore –
M.A. Hanna, International Harvester, Inter-
State Iron, Cleveland Cliffs Iron, Shenango
Furnace, Republic Iron and Steel and, of
course, "the Oliver" – were doing most of
the iron mining near Buhl after 1903.[7]

Map of Northeast Minnesota
showing Buhl, Kinney, Spina,
Aurora, Nashwauk, Keewatin
and towns, railroads and the
Canisteo District (in light
shade, lower left). MAP
PROVIDED COURTESY OF THE STATE
OF MINNESOTA

173

In November 1910, a vote taken at the saloon of Solomon Ketala produced the Village of Kinney. VOSS COLLECTION, IRON RANGE RESEARCH CENTER

It was a new kind of mining that these well-financed firms brought to Iron Country. Mines that might have been underground workings were laid open with sophisticated machines and relieved of their hematite with giant electric- and steam-powered shovels. Inter-State Iron installed an enormous grab-and-overhead carrying system to strip away the entire surface from the Grant Mine, while a five-man crew, using an electric shovel with a 10-ton dipper at the Wabigon Mine, set an all-time record for cheap mining when they scooped up a half-million tons of ore in two seasons. In these mechanized mines, not only was ore removed at an unprecedented rate, it was removed completely.[8]

The new kind of mining spawned old-style locations: Grant, Seville, Hartley, Sharon, Croxton, Whiteside, Kinney – small clusters of miners' dwellings and boardinghouses next to almost every mine. Two petitioned for incorporation and became legitimate villages. In 1913, Hartley location became the Village of Spina and, after a failed attempt at incorporation in 1909, a vote taken "at the saloon of Solomon Ketala" on November 1, 1910, produced the Village of Kinney.[9]

Industrial scale mining created problems in this crowded belt of mines, locations and villages, all located within a strip of land six miles long and little more than a mile or two wide. The ever-enlarging pits, with their company offices, machine shops, blacksmith shops, warehouses, draglines, anchor towers, wash plants, railways, trestles, loading pockets, piles of lean ore and expanding dumps of overburden, left little room for towns to grow. Not only that, there was barely enough space for mines to expand without trespassing on each other's property. The county board of commissioners aptly named the township "Great Scott."[10]

While Spina wrestled with the problem of village limits and a growing mine dump, the village of Kinney managed to expand its boundaries to include nearby mine property and thus increase its valuation. By this time, it was common practice for Iron Country towns to extend their corporate limits to include as many mines and undeveloped mineral lands as possible so that local taxes could be levied against them.

Mining companies, on the other hand, did everything they could to stop these expansions, and Kinney's second attempt six years later was successfully blocked in the courts by Cleveland Cliffs Iron Company. From then on, the two villages faced mining company opposition every time they attempted to make an improvement. Pressed in on all sides by expanding mines, Spina, unable to grow, gradually faded away, but Kinney survived. In 1920, 1,200 people were living within the town limits and its assessed valuation approached $2 million.[11]

According to a description of the time, "The Kinney Mine is a big hole in the ground, but the village of Kinney is rapidly reaching the high standard in town-planning

174

and administration that has brought other range places into high repute. Kinney has excellent schools, has an up-to-date lighting system with an adequate 'White Way,' is well-paved and has a good sewerage system. It has a well-patronized state bank, some good stores and some fine residences."[12]

It was Buhl that expanded and prospered the most. Although its population barely exceeded 1,000 in 1909, the village was already on its way to becoming an important Mesabi town. On the site were nearly 100 newly built homes, several boardinghouses, a city hall, firehall, two good hotels, several grocery stores, department store, confectionery, law office and eight saloons. By 1910, the town had an electric light plant, piped-in steam heat for all of its buildings and one of the best water systems on the range.[13]

During the next 10 years, the town grew significantly; village limits were expanded, assessed valuation rose to almost $10 million, tax money flowed in, streets were paved, a magnificent high school was built and both population and retail trade doubled.

In 1916, *The Buhl Advertiser* boasted proudly, "There is little doubt that Buhl is

coming into its own and the day for good business conditions for Buhl is here...."

Not all of the good business was due to mining. In June 1914, the U.S Supreme Court handed down a decision prohibiting the sale of liquor in territory created by the Chippewa Treaty of 1855 and the following November Cato Sells, commissioner of Indian Affairs, ordered the closing of all bars and saloons in the treaty zone. Sixty-one Minnesota communities were to be affected by the decision, including the Iron Country towns of Chisholm, Hibbing, Keewatin, Nashwauk, Taconite, Calumet, Marble, Bovey, Coleraine, Grand Rapids, Deerwood, Crosby, Ironton and Cuyuna.

Buhl, located just outside the treaty territory, was not. However, "the lid," as it

For a time Buhl, with its paved streets, waterworks, electric lights and modern buildings, was one of the leading range towns. Photograph taken in the early 1930s. Voss COLLECTION, IRON RANGE RESEARCH CENTER **Bottom:** Buhl was already a well developed town when this photo was taken in the early 1920s. IRON RANGE RESEARCH CENTER

On November 25, 1903, at the grocery store of Knuti and Ongala located in a small cluster of buildings just off the Mesabi Trail, 38 votes were cast to incorporate the Village of Aurora. **Bottom:** The Skibo Timber Company located on the St. Louis River east of Aurora provided much of the lumber for the growing town. Photograph taken in 1918. Nute collection, Northeast Minnesota Historical Center

was called, did not close immediately – nor did it close equally. Led by Hibbing Mayor Victor Power, village councils in Hibbing and Chisholm managed to delay the closings for a year, but on November 29, 1915, 71 liquor establishments in the two towns were shut down by federal order.[14]

The number of saloons in Buhl doubled, and for almost five years the town was packed nightly with hard-drinking crowds from Chisholm, Hibbing and other places in dry territory – some from as far away as Nashwauk. They came by rail, riding the Mesaba Railway's electric streetcars and by automobile and bus from Hibbing along the newly built Babcock Highway. There were so many people in the bars of Buhl that "bucket brigades" had to be formed to get the filled glasses of beer from bartenders to customers located "back out in the crowd."[15]

Because streetcars and buses were also used to transport liquor into dry territory for resale in the back rooms of newly established soda pop parlors, they were soon monitored by federal agents. By this time, an inordinate amount of traffic had worn down the road between Buhl and Chisholm. The town's

reputation for fun and frolicking was such that the west-bound trolley from Mountain Iron was packed with merrymakers from towns that were not even affected by the ban. Then, on January 1, 1920, the 18th Amendment and Prohibition put a sudden end to what was probably the most prosperous time in Buhl's history.[16]

Despite the sudden loss of income, it was said in 1921, "Buhl has much of which to be proud. Its municipal building, library, park and school system rank with the best to be found on the Mesabi Range…. Buhl, with its paved streets, water works, electric lights, beautiful schools and churches,

handsome public library and other modern structures, is one of the leading towns of the range group."[17]

The Incorporated Village of Aurora

On the eastern Mesabi, the search for new sources of ore also intensified, but here hematite deposits, although high in iron content, were smaller, deeper and more irregular. The result was a rash of small mines, most of them underground workings. The Meadow, Hudson, Miller, Mohawk, St. James, Perkins, Stephens, Adriatic and Fowler mines were all shipping ore by 1910.[18] They joined scores of other new mines all across the Mesabi and ore shipments from the range rose from 9 million to almost 30 million tons a year – and yet the steel mills called for more. The demand for Mesabi hematite seemed insatiable.

The activity spawned another new town, this time on the east Mesabi. On November 25, 1903, at the grocery store of "Knuti and Ongala" in a small cluster of buildings called Norlander located just off the old Mesabi Trail, 38 votes were cast to incorporate the village of Aurora. Already 174 people were living within the new village limits and the incorporators were sure that the town would quickly become a major trading center. Tom Flaherty, first to

sign the petition for incorporation, also became Aurora's first village president.[19]

However, it wasn't long before it became clear that the town was badly located. It was too close to the mine, the wagon road to it was at times almost impossible to navigate and the railroad was a mile away.

In 1905, Edmund Longyear platted a new site closer to the Duluth and Iron Range track and the entire town was picked up and moved to the new location. The town boomed. Within two years, Aurora's population exceeded 2,000 and the town boasted a bank, a newspaper, two churches, an excellent school and "one of the most modern business sections on the Mesabi."

By 1910, Aurora had all of the conveniences of any Minnesota city – and enough saloons to qualify it as a genuine iron range mining town.[20]

In 1905, Edmund Longyear platted a new site for Aurora closer to the D&IR track, and the entire town was picked up and moved to the new location. NUTE COLLECTION, NORTHEAST MINNESOTA HISTORICAL CENTER **Bottom:** The Hearding High School in Aurora, completed in 1911 and named after iron range pioneer, John H. Hearding. VOSS COLLECTION, IRON RANGE RESEARCH CENTER

THE HIGH SCHOOL AT AURORA MINN.

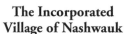

BUSINESS ST. AURORA. MINN.

After 1910, Aurora had the conveniences of most Minnesota cities – and enough saloons to qualify it as a genuine iron range mining town. AURORA CENTENNIAL COMMITTEE, IRON RANGE HISTORICAL SOCIETY

The Incorporated Village of Nashwauk

Continued exploration led to new sources of ore west of Hibbing – the Stevenson in 1901, Utica in 1902, Leetonia in 1903 – and the first mines in Itasca County. The earliest of the Itasca mines, the Hawkins, was explored as early as 1900 by Itasca Mining Company, formed by O.D. Kinney, George Crosby and Senator E.B. Hawkins. It was opened as an underground mine by Deering Harvester in 1902. A year later, a second underground working was operated by the La Rue Mining Company. In 1903, the Great Northern Railroad considered the ore in the two mines rich enough to connect them to a nine-mile shipping spur from Hibbing.[21]

While all this was going on, mergers and consolidations were taking place all across the nation, the Hawkins Mine was absorbed into the holdings of International Harvester Company, one of the great industrial combinations of the time. With enormous capital backing, Wisconsin Steel Company, a mining and steel-making arm of International Harvester, brought in expensive heavy equipment and within three years stripped away 2.5 million yards of surface overburden from the mine, turning it into an open pit.[22]

In 1902, the Nashwauk Realty Company, composed of Joseph Sellwood, George Hartley, O.D. Kinney, George Crosby, Senator Hawkins and Edmund Longyear, platted the townsite of Nashwauk

next to the mine. Its name, *nas-e-wauk,* means "the land between" in Algonquin, a title once used by lumbermen to refer to this part of the Mesabi, where there were prime stands of timber, but no rivers down which to float logs. Nashwauk became an official village on January 12, 1903, not long after the first ore came out of the Hawkins. A census taken two years later counted 687 people living within the town's limits.[23]

Although its name probably originated in the offices of timber buyers, the village was a mining town in every way, much like Aurora and some of the older range towns. If anything, the people of Nashwauk might have been more aware of their dependence on the mines. Nearby hematite deposits, although soft and relatively easy to remove, tended to be streaked with sand, and large areas contained ore of such low grade that it was rejected at the steel mills.[24]

In 1906, after the Hawkins and La Rue mines had shipped the best of their ores and Butler Brothers had stripped away the surface from the Hoadly Mine, development slowed to a standstill, awaiting the development of a means to wash away some of the impurities in the ore. Only after a successful wash plant was established at O'Brien Lake in 1910 and another installed at the La Rue Mine did large ore shipments occur – and only then did the town grow and prosper.[25]

Captain Robert W. Batchelder's arrival in 1909 as superintendent of the Hawkins is

representative of a new kind of captain that began to be seen in Mesabi mines after 1905. Unlike the earlier men of practical experience, Captain Batchelder, a native of Wisconsin, had an engineering degree from the Michigan College of Mines in Houghton and his expertise was crucial to the design, construction and operation of Wisconsin Steel Company's highly successful ore concentrator located two miles south of the mine.

The plant churned out ton after ton of washed ore with a steady iron content of 53 percent. Even though the concentrated ore's content was less than that of the older Mesabi mines, there was an enormous amount of it and furnacemen could count on its consistency. Twenty-five million tons would eventually come out of the Hawkins.[26]

In 1920, Nashwauk had a population approaching 3,000 and was hailed as the largest mining town in Itasca County. Its ethnic mix was similar to that of other range towns and it had one of the most active business centers on the western Mesabi. Along the town's Central Avenue could be found a meat market, grocery, hardware, bakery, clothing store, furniture store, bank, confectionery, barbershop, tailor and photography studio and an array of restaurants, saloons, boardinghouses and hotels.

The most impressive building in town was the Ollila Hotel, a three-story brick structure with steam heat, pool hall, restaurant and bar. Nashwauk, with its fenced-in yards and main street lined with wood-frame, false-fronted buildings differed little in appearance from other Iron Country towns and, like most, the village was not without its excellent water-and-light plant, paved streets, fine churches and palatial city hall and school.[27]

The Incorporated Village of Keewatin

Keewatin, located at the eastern edge of Itasca County a few miles west of Hibbing was incorporated on July 31, 1906, some 3½ years after Nashwauk. Its name, commonly thought to be derived from the Ojibway word *gi-we-din*, meaning "northwest wind," more likely came from the field notes of a geologist referring to the original and much altered iron-rich rock of the Mesabi.

Prior to incorporation, it was a busy logging center, complete with a general store, post office, bakery and a popular establishment known as the Pine Tree Saloon, run by an Irishman named Patrick J. McGuire. Although it is claimed there were already eight saloons in Keewatin in 1903, the town grew slowly and its streets had not

Nashwauk was incorporated as a village in 1903, not long after the first ore was shipped from the Hawkins Mine. Voss Collection, Iron Range Research Center

Main St., Nashwauk, Minn.

MISSISSIPPI.MINE KEEWATIN MINN.

Street Scene, Keewatin, Minn.

The Mississippi underground mine, operated by Oliver Iron Mining Company from 1910-14, spawned a well-populated "location" close to Keewatin. **Bottom:** Although a logging center for years and incorporated as a village in 1906, Keewatin's growth was slow until the Great Northern Railroad reached the town in 1909. VOSS COLLECTION, IRON RANGE RESEARCH CENTER

yet been cleared of pines when the first drill crews arrived.[28]

Iron ore was found and mines developed rapidly. Tesora Mining Company opened the Forest Mine in 1904 and was followed by Platt Iron Mining Company's Alexander Mine in 1905. A year later, Corrigan-McKinney Steel Company opened St. Paul Mine and spawned the large St. Paul location. However Keewatin itself experienced few immediate improvements. In fact, there was a time when homes in the location were plumbed and wired for electricity while citizens in the village lit kerosene lamps and drew their water from a nearby creek.[29]

Although sidewalks were built in 1907 and a boardwalk extended to the nearby St. Paul location, Keewatin didn't really grow until the Great Northern Railroad reached the town two years later. Advertised in 1910 as the "new town on the Nashwauk branch of the Great Northern Railroad," Keewatin attracted entrepreneurs and merchants from many places, including a few from towns already declining, places like Sparta, McKinley and Spina. Surrounded by a

relatively large population housed in the Mississippi, Bennett, Bray, Forest and St. Paul locations, Keewatin seemed an ideal place to locate a business.[30]

Keewatin prospered as the business center for the locations until well after World War I. Its main street included an active lumberyard, major hotel, hardware and furniture store, clothing store, confectionery, cigar store, tailor shop, several grocery stores and restaurants and a few saloons. Its all-brick village hall was described as one of the finest in Itasca County and in 1912, just six years after it was incorporated, the town had a water and sewage system equal to any on the range and an electric generating and heating plant capable of serving every home and business in the community.[31]

The amount of merchantable hematite in the vicinity of Keewatin and Nashwauk was limited. Although there was enough of it to initiate mining, much of what remained was low grade hematite that could not be turned into steel. It didn't take too many years for mine operators to see that the same would soon be true in other parts of the Mesabi. By 1904, there were few who doubted that, as mining continued, the ores would become increasingly lean. A way was needed to raise its iron content. United States Steel took the lead in perfecting the technology to do this and a new mining district resulted – the Canisteo.

The Canisteo Mining District

Everyone in the steel industry knew about the lean sandy hematite on the western Mesabi. Ten tons of the material had been dug from the old Arcturus Mine in 1897 and shipped through Grand Rapids to the Illinois Steel Company mill in Chicago, where it was quickly pronounced unsuitable for smelting. There were attempts to wash the sand out of the ore. J.W. Leech of Pittsburgh put together an ore-washing plant near the Arcturus in 1902. It washed out the sand all right – and most of the iron ore, too.[32]

In 1904, two Duluthians, Chester Congdon and Guilford Hartley, formed a partnership to develop a way to concentrate western Mesabi ore and market it. Congdon

named their firm the Canisteo Mining Company. *Canisteo,* an Iroquois word, means "head of the waters." The two men came from completely different backgrounds. Congdon, a lawyer, came to Duluth in 1892, where he served for a time as an Oliver Iron Mining Company attorney. In that capacity he learned enough about mining and steel mill needs to see value in western Mesabi ore.[33]

Hartley was born in Canada and came to the United States at the age of 18 to work in a lumber camp near the future site of Grand Rapids. His early years were spent in the woods at the west end of the Mesabi. After learning all he could about lumbering, he moved to Brainerd and went into business for himself. After serving in the State Legislature of 1883, he moved to Duluth, arriving at about the same time the first train load of ore was shipped to Two Harbors from the Vermilion Range. He heard talk everywhere about iron ore; Duluth in 1884 was a place where money could be made by speculating on potential mineral land. Hartley did and became wealthy.

Hartley and Congdon had a few things in common. Both were men of means and both were interested in mining the west end of the Mesabi. They bought the old Arcturus property and constructed a small

This 100-ton railroad steam shovel with crew was busy in a Canisteo district mine during the 1920s. The western Mesabi mining district prospered after ore concentrators were developed to upgrade iron content and wash sand from the ore that was mined there. HILL-ANNEX COLLECTION, IRON RANGE RESEARCH CENTER

experimental ore-washing plant nearby. But as rich as they were, they didn't have the kind of money needed to perfect and build a plant that could handle the heavy iron ore on a commercial scale. They turned to a company that did: the Oliver Iron Mining Company.[34]

By this time, Hartley and Oliver's president, Thomas F. Cole, were good friends. They hunted and fished together, they co-directed activities at Duluth's Kitchi Gammi Club and spent a lot of time cruising Lake Superior on Cole's yacht, the *Alvina*. It wasn't hard for Hartley to convince Cole that the Oliver should buy their plant and property.[35]

Cole's biography reads like a Horatio Alger story. He was born on Michigan's Keweenaw Peninsula to Cornish immigrant parents on July 19, 1862. When he was 6 years old, his father was killed in a mine accident and the family was poverty-stricken. Cole left school to work in the mine. He was then 8 years old. He earned 50 cents a day picking rocks out of copper ore at Michigan's Phoenix Mine. At the age of 9, he got a job at the Cliff Mine stamp mill and at 15 was a brakeman on the Hecla and Torch Lake Railroad. Although he came to know a whole lot about copper mining and was once called the best worker on the railroad, he could barely read or write. He attended night school. When he was not quite 20, he got a job as a clerk at the Chapin, the largest iron mine on the Menominee Range. This was the beginning of his rise to Oliver Iron Mining Company's top position.[36]

He took a position as captain in a Gogebic iron mine and within a few years was superintendent of the place. He joined Henry Oliver's company just as it was beginning to mine on the Mesabi. When the company became a subsidiary of United States Steel, Cole, at the age of 40, was named president. In the spring of 1904, he traveled to the western Mesabi and personally inspected the Hartley-Congdon property and plant. It was then that he decided to develop the western Mesabi without waiting until the high-grade ores were gone.

Cole moved decisively and quickly. He convinced United States Steel's New York directors that they should spend $10 million on the venture and was soon buying up all the land and mineral rights he could find west of Nashwauk. When winter came in

1904, the Oliver Iron Mining Company held a large block of land between Oxhide Lake and the Mississippi River. Cole named the new mining district Canisteo, after the Hartley-Congdon partnership.[37]

It was a deserted region, a logged-out land of pine stumps, brush and poplar saplings. A lonely winding wagon road ran the length of the district connecting the busy Mesabi mining towns with the river port of Grand Rapids.

Bovey (1904-1910)

A year later, the road was filled with men looking for work. A rumor had spread that the Oliver was going to mine. Already, a town was booming. They called it Bovey, after Charles Bovey, the man who had stripped the site of its white pine 10 years earlier. It was the brainchild of three men: Minneapolis lumberman Charles Bovey, Edmund Longyear and Duluth's Guilford Hartley.

In early 1904, the three men formed the Bovey Townsite Company and, by the end of April, Longyear had the site platted. A month later, lots were selling like hot cakes. When July came, the place was a legally incorporated village. It was still 1904.[38]

Bovey, like other range towns, grew quickly. It took only a year and a half for the town to have eight hotels, nine restaurants, five general stores, two clothing stores, a print shop, confectionery, blacksmith shop, meat market, grocery, bank, hospital, opera house, hardware store, soda factory and 17 saloons.

"Our town is growing so fast that even our own people can't keep up with what is going on," wrote the *Itasca Iron News* in 1905. There were saloons in Bovey even before stumps were removed from the streets and, by the time the stumps were gone, there were even more saloons – but no system for sewage. There was typhoid.[39]

Saloons always played a role in shaping the reputation of iron range towns. And Bovey's reputation was just plain bad. Poker, faro, klondike and roulette were the preferred sports in town and no place of business was without its slot machine. Bovey was one of the last towns in the state to put an end to open gambling.[40]

Permanent jobs in the developing mines were scarce during Bovey's first years, yet the town continued to grow. Such was the

reputation of the giant mining company. Since there was no railroad to the place, all building supplies, retail goods, provisions, saloon needs and mining hardware had to be hauled in over 11 miles of what some called "the roughest wagon road ever seen." Its mud holes, bumps, rocks, ruts and stumps were the source of news articles in local papers. "There is more traffic over the Bovey-Rapids road than any road in the county. Yet it is unsafe to drive over in an empty wagon and it is about all a man can do to walk over it," wrote one reporter in 1905.[41]

Although it was claimed "the road inspired more profanity than any other road before or since," a twice-a-day mail service was established in the fall of 1905. Stagecoaches carrying mail to Bovey left Grand Rapids at 7 a.m. and 3 p.m. every day of the week, including Sunday.[42]

Few federal marshals or other lawmen traveled that bumpy road to Bovey during those first years. As a result, gambling houses, dance halls and all-night saloons more or less ran the town. That is, until the railroad arrived. A 55-mile-long "Alborn Branch" of the Duluth, Missabe and Northern Railroad was completed in 1906 and the Oliver mines began shipping ore the following year.

The town became home to hundreds of miners and their families. Modest miners' cottages and boardinghouses appeared where just a short time before there had been nothing but brush and stumps. Streets were graded, a new school was built and they even put up a church – something Bovey didn't have during its first two years. The *Itasca Iron News* boasted, "Our people are practical, their dress is plain and they have no swagger."[43]

The Trout Lake Concentrator

The Holman, Canisteo, Diamond and Hartley mines all began shipping ore in 1907. They were followed by the Walker Mine in 1909, the Hill Mine in 1910 and Arcturus Mine in 1917. There was plenty of sand in the ore, but this didn't deter the mining because the great Trout Lake Concentrator washed out the sand and did it well. Its construction in the winter of 1909 is credited to John C. Greenway, superintendent of Oliver Western Mesabi Operations.[44]

Greenway, a Yale-educated Alabaman, arrived on the range in 1905. He had previously been employed by Carnegie Steel and during the Spanish-American War served as one of Theodore Roosevelt's Rough Riders. Cole picked him as "the kind of man who would do what was necessary to make

In 1907, the stumps were gone from Bovey's streets, but there was no system for sewage and animals roamed freely in the townsite. UNITED STATES STEEL CORPORATION COLLECTION, IRON RANGE RESEARCH CENTER

John Uno Sebenius, Oliver Iron Mining Company's chief mining engineer, developed information on ore bodies and tonnages used to develop mines in the Canisteo District. NORTHEAST MINNESOTA HISTORICAL CENTER **Bottom:** John C. Greenway, superintendent of Oliver Iron Mining Company's Canisteo District. Photograph taken in 1910. He developed the giant Trout Lake Ore Concentrator and created the town of Coleraine. UNITED STATES STEEL CORPORATION collection, IRON RANGE RESEARCH CENTER

the Oliver's western Mesabi mines pay."[45]

At the time Greenway arrived, no one knew much about western Mesabi ore. It was the only part of the range that had never been explored with diamond drills. Its hematite was so soft and sandy that when the casing was lifted from a drill hole, the ore simply ran out of the end. Without a drill core to study, Oliver's experts couldn't even agree on the size of the ore deposit, let alone on the best way to mine it.

The experts did agree on one thing. Something had to be invented to get the sand out of the ore and this would require money. Yet there would be no money as long as the size of the ore body remained a mystery.

With Greenway in 1905 was a brilliant Swedish engineer by the name of John Uno Sebenius. Using test pits instead of drill holes and combining engineering skills learned in Sweden with years of iron mining experience, Sebenius was able to systematically explore the Canisteo's geology and correctly calculate the exact amount of ore existing in a given property. The knowledge allowed the Oliver to make precise plans for mining and encouraged the company to invest large sums money in processing the ore.

As Oliver's chief mining engineer, Sebenius refused to open a pit before a complete geological study and better measurement of ore tonnage had taken place. Understanding of ore deposits led to more open pits and a further decline in underground mining.[46]

The Swedish engineer's success in estimating amounts of ore beneath the ground in given areas diminished the role of traditional "work experienced" mining captains. The years following 1905 saw fewer captains in Mesabi mines and a steady rise in the number of professional engineers.

While Sebenius estimated ore tonnages, Greenway studied everything he could related to washing and concentrating (also called beneficiating) ores, including the workings of the old Hartley-Congdon wash plant at the Arcturus. For a concentrating plant to be successful, it needed to be relatively inexpensive to build and have as few moving parts as possible – but at the same time it had to be capable of handling huge quantities of extremely heavy iron ore. He found his solution in so-called "log washers" used to remove clay from ore in Alabama iron mines.[47]

In 1907, Greenway had a small experimental log-washing plant constructed near Trout Lake. With the help of Princeton educated engineer L.D. Ricketts and financial support from the steel corporation, Greenway managed to improve and fine-tune the plant to a point where it functioned with little waste and few breakdowns. Work began immediately on a permanent plant. The result was the world-famous Trout Lake Concentrator, completed in April 1910, which raised the

iron content of ore from Canisteo mines to an acceptable level of 57 percent.

The plant was impressive and drew comment in mining and engineering journals all over the world. Constructed of heavy steel and enclosed in corrugated iron, the 125-foot-high mill building was almost as long as a football field and more than half as wide. It contained five production units and was connected by a 650-foot steel trestle to a gradually rising approach almost a mile long, formed from overburden removed from the Canisteo and Walker mine pits.

All of the machinery was driven by electricity drawn from a power and water pumping station located more than a mile

away on the shore of the lake. Crude ore from the Walker, Holman, Hill and Canisteo mines was hauled over the approach and trestle to the top of the plant, where it was dumped into huge bins from which the ore was sluiced out by jets of water and gravity-fed through screens and revolving trommels to a "picking belt," where workers picked out pieces of rock and taconite waste. From there, it passed through a series of "log washers," "turbos," "settling tanks" and "dewatering tanks" designed to separate the concentrate (refined ore) from the tailings (waste material) and dry it. The concentrate was then discharged into 90-ton collection bins from which it was loaded into ore cars

Greenway's experimental "log washer plant" near Trout Lake was completed in 1907 and proved that the beneficiation of ore could be a commercial success. VOSS COLLECTION, IRON RANGE RESEARCH CENTER **Bottom:** The Trout Lake Concentrator, Minnesota's first commercial iron ore concentration plant, was completed in 1910 and immediately began production. By the time this photo was taken in 1943, it had already processed tens of millions of tons of iron ore concentrate. UNITED STATES STEEL CORPORATION COLLECTION, IRON RANGE RESEARCH CENTER

By 1918, Oliver Iron Mining Company's "model village" of Coleraine was a well established mining center.
Bottom: Greenway Lodge was a social center in early Coleraine. AUTHOR'S COLLECTION

GREENWAY LODGE

waiting on a track located below each bin. The tailings were discharged into Trout Lake. Rocks picked off the belt were hauled to a "waste dump" by electric motor.

The plant was operated in two 10-hour shifts during the shipping season and each of its five units was able to process more than 200 tons of crude ore an hour. The total cost of the mill and equipment was approximately $1.5 million.[48]

From an economic point of view, the Trout Lake Concentrator was a total success and a marvel of its time. Its completion marks the beginning of a long process to find a way to concentrate iron from the lean and taconic ores of the Lake Superior District. It would continue until 1973.

Coleraine

During the same year it shipped its first concentrates, the Oliver began building a town on the shore of Trout Lake. It was a beautiful town. They named it Coleraine after Thomas Cole.

John Greenway, already a favorite with Cole and certain executives of United States Steel, was given a free hand in planning and developing the town. Public criticism of big business was at an all-time high and Greenway was determined to make Coleraine a model of what a large corporation could do to better the lives of its employees and their families.

According to a newspaper of the time, Coleraine "would be designed to appeal to the best classes of people." It would be a place where residents could "find a contentment in their home life, which rough and uncouth mining towns seldom allow."[49]

Greenway also decided that Coleraine should be tightly regulated by the company. It would not be a place where "just anyone can live or start up a business." He picked the businesses and set them up on a special street which he named "Roosevelt" to honor his Rough Rider commander. Other streets he named after company officials.[50]

Nothing was built in Coleraine without company approval. The company graded the streets and laid out all of the town's water and sewer lines. Free lots were given to churches and the Oliver willingly financed the building of a hospital, athletic field and town park. The town in 1909 was portrayed as "an oasis of Americanism in a sea of lawless towns and foreign speaking miners." It was nothing like

Bovey – or Hibbing – or Virginia. Sitting in their New York offices, executives of United States Steel were delighted.[51]

Taconite, Marble and Calumet

Expansion of mining in the Canisteo District led the Oliver Iron Mining Company to establish two more company towns, Taconite near the Holman Mine and Marble next to the Hill Mine.

During the years 1905-1909, the company built 73 homes and a boardinghouse in Taconite and 35 more in Marble. Although John Greenway had a hand in their establishment, the two towns were probably designed more to forestall the spawning of squatters locations than anything else. Even though some substantial homes with spacious yards were constructed and sale of liquor forbidden, the emphasis on positive environment, screening of businesses and town planning seen in Coleraine was not evident in either Taconite or Marble. During their first years, the two towns were little more than large company locations.

Calumet was different. It began in 1908 as a typical Minnesota mining boom town. Located close to the Hill Mine and platted by the Power Improvement Company, the town began mainly as a street lined with the usual mix of saloons and boardinghouses,

but before it could be officially incorporated, a fire broke out and destroyed most of the town. Construction of a new Calumet began immediately and was well under way in 1909, the year change came to the Canisteo.

The Year of Change (1909)

There had never been talk of incorporation in Coleraine. Coleraine was Greenway's town. Residents had no voice whatsoever in the town's government. They didn't need any. Greenway and the great corporation saw to all their needs. That is, until 1909.

In that year, the inevitable happened. Tom Cole retired. His vice president, William Olcott, replaced him. Cole had relied on Greenway for the entire

Marble's Main Street featured a number of prominent structures by 1909. ITASCA COUNTY HISTORICAL SOCIETY
Bottom: Although Taconite would never become a major population center, in 1908 it served as home to a number of families who put down deep roots and remained there. IRON RANGE HISTORICAL SOCIETY

After a 1908 fire, Calumet was quickly rebuilt into a full blown village a year later. ITASCA COUNTY HISTORICAL SOCIETY

development of the Western Mesabi. Olcott fired him. The mining world was shocked. Rumors circulated. Then Greenway was back. Neither Olcott nor Greenway were willing to talk much about what happened.[52]

One explanation suggests that the United States Steel Corporation was experiencing growing pains at the time. Presidents of once-independent companies that had become United States Steel subsidiaries still thought they were the ones who should decide how the job should be done. They resented directives from corporation executives in New York City – they called them "the bankers." There were rivalries. There were power plays.[53]

Greenway's mysterious dismissal and quick return may have been a side effect of one of these growing pains. Whatever the cause, the whole episode was enough for Greenway to decide to leave the range forever. He remained only a few months – until completion of the Trout Lake Plant. Olcott, however, remained as president of the Oliver and was for years a prominent figure in Duluth. His home, patterned after a Georgia mansion, was once described as "the most aristocratic dwelling in the city."

In early 1909, mining company officials learned that Chisholm legislator Joseph Austin had placed a bill before the Legislature to allow range towns to include mining company properties within their boundaries, thus subjecting nearby ore

reserves to municipal taxation. At the time, Bovey was the only independently incorporated village in the Canisteo District. If the bill passed into law, there was nothing to stop Bovey from expanding its limits to include all nearby ore reserves. When it became clear that the bill would easily pass into law, Oliver officials became alarmed.[54]

They quickly moved to get Coleraine incorporated. It became an official village one day before the bill became law and quickly took within its limits all of the company land in the vicinity – and then some. Only the Trout Lake Concentrator, still under construction, was left outside the new village limits.

Coleraine wasn't the only company town to become an independent village in 1909. Taconite and Marble were also incorporated – and for the same reason. Calumet, too, incorporated that same year, but Hill, Holman, Canisteo and Walker mine taxes were stopped from going to either Bovey or Calumet.

Greenway explained it this way: "We felt that our mines were going to go to one town or another and we wished to have them go to the town where the best element lived and where the company spent its money."[55]

In 1909, there were predictions of great population growth for the new towns of the Canisteo. Coleraine's population was projected to grow to 10,000. Taconite had a building on every lot and expansion seemed inevitable. Impressive brick buildings were constructed

along Marble's Alice Avenue in anticipation of the many people expected there. There was even a three-story hotel. Meanwhile, Calumet proceeded to take on the trimmings of a typical iron range town. There were 15 new saloons along its main street within six months of the time it incorporated.[56]

The predictions didn't materialize. Coleraine's population never exceeded 2,000. Taconite and Marble peaked at 800 and Calumet took 30 years to rise to a population of just less than 1,000. The development of machines to make lean ore richer and mining faster replaced human labor. Once the stripping and developmental work was finished, demand for large numbers of unskilled labor dropped and the towns simply stopped growing.

Even after it incorporated, Coleraine remained a company town. Oliver and United States Steel officials continued to see it as an example of the positive effect that the large corporation could have on American life. According to residents, it was a wonderful town to grow up in. Saloons were carefully controlled, there were no roulette wheels, professional gamblers or houses of prostitution. It was from the beginning a place for families.

Coleraine's Greenway School, with its carefully selected staff, offered the best in education to the children of company employees. Beautiful homes lined the shore of Trout Lake, lots were spacious and band concerts in the park drew crowds on Sunday afternoons.[57]

Meanwhile, iron ore production at Oliver's Canisteo, Holman, Hill and Arcturus mines reached new heights. Other companies with financial resources – Interstate Iron, Mesaba-Cliffs, International Harvester – opened mechanized mines and wash plants of their own. But the operations of the Oliver surpassed them all. The company's ores flowed steadily to the shore of Trout Lake, where stood the largest and most advanced iron ore beneficiation plant in the Lake Superior District. The age of the giant mining company had arrived.

The success of ore concentration/beneficiation opened a new era in iron mining and guaranteed its continuation for many years. By 1924, there were 36 ore beneficiation plants operating on the Mesabi Range and six more on the Cuyuna. Forty years later, the number of beneficiation plants in Iron Country had risen to 68 and shipments of concentrates exceeded those of direct ores.[58]

The Cuyuna Range

Although the Oliver Iron Mining Company never operated a producing mine on the Cuyuna, its brief participation in the search for iron ore in 1904 and again in 1906 was enough to lend credibility to the effort. The mere appearance of the great company was enough to stimulate the sale of stock in the small exploratory Orelands Mining Company. The sale of stock allowed the company to buy needed equipment and go on to hit pay dirt in 1907 at a place called the Kennedy Mine.[59]

The Cuyuna Range differed from the rest of Iron Country in significant ways. It was flat. There were no outcroppings. The iron lay deep under a layer of glacial drift and took the form of two rather narrow hematite belts about three or four miles apart sometimes referred to as the North and South Ranges. The ore varied in its consistency. In some places, it was hard like that on the Vermilion. In other places, it was soft like Mesabi ore. Unlike the Mesabi or Vermilion, Cuyuna ore was suspected before it was seen.[60]

The first suspicions were aroused shortly after 1859, when a survey crew laying township lines near Nokay Lake in Crow Wing County reported problems with their compasses due to "a considerable local attraction … no doubt … from bog iron in the marshes."

Although the remains of test pits close to the Mississippi River's Oxbow Rapids are said to have been sunk in 1862 by some unknown iron prospector, credit for being the first person to actually see Cuyuna iron ore is given to a young Finnish immigrant named Henry Pajari.[61]

In the summer of 1882, about the same time Iron Country's first mines were being opened near Tower, Pajari, a 25-year-old Michigan miner, was on a "slow freight train" bound for western Minnesota, where he planned to homestead some land in Otter Tail County. As the train slowed to its regular stop to take on water at Deerwood Station, Pajari noticed some fragments of rock alongside the track that looked to him

PENNINGTON MINE
IRONTON   MINN
NO 806 GRAY STUDIO   AITKIN MINN

The Cuyuna Range lived up to all expectations. Its ore shipments rose from 733,000 tons in 1913 to 2.5 million tons in 1918. Manganese in the Cuyuna ore made it especially desirable for furnace operators. The Pennington Mine near Ironton operated as an open pit, but a number of underground properties also operated on the Cuyuna. HILL-ANNEX COLLECTION, IRON RANGE RESEARCH CENTER

like iron ore that he had seen in Michigan. He got off the train, walked to a place where the railroad cut through a small ridge and picked up some specimens. There was no doubt – in his hand were fragments of hematite.[62]

He changed his plans on the spot. He returned to Michigan with the specimens, obtained financial backing and came back to Deerwood with a dip needle and an assistant named Herman Bjorklund. The two men made several attempts to sink test pits west of the station but, when the pits filled with water and no additional ore was found, Pajari's backers convinced him to give up the venture. Pajari, therefore, lost his chance to open the first iron mine on the Cuyuna. He also lost his dip needle.[63]

Credit for opening the range is usually given to Cuyler Adams. Born in Canton, Illinois, in 1852, Adams suffered health problems as a child. At the age of 18, following the advice of doctors, Adams went to Lake Vermilion to improve his health. He spent a year with Bois Forte trappers, learning how to hunt, catch fish and find his way in the woods. His health improved.[64]

His luck improved, too. After exchanging a large amount of depressed Northern Pacific Railway stock for North Dakota farmland in 1878, Adams went into the wheat growing business for a few years and then had the land divided up and sold, realizing a profit of close to $100,000. He used some of the money to buy a parcel of land in Crow Wing County not far from Deerwood Station. In 1882 while laying out his property lines, he noticed something very strange about his compass.

"It was noon and his shadow fell across his compass. He observed, at first casually and, then with astonishment, that his shadow and the needle of the compass did not both point in the same direction as they should have done at that hour."[65]

When he walked some distance away, he noticed that the compass and shadow were again aligned, as they should have been at that hour of the day. After a systematic search of the area with compass in hand, Adams outlined what he suspected to be a large formation of iron ore. There followed several years of exploration with a dip needle and extensive library research, during which time Adams carefully recorded every detail of his findings. Finally, he was convinced he had located a vast body of iron ore – and he had done it without ever seeing it.[66]

On March 3, 1903, along with Deerwood summer home owner William C. White and Duluth and Iron Range railroad executive William McGonagle, Adams incorporated the Orelands Mining Company. Two months later, the company was diamond drilling just south of Deerwood Station. Adams and his partners were also trying to sell mining stock to Duluth and Brainerd businessmen. Very little was sold – it was difficult for anyone to believe the gently rolling countryside with its small farms, fenced in fields, lakes and marshes was potential mining country.

The attitude of Duluth businessmen was succinctly captured in an article appearing in the *American Magazine* 19 years later, "Iron ore near Deerwood? Impossible! … You might as well sink a shaft under Superior Street!"[67]

Brainerd businessmen were equally cautious. Brainerd had been the county seat since the town was platted in 1871. Brainerd people knew the area and no one had ever reported seeing iron ore. Brainerd people had seen the lumber industry come and go. No one got rich from it. Mining would be no different. A person would have to be crazy to buy stock in a company trying to find ore where no one had seen any.[68]

It was then that the Oliver announced its plans to explore for ore in Aitkin County. That's all that was needed. If United States Steel was interested in the region, there must be ore. Orelands' mining stock now sold quickly. In April 1904, Oliver withdrew its equipment, leaving 12 oreless drill holes behind. But the Orelands Company had the funding it needed to continue its operation.

Little more would be seen of the Oliver on the Cuyuna and the range would be explored by companies not directly associated with United States Steel. Beginning in 1905, the region was besieged by drill crews. New mining companies came into being and old names appeared among the explorers. Chester Congdon and George Hartley acquired property in Irondale Township; Louis Rouchleau, David Adams and Neil McGinnis began exploring

southward from the Mesabi toward Brainerd; and George Crosby began picking up potential mineral land in Crow Wing County.

Meanwhile, W.C. White, R.R. Wise and Judge G.W. Holland organized the Brainerd Iron Company and Franklin Merritt, son of Napoleon Merritt, along with John McAlpine, Patrick Hines and J.C. Campbell, drew up incorporation papers for the Cuyuna Mining Company. Mining fever spread as far south as Little Falls.[69]

Firms well known on the Mesabi sent representatives to the Cuyuna: North Star Iron, John A. Savage, Inland Steel, Coates and Tweed, M.A. Hanna. "Nearly every big operator or mining concern known in Duluth is interested in the development of this range," proclaimed the *Duluth Daily News* in October 1908.

They had reason to be. In September 1905, Hobart Iron, a mining arm of Pickands Mather and Company, sank a shaft through 120 feet of glacial drift near Nokay Lake and struck iron ore.

"The entrance of Pickands Mather Company, a very conservative firm from Cleveland, Ohio, proved a great surprise to many and silenced quite a company of doubters," wrote John Morrison in the *Duluth Evening Herald* in July of that year.[70]

By this time, the new range had a name. In the summer of 1905, noted geologist Charles Lieth, who had done extensive work describing the Mesabi iron formation and who had personally gone over the new range with Adams, asked him what he proposed to name it. Adams' wife, Virginia, suggested a combination of the first syllable of Cuyler's name *Cuy* with the name of his favorite dog *Una* – *Cuy-una*. Professor Lieth approved and from that time the name was used in all official publications.[71]

Then, at the height of the excitement, Pickands Mather and Company encountered water under high pressure at the Hobart and abandoned the mine. This was followed by Oliver's second failure near Rabbitt Lake. Iron ore enthusiasm died. If two of the biggest mining firms in the country couldn't make a go of it on the Cuyuna, what chance did a small local independent company have?

The Orelands Company was holding a block of potential mineland almost 20 miles long, but was suddenly without funds and

The first iron ore to leave the Cuyuna Range was shipped from the Kennedy Mine in April 1911. This photo is from 1915. CATHERINE RUKAVINA, IRON RANGE RESEARCH CENTER

investors. Co-founder Bill White's desperate effort to interest eastern steel makers in the property caught the attention of S.A. Kennedy, president of Rogers-Brown Iron Company of Buffalo, New York, a company well known on the Mesabi for its work at the Iroquois and Susquehanna mines. On July 3, 1907, the New York company signed a lease to mine the Orelands' holdings near Rabbit Lake. A year later, the Cuyuna's first producing iron mine, the Kennedy, was stockpiling marketable ore.[72]

Like the Mt. Iron Mine 16 years earlier, the Kennedy needed a railroad. The first machinery and supplies had to be hauled in over a six-mile wagon road from Deerwood Station on the Northern Pacific Railroad. The *Brainerd Dispatch* estimated that "it cost as much to get coal from Deerwood to the Kennedy as it did to bring the fuel from Pittsburg to Deerwood."[73]

Like the Merritts before him, Cuyler Adams was sure that once the mine began showing merchantable ore, it would be easy to secure the necessary financial backing for a railroad to Lake Superior. In 1909, along with two attorneys for the Minneapolis, St. Paul and Sault Ste. Marie Railroad, better known as the "Soo Line," Adams incorporated the Cuyuna Iron Range Railroad Company.

Railroad construction began, but as more and more mines were brought to production, Soo Line officials, thinking that an iron bonanza might be in the making, bought Adams out for $500,000 and

completed the spur to the Kennedy Mine. The first shipment of ore from the Cuyuna Range left the Kennedy on April 11, 1911. It began with the usual festivities.

"Finally, on Thursday, April 11, 1911, the great day arrived when an ore train was to leave the Cuyuna Range for Superior docks. With bands playing and whistles blowing, with cars decorated with placards and banners, with 'everybody there,' the train left the Kennedy Mine. Monster engines drew 42 cars of ore."[74]

As it turned out, that first shipment was nothing like those glorious first shipments from the Vermilion and Mesabi. The train was stopped six miles away at Ironton and sat on the track for weeks. It took the entire month, and then some, just to get the 42 ore cars to Superior and once there the train was put on a siding to await completion of the ore dock.[75]

That was enough for Adams. He and his sons incorporated a second mining railroad, the Cuyuna Northern. The new company was formed on September 20, 1911, and a year later sent a shipment of ore from the Cuyuna-Mille Lacs Mine to the dock at Superior's Allouez Bay. Three years later, this second railroad was sold to the Northern Pacific, a company that had done its own iron exploring and held many parcels of potential mineland – and more than a mild interest in developing the Cuyuna.[76]

By 1913, the Northern Pacific owned a 1,200-foot-long, 70,000-ton capacity ore dock in Superior, had railroad spurs connected to several potential mines and was running passenger service to a new mining town called Ironton. In the meantime, the Soo Line developed its own spur to another town nearby. They called it Crosby. Anticipating heavy iron ore traffic, the Soo Line constructed a 2,412-foot-long, 120,000-ton-capacity ore dock at Superior. Not to be outdone, the Great Northern Railroad built three ore docks at Allouez Bay, all about 2,000 feet long, giving the company a total loading capacity of 300,600 tons.[77]

The Cuyuna lived up to all expectations. Its ore shipments jumped from 733,000 tons in 1913 to almost 2.5 million tons in 1918. Steel makers fell all over themselves trying to get contracts for Cuyuna ore. There was reason – the ore's manganese. An especially hard and durable kind of steel could be made using ore like this.

Although manganese in small quantities was a normal part of most steel making, a special conversion process using larger amounts produced a form of steel containing as much as 13 percent to 14 percent manganese. Manganese steel, as it was called, was used to make bearings and other steel products subject to very hard usage.

Iron ores containing high percentages of manganese were much in demand during World War I, especially after shipments from Russia, the main supplier of high-grade manganese ores, stopped. Although Cuyuna Range deposits were comparatively small and erratic, intensive hand sorting took place in some of the mines to bring the content up, resulting in shipments running as high as 20 percent to 40 percent manganese. However, hand sorting lowered the overall tonnage and degraded the iron content, causing shipments like these to be the exception, not the rule. Iron ore from most of the Cuyuna's so-called manganiferous mines tended to have a manganese content anywhere between 3 percent and 17 percent. Yet, for a few years, the Cuyuna Range was recognized as one of the nation's important sources of manganiferous iron ore.[78]

In 1923, the range had 29 operating mines and was shipping almost twice as much ore as the Vermilion Range. A year later, the greatest mine disaster in the history of the Lake Superior Mining District occurred at one of the Cuyuna's manganese iron producing mines.

Tragedy at the Milford

Most of the mines on the Cuyuna's "North Range" produced some marketable manganese ore. Although some came from open pits, most was raised to the surface from small shallow underground mines. The Milford was one. Opened by Franklin Merritt in 1914, it was owned by George Crosby and operated by Whitmarsh Mining Company.

Probably of more importance to the 115 men working there in 1924 were the single shaft to the surface, the unprotected cage and the slowly bending green timbers holding back walls in the drifts below.

But concerns like these were heard in other underground mines. Captain Evan Crellin was in charge of the workings. Crellin, son of well-respected Eveleth mining captain John Crellin, was a man of 19-years experience with a reputation for being "the best man to work for on any range."[79]

It was February – February 5, 1924, to be exact. A quiet winter day. The 3 p.m. afternoon sun was already casting shadows across the soot-layered snow and miners' wives were busy in the kitchens of the two short rows of identical cottages that made up the Milford Location. The kids were still in school.

It was now 3:45. Below the snow-covered ground, 165 feet down, the day shift – 48 men – were just 15 minutes from going off duty. Mine superintendent Harry Middlebrook was away on business and Captain Evan Crellin was in the process of giving visiting mining engineer Ronald McDonald a tour of the underground workings.

Suddenly there was a rumble and a wind. It seemed to come from every direction. It grew into a roar. There were cries, "Water, Water!" Men ran as fast as they could to get to the shaft. But the skip and cage were at the surface. They would have to climb. One-by-one, they mounted the ladder. It was 165 feet to the surface.

It took only a few minutes for the entire mine to flood and the water now rose swiftly up the shaft – faster than anyone could climb. One-by-one, the climbing men were pulled under. Twenty-five minutes after the first rush of wind, the water was within 15 feet of the surface. Seven men got out. Forty-

By 1924, nearly half of the ore coming from the Cuyuna Range needed to have its iron content raised and iron ore concentrators became a common sight in most of that range. Because ore was wet, drying plants were also common throughout the district. VOSS COLLECTION, IRON RANGE RESEARCH CENTER

one didn't. Captain Crellin was one who didn't. Ronald McDonald, who just happened to be visiting, was another.[80]

It was immediately recognized as the worst iron ore mine accident in the history of the Lake Superior District and word of the Milford Mine disaster spread all across the country. Within days, every miner in every mine in the Lake Superior District knew the story of the Milford and the 41 men who died there. The mine didn't produce much manganese ore that year. It took almost the whole year just to pump it out and recover the bodies.[81]

By late 1925, the mine was shipping ore again. A new firm, Amherst Mining Company, organized by George Crosby Sr., George Crosby Jr., William Harrison and W.A. Rowe, took over the mine under its original name, Ida Mae, and it went on to ship more than a million tons of manganese ore before it closed in 1932.[82]

However, the deaths of 41 men in a single accident caught the attention of the nation and questions were raised as to cause and guilt. Minnesota Governor Jacob Preuse appointed W.E. McEwen, Ed Smith, Dwight Woodbridge, J. Wilbur Van Evra and R.R.

Baily to an investigative committee to determine the cause of the accident.

The committee held hearings from May 9 to July 12, 1924, and determined that a portion of a narrow neck of swamp above the mine and leading out to nearby Foley Lake crushed the roof of the mine workings, allowing water from the lake to pour into the mine. The committee further determined that the flooding was caused by conditions so unusual that no one could have foreseen them happening. Therefore it was unable to find any agency or any person on which to place blame.

Captain Crellin was, in fact, commended for the way he looked after his men, both in life and the way he spent his last moments trying to save them. Whitmarsh Mining Company was, in the end, absolved from all responsibility and a number of mine safety improvements were recommended.[83]

The Portsmouth Sintering Plant

By 1924, almost half of the ore coming out of Cuyuna mines had to be concentrated in some way. Beneficiation methods to increase the iron content of ore had improved some since the early days on the Canisteo. The Savage Ore Drying Plant, Mahnomen Wash Plant, Moroco Wash Plant, Louise Crusher and the Portsmouth Plant all served to concentrate the iron content of ores from nearby mines. Methods included not only crushing and washing the ore, but also drying and a process called sintering, which produced fused chunks of iron ore by firing.[84]

The Portsmouth plant was built in 1924 and was described as the largest of its kind in the world. For more than 40 years, it was a Cuyuna landmark. After dark, the red glow from hot sinters pouring through chutes into ore cars would light up the night sky over Crosby.

Although most Cuyuna ore had a high moisture content, ore from the Portsmouth mine pit was particularly wet. The plant heated the wet ore to a high temperature, driving off the water and 30 percent of its weight. The final product took the form of cinder, or "sinter," and its red-hot glow lingered long after it was loaded into ore cars. Although the process was criticized by some as "expensive," the sinter it produced had a steady iron content of 60 percent to 62 percent.[85]

The Mining Towns of the Cuyuna (1908-1918)

The Cuyuna Range was developed in a region that had already been more or less parceled off for lumbering and farming. Brainerd and Deerwood Station were already there when the first mines were developed. However, the mining boom produced several new towns: Cuyuna in 1908, Crosby in 1909, Iron Hub and Ironton in 1910, Manganese in 1911, Orelands, Riverton, Klondike and Julesburg in 1912, Iron Mountain and Steelton in 1913, Wolford in 1917 and Pershing in 1918.[86]

It was in procuring land for the new mining towns that townsite developers confronted their greatest challenge. Unlike the Mesabi and Vermilion ranges, mining on the Cuyuna began in a region where land was already homesteaded and for the most part turned into small farms. It was well known that most local farmers were willing to talk mining lease for a price, but sell their land? Never! As a result, land for mines and townsites was scarce and expensive. Thus,

every investment in a mine was preceded by extensive drilling and every purchase of land was an enormous gamble.

The new towns developed all at once. Streets were laid out where weeks before there had been only woods and farmers' fields. Hastily built hotels and boardinghouses became homes for crews of miners and laborers, many of them immigrants. As in most mining towns, there were saloons, gambling halls, vice and violence. But most of all there was energy – and optimism.

"Ironton is a coming city surrounded by large and rich ore bodies on the Cuyuna Iron Range. Only two months old, it expects to have 2,000 in population in a year."[87]

"Manganese was platted last December and nearly all the lots sold in seven weeks…. Buildings are going up and every indication of life and prosperity prevails."[88]

"If there is ever a town of the Cuyuna Range that started out under favorable conditions, it is Oreland…. Among the buildings recently erected is Hotel Orelands of the Brainerd Brewing Company. There are oak walls, polished maple floors, ornamental steel ceilings and the entire building is illuminated by electricity."[89]

Crosby (1908)

One of the new towns was different. Like John Greenway's Coleraine, it was carefully planned from the beginning. It was the product of George H. Crosby, Duluth financier and veteran mining man. Crosby was an early explorer for iron on the Mesabi, when that range was just opening up. After locating a few mines, which he sold to obtain capital for further exploration, he went on to lease land west of Hibbing at the edge of what became the Canisteo Mining District. One of his leases, the Hawkins Mine near Nashwauk, became a major producer of iron ore. It also was the beginning of the Crosby fortune. His later interests included mines in Arizona, California and Washington – and in 1908, the town of Crosby.[90]

There is no doubt that Crosby was aware of Greenway's work at Coleraine. He, too, was determined to avoid the mistakes and excesses of the earlier Mesabi mining towns. He planned his town carefully.

In 1908, with the help of Brainerd Attorney Leon Lum, Crosby was able to buy a large tract of land near Serpent Lake. It was a beautiful place. It was also a place where some people thought there might be iron ore. The first thing he did was to diamond drill the entire area. He found no ore.

It was only after the drilling was done that Crosby began building his town. The site included some small farms and, on what were once plowed fields, Crosby located his main street. The financier paid for all the improvements that followed: graded streets, eight wells for drinking water, sewer lines, sidewalks with cement curbs, lots for buildings, community park, public beach, children's playground, baseball field, a bandstand and 100 low-rent miners' cottages. Then, exactly at the height of the mining boom, he began renting out the cottages and selling lots.

The lots sold quickly and in a short time the newly built miners' cottages were filled with families of men employed in nearby mines. Although small by modern standards, the cottages came complete with electricity, running water, indoor toilets and screen doors and were considered a wonder of the time.

"There is no king or magnate in the world whose grandfather was as well-housed and as safely surrounded as a Crosby miner in his cottage that rents for $12 a month," boasted Crosby's promotional bulletin published in 1914.[91]

Four shipping mines, all within a mile of town, made Crosby the place to locate a business. Standard Oil established a distributing center in town, a 60-room hotel was built, retail stores were established along the main street and, within five years of its inception, Crosby had a population of 3,000 and was proclaimed the business center of the Cuyuna.[92]

Although the mines and towns of Cuyuna were never run by companies directly associated with United States Steel, need for the Cuyuna's special kind of ore kept relatively small Cuyuna iron mines operating. New uses for hard manganese steel in the production of machines, tools and automobile engines during the second decade of the 20th century not only diversified steel markets but for a time brought a measure of prosperity to the Cuyuna. In 1916, the range was well known among steel makers for its special kind of iron ore.

All of Iron Country was booming in 1916. More than 46 million tons of iron ore flowed down the lake that year. The age of the great corporation had arrived and it seemed that it had produced jobs for anyone willing to work. By this time, tens of thousands of immigrants had come to Iron Country. They were willing to work and work hard. But was it enough just to be a hard worker? Problems created in the towns and mines of Iron Country by the new age of mining were just beginning. ■

CHAPTER 11

Immigrant Labor, Unions and Range Politics

They came by the thousands. Immigrants from all parts of Europe. Immigrants in search of a new way of life. Their purposes for coming were clear. "You can get rich in America." "There's work for everybody in America." "The streets are paved with gold in America."

They came out of the Arctic copper mines of Norway, the chalk pits of Slovenia and the peasant farms of Italy and eastern Europe. Their dream was the same – to find a new and better way of life in America. Their reasons for leaving were many. "We were so poor." "My older brother got the farm." "I wouldn't be a soldier for the Czar." "There was no chance for my children to go to school in the old country."

They found America in the stark towns of Iron Country. They came in large numbers – young men hired by the mines – even younger women, who found work in the region's numerous camps and boardinghouses. In 1885, there were less than 5,000 people living north of Duluth. Almost all were on

the Vermilion Range. Fifteen years later there were more than 25,000 people in the region. Most were on the Mesabi Range. Most were immigrants. During the next 10 years, the immigrant population tripled. In 1910, nearly 80 percent of all people residing in Iron Country were born in a foreign country. The flow of immigrants continued until the mid-1920s.

Virginia: Queen City of the Mesabi

Populations in Iron Country towns swelled. In 1915, there were 4,500 people in Ely, 8,000 in Eveleth, 10,000 in Chisholm and 15,250 in the crowded village of Hibbing. But Virginia surpassed them all – population 16,000.[1] In 1915, Virginia, with its three banks, four opera houses, three sawmills, four hospitals, 11 schools, 12 churches, all brick blocks and 17 miles of paved streets, was by far the most urban community north of Duluth. It was terminus for six railroads – the Duluth, Missabe and Northern; Duluth, Winnipeg

In 1910 the Virginia and Rainy Lake Lumber Company boasted the largest white pine mill in the world. VOSS COLLECTION, IRON RANGE RESEARCH CENTER

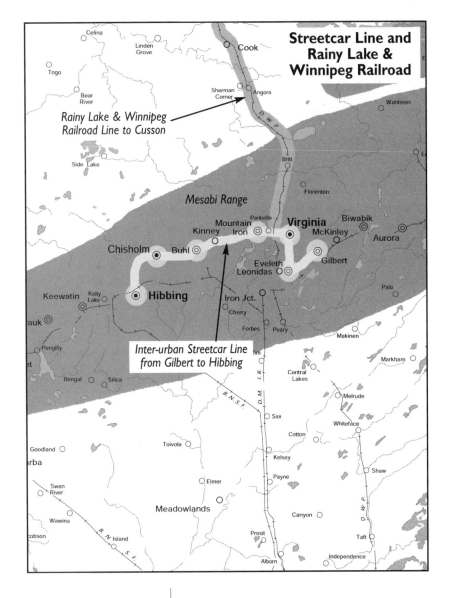

Streetcar Line and Rainy Lake & Winnipeg Railroad

Rainy Lake & Winnipeg Railroad Line to Cusson

Mesabi Range

Inter-urban Streetcar Line from Gilbert to Hibbing

This map of the Mesabi Range shows the towns, including Cusson, and the route of the Duluth, Rainy Lake and Winnipeg Railroad, as well as the Inter-urban Streetcar Line from Gilbert to Hibbing. MAP PROVIDED COURTESY OF THE STATE OF MINNESOTA

and Pacific; Duluth and Iron Range; Great Northern; Duluth, Rainy Lake and Winnipeg, and Mesaba Railway. Daily passenger trains connected the city to all parts of the United States and Canada.[2]

The Virginia and Rainy Lake Lumber Company

Virginia was also headquarters for the Virginia and Rainy Lake Company, which in 1910 boasted the largest white pine sawmill in the world. The mill produced 500,000 board feet of rough lumber, 250,000 board feet of planed lumber and 600,000 feet of lath every 24 hours. The company kept an estimated 90 million board feet of lumber in three large storage yards. The yards were crisscrossed by miles of narrow gauge track and tramways. Electric tram cars ran day and night carrying lumber to and from the mill site. A thousand men were employed at the mill and another 2,000 in the company's lumber camps.[3]

The camps swarmed with immigrant 'jacks. They were of almost every nationality. A large number were Finns. Pay was notoriously poor, averaging less than $2 a day, but the food was good and there was plenty of it. Cook shacks were kept open for coffee and doughnuts and camp cooks made an art out of their pies, cakes and puddings. Travelers could always find a good meal and a night's lodging at a Rainy Lake camp.[4]

For 19 years, logging trains arrived in Virginia daily and Silver Lake was covered with a perpetual layer of logs. During winter, the lake was kept from freezing by driving steam from the company powerhouse into the water. They called it "hot ponding." The logs arrived via the company's Duluth, Rainy Lake and Winnipeg Railroad, which ran all the way from Virginia to Rainier on the Canadian border. Cusson, located in the heart of logging country, was the most important station on the line. During the height of the logging era, it was nothing less than a small town.[5]

From Cusson, a network of tracks ran to more than a 140 camps situated at such places as Arbutus, Echo Lake, Kabetogama, Elephant Lake, Namakan and all along the Canadian border. During the years 1910-1929, the railroad delivered more than 2 billion log feet of timber to the great mill in Virginia.[6]

The multimillion dollar operation was put together by two of the greatest timber barons of the age, Edward Hines and Frederick Weyerhaeuser. When it closed its doors in 1929, it had logged out 36 townships and left behind more than 140,000 acres of clear cut land. Five thousand of these acres were sold to farmers and lakeshore developers. The rest reverted to the state as part of the tax delinquent rolls.[7]

The Inter-urban Electric Streetcar Line

By 1910, Virginia was the commercial center of the Mesabi. It was located in the the most heavily populated region of Iron Country – a 30-mile stretch of towns and locations between Gilbert and Hibbing. Here were the Mesabi's greatest mines and 75 percent of its population. The region teemed with recent arrivals and a dozen languages could be heard on the streets.

There were people but few roads in 1910. Most of the locations were isolated places and steam railroads showed little interest in delivering passenger service to them. On the range, railroad profits came from iron ore, not people. A good system of public transportation was needed.

There were entrepreneurs who were aware of the need. In November 1910, the Mesaba Electric Railway Company was incorporated to develop streetcar service throughout the Mesabi heartland. Although the company established headquarters in Virginia and the list of local investors included such people as W.P. Chinn, Richard Chinn, Samuel J. Cusson, E.H. McIntyre, John Lamont, Chester Rogers, Dana C. Reed and Albert B. Coates, it was mostly the product of Boston financial interests. The company's first officers were Oscar Mitchell, Duluth, president; Robert Watson, Philadelphia, vice president; Philip L. Saltonstall, Boston, treasurer; and Henry S. Newton, general manager.[8]

In early 1911, when the survey for the line began, an immediate problem was encountered. There were too many open pit mines. It was impossible to develop any kind of reasonably straight track without having to go through a mine pit. The problem was solved with many wide curves, 22 bridges and trestles and a whole lot of investment money.[9]

Construction began in 1912. An office, maintenance shop, paint shop and car barn were built west of Olcott Park on Virginia's

For 19 years Virginia's Silver Lake was covered with a perpetual layer of logs. **Bottom:** The Virginia and Rainy Lake Lumber Company's railroad center at Cusson was a busy townsite during the height of the logging era. VIRGINIA AREA HISTORICAL SOCIETY COLLECTION, IRON RANGE RESEARCH CENTER

A Mesaba railway eastbound trolley pauses at Virginia-Center Station on Wyoming Avenue (Third Avenue today) in 1914. VOSS COLLECTION, IRON RANGE RESEARCH CENTER

north side. From there, the track was extended in two directions, west to Hibbing and east to Gilbert.

An electric trolley system was put together and two 600-volt, steam-driven generators were set up close to the Virginia and Rainy Lake Mill, where chips and shavings could be used as a cheap source of fuel. A conveyor from the mill fed directly into the power station's firing room and water for steam was drawn from Silver Lake. Substations were established at Gilbert and Chisholm and, after 1921, at Hibbing.[10]

The streetcar made its first run between Virginia and Eveleth on December 24, 1912, and by the end of January, hourly service from 6 a.m. to midnight extended across the line. From Virginia, fares were 10 cents to Eveleth, 20 cents to Gilbert, 5 cents to Parkville, 10 cents to Mountain Iron, 25 cents to Buhl and 50 cents to Hibbing. The response exceeded all expectations. Soon everyone was riding the streetcar: mine inspectors, mothers with children, businessmen, salesmen, shoppers from the locations, men in search of work and miners on their way to work.[11]

During shift-change, two-car trains jammed with miners ran the length of the line. On weekends and holidays, three-car trains were sometimes used. During weekdays the heaviest traffic was always between Eveleth and Virginia.[12] But there were Saturday nights in summer when public dances at the Sparta Pavilion on Ely Lake drew record streetcar crowds.[13]

"The cars often reached speeds up to 40 miles an hour and there were times when people, cars, trucks, cows, chickens and even other trolleys got in the way ... demerits were issued to a conductor taking a car from the barn without a cow catcher."[14]

The electric railway was 30 miles long and there were 46 stations along the route – that is, if you count the ice cream parlor near the corner of Wisconsin and Broadway in Gilbert. There, the street car turned around and became a "westbound." It then proceeded on through Genoa Location and Station 44 to Eveleth, where it turned north on Adams Avenue and continued on to Virginia.[15]

Virginia had more streetcar track than any other town on the line. It was here, between Virginia Center and Northside Station, that streetcars were often the most crowded. West of Virginia the streetcar passed through Parkville, Mountain Iron, Kinney-Spina Station, Lucknow Location and entered Buhl along Culver Avenue. After

a stop at the Buhl Drugstore, it proceeded on to Chisholm. After a number of stops at stations along the line, it rumbled into Chisholm along a 2,000-foot wooden trestle across Longyear Lake. At the substation on the corner of Chisholm's Central Avenue and First Street, there was always a crowd of miners at shift-change waiting for an "eastbound" or "westbound" to appear.

The run from Chisholm to Hibbing was through a "no man's land" of mines, dumps and locations. Although the distance between the two towns was short, here the track was long. The streetcar had to wind its way through an extremely active mining area before it could make its final stop at Hibbing's McKinley Street Station.[16]

Continued mining forced both Hibbing and the streetcar line to relocate. A 90-day cancellation clause in the streetcar's right of way contract with the Oliver was enacted in 1919. New track was laid and a substation and terminal building built at the corner of Sixth Avenue and Howard Street on the new townsite. After 1921, the streetcar passed by Glen Location and ran through Kitzville and Brooklyn before entering Hibbing at Howard Street.[17]

When first established, it was planned that the Mesaba railway would span the entire length of the range from Aurora to Grand Rapids. The incorporators also hoped to deliver electricity to every town in the mining district. It didn't happen. Rapid development of motor cars, all-weather roads and efficient hydroelectric plants ended plans for expansion. By 1921, the company was operating in the red. On March 7, 1924, it went into receivership and on April 16, 1927, the last inter-urban streetcar made its final run.[18]

Mesabi Bus Companies and the Greyhound

When Andrew Anderson, former diamond driller turned car salesmen, found that he couldn't sell the first car shipped to his Hibbing Hupmobile agency, he began using it to sell rides to nearby locations.

A Mesaba railway westbound on Chisholm's Lake Street in 1912. COSTANZI COLLECTION, IRON RANGE RESEARCH CENTER **Bottom:** An Inter-urban streetcar passes down Hibbing's Third Avenue on its way to its final stop at McKinley Street Station. VOSS COLLECTION, IRON RANGE RESEARCH CENTER

When Hibbing's Andrew Anderson found that he could not sell the first car shipped to his Hupmobile Agency, he began using it to sell rides to nearby locations and became one of the earliest such businesses that eventually were merged into the Greyhound Corporation.

LYONS COLLECTION, IRON RANGE RESEARCH CENTER

Business was so good that it wasn't hard for "Bus Andy" to find partners and expand the service. In 1915, Anderson along with partners Carl Eric Wickman, Fred Lindbergh, Arvid Heed and Ralph Bogan formed the Hibbing Transportation Company. The five officers of the company were also the bus drivers. They beat out competition, made money and expanded the service. On December 17, 1915, they changed the name of their firm to the Mesaba Transportation Company.[19]

The motor bus business boomed and rival bus companies appeared in other range towns. In 1915, the same year that "Bus Andy" formed the Hibbing Transportation Company, Victor Maryland founded the Auto Transportation Line to connect Aurora, Biwabik, Belgrade Location, McKinley and Elba Location to the streetcar station in Gilbert. He located his office in Virginia, changed the name of his company to Maryland Transfer Line and extended bus service to Tower and Soudan on the Vermilion Range in 1918. In 1920, John and Kent Fitzgerald established another bus line in Eveleth – the Range Rapid Transit Company. Not only did they provide miners with transportation to nearby mines, they also established regular bus service to Duluth, before finally selling out to the Mesabi Electric Railway Company.[20]

There were other ventures, mostly one-man operations based on customer demand and cash fares. It was not uncommon in 1918 to see a motor bus or two parked near a streetcar station waiting for the next tram to arrive. There were no regulations to comply with. All one needed to get into the business was a bus. Fixed timetables seemed unnecessary, because a bus could go anywhere to pick up fares – anywhere in summer, that is. In winter, buses had to plow their own roads. Regular runs were eventually established, but there was no guarantee that the bus would arrive on time. If it couldn't pick up enough passengers, it didn't arrive at all.

But Mesaba Transportation Company buses did arrive – sometimes even on time. Timetables and schedules were developed and, by 1917, Mesaba Transportation was the largest and most prosperous motor bus company on the range. Its buses ran every 30 minutes between Alice and Hibbing and on-the-hour to Keewatin, Nashwauk and a dozen nearby mining locations.[21]

As service increased and routes became longer, larger buses were needed. But roads to locations – even between the larger range towns – were bad and impassable in the winter. Buses got stuck. They broke down. So in 1919, the firm formed its own bus manufacturing company – the Mesaba Motor Company.[22]

Iron range blacksmiths and mechanics were hired to construct special buses more suited to the harsh environment of Iron Country – buses that could make it down those mining roads – buses that were more comfortable to ride – buses with heating systems. Carl Eric Wickman would eventually buy out the interests of his partners and take sole control of the Mesaba Motor Company.[23]

As public demand for improved services grew, the only way bus companies could survive was to merge. In 1922, Wickman, still heading the Mesaba Motor Company, moved to Duluth, where he purchased the White Bus Lines and began providing long-distance service from Grand Marais to Minneapolis. In 1924, Wickman merged his interests with several Midwest bus companies and became president of Northland Transportation Company. More mergers followed and Northland became part of Motor Transit Corporation, a consolidation that became the basis for the nationally known Greyhound Corporation.[24]

The Politics of the Iron Range

At the same time Virginia was establishing itself as the commercial center of the range, Hibbing grew into its political center. The politics arose as a reaction to mining. During its first 20 years, Hibbing was dominated by the mines. Pits pressed in on the town and mine blasts shook buildings and damaged homes of residents. Public improvements were either approved or put on hold by decree of nearby mining companies, but mine properties were never listed on the public tax roll.

It was to this Hibbing that two brothers came to practice law. They were the sons of John Power, a popular Irish-American attorney and powerful politician in Michigan iron mining districts. Bill, the older brother, came first and replaced mining captain John Redfern as village president in the village election of 1902. Defeated in the election of 1903, Bill Power was returned to office in 1904 – this time on a platform of paving Pine Street.[25]

The project was begun without the approval of any of the mining companies.

In winter, the early buses had to plow their own roads.
PEDERSON COLLECTION, IRON RANGE RESEARCH CENTER

When corporation lawyers threatened injunction, Power had the entire length of Pine Street plowed up, making it impossible for companies to haul their heavy mining freight through the middle of town, something they had always done. They gave in. Pine Street was paved – and Power was replaced in the next election. But everyone knew Bill Power had beat the mining company.[26]

Even so, Hibbing remained a company-controlled town. Businessmen were still reluctant to put up a building for fear that a steam shovel would soon be digging up the lot. The town grew more crowded every month, but worst of all were the mine blasts.

According to one Hibbing miner, "You sit with your little family around the table, partaking of the humble repast your daily pittance allows you. Suddenly, a mighty roar and blast shakes everything in view and, a few seconds later, there comes crashing through your roof ... rocks and debris, endangering your life and the lives of your loved ones."[27]

More than half of Hibbing's residents in 1905 were recently arrived immigrants – people without citizenship – people who couldn't afford to quit their jobs – people who couldn't afford to complain.[28] The company position was clear. All these people were in Hibbing because of mining. Without the mines there would be no employment, without employment the people would starve. If mining caused some property damage, it was a small price to pay.

Victor Power began his law practice in 1904, the same year that his brother plowed up Pine Street. He took on every case of mining company damage he could find. There were many. He won some of them.[29]

In 1909, he defended the village of Spina against a suit by Republic Iron and Steel and Seville Mining Company for trespassing on their property. The companies claimed that some of the village's lots crossed their property lines. The court ruled that under the new law passed by the state Legislature an incorporated village like Spina could now vote to expand its boundaries to include mining properties. The village voted, company land was included in the village limits and Power's political stock rose.[30]

"Mine people do not like this condition (of self government). It does not jibe with

their ideas of proper government and they are doing their best to throw a scare into people who have bought property and built houses," said Power in 1909.[31]

In 1913, a somewhat reluctant Vic Power was a write-in candidate for Hibbing village president. He was part of a "progressive ticket" formed to hold mining companies more accountable for village improvements – mostly to provide a better lighting system for the town. He won. He would be re-elected to the office for 10 consecutive terms.[32]

Victor Power won few votes from "company men." Even before he took office in 1913, Power so angered Oliver officials over an injunction curbing their blasting that they threatened, "unless you have this injunction dissolved, grass will grow on the streets of Hibbing." Power replied, "Go ahead, we'll have men on the street to cut that grass."[33]

The mines shut down just before the election. Power won and, when he took office, the unemployed went to work for the village. The bill went to the companies in the form of taxes.

Clearly the biggest accomplishment of the Power administration was the discovery of mining company property within the village limits, property that had never been listed on the tax rolls. It didn't take Vic Power long to change that situation. The new taxes transformed Hibbing from a ragged mining village into a comfortable municipality filled with public improvements. Besides, if a man lost his job in the mine, he could always go to work for the village.[34]

Power became the idol of the range. Called by some "the Little Giant," his accomplishments became legendary. Duluth historian Walter Van Brunt credited Power for significant improvements in the village. According to his 1921 history of the county, "Hibbing is no longer a mining camp; it is a metropolitan, cosmopolitan city, in which the (immigrant) miner may, and does, hold his head high and provide for his family a typical American home."

During Power's years, the entire range seemed to go on a spending spree. Villages and cities expanded their limits to include mining company property. Tax money rolled in and mayors like Jacob Saari in Eveleth and

Michael Boylan in Virginia launched ambitious programs of public improvements. Chisholm, Buhl, Aurora and Gilbert soon had beautiful schools and public buildings. Eveleth built a large ice arena and outfitted the best hockey team in the tri-state area – all paid for out of taxes on iron ore.[35]

Politics for the years 1910-1921 completely reversed the mine-dominated decision-making processes of previous years and differed from politics in most other places in one specific way: "Let's get all that we can! If we don't, it will go to buy cigars for them damn capitalists down East," campaigned one iron range politician in 1915.[36]

Local affairs dominated and ad valorem taxes soared as towns competed to see which municipality could achieve the greatest number of public improvements. Led by Oliver, the mining companies responded. In 1913, they organized the Lake Superior District Tax Association to fight the actions of the range municipalities. They filed injunctions against town governments, they incorporated villages – Franklin, Fraser, Cooley, Fayal, Leonidas – all for the single purpose of removing their ore properties from the taxing powers of range municipalities. They even tried to get some of Hibbing's tax

base by forming a new town at their mine site called Mahoning. Power beat them again.[37]

In 1921, company lobbyists convinced the state Legislature to place a per capita limitation on the amount of taxes that could be collected on their properties. This brought an end to the "Power era," but by this time a decade of public works had transformed many of Iron Country's crude mining towns into modern urban centers.[38]

Iron range politics sometimes went beyond simply taxing mining companies. In 1905, state Representative Jacob Saari of Eveleth was instrumental in getting the Legislature to establish the office of St. Louis County Mine Inspector.[39] It was needed.

Working Conditions in the Mines (1907-1916)

In 1907, out of a total work force of 10,139, the Oliver Iron Mining Company had less than 300 employees who could speak English fluently. The list of foreign miners included 2,525 Finns, 1,881 Croatians, 1,279 Austrian-Slovenians, 864 Italians, 521 Scandinavians, 359 Slovaks, 210 Montenegrins, 210 Bulgarians, 151 Poles, 146 Bosnians, 129 Dalmatians and 95 Serbs.[40] There were other nationalities scattered among

"Relief stores" for strikers established in 1907 and 1916 served as catalysts later for more permanent cooperatives. HILL-ANNEX COLLECTION, IRON RANGE RESEARCH CENTER

205

the crews, but all had one thing in common – they were willing to work and work hard.

They found hard work in the mines of the Mesabi – they also found danger. Although most of the ore was mined from open pits and underground workings were usually well-constructed, there were serious safety flaws. Possibly the biggest hazard was that most of the men working in the mines were recently arrived foreigners. They couldn't understand English.[41]

Orders and directions were not always understood. Miners wandered into unsafe areas. There were premature blasts. Men got in the way of moving ore cars. They were caught in machinery. There were falls. Sides of pits gave way. There were cave-ins. There were deaths – lots of them.[42]

According to one Slovenian immigrant who worked for a time in the Genoa underground, "There were places in the mine where the carbide lamps got dim. It was hard to breath. But the worst thing of all was the sound of the timbers. They creaked and groaned all the time. I would say to myself, will I get out of here alive today?"[43]

Although pay scales varied during the years of the 20th century, it was usual for Mesabi miners to work 10-hour shifts, six days a week. Wages were paid monthly, usually in gold or silver. They averaged from $12.50 to $20 per week – even more for a select few. But the work was seasonal and, when winter came, there were always layoffs. A contract system of pay was used in underground mines. Under the contract, miners were organized into "gangs" and each gang was assigned a "pitch," or a place to work. The gang was given a quota – the number of cars they were expected to load – and a "rate" – so much per car.[44]

A miner's pay at the end of the month was based on his share of the number of cars loaded at the given rate – minus the cost of explosives, fuses, blasting caps, candles and carbide used during the month.

A bonus rate was paid for all cars over the quota, but as one Oliver employee recalled, "There were three of us miners on the contract. We had to load four cars each shift to make our base pay. For every car over, we were paid a dollar. We worked like crazy and was getting two or three cars over the quota each shift and were making a lot of

money. The next month our quota was raised to six cars and we were getting 80 cents for everything over. We didn't work like crazy after that."[45]

Mesabi underground miners hated the contract system. Many believed that favorites of the boss were given pitches in the richer softer ore. They loaded more cars. Their pay was better. There was talk of corruption, extortion and bribes – presents of cigars and bottles of whiskey, even money – for a good place to work. Croatian and Serbian laborers in one Mesabi mine complained openly that they had been forced to pay as much as $20 to a mine official in order to get their job. There was a case in Hibbing in which 15 laborers were laid off and immediately re-employed – after each paid the employment boss $5.[46]

According to former U.S. Immigration Commission special agent LeRoy Hodges, in his report of 1912: "When a Servian [sic] laborer complained in person to the general superintendent of his company that he had been forced to pay one of the foremen for his job, that official replied: 'If you have so much money that you can pay for a job, that is all right, for the foreman has a lot of little children and needs the money.'"[47]

Although most of the abuses occurred at the "petty boss level," it seems unlikely that high company officials were not aware of the problem. A 1908 Oliver Iron Mining Company memorandum to the superintendent of the Holman Mine suggested a quick solution. "In case any foreman, regardless of his position, is accepting money for giving work to an employee, he must be discharged at once."[48] However, by this time, a major strike had occurred.

The Strike of 1907

There was discontent in Iron Country mines in 1907. Uprisings and attempted strikes at one mine or another during earlier years had been quickly put down by company guards and local town marshals and, if things became too threatening, like the one at Mountain Iron in 1894, a sheriff's posse was organized and strikers were run off the premises. In the resulting melee, a Finnish miner was shot and killed by a St. Louis County deputy sheriff. There was no investigation.[49]

Strikes at the Chandler Mine in Ely, Fayal Mine near Eveleth and Hull-Rust Mine

at Hibbing in 1904 and 1905 all resulted in violence. There were threatened lynchings, rocks were rolled down mine pits on workers refusing to strike, there were beatings, there was gunfire – strikers were shot. All of the strikes failed – and failed miserably. The combination of town marshals, sheriffs and deputized company guards was too much for unorganized immigrant miners striking in individual mines. "The reason the companies are so cruel to us is because we aren't organized," complained one Slovenian miner in 1906. "Only through organization can the worker live like a man in freedom."[50]

The American Federation of Labor (AFL), largest union in the country, was not interested in organizing unskilled foreign miners, but there was a union that was. The Western Federation of Miners sent organizers to the range in 1906. The WFM was a militant industrial union formed in the 1890s to counter company use of gunmen, vigilantes and deputized marshals to break strikes in western gold and copper mining camps. The union was then under the direction of "Big Bill Haywood," who was not afraid to apply the union's policy of

"direct action." Pitched battles between strikers and mine guards at Coeur d'Alene, Idaho, and Leadville and Cripple Creek, Colorado, resulted in bloodshed, arrests, jailings and long-smoldering hatred of the men who owned the mines.

"Those barbarous gold barons," said Haywood at a 1903 Colorado strike rally, "they do not find the gold, they do not mine the gold, they do not mill the gold, but by some weird alchemy all the gold belongs to them."[51]

Haywood had reasons for wanting to organize the miners of the Mesabi Range. In his mind, a strike on the iron range would make trouble for Rockefeller, whose interests included not only western copper mines, but also iron mines in Minnesota. Haywood had a second and more important reason to organize Mesabi miners. They had been used as "scabs" in some of the western mines. A good way to protect unionized miners' jobs in Colorado and Idaho was to have a union on the Mesabi.[52]

He sent organizers to the range, but they had little success. Iron Country miners distrusted the English-speaking union organizers as much as they distrusted the

Virginia's Socialist Opera Hall served as central headquarters for IWW Local No. 490 during the 1916 Mesabi miners' strike. Bukovas collection, Iron Range Research Center

207

English-speaking mine bosses. In 1907, Haywood sent Italian socialist Teofilo Petriella to Hibbing for one more try at organizing the iron range. Petriella, himself an immigrant, understood the situation at once. He set up his office in Hibbing and began developing locals with three sections – Finnish, Slavic and Italian. He placed a man who could speak the language at the head of each section. Membership soared.[53]

By June, there were 14 active WFM locals on the range. They talked direct action. Leaders blamed the Oliver for the corruption and poor working conditions in the mines. Word spread rapidly that there would soon be a strike on the Mesabi and it would be directed against the Oliver Iron Mining Company. The word was greeted with a certain amount of enthusiasm; red flags were hung from windows along Virginia's Chestnut Street, anarchist speakers gathered at street corners in Eveleth calling for a general strike, anti-"steel trust" speeches were heard at Mesaba Park near Chisholm and handbills describing "workers poised to mount the barricades" were handed out in Hibbing.[54]

There were no red flags or speeches on street corners in the blossoming company town of Coleraine. Tom Cole, under instructions from United States Steel executives in New York, sent word to John Greenway "to make a stand."

Special deputies hired in Duluth were brought into the district – 500 of these temporary guards are said to have appeared in Bovey alone – and pressure was applied on local businessmen not to extend credit to any worker attempting to strike. Along with this, newspapers in Grand Rapids and Bovey waged a relentless and clearly effective war of words against industrial unionism. As a result, the WFM made few inroads in the Canisteo District and "work in the mines continued unabated" all through the summer of 1907.[55]

On July 17, the Oliver discharged 200 men. A dockworkers strike had tied up shipping on the Great Lakes and the lay-off might have been seen as a normal mining company action, had not the men been card-carrying WFM members. On July 18, leaders of locals gathered in Hibbing and drew up a list of demands that were

presented to Oliver Iron Mining Company the next day. The demands included an eight-hour work day, elimination of the contract system of pay, modest wage increases and an end to kickbacks to bosses for a good place to work.[56]

The notice to strike was issued on July 20. It read "strike but no violence" and was posted on all roads leading to Oliver mines. It's hard to know how many miners responded because mass layoffs were taking place at the same time, but in the end something like 17,000 miners were off the job. Shovels stood motionless in Hibbing pits, drills stopped clattering outside of Chisholm and boiler fires went out in Eveleth and Virginia mines. All Oliver operations came to a standstill. It had never happened before.[57]

Management of the strike was taken over by local union organizers John Maki, John McNair, Nick De Stefano, Oscar Luihunen, Aate Heiskanen, A. Takela, Frank Lucas, John Movern, R. Lundstrom, E. McHale, F. Manarini and J. Conners – led, of course, by Petriella from his Hibbing strike center. The WFM call for solidarity was answered with a certain amount of enthusiasm and the mining industry found itself facing a serious labor rebellion.[58]

The Oliver Iron Mining Company contacted Minnesota Governor John A. Johnson and urged him to send state troops to the range as fast as possible to "prevent bloodshed and destruction of company property." Mine guards were organized to patrol all Mesabi mines, marshals were deputized in range towns and rifles handed out. Professional strikebreakers from New York and Chicago arrived by train and tensions mounted as the Oliver waited for Johnson's reply.[59]

Meanwhile, the Western Federation of Miners sponsored rallies in Hibbing, Virginia and Eveleth and hundreds of miners gathered at fund-raising meetings held in the halls of Mesabi Range towns. The Socialist Party brought in one of the greatest strike mobilizers of all time, Mary Harris Jones – "Mother Jones." She was then 77 years old. She would live to be 100. She made her opinion of the mining industry clear, "Those high-class burglars know the life and limb of the miner is unprotected by the laws. They

know miners' families live in company-owned shacks that are not fit for pigs!"[60]

Long columns of strikers paraded from town to town, location to location, mine to mine, calling other workers from their jobs. The situation became even more tense. Town marshals and deputized guards nervously patrolled the mines. St. Louis County Sheriff William Bates issued an order forbidding all future parades and public demonstrations.[61]

Governor Johnson didn't send troops. He decided to come to the range himself to meet with all parties. He talked to strikers in Hibbing, Mountain Iron, Eveleth and Virginia and conferred with mine officials, range politicians, policemen and town merchants.

On July 24 in Duluth, he listened to the following appeal on behalf of the strikers from a young Finnish miner named John Valimaki: "I am 24 years old. I came to this country from Finland with my father in 1901 and I have been a citizen just three days and I learned to read and write at home. In this state, there are 8,000,000 [sic] workers waiting for a chance to work and advance themselves. I am a socialist and I believe these mines should belong to the workers and not to mining companies.

"In short, I believe in work for the general good. We carry the red banner which is a symbol of our blood. We are not anarchists.... None of them are found in the mines. The socialists are a political party. As workers we belong to the Western Federation of Miners. All the socialists in the mines belong to it, but not all who belong to it are socialists.... We are striking for wages, but principally for an eight-hour day...."[62]

Governor Johnson went back to St. Paul. He still didn't send a militia. Instead, he assured both sides of protection by law and issued a proclamation guaranteeing miners the right to peaceful assembly in their halls – but no parades. With this guarantee, the union saw no reason to act outside the law. Although there were isolated incidents of violence and the iron range press and business community were openly hostile to the striking "foreign miners," the strike was – for the most part – peaceful.[63]

Facing prospects of a long-term strike and little opportunity to use their mine guards, the Oliver began importing new foreign labor. Trainloads of Montenegrins,

Serbians, Croatians, Greeks, Bulgarians, Slovenians, Bosnians and others – all fresh from the old country – were brought in to fill positions vacated by striking miners. They were housed in hastily built camps at Mountain Iron, Eveleth, Buhl – wherever there was an Oliver mine.[64]

By mid-August, most Oliver mines were again producing ore and tar-paper barracks had become a common sight on the Mesabi. By the end of the month, some of the smaller mining companies were able to resume full production, using only imported labor. The new arrivals probably had no idea they were being used to break a strike. Anyway, from their point of view, the pay at the mines was far better than they ever had seen in the old country.

From the company point of view, the new arrivals were not the most efficient workers that could be hoped for, but they were enough to discourage the strikers. One by one, men began returning to work and the strike melted away. Petriella himself went to Duluth to try to talk the new arrivals into not going to the Mesabi, while Finnish strike leaders urged their union brothers not to go back to work. But finally, even the Finnish socialists, who held out the longest, had to admit the strike was over.[65]

Strike leaders were blacklisted and hundreds of Finns, Italians, Croatians and Slovenians left the iron range forever. Reports of the exodus began appearing in the press in late August and by September *The Virginian, Eveleth News, Labor World* and *Duluth Daily News* were all reporting large numbers of people leaving the range. It was predicted that the labor force at the mines would be depleted by as much as "5,000 workers."[66]

Yet, many stayed on. Some miners simply returned to their old jobs, while others moved on to the next town or the next range in search of work. A few strikers became saloon keepers or merchants, but a larger number found work in the many lumber camps still operating on both sides of the Mesabi. Some, mostly Finns, managed to survive among the rocks and muskeg of the surrounding countryside on tiny homestead farms.[67]

In Hibbing, Chisholm and other Mesabi towns, new immigrant people replaced the old and the ethnic complexion changed – a

An Industrial Workers of the World parade in Hibbing on June 21, 1916. MAKI COLLECTION, IRON RANGE RESEARCH CENTER

little. In all of the towns there remained those who didn't forget. To them, there were two Mesabi ranges, the Mesabi of the "company men" and the Mesabi of the "worker." One did not talk union in public between 1907-1916 – and it wasn't always safe to be a company man. On January 20, 1908, the home of Captain T.J. Nicholas of the Mohawk Mine near Aurora was blown to smithereens with 15 sticks of dynamite. There were arrests; hatred festered.[68]

Labor unrest during these years was not confined to the Mesabi. In April 1913, Cuyuna Range miners employed by Inland Steel and Rogers-Brown Ore Company suddenly and without warning walked off the job demanding an end to contract pay, an eight-hour work day and company payment of hospital fees.[69] The strike was put down in the usual manner – there were scuffles, jailings and threats of additional militant actions. Then came the abortive – and tragic – copper miners' strike in Michigan, which began in July 1913 and lasted until April of the following year. After it was over, there was talk in Iron Country of "industrial war."[70]

The Strike of 1916

After 1907, conditions on the Mesabi gradually worsened. In the towns, the cost of living rose. Houses that had once rented for $20 a month were now $40 and $50. Food prices climbed. In March 1912, the work day was reduced from 10 hours to eight hours, but the contract system remained in force, bribes to petty mine bosses continued and wages fell below the $800-a-year poverty level.[71]

Mesabi mines had no problem finding workers. Immigrants in search of work arrived daily and, if a miner didn't like the mine, the company was happy to see him move on. After all, there were plenty who were willing and able to take his job. Little had changed since 1907 and, according to one Chisholm miner, "… every miner who makes $3 there, he had to tip the captain. I know of certain captains … where they are making tips of $5 and $10 from fellows … and then going into saloons, they have to buy drinks and cigars and I can prove that even if the mining captains like the woman of some of these miners, in order to keep his job, he has to keep his eyes shut to that … and if they see he makes more money, they cut him down and he has to work harder. I challenge anybody to say that any miner who works in the mines at contract for 10 years is fit for any labor after he gets to be 35 or 40 years."[72]

(Editor's Note: In fairness, at least to part of the above statement, it should be noted that there are anecdotal tales of ambitious husband and wife teams that enticed a powerful "mining man" into an adulterous situation, then extorted money from the executive not to reveal his indiscretion. In a case or two, names that later appear prominently in the city are mentioned in these tales.)

Then World War I broke out in Europe. The flow of immigrants stopped and, at the same time, the demand for iron ore increased. By 1915, there was a labor shortage. Mine operators drove their men harder, contract quotas were increased, but pay scales didn't improve.[73]

On June 2, 1916, workers at the St. James underground mine in Aurora, disgusted over what they perceived as "bad working conditions" and "poor pay," walked off the job. Led by Italian miner Joe Greeni, angry Finns, Italians and Slovenians went from mine to mine, stope to stope, shouting, "We've been robbed long enough! Its time to strike!"

Within two days, all of the mines at Aurora were closed and every miner was a striker. A committee was formed, grievances listed and an appeal sent to the local mine officials asking if a meeting could be held to make adjustments. The request went unanswered and the Aurora strikers, hundreds of them, along with their families, began a 75-mile march across the range spreading news of the strike. The response was astounding. All across the Mesabi, mine by mine, miners spontaneously left their posts and went home. There were no strike organizers, no strike committees. The

The funeral procession for John Alar passes down Virginia's Chestnut Street, on June 26, 1916, flourishing a banner reading, "Murdered by Oliver Gunmen." PAGLIARINI COLLECTION, IRON RANGE RESEARCH CENTER

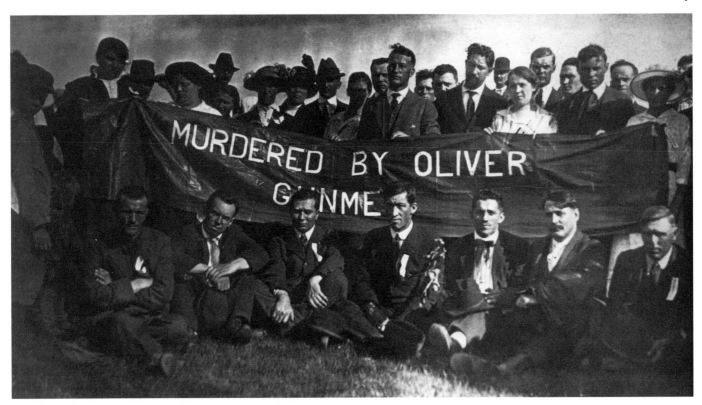

Banners boldly proclaimed "Murdered by Oliver Gunmen" at John Alar's funeral on June 26, 1916. (Carlo Tresca, a high-ranking IWW spokesman, is 4th from right, directly behind banner.) PAGLIARINI COLLECTION, IRON RANGE RESEARCH CENTER

walkout was clearly in response to low pay, difficult working conditions and the hated contract system.[74]

It isn't that there hadn't been union organizers on the range since the strike of 1907. Representatives of the American Federation of Labor had made visits to iron range towns at the request of some Mesabi miners and organizers had been in Virginia trying to get Italian timber workers to join the Industrial Workers of the World (IWW). The so-called "Italian timber workers" were really miners who were trying to supplement their income by working in lumber camps during the winter layoff.

As soon as the strike broke out, it became clear that, although it sympathized with the walkout, the AFL was not in a position to help. It was also clear that no help would be coming – or was wanted – from the Western Federation of Miners. The only union ready and willing to jump into the fray was the IWW.[75]

The IWW had become famous for its successful, but violent, textile strike conducted in Lawrence, Massachusetts, in 1912. However, since that time, it had suffered several losses and was going through a period of internal struggle. Bill Haywood, who now headed the union, was openly committed to the concept of class warfare and saw the Mesabi walkout as a possible beginning of widespread labor war against

industry and an opportunity to unify the IWW. From his headquarters in Chicago, he sent his best organizers to the range.[76]

The first to arrive was James Gilday, chairman of the committee that had organized the IWW-dominated Agricultural Workers Organization. He was followed by Sam Scarlett, a talented orator and fanatical IWW organizer from Canada; fiery Italian anarchist and IWW mobilizer Carlo Tresca; Slovenian-speaking Lithuanian Joe Schmidt, who had earned his reputation for militancy in the Lawrence strike of 1912; and IWW organizer and Haywood confidant, Arthur Boose.

On June 24, Frank Little, well-known organizer of western copper miners, was also sent to join them. He brought with him a $36 check to cover organizing expenses and instructed Scarlett to take command of all IWW activities related to the strike. Tresca was to be second in command and Schmidt, third.[77]

By the second week in June, the walkout was complete. Estimates of the number of men on strike varied between 10,000 and 20,000. When the IWW organizers arrived, they found capable leaders already at work at a newly formed strike center set up in Virginia's Socialist Hall. Joe Greeni from Aurora was there, along with John Seppanen of Virginia, Finnish Socialist William Wiertola and George Andreytchine, a Bulgarian civil engineer from an Oliver mine at Hibbing.

The Socialist Hall continued to serve as central headquarters for IWW Local No. 490 and, at Haywood's suggestion, individual strike committees were set up in every town. However, management of the strike remained with a 15-member central strike committee presided over by Tony Shragel of Virginia, Fulvio Petinelli of Eveleth and M.E. Shusterich of Chisholm.[78]

"Orderly demonstrations" and parades were planned in Hibbing and Virginia, a "strikers' police force" was formed to prevent anyone from interfering with the demonstrations, strikers' "relief stores" were set up in Nashwauk, Hibbing and other towns and demonstrators were instructed to "keep their hands in their pockets" and avoid violence at all times. However, Sam Scarlett himself struck a violent note when he assured a crowd of applauding miners at Virginia's Socialist Opera that "there is a point where non-violence will cease.... If any committee or anyone else in Virginia starts violence, the strikers will finish it ... and for every striker shot down by a company gunman, summary vengeance will be meted out."

Meanwhile, hundreds of miners filed into nearby Finnish halls to help draw up a list of demands to present to the companies.[79]

Oliver responded by recruiting and arming 1,000 mine guards who were quickly deputized by the sheriff of St. Louis County, John R. Meining. Other companies followed suit. They had learned their lesson in 1907. They were not waiting for the governor of the state to send up a militia. The deputized guards became a small army and, more or less, took over the range.[80]

On June 21, guards in Hibbing confronted a parade of 1,000 strikers carrying red flags and banners and the demonstration quickly turned into a riot. The next day, after a scuffle between guards and picketers in Virginia, Croatian miner John Alar, father of three children, was shot three times in the back. No one was arrested. His funeral took place on June 26 at the Socialist Opera and the procession to Calvary Cemetery, said to have been the largest ever in Virginia, included an estimated 3,000 mourners. It had been the wish of Alar's widow that a priest perform the last rites, but none was found who was willing to do so.

The Workers' Hall in Hibbing, was the planning center for demonstrations and parades during the 1916 strike. MAKI COLLECTION, IRON RANGE RESEARCH CENTER

213

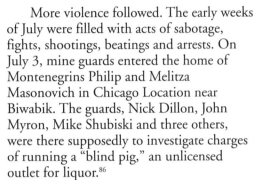

In the procession, marchers carried a red banner with the words "Murdered by Oliver Gunmen," and at graveside, Carlo Tresca asked all in attendance to solemnly swear, "That if any Oliver gunmen shoot or wound any miner, we will take a tooth for a tooth, an eye for an eye, a life for a life." The range hovered on the brink of industrial war.[81]

On June 28, the list of demands was presented to the mining companies. The list included an eight-hour work day timed from when the miners entered the mine until they were outside the mine, pay day twice a month, immediate payment when a miner quit, abolition of the Saturday night shift and an immediate end to the contract system of pay. On the list were also modest pay increases: $2.75 a day for open pit mining, $3 a day for underground mining and $3.50 a day for wet underground work. The IWW did not ask for union recognition, nor did it call for a contractual agreement from the companies.[82]

Instead, it issued a declaration of war: "War has been declared against the steel trust and independent mining companies of Minnesota by the Industrial Workers of the World. The iron miners are mustering. Twenty thousand have left the mines and pits. More than 7,000 have already been sworn in. The steam shovels are idle. The drills are silent.... These barehanded iron miners, driven to desperation, have declared industrial war against the United States steel corporations...."[83]

On June 30, Governor J.A.A. Burnquist telegraphed the St. Louis County sheriff and ordered him to arrest all labor rioters, to prevent all unlawful assemblies and to use all of his powers to maintain order. Tresca, Little and Joe Gilday were immediately arrested and placed in the Virginia jail but were quickly released when 3,000 strikers converged on the city.[84]

Meanwhile, in Hibbing, two armored cars containing sharpshooters armed with rapid-fire Winchesters began making daily patrols of Hull-Rust and Mahoning mine properties and each night a small army of 300 well-armed men stood guard. Signs went up on Oliver properties at Virginia warning: "Any Striker Who Steps on Mining Property Does So At the Risk of His Life." The warning was backed by Oliver police carrying Winchester carbines.[85]

More violence followed. The early weeks of July were filled with acts of sabotage, fights, shootings, beatings and arrests. On July 3, mine guards entered the home of Montenegrins Philip and Melitza Masonovich in Chicago Location near Biwabik. The guards, Nick Dillon, John Myron, Mike Shubiski and three others, were there supposedly to investigate charges of running a "blind pig," an unlicensed outlet for liquor.[86]

There was a scuffle. Melitza Masonovich was thrown to the floor. Three Montenegrin boarders joined in the scuffle. There were gun shots. John Myron fell dead on the floor. John Ladvala, Biwabik soda pop dealer who happened to be in the area, was also killed. The Montenegrins were immediately arrested and charged with the murder of Sheriff Deputy John Myron. The IWW leaders were also blamed for the killing. It was alleged that, even if they were nowhere near the incident, they had caused the murder by their speeches. No charges were drawn up for the death of Ladvala.[87]

Mass arrests followed. Local leaders were picked up: Leo and Mike Stark, Joe Nickich, George Andretchine, others. At Virginia, "Scarlett, Tresca, Schmidt, Little, Gilday and other IWW organizers" were taken from their hotel at 3 o'clock in the morning, manacled and put on a southbound train to Duluth, where they were charged with first-degree murder. The arrests seemed to take the life out of the strike.[88]

However, iron range merchants and businessmen, many of whom sympathized with the strikers, began calling for a council to mediate the strike. Although mayors Victor Power, Michael Boylan and others were openly anti-IWW, they also objected to liberties taken by some of the deputized mine guards. They formed a "Range Council of Municipalities" and began listening to miners' complaints. The Range Council went on record condemning the use of armed guards and opposing Burnquist's order to arrest strikers and try them in Duluth.[89]

In mid-July, in an attempt to bolster the sagging spirits of striking miners, Haywood sent Elizabeth Gurley Flynn to the range. The 25-year-old IWW organizer, well known for her success in rallying strikers

Captain Bill says:—

"It seems to me that there are enough safety rules and appliances; safe tools and equipment are ample; but most of our accidents are caused by men themselves doing something just a little bit wrong, using poor judgment, or *taking a chance.*

OLIVER IRON MINING COMPANY

Eveleth District   Bulletin No. 41

during the Lawrence textile strike of 1912, had been on the Mesabi before, shortly after the strike of 1907. Haywood was hopeful that her speaking talent and organizing ability would be enough to hold the strike together until aid could be delivered to the striking miners. She traveled from one end of the Mesabi to the other in an old bakery truck driven by a couple of Italian strikers. She spoke wherever she could find a group of miners.[90] Her impact on the morale of strikers was profound.

"When Elizabeth spoke, the excitement of the strikers became a visible thing. She stood up there, young, with her Irish blue eyes, her face magnolia white, her cloud of black hair.… It was as though a spurt of flame had gone through the audience, something stirring and powerful, a feeling which made the liberation of people possible."[91]

She was joined by Joe Ettor, Ed Rowan and Joe Gruni, all of whom made passionate speeches pleading with Mesabi miners to continue on with the strike. It is said that the speakers moved a thousand strikers, many with wives and children, "Finnish women

pushing their baby carriages along," to march in Virginia for almost 12 hours "in over 100-degrees heat" on July 27, 1916.[92]

However, speeches were not enough to hold the strike together. With its leadership jailed and IWW failure to deliver aid to striking workers, the strike collapsed. The men went back to work in August.

Meanwhile, the violence attracted national attention. Mediators were sent to the range and a federal investigation followed. The Department of Labor recommended reforms and reports in local papers suggested that United States Steel Corporation was now ready to moderate its position and become more concerned with the plight of its workers. A month after the strike, day wages and contract rates in underground mines "were increased by 15$\frac{1}{2}$ to 20 percent," and in November, Oliver announced a second pay raise amounting to almost 10 percent.

Although the contract pay system in underground mines was never completely eliminated, most mining companies eventually allowed contract miners to select their own partners and fixed the rate only at the beginning of each month. In the end, except for semi-

Oliver Iron Mining Company took the lead in trying to improve safety and working conditions for its employees.
UNITED STATES STEEL CORPORATION COLLECTION, IRON RANGE RESEARCH CENTER

OLIVER IRON MINING CO. (SAFETY PICNIC)
TUG OF WAR - STEAM SHOVEL VS. LOCO-MEN
EVELETH DIST. ELY LAKE PARK EVELETH

"The Oliver" sponsored picnics, outings and contests for employees and their families. UNITED STATES STEEL CORPORATION COLLECTION, IRON RANGE RESEARCH CENTER

monthly pay, most of the commissioners' recommendations were instituted.[93]

The strike occurred at a time when steel markets were rising. There is no doubt that the mining companies wanted to get the men back to work as soon as possible. With America's entry into World War I, with markets at an all-time high, with the labor pool at an all-time low, the mines of Iron Country wanted – and needed – a contented work force.

Iron Country of the 1920s

If the steel industry learned anything from the strike of 1916, it was to never let a strike like that occur again – and a strike like that didn't occur again – at least for another 30 years. The Oliver Iron Mining Company took the lead in trying to make things better for its employees. It sponsored picnics, outings and contests. There were employee stock ownership programs, bonus payments and generally improved working conditions in most of the mines. The 1920s were the years of the Oliver Clubs, company gold watches – and the company cop.

Oliver guards worked round the clock to protect company property. Heavy gates with guard posts were set up on roads leading to the mines and trespassers were arrested and, in one or two cases, even shot. Company cops patrolled the streets of locations, curfews were strictly adhered to and company officials joined with the Rotary, Elks and American Legion in promoting and supporting youth hockey programs, curling bonspiels, local baseball teams, theatricals, Boy Scout troops and sports festivals of all kinds in an effort help make the various nationalities of Iron Country better citizens – and, hopefully, better and more loyal workers.

To the average working Joe in the 1920s, the mines offered little hope for advancement or personal satisfaction – nor did they do much for one's personal esteem. This was not only true for miners, but, to a certain extent, for their families as well. Satisfactions like these had to be sought outside of the mines, locations and homes. Rangers of the 1920s embraced the athletic and cultural opportunities with an enthusiasm beyond all expectations. To the people of Iron Country they were "a welcome diversion from the drudgery of the mines."[94]

Iron Country towns took on an air of permanency during the 1920s. Streets were paved. Brick and concrete buildings replaced the shacks and frame structures of earlier times. Residents took renewed pride in their schools and public buildings.

Miners and their families became avid participants in many aspects of 1920s American culture. They listened to Will Rogers and Ed Wynn on the radio, thrilled to the exploits of Charles Lindbergh and Babe Ruth, rode the streetcar to Virginia to root for the "Ore Diggers" at Ewens Field and took the 6 p.m. tram to Hibbing to watch Clara Bow and Rudolph Valentino at the movies. They were flappers and jazz lovers, wore one-piece bathing suits and danced the Charleston – and violated prohibition just like every other American community.

Yet, within some Iron Country homes, old ways persisted, foreign languages could be heard at the dinner table and parents and grandparents to some extent still thought of themselves as strangers in a foreign land.

The IWW was gone from Iron Country by 1921. After one more attempt at a strike against the Virginia and Rainy Lake Lumber Company in 1917, the union left the range, defeated.[95] Anti-war positions taken in 1917 and 1918 had turned the forces of the nation against industrial unionism. There were jailings of aliens, "left wingers" and "slackers"

– of which Iron Country seemed to have a somewhat disproportionate share. The conservatism and isolation dominating American politics during the 1920s was felt strongly on the range, unions were discredited and foreign speaking miners were seen as potential threats to property and production.

Iron range public schools sponsored Americanization classes designed to turn the suspect "foreigners" into "responsible English-speaking citizens." Children in St. Louis County rural schools wore pins with the words "We only speak English in our Family," and Oliver Iron Mining Company put up posters reminding workers that citizens stood a far greater chance for pay raises than did aliens.

Night schools for learning English and American ways became part of 1920s public education in Eveleth, Virginia, Buhl, Chisholm, Hibbing, Nashwauk and most other range towns. A special effort was made to draw women into the program, and to do this, classes were extended to the company locations. At Kittsville, Carson Lake, Leonidas and other location schools, teachers found parents unable to express themselves in English, ancient superstitions like "pinning the tail of a rabbit on the shoulders of a baby to keep the child's eyes straight,"

A two-car train travels westbound on Third Avenue in Virginia. The railroad was a primary mode of transportation for workers and other Iron Range travelers before good roads were developed between range communities. It connected virtually all of the towns and locations of the Mesabi Range. KIRBY COLLECTION, IRON RANGE RESEARCH CENTER

Iron Range schools sponsored Americanization classes, designed to turn foreign immigrants into English-speaking Americans. SALVINI COLLECTION, IRON RANGE RESEARCH CENTER

and very little understanding of the importance of citizenship.

As one teacher explained, "We start our work in the belief that the home is the heart of America and,… unless the spirit of the home is truly American, nothing has been gained. The mother must not be forgotten in the Americanization process…."[96]

It came as no surprise to many in the 1920s that the Oliver Iron Mining Company was involved in activities other than sponsoring picnics and Americanizing immigrant people. In 1928, the company was accused of running a spy system designed to rid itself of potential "trouble makers" and discourage the establishment of unions on the range.

In a book called *Spies in Steel*, Frank L. Palmer, labor reporter for *Federal Press*, investigated claims of a former Oliver employee and exposed an intricate network of company-paid spies that reached into almost every organization on the range, even churches, and reported all anti-company

sentiment encountered. Rangers had long suspected that this was the case.[97]

The years 1919-1929 saw little unionization and even fewer labor disturbances and it wasn't until after the passage of the Wagner Act in 1935 that any real union movement was again seen on the range. In November of that year, John L. Lewis led eight affiliates of the AFL into forming a Committee for Industrial Organization (later the Congress of Industrial Organizations) – the CIO.

The years 1936-1938 would mark the greatest surge of union activity in the history of Iron Country. A Steelworkers Organizing Committee, under the direction of such men as Joe Van Nordstrand and Martin Mackie, led miner after miner into the ranks of the CIO. Organizing took place, first in secret and then, in 1938, openly and, after 1941, it was an act of patriotism to join the CIO. Labor and industry had combined forces in the greatest wartime production effort the world had ever seen. ■

CHAPTER 12

Depression, War, Taconite and More

In 1929, the mines of Iron Country were on their way to a record shipping season. Steel production was at an all-time high and ore was being removed at an unprecedented rate. The range was a place of beneficiation plants and mechanized mines. Where crews of pick and shovel miners once worked, there were now giant electric shovels, conveyor belts, electric tuggers, power loaders and mechanical scrapers.

In 1917, it took more than 20,000 Mesabi miners to produce a record 41 million tons of ore. In 1929, 12,500 miners produced 43 million tons. Machines not only improved production, but seemed an answer to many labor problems. They never complained, never tired, were more efficient and far more profitable than human labor – and they never went on strike.

If there were less men in the mines in 1929, it didn't seem to matter. Iron Country towns had expanded and diversified. There were other jobs – bricklayers, carpenters, plumbers, painters, letter carriers, meat cutters, teamsters, machinists and a host of other occupations. It seemed a time of prosperity and opportunity, not only in Iron Country, but everywhere in America.

The Great Depression (1930-1937)

Between 1925-1929, the average price of common stock on the New York Stock Exchange more than doubled. Speculation strained credit to the breaking point. Then came October 29, 1929. The market crashed. Millions lost their savings. Businesses and banks closed. Public and private debts rose to staggering sums.

Iron Country ore production fell from more than 47 million tons in 1929 to barely 2 million in 1932. Employment in St. Louis County mines dropped from 12,000 to less than 2,500.[1] An eerie stillness set in. Stripping of overburden stopped, shovels and locomotives stopped operating, crushers went silent and, although maintenance crews kept machinery oiled and ready for use, the pits were strangely empty and underground mines dark.

Retail sales in range towns slowed to a standstill and the entire nation slid into depression. There had been depressions in Iron Country before, but none like this. Debts mounted, steel mills cut production, mines closed, sawmills shut down, there were mass layoffs, tax collections sagged and government services were cut.

Mining companies tried to give their more valued employees a day or two of work now and then, but for most people there were no jobs. Men clustered on street corners or waited in line at the relief office. At the outskirts of Virginia, a tar-paper and packing crate town appeared. They called it "Hooverville." It was one of many to form in America during the Depression.[2]

President Herbert Hoover got the blame for the hard times. This wasn't entirely justified, but it could be argued the Hoover administration underestimated the seriousness of the situation. Most people did. It seemed inconceivable that America's economy could go through a decade of such good times and then collapse without warning. Prosperity had to be just around the corner – all that was needed was confidence.

In Iron Country, people waited for the prosperity to arrive. There were no evictions from company houses in the locations. Unemployed miners and their families expanded their gardens; they hunted, fished and cut trees from company land to heat their homes. Meanwhile, relief rolls grew.

In Hibbing and in other range towns, people turned to their schools – the finest schools in the world. Learning opportunities expanded and school buildings became centers for public meetings – and often

The federal Civilian Conservation Corps program sent hundreds of young men into the woods to work on conservation and other public improvement projects. CIVILIAN CONSERVATION CORPS COLLECTION, IRON RANGE RESEARCH CENTER

much needed employment. There wasn't a cleaner floor in the world than that of an iron range school during the Depression.

There were some in Iron Country who saw the Depression as a sign that America's free enterprise system was failing. The "steel trust" was to blame. It had to be brought into line. Old strike leaders from 1907 and 1916 emerged. They abandoned the IWW policy of "direct action" and now called for "political action" – and political action came in the form of Minnesota's Farmer-Labor Party.

Iron Country's first Farmer-Labor club was formed in Hibbing on January 25, 1923, ironically to oppose re-election of Victor Power as village president. Although Power's efforts to make Hibbing "the richest little village in the world" had won him much admiration and support, it also gave rise to detractors – many from the ranks of labor. Convinced that Power had become too "self important" and possibly "had taken up with the mining companies," the anti-Power people worked hard to win votes to their cause. But the "Little Giant" treated the

Hibbing Farmer-Laborites the way he had once treated the mining companies. He beat them and returned to office.[3]

The Farmer-Labor Party turned out to be much more than a local club. It advocated public ownership of large-scale industry, consumer and producer cooperatives and private ownership of small businesses and farms. It became the largest political party in the state and, in 1932, ran Minneapolis attorney Floyd B. Olson for governor.

Campaigning in Ely in the fall of 1932, Olson said to Iron Country's unemployed, "Do not be alarmed by any threat of the mining companies to move out of the state…. We can operate our state mines if necessary."[4]

This was what Iron Country's unemployed miners wanted to hear. They flocked to the ranks of the Farmer-Labor Party. They liked Floyd B. Olson – and they liked what they were hearing from the Democratic Party's candidate for president, Franklin Delano Roosevelt.

"Values have shrunk to fantastic levels; taxes have risen; our ability to pay has failed;

220

government of all kinds is faced by serious curtailment of income; the means of exchange are frozen in the currents of trade; the withered leaves of industrial enterprise lie on every side ... the savings of many years in thousands of families are gone. More important, a host of unemployed citizens face the grim problem of existence.... The unscrupulous money changers stand today indicted in the court of public opinion.... They have no vision ... and where there is no vision the people perish.... This nation asks for action and action now."[5]

Roosevelt won in a landslide and Floyd Olson and other Minnesota Farmer-Laborites were swept into office. Many thought that they would now see government action to reopen the mines and put the men back to work. It didn't happen. Much of the Farmer-Labor platform was picked up by Roosevelt's "Brain Trust," modified and molded into New Deal legislation.

When 1935 came to an end, production in Minnesota iron mines had risen to 20 million tons and people on the range were talking in New Deal terms – WPA, PWA, CCC, government programs to put people back to work. The Civilian Conservation Corps sent hundreds of young men into the woods to work on programs of conservation in the CCC camps. Few range communities were without their WPA project. It seemed that if there was a need, there was a government program for it. No doubt there were many who doubted the wisdom of FDR's spending programs, but by 1936, retail sales in range towns had improved and there was talk of an upward trend in the steel industry.[6]

As far as the men in the mines were concerned, the most impacting actions of the New Deal were the National Recovery Act of 1933 and the Wagner Act of 1935. Labor's right to organize and bargain collectively was recognized by law.

Beginning in 1936, the CIO, led by John L. Lewis, launched a campaign to organize the entire steel industry, "from the mill to the mine." At the same time, United States Steel, the largest of the steel producers, once described as the "the citadel of the open shop," made it clear it would never require employees to belong to a union in order to gain employment in its mills. Iron Country

responded with the greatest surge of union expansion in its history.[7]

Inclusion of the "7-a Clause" in the National Recovery Act legalized the organization of unions for the purpose of collective bargaining and encouraged the AFL to send representatives of its Mine, Mill and Smelter Workers Union to the range. They managed to organize a few local chapters, but the companies responded with tighter enforcement of their labor policies and the formation of a number of "company unions."

There were no further developments until 1937, when the Amalgamated Association of Iron, Steel and Tin Workers of North America, a CIO affiliate, brought employees of Butler Brothers and International Harvester at Nashwauk and Keewatin into their union.[8]

Nashwauk and Keewatin became the strongest CIO towns on the range. Town trustees, clerks and even mayors were voted into office from the ranks of the CIO. The union worked hand in hand with the now fast-growing Farmer-Labor Party. In 1936, following the unexpected death of Governor Olson, the Farmer-Labor Party, led by Elmer Benson, won 72 percent of the range vote and Eveleth CIO organizer John T. Bernard was sent to Congress.[9]

Born on the French island of Corsica, John Toussaint Bernard came to Eveleth in 1907 at the age of 14. He worked for a time as an underground miner in the Spruce Mine. After serving in World War I, he became a member of Eveleth's Fire Department, a position he held until election to Congress in 1936. He rose swiftly within the ranks of the Farmer-Labor Party and made no secret of his pro-labor sentiments. "I believe that labor should have the right to collective bargaining in fact as well as in name and that those who produce our wealth are entitled to an equitable share."[10]

Bernard served only one term in Congress. He was defeated in 1938 by AFL-endorsed Republican Bill Pittinger. Friction between the CIO and AFL, along with bitter internal political fights after 1937, weakened the Farmer-Labor Party to the extent that it was unable to elect a statewide official until it fused with the Democratic Party in 1944.[11]

During his short time in office, John Bernard earned the distinction of being the

only member of Congress to vote against an embargo of arms to either side in the Spanish Civil War. The Spanish government was trying to fight off a military take over by General Francisco Franco, who was at the time receiving arms and military support from dictators Benito Mussolini of Italy and Adolph Hitler of Germany. Most Americans, including the president, favored neutrality. War was brewing in Europe.

The War Years (1939-1945)

In 1939, Germany attacked Poland. In 1940, the Soviet Union moved troops into the Baltic states and went to war with Finland. By the end of 1940, much of Europe, including France, had fallen to the armed might of Nazi Germany and Fascist Italy. Great Britain stood alone. What if Britain couldn't hold out?

Iron Country families listened closely on their radios to the measured words of Britain's new prime minister, Winston Churchill: "We shall not flag or fail, we shall go on to the end. We shall fight in France. We shall fight on the seas and the oceans.... We shall fight in the fields and the streets, we shall fight in the hills. We shall never surrender.... "[12]

As frightening as it was, war in Europe did help to bring a measure of economic relief to the range. In 1939, a reluctant Congress lifted the arms embargo and Britain and France began placing orders for war materials on a cash-and-carry basis. Production in Minnesota iron mines rose from less than 15 million tons in 1938 to 33 million tons in 1939. By the end of 1940, it was almost 49 million tons and 9,000 miners were again at work.[13]

In March 1941, prodded by President Roosevelt, Congress passed "Lend Lease," an act providing armaments "to any country deemed vital to the defense of the United States" – namely Britain. From then on, the nation's automobile manufacturers and steel producers were pushed steadily toward retooling for war.[14]

The iron mines were among the first to feel the change. Iron Country ore production jumped to more than 64 million tons.[15] Never before had so much iron ore been mined in such a short time. Sixty million tons came from the Mesabi Range.

Then war came. On a bleak December day threatening snow, Iron Country families gathered at their radios to hear the solemn words of America's president:

"Yesterday, December 7, 1941 – a date which will live in infamy – the United States of America was suddenly and deliberately attacked by naval and air forces of the Empire of Japan. The United States was at peace with that nation and, at the solicitation of Japan, was still in conversation with that government and its emperor, looking toward maintenance of peace in the Pacific.... The attack yesterday on the Hawaiian Islands has caused severe damage to American naval and military forces. Very many American lives have been lost...."[16]

If there had been mistrust of the man in the White House, if industry had been reluctant to incur the expense of converting from cars to tanks, there was no doubt about industry's motives after Pearl Harbor. "With confidence in our armed forces – with the unbounded determination of our people – we will gain the inevitable triumph – so help us God," promised President Roosevelt on that fateful day.

Despite the confident words, there were reasons for Americans to feel vulnerable. It had been only a year since the United States had been given its rank among the military powers of the world – 19th. In 1940, the total number of active-duty servicemen was less than 500,000, the army's tanks and guns were outdated, most of its planes were too old for active service and it was rumored that there were no more than four up-to-date anti-aircraft guns in the entire country.[17]

Despite this, the United States was in better shape to fight a war than at any other time in history. The reason was that this country had an operating steel-making infrastructure that was complete in every detail. Easily mined Iron Country ores could speedily be shipped by rail to loading docks at Two Harbors, Duluth and Superior and carried down lake by a fleet of hundreds of existing ore carriers to steel mill receiving ports at Chicago, Gary, Detroit, Toledo, Sandusky, Cleveland, Ashtabula and by a stretch of rail to the chief center of steel production during the war, Pittsburgh.[18]

For more than a half-century, ores had been steadily flowing to the open hearths

and blast furnaces of the eastern Great Lakes. It was an infrastructure that had been tried and tested, one that met the steel needs of America's industries, one that grew steadily with this nation as it rose to industrial greatness. If there was a question as to its ability to meet the needs of unprecedented global scale warfare, it was quickly answered.

Under the guidance of the War Production Board, the steel industry produced for war. Steel production (which had been only 28.35 million tons in 1938) rose to 52.8 million tons in 1939, almost 67 million tons in 1940, 82.84 million tons in 1941, 86.2 million tons in 1942 and more than 89 million tons in 1943. By comparison, the 1943 combined steel production capacity of Germany and all other Axis nations was estimated to be no more than 51 million tons.[19]

The need for weapons of modern warfare, acute in 1940, was remedied. Between July 1940 and December 1941, American industry produced 1,341 naval ships, 136 merchant ships, 126,113 machine guns, 4,258 tanks, 23,228 military airplanes. In 1942, industry produced 8,059 warships, 760 merchant ships, 666,820 machine guns, 23,884 tanks and 47,859 military airplanes.[20] Much of the raw material came from Iron Country's mines – 188,310,000 tons of it.[21] Never before had so much iron ore been mined in such a short time, never before had so much steel been produced and never before had so many ships, guns, tanks and planes rolled off assembly lines.

In 1942, there were war jitters on the iron range. Japanese forces seemed unstoppable. The Philippine Islands were invaded. Bataan and Corregidor fell. The Aleutian Islands were invaded and there was talk of possible air raids on the mines. Civilian Defense wardens with arm bands and binoculars climbed to the tops of buildings and stationed themselves in fire towers to watch for enemy planes. There were blackouts.

All men between 18 and 45 years of age were required to register for the draft. There were hundreds of voluntary enlistments from range towns. An army of 10 million was in the making. Congress authorized the enlistment of women in early 1942 – after a "spirited fight."[22] Iron Country women

joined the services and became WAACs, WAVES, SPARS and WAFSs (respectively: Women's Auxiliary Army Corps, Women Appointed for Voluntary Emergency Service, *Semper Peratus* Always Ready Service, Women's Auxiliary Ferrying Squadron).

The range faced a mild labor shortage in 1942. With so many men in service, women, for the first time, went to work in the mines. They loaded ore cars, they welded dipper teeth, they manned the pumps, mucked the ore and did a hundred other things that had to be done. A shortage of men was felt in other places. Male teachers disappeared from schools and women bus drivers became common. There were other shortages. Ration books appeared in every home – blue stamps for canned goods – red stamps for meat. Sugar and gasoline were rationed.

Placard seen in public buildings during World War II urged young men and women to enlist in the war effort. IRON RANGE RESEARCH CENTER

Businesses like Chisholm's
First National Bank promoted
the war effort during World
War II. VEDA PONIKVAR, IRON
RANGE RESEARCH CENTER

Never before, or since, has Iron Country seen such patriotism. There were no slackers. There were no anti-war demonstrators. Even the local communists supported the war effort. Placards appeared in public buildings declaring "Uncle Sam Wants YOU!" and billboards called for everyone to do their part – "The boys on Bataan don't work a 40-hour week" – "Keep 'em Flying." A common poster of the time, "Men Working Together," portrayed a soldier, a sailor – and a steelworker.

In early 1942, iron ore miners came under the wartime no strike pledge. Disputes were handled by the Government's War Labor Board. As production in iron mines rose, work became an act of patriotism and a six-day week was soon considered the norm. There was overtime. Lots of it. Miners' pay checks had never been so large.

New mines were opened, some in unlikely places. A lake was drained near Aurora and the Embarrass River diverted to expose a deposit of hematite. It was opened as the Embarrass Lake Mine and contributed

15 million tons to the war effort. Old mines were stripped and expanded: the Canton, the Schley, the Sharon, the Holman and Hartley – and the great Hull-Rust. Even the old Mahoning was scrammed for every ounce of hematite that could be found. All across Iron Country, mines poured out their natural ores as never before.[23]

During 1943 and 1944, Iron Country mines continued to produce iron ore at a rate of nearly 70 million tons a year. The tide of battle turned. Hitler's Europe was invaded, the Japanese Navy was destroyed and American troops took back the islands of the Pacific. And then, in 1945, it was over.

Speaking from the battleship *Missouri* in September 1945, General Douglas MacArthur accepted the Japanese surrender and issued the following warning: "A great tragedy has ended. A great victory has been won … a new era is upon us.… The utter destructiveness of war now blots out this alternative. We have had our last chance. If we do not devise some … more equitable system, Armageddon will be at our door."

The rusting wreckage of steel formed from Iron Country's mines lay strewn across the planet – smashed and broken tanks, trucks, ships, guns – the remains of a thousand different military devices. And most of Minnesota's natural ores were gone.

The Postwar Steelworker Strikes (1946-1952)

At the end of the war, iron range mine worker concerns were not so much about the ore running out. They were about the high cost of living, low wages, accident insurance and pensions.

These concerns resulted in industrywide strikes in 1946 and 1949. They were not at all like the strikes of 1907 and 1916. There was no talk of industrial war. There were no deputized mine guards. There was no violence and public sympathy was with the men. Steelworker wages were frozen during the war, while the cost of living rose. Now that the war was over, the men deserved a raise. Iron range merchants happily contributed money to buy coffee for strikers on the picket lines.

This is not to say that the walkouts were free of controversy, hard feelings and a certain amount of dissension. The steelworkers strike of 1946 was about a pay raise and within 26 days had won an industrywide 18½-cents-an-hour increase. However, that March, after the strike ended, the only miners on the range called back to work under the new contract were those employed by Oliver Iron Mining Company, Inter-State Iron Company and Wheeling Steel Corporation. Other companies failed to follow the lead of the Oliver as they normally did – at least they were slow to come to agreement and, for a short time, the iron range union faced a confusing and disheartening situation. Steelworkers at the mills and some members in the mines were back at work with a raise, other miners were not.[24]

Call backs continued during the weeks that followed and, by the end of May, all of Iron Country's miners were back on the job with a pay raise – that is, all, except those employed by International Harvester. They remained on strike for almost another year before their issues were finally resolved. There were hard feelings. There was controversy.

What was clear was the fact that union miners in Iron Country were inexorably tied to the nationwide steelworkers union with most of its membership in steel plants. Could it be that the union leadership was more concerned about steelworkers in the mills than those in the mines? There was talk about forming an all-miners union. However, in the eyes of the iron range leadership and what turned out to be most of the members, the big union had proved its worth with the assistance it gave to miners still on strike after the March agreement.[25]

The Strike of 1949 was about a pension plan. The steelworkers union wanted the plan to apply to all of its members and be entirely paid by the companies. When the companies refused and the union threatened to strike, President Harry Truman invoked the Taft-Hartley Act and appointed a fact-finding board to investigate the disagreement. The Taft-Hartley Act had been passed in 1947 over the president's veto by the strongly Republican 80th Congress. It outlawed the closed shop, authorized an 80-day injunction against strikes considered harmful to national security and, among other things, required a 60-day cooling-off period before any strike could take place.

However, in this case, Truman's committee found that steel companies could well-afford the plan being asked for by the union. In October, after companies responded with only a partial plan, the steelworkers walked off the job and Minnesota's iron miners went out with them. The strike, however, was quickly settled, a pension plan became part of the contract and the entire Iron Country community breathed a sigh of relief.[26]

The strike of 1952 was different. America was again at war – this time in Korea. That June, iron range steel workers went out again as part of a nationwide steel strike. There were efforts to get President Truman to invoke the Taft-Hartley Act and force the men back to work. This time, Truman refused and the strike dragged on. It was a gloomy summer, businesses reported losses, sales declined, weeks passed – still no end in sight. Families began leaving.

The strike lasted 55 days. It was not popular. There was dissension in the rank and file. Issues were complicated and hard for the general public to understand. Many

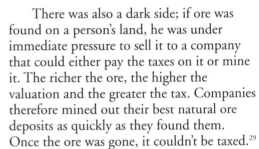

thought it was wrong to strike during a time of war. Loyalty and patriotism were questioned. Despite this, the steelworkers union won a pay raise, expanded its membership and every mine on the range was unionized.[27]

There would be more strikes. But during the 1950s, the iron range steelworkers union changed in significant ways, as did unions all over the country. The AFL and CIO merged and became increasingly influential and prosperous. Negotiating teams and political action committees replaced the strike committees and militancy of earlier times. Many of the traditional goals of organized labor had been achieved. But, in Iron Country, a new threat loomed ahead. The natural ores on which miners based their jobs had run out.

The Formation of the IRRRB

It was hard for people living on the range to imagine the ore running out. It seemed that whenever mining companies wanted ore they found it. They dug it up from under mine dumps, under towns, under lakes and swamps – in places where everyone was sure there was no ore. The reality was different. There was no more natural ore to discover and the mining industry knew it. In fact, the mining industry had been doing everything it could to see that the ores would run out – especially the rich ores.

The reason was the tax situation. In 1940, mining companies paid three kinds of taxes – a royalty tax, occupation tax and ad valorem tax. Royalty and occupation taxes were based on the amount of ore being mined. But it was, as it had been before, the ad valorem tax, the tax on ore still in the ground, that bothered mine owners. It was a tax they had to pay year after year, even if they didn't mine.

At the same time, it was the *ad valorem* tax that allowed range towns to prosper and gave the region's schools their reputation for being some of the best in the nation.[28] It was the ad valorem tax that provided the funds to help unemployed miners find work in the villages and schools during the Depression. It was the source of income around which mayors and city councils planned their budgets. It was described by some as the lifeblood of the iron range.

There was also a dark side; if ore was found on a person's land, he was under immediate pressure to sell it to a company that could either pay the taxes on it or mine it. The richer the ore, the higher the valuation and the greater the tax. Companies therefore mined out their best natural ore deposits as quickly as they found them. Once the ore was gone, it couldn't be taxed.[29]

It wasn't that the mining industry didn't do everything it could to get the law changed. After winning a per capita limitation on taxes in 1921, bill after bill was introduced in the state Legislature to curb town spending. Iron range legislators fought off every bill – that is, until 1940. That year, the unexpected happened. United States Steel's Oliver Iron Mining Company, which had never released a pound of ore to anyone else, announced that it would start selling its ore on the open market. The Oliver was holding most of the high grade ore on the range. The company was dumping it.[30]

The range legislative delegation was faced with a tough decision. Giving up the ad valorem tax meant a significant loss of money for schools and communities. Protecting it could mean mine closings and ghost towns.

Facing prospects of revenue losses, a group of Mesabi Range legislators and businessmen, led by then state Senator John Blatnik of Chisholm, lobbied Minnesota Governor Harold Stassen to adopt a program of rehabilitation for the range.

Governor Stassen responded by recommending the formation of an Iron Range Resources and Rehabilitation Commission to search for ways to diversify the region's economy. The Legislature gave Stassen what he wanted. On April 27, 1941, he signed a bill into law establishing the office of commissioner of Iron Range Resources and Rehabilitation. Funding would be drawn from iron ore occupation taxes paid to the state by mining companies.[31]

The commissioner was charged with the task of determining the needs of areas negatively affected by the decline of mining and initiating projects and programs to meet those needs. Stassen's choice for IRR&R commissioner was former Minnesota resources executive secretary Herbert Miller, who opened an office in St. Paul on July 1,

1941. Charged with a seemingly impossible task and answerable directly to the governor for his actions, Miller, a non-Iron Ranger, quickly established a second office in Chisholm and set up several advisory committees to help him decide on ways to proceed.

The use of an advisory committee to assist the commissioner took on more formal proportions in the 1943 session, when the Iron Range Resources and Rehabilitation Commission was formed to make a study of policies and plans for future development of low grade ores. It consisted of three senators, three legislators and the commissioner of the Department of Conservation – later changed to the Department of Natural Resources.[32]

Early IRRR commissioners involved themselves in studies and surveys – and in helping out with the war effort. After the war, the Iron Range Resources and Rehabilitation Commission became officially known as the Iron Range Resources and Rehabilitation Board (IRRRB) and provided loans and grants for forestry, agriculture, tourism and research to find ways to develop the vast lean ore deposits of the Mesabi.

IRRRB attempts to diversify the region through agriculture were not very successful. The iron range was not farm country. An exception might have been a loan to Jeno Paulucci in the late 1940s. Paulucci, a Hibbing-born entrepreneur, needed the money to buy a peat bog south of Eveleth. He grew celery in that bog and shipped it to a Chinese food plant in Duluth. Although there were some who scoffed at what seemed "a ridiculous waste of mining taxes," the scoffing stopped when Paulucci repaid the loan with interest and sold his Chun King company to R.J. Reynolds for more than $60 million.[33]

The agency's main focus was on finding uses for the Mesabi's low-grade ores. During the 1940s, the commission granted $650,000 to Continental Machines Inc. to construct a pilot plant at the eastern end of the Mesabi Range near Aurora to test the commercial feasibility of a process developed by Charles W. Firth of the University of Minnesota's mines experiment station to produce a fine iron powder from the vast amounts of low-grade iron carbonate slate underlying much of the region.

Iron in the form of powder had been in great demand during the war for the manufacture of machine gun parts, aircraft weapons and precision instruments. In the summer of 1946, amid glowing reports on the project's possibilities, a plant was constructed, a crusher set up on a nearby bluff and a water supply pipeline extended two miles north to the Embarrass River. The unexpected death of the inventor before his furnace was blueprinted led to redesign costs, litigation and finally an end to the project, leaving the agency with an empty building and a loss of more than $700,000. It was, however, the IRRRB's continued funding to the University of Minnesota's mines experiment station that made the biggest impact on the region; a way was found to concentrate low-grade taconite into iron-rich pellets.[34]

The Mother Rock of the Mesabi

In 1941, the same year that the IRRRB was formed, the range delegation, in an unprecedented move, asked the Minnesota Legislature to enact a law that would take taconite off the ad valorem tax rolls. They had been convinced by Doctor Edward Wilson Davis, head of the mines experiment station, that the future of mining – and the range – lay not with high-grade ore, but with taconite.

Known today as the "father of taconite," Davis is credited with a major role in the development of a process for commercial taconite production. Taconite has been described as "the mother rock of the Mesabi." About one-third of it is iron ore and the other two-thirds waste. It stretched across northern Minnesota in an extended sheet more than 100 miles long and several miles wide. The amount of iron produced by every Iron Country mine that ever existed was but a small fraction of all that was locked up in the taconite formation.[35]

To developers who knew the mining business, the prospects were mind boggling. If the iron in the taconite could be concentrated and smelted like natural ore, it didn't matter if the hematite mines were depleted. The entire iron formation could be mined.

But to make taconite marketable, companies had to learn complex techniques and invest millions of dollars in sophisticated plants and equipment. New methods of

Walter Swart was vice president and general manager of the Mesabi Iron Company, the first commercial company to successfully process taconite into a finished product for blast furnaces. Opened in 1919, it encountered too much competition from natural ore and closed in 1924. IRON RANGE RESEARCH CENTER

drilling and blasting had to be invented, special ore crushers had to be developed. The biggest task of all was to find a cost-effective way to separate the iron from the rock. This was not a problem of mining, it was a problem of manufacturing.[36]

The World's First Taconite Processing Plant

Since the days of Peter Mitchell and the Ontonagon Syndicate in the 1870s and 1880s, the lean iron deposits at the east end of the Mesabi had fascinated prospectors and investors. Even though the ore was lean, even though it was locked up in hard gray rock, there was so much of it that it was irresistible to speculators.

And that's what the first years of taconite development were about. Speculation. In 1873, the Ontonagon pool acquired 9,000 acres of eastern Mesabi taconite for next to nothing, became the Mesaba Iron Company in 1882 and looked for buyers. George St. Clair of Duluth bought the property for $100,000 in the early 1900s. Because Minnesota law limited the land a company could hold to 5,000 acres, St. Clair had to take on partners and form two companies – the East Mesabi Iron Company and the Dunka River Iron Company.[37]

One of his partners was Duluth attorney John G. Williams. Williams was also a regent of the University of Minnesota and managed to interest William R. Appleby, dean of the university's mines experiment station, in the potential of taconite. It was Dean Appleby who introduced Dr. Davis to the possibilities of taconite.

Davis later recalled, "The dean called me in, as a new instructor in mathematics, to introduce me to the regents. At that meeting, Williams told us about a great area of mineral land of which he was part owner. It was, he said, on the eastern Mesabi Range between the

town of Mesaba and Birch Lake and it was entirely composed of taconite.... We listened politely, if somewhat skeptically, and Dean Appleby, always the diplomat, suggested that Williams send a sample of this rock to the newly formed Mines Experiment Station...."[38]

In 1912, St. Clair and Williams hired Duluth mining engineer Dwight Woodbridge to explore their property and suggest ways to mine and process the taconite. Woodbridge reported that, although he found no hematite worth mining, there was more iron locked up in the taconite than in all the deposits of high grade ore in the state put together. But it was worthless – unless, of course, a way could be found to make a concentrate out of it.

Samples were brought back. They were studied by experts. Scholarly papers were published suggesting ways to improve the ore. Chunks of taconite were sent to various laboratories and experiment stations. They were crushed, ground into powder, washed and heated in attempt after attempt to get the iron out of the rock. Nothing worked.

While all this was going on, a Boston-based brokerage firm by the name of Hayden, Stone and Company picked up some of the rock and handed it over to Daniel C. Jackling, a Utah copper mine owner. Jackling was asked if any of his copper processing methods might be used to separate the iron from the rock.[39]

Jackling had seen Woodbridge's report and was already convinced that taconite presented significant economic possibilities. He sent a close associate of his, Walter G. Swart of New York, to look over the St.Clair-Williams property to see if it was worth developing. Swart, a graduate of the Colorado School of Mines, had known Jackling since the two shared a copper mining office in Cripple Creek, Colorado.[40]

Swart arrived in Minnesota in the spring of 1915 and proceeded immediately to Birch Lake to see the deposits for himself. St. Clair, Williams, Woodbridge and geologist Horace Winchell accompanied him. The men brought back samples of taconite and took them to the University of Minnesota School of Mines in Minneapolis. There, Edward Davis was already achieving some success removing iron from pulverized taconite with a magnet held under water.[41]

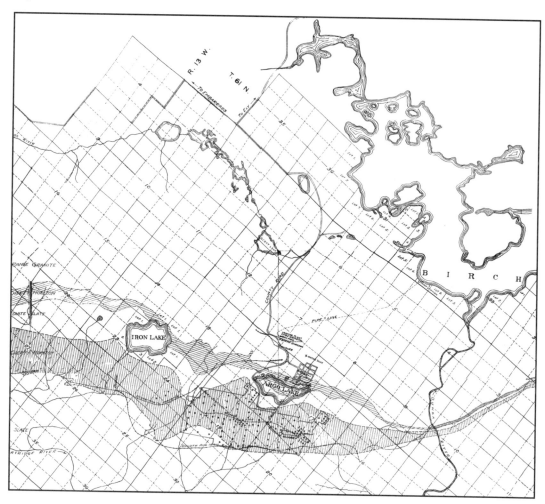

Mesabi Iron Company Properties, taken from Mesabi Iron Company surveys, shows the old townsite of Babbitt, the locations of the plant and mine, as well as the properties of the Dunka-Mesaba Securities, Cloquet Lumber Company and Romberg properties located from the west end of Birch Lake, and including Iron Lake and Argo Lake. From "Report on Mesabi Iron Company at Babbitt, 1931" by Walter Swart. IRON RANGE RESEARCH CENTER, CHISHOLM.

According to Davis, "My first wet test was made in October 1914 on pulverized crude ore assaying 29.11 percent iron. Laboriously made in water with a hand magnet and many washings, it produced a concentrate assaying 68.88 percent iron and 3 percent silica."[42]

Swart was impressed with Davis' work. He sent Jackling a glowing report. "There is no doubt in my mind that this is a game worth playing and that it can be played to a successful finish. It seems now only a question of men, money, methods and detail."[43]

Words such as these had been heard in Iron Country before. They didn't always lead to success. But Swart, Jackling and their copper mining associates were determined to market the unmarketable – the lean magnetic iron ore of the east Mesabi. In 1915, a group of investors including Daniel C. Jackling, Charles Hayden, Galen Stone, Seely Mudd, Bernard M. Baruch, Percy Rockefeller, Louis S. Cates, John Ryan, Ambrose Monell, William Corey, Horace Winchell, Dwight Woodbridge and Walter Swart organized the Mesabi Syndicate. Swart was picked resident manager. He set up his office in Duluth's Sellwood Building and

sent a crew to the Mesabi to open a taconite mine. In 1916, he bought an old lumber mill at the foot of 39th Avenue West and turned it into a taconite processing test plant.[44]

The mine was located near the remains of an abandoned logging camp on a railroad spur called "Sulfur Siding," about 15 miles northeast of Mesaba Station. The old Peter Mitchell test pits were not far away. Several of the camp's buildings were refurbished into living quarters for the men mining the ore for the Duluth plant. The mine would be unlike any other in Iron Country. According to one description, "the mine is really a quarry … the rock hard and tough … and the cost of breaking it is higher than in many quarries."[45]

The mine and test plant operated until 1919. During this time, a promising form of concentrate was developed. It looked like a clinker from an old coal stove, but it was low in phosphorus and high in iron content. Surely it would compete favorably with natural hematite ore. They gave it the name "Mesabi sinter" and during World War I shipped 1,840 tons of it to an eastern steel mill where it was turned into steel for armor piercing shells.[46]

Barely under construction in 1920, old Babbitt was never a prepossessing location, described by one visitor as a collection of modest houses barely better than shacks.
NORTHEAST MINNESOTA HISTORICAL CENTER

That was good enough for Jackling. The Mesabi Iron Company – spelled with an "i" – was born. Hayden became chairman of the board, Jackling, president, and Swart, general manager. Preliminary work for building Iron Country's first taconite plant was under way in late 1919.

The Duluth facility was dismantled and equipment either sold or shipped to the Sulphur Siding camp, where Swart had set up his office and drafting room. Actual construction began in 1920. Track was extended to the millsite, materials and construction crews brought in and work proceeded cautiously. Since only one processing unit was to be built, great care was taken in selecting a site that would allow for additional units and expansion of the mine.[47]

Locating the mine was probably the easiest task. It would be opened close to the remains of test pits where, 45 years earlier, explorer Peter Mitchell had described his "mountain of iron." Here, acres and acres of smooth taconite rock lay open to the sunlight, but it was as formidable a task to quarry it as it had been for Mitchell when he put down his 6-foot-deep test pit. [48]

It was a bleak and lonely place. A fire had swept through the region in 1917, leaving only the charred remains of fallen trees and stumps. Even the mosses which once covered parts of the iron formation had burned away, along with the blaze marks of trails, markers of survey lines, trappers' shacks and other signs of human activity. If there ever was a "no man's land" in northern Minnesota, this was it.

There was a gravel road from Aurora to Ely that ran through nearby Embarrass, but it was a brave person willing to drive a car on it and there was no connection to either the mine or the mill. The only way to

civilization was by way of 17 miles of logging spur to Mesaba Station on the Duluth and Iron Range Railroad. If there was going to be any commercial mining of taconite in this country, a town would have to be built.[49]

Under Swart's direction, a site was cleared near the plant, a depot constructed and building equipment hauled in by rail. Sites for the town, plant and station were leveled and graded by crews of pick-and-shovel workers aided by teams of horses with wagons and scrapers. A large bunkhouse and star-shaped "mess hall" were built to accommodate a work force of about 400 men, who all ate their meals at the same time. It was said that, when the cook bell rang, workers could be sure food was already on the table and a person was "in danger of being trampled" in the mad rush that followed.[50]

Babbitt grew quickly. The site was cleared in 1920 and a year later 400 people were living on it.[51] Jackling wanted to name the place "Argo" – after Jason's ship in his search for the golden fleece. But there was already a town called Argo in Minnesota, so they gave it the name "Babbitt," to honor the memory of then recently deceased Judge Kurnal R. Babbitt of New York, Jackling's former attorney. According to Edward Davis, who served as consultant to the project, "by 1924, there were 25 dwellings in Babbitt, 28 in West Babbitt and 16 in Pleasant View."[52]

That same year, iron mining engineer Arthur Parsons said this about the town: "Babbitt is not to this day what might be called a prepossessing place. The country is … forbidding and only the barest necessities have been provided. Mr. Swart himself lives in a three-room cottage; and the combination town hall, movie house and church is little more than a shack. This will all be changed, however, when the ledger begins showing black instead of red."[53]

As the work force grew, the additions of West Babbitt and Pleasant View came into being.[54] In West Babbitt, the company leased out lots and sold construction materials at cost to anyone willing to build. Most of the dwellings in this part of Babbitt turned out to be little more than tar-paper shacks. However, in Pleasant View and "Babbitt proper," the company went to work building homes. Not that the homes were marvels of modern construction – they were all alike – two bedrooms, kitchen, living room and bath – no basements. But they all had electricity and indoor plumbing and the view across the Embarrass Valley was spectacular. On clear nights the lights of Tower and Ely could be seen in the distance.[55]

In Babbitt proper were the company office, dining hall, dormitory for single men and Babbitt's first school – a two-room affair with 68 children attending. All buildings were set on rock so solid that even the water and sewer lines had to be laid out above ground. They were boxed in and insulated for cold weather. In winter, water for homes had to be circulated through a boiler to keep it from freezing.[56]

Impermanence was everywhere. Every house the company built seemed designed so it could be moved at a moment's notice. If a larger building was needed, two houses were simply joined together. The company used five to form its office.

Production of taconite sinter began on June 21, 1922. The plant was located on the north side of the ridge, a mile and a half from the mine. Locating it closer would have placed it too near the divide separating the Lake Superior and Hudson Bay drainage basins. Although water for processing the ore could be drawn at times from several sources, law prohibited the moving of water from one side of the divide to the other, so Birch Lake, the only dependable supply, became both the source and repository for most of the water used in the plant.[57]

A four-mile narrow gauge railroad was constructed to join the sinter mill to the mine. The taconite was mined by the same method used in New York traprock quarries. A cut was made into solid rock creating a face about 20 feet high. Slices were taken from the face by careful drilling and blasting to eventually form a shallow mine pit. Holes for blasting were spaced so that the taconite could be broken into chunks just large enough for steam shovels to handle.[58]

The Mesabi Iron Company mill was impressive and far ahead of its time. Rock

Mining the flinty taconite ore at Babbitt in 1919 was made more difficult by drills that were inadequate to pierce the rock to create blast holes. Blasting was necessary to break up the solid rock of the ore formation. LAKE COUNTY HISTORICAL SOCIETY **Bottom:** In 1921, Babbitt retained the look of rugged impermanence that would mark it until the 1924 closing of the nearby plant. At that point, the town was abandoned and became a ghost town. CONRAD HOLTER, IRON RANGE RESEARCH CENTER

from the mine was crushed and rolled into pea-sized granules. The granules were moved by conveyor through a dry cobber and a series of wet magnetic separators to remove waste. The material that remained was ground to the consistency of fine sand and run through another magnetic separator, leaving a concentrate of 60 percent to 61 percent iron. The concentrate was then dewatered, mixed with anthracite coal and sintered in a furnace.[59]

It seemed in 1920 that ore buyers would find Mesabi sinter irresistible. The iron content was high (around 60 percent) and the phosphorous content was low (less than .025 percent). It seemed to meet "Old Range Bessemer" standards. It should fetch a good price on the market. It had to. Jackling and his investors were counting on it.

"Besides," remarked the always optimistic Swart, "unlike other Lake Superior ores, Mesabi Iron Company sinter does not freeze in the winter."[60]

But by 1923, things had changed. Industrywide corporations were now in charge. Steel mills bought their ore from subsidiary mining companies. There was little room in the market for a small independent organization like the Mesabi Iron Company. More important was the fact that all of this consolidation in the steel industry had made it possible to replace most of the old Bessemer converters with more productive – and more profitable – open-hearth furnaces. As a result, low phosphorus "Bessemer" ore, the kind of ore that smelted well in a Bessemer converter, lost its importance – and its premium price.[61]

What steel producers wanted now was ore low in silica, ore that was soft and more completely oxidized. If the iron content was a little lower, it didn't matter. In fact, the average iron content of natural ore being shipped down lake in 1921 was only 52.07 percent, but it didn't form costly slag deposits in the open hearths. A cause of slag in an open hearth was silica – and Babbitt sinter was loaded with it. Not only that, because of its hardness and irregular shape it smelted slowly and inconsistently. Furnace operators didn't want it.[62]

Walter Swart was aware of the problem. It was his hope that if he could get the silica content down and raise the iron content to something like 64 percent, Mesabi sinter

would be more marketable and maybe even fetch the premium price that backers were counting on. They would grind finer, wash harder and expand the plant. A 60,000-ton contract was made with Ford Motor Company, but in order to get the contract the company's sales representative had to advertise Mesabi sinter as having an iron content of 64 percent. Mesabi Iron's first shipment, 5,076 tons to Ford in October 1922 assayed at 62.02 percent iron, 9.34 percent silica – not great – but promising.[63]

Swart reported improvements, "The months from July 1922 to February 1924 were practically all consumed by what might be called experimental operation, whipping the plant into shape, correcting such things as improperly designed gyrating crushers, sintering machine deficiencies and hundreds of minor difficulties. In February 1924, the output began to rise consistently and costs went down correspondingly. This took place, too, while the plant was being reconstructed to a capacity of 800 tons of sinter per day, the construction work naturally interfering pretty constantly with the best operating conditions."[64]

There would be more shipments. Donner Steel Company bought some sinter in 1923 and again in 1924. Another shipment sent to the Ford Motor Company in May 1924 assayed at 64.39 percent iron with a silica content of 8.38 percent. It was a plant record and sold at premium.[65]

It was a record that was difficult to maintain. Raising the iron content and lowering the silica content by grinding finer and washing harder caused even more of the already low percentage of iron in the rock to be washed away with the tailings. The result was more waste and less sinter per ton of crude taconite. Getting the plant to produce at the premium level needed to sustain the operation meant marginal profits at best.

Meanwhile, other problems – breakdowns, penalties, increased transportation rates because sinter didn't pack well in railroad cars, storage charges at dockside for material waiting to be sold – all helped to keep the plant operating haltingly – and in the red.[66]

In the spring of 1924, the Lake Erie base price for premium ores dropped from $6.45 a ton to $5.65 a ton and remained down for the next 25 years. Convinced that they were

trying to compete with ore producers who could influence the base price, Mesabi Iron Company's directors quickly became discouraged and Iron Country's first commercial taconite plant closed its doors before it really got going.[67]

It was all over by June 10, 1924. A few men were retained at the plant to oil and paint equipment, but the village of Babbitt was abandoned even more quickly than it had come into being. By September, it was a ghost town.

Jackling went on to other ventures, but for Swart, Williams and many others, it was a sad defeat. Rumors persisted that the iron mining industry had somehow "engineered" the failure of the taconite company.

In a letter to Swart in 1931, Jackling seemed to hint at manipulation. "The enterprise is sound under any conceivable conditions … competitive or otherwise, provided it can be operated on a large enough scale and can find a free market … at prices

relatively representative of their value … as compared to iron ores in general."[68]

Although it was the drop in ore prices in 1924 that ended the operation, there is little else in the record to indicate that this was anything more than coincidence.

The University of Minnesota Mines Experiment Station (1925-1945)

After 1924, and for many years thereafter, taconite seemed to be a dead issue. If a well-financed group like Jackling and his highly regarded technicians couldn't make a go of it in taconite, who could?

To many, the whole idea seemed a waste of time and money. Yet, there were some who refused to give up hope. Still lured by taconite's promise of prosperity, the staff at the University of Minnesota's mines experiment station pressed on. They decided that if they were going to make a marketable product out of taconite, they needed to find the exact cause of the Babbitt project's collapse.

Beginning with a pilot plant on in 1952 at Babbitt, Reserve Mining Company moved swiftly to test, prove and begin construction of a larger commercial operation co-located at the Babbitt minesite and the shoreline of Lake Superior at Silver Bay. The plant began production in 1956. LAKE COUNTY HISTORICAL SOCIETY

After careful study, the group concluded that the main reason the project failed was that the Babbitt plant produced a sinter that was only the equal of "old range ore." What was needed was a product that was superior – so superior that steel producers would prefer it to any natural ore they could find.[69]

The effort began in 1925. Edward Davis and Dean William Appleby successfully appealed to the state Legislature for financial help. Machinery was purchased, the staff increased and carloads of taconite were brought to the university for experimentation. Technical experts were called in and blast furnace men and steel plant engineers from eastern steel mills were consulted.[70]

As the years passed, taconite agglomerates of all kinds, sizes and shapes were developed – taconite cylinders, taconite briquettes, sinters, balls, cakes, nodules – pellets. Gradually, the fundamentals of a superior product were formed:

1. It had to have a high iron content – at least 64 percent. To get this, the ore had to be ground into a powder as fine as flour with two-thirds of it rejected as low-grade, nonmagnetic tailings.

2. It had to smelt quickly and smoothly in the steel mill. For this to happen, it had to be of a shape that would allow hot furnace gases to reach every particle equally. Spherical particles all about the same size would allow this to happen.

3. The spherical particles had to be formed in a relatively inexpensive way and hold their shape on their way to the steel mill. Pellets of taconite about three-fourths of an inch in diameter and fired at 2,300 degrees F under high oxidizing conditions met this requirement.

Of course, there were many other technical problems yet to be to solved but by 1945 as World War II was ending, Davis and his staff knew that they had a way to make a superior product. According to Davis, "We had demonstrated that this could be done, but we had not devised equipment for commercial operations."[71]

By this time, they were no longer alone. Every iron and steel firm in the nation was interested in taconite – Bethlehem Steel, Algoma Steel, Cleveland Cliffs, Inland, Jones and Laughlin, Pickands Mather, Armco,

Republic, Butler Brothers. The companies would create the commercial equipment. Even the Oliver Iron Mining Company, which had dominated Iron Country's natural ore market for 50 years, began experimenting with equipment to concentrate the taconite.

It was time. The development of the St. Lawrence Seaway was under way. Foreign ores could soon be brought to Great Lakes steel mills. According to Dr. Davis in 1964, "If the vast foreign deposits and the St. Lawrence Seaway had become available earlier, or if the university had decided to drop the taconite study, I believe that taconite would probably still be just an interesting possibility."[72]

The Reality of Commercial Taconite Mining (1948-1972)

Taconite mining was already on its way to becoming a reality in 1948, when Erie Mining Company, an organization formed by Bethlehem Steel, Youngstown Sheet and Tube, Interlake Iron and Steel Company, Steel Company of Canada (Stelco) and Pickands Mather and Company built a taconite processing pilot plant at Aurora. Formed in 1940 and operated by Pickands Mather, Erie Mining had a single purpose: to acquire taconite properties for the purpose of future mining. Pickands Mather established a laboratory in Hibbing in 1942 to try to find ways to separate the iron from the rock. Helped by the findings of Dr. Davis and the University School of Mines, efficient magnetic separators were gradually developed and, in 1948, plans were laid for the commercial scale pilot plant.[73]

From 1948 until 1952, the Aurora plant was the only one on the range using commercial-sized machines to produce taconite pellets. It operated haltingly. There were problems with the furnace, the pellets stuck together – but they were pellets – and they made good steel. In 1952, Erie announced that it was ready to build a full-scale production plant near the site of the old village of Mesaba. The plant would eventually produce high-grade pellets at a rate of 7.5 million long tons a year.[74]

However, no company moved faster to establish commercial taconite production than did Reserve Mining Company. In

The Erie Mining Company "powder iron plant" near Aurora as it appeared in 1946. The pilot plant was the first of the modern era to test laboratory techniques for turning taconite into usable feed stock for blast furnaces. By 1952, confidence in the flowsheets was sufficient that the company announced its intention to build a huge plant to produce 7.5 million tons of pellets per year. VOSS COLLECTION, IRON RANGE RESEARCH CENTER

1951, a year before the Erie announcement, Reserve was already developing a mine, pilot plant and town near the site of Babbitt.[75]

Reserve Mining Company had been organized as early as 1939 by Oglebay, Norton and Company of Cleveland, mainly to acquire and hold the taconite lands of the old Mesabi Iron Company. The idea was to wait until the natural ores were gone and then reintroduce the concept of taconite sintering – a process that had worked well, but couldn't compete with the natural ores of the time – thus the name Reserve. But when it became clear that some of America's largest producers of steel were interested in the concept of taconite pellets, Reserve moved fast.[76]

Under the direction of Crispin Oglebay, grandson of one of the founders of the Cleveland firm, financial backing was obtained from the Armco and Republic steel firms.[77] Things moved quickly after that. The test plant was housed in old Mesabi Iron Company buildings already on the site and a whole new townsite was platted on land that had once been the certified seed potato farm of Virginia's Doctor Charles Lenont.

Babbitt Reborn

New Babbitt was a product of modern community planning. Working closely with Reserve Mining Company, planners from Pace Associates of Chicago and the University of Minnesota School of Architecture studied mine expansion plans and projected employment figures, while carefully laying out the site for the new location of Babbitt. Yards were spacious, streets were wide and, unlike old Babbitt, water and sewer lines were laid below ground. Sites for schools, churches, parks and a shopping center were all laid out before the first buildings were put together. Although the very first homes were built on site, most were prefabricated in Biwabik by Model Homes Incorporated and moved to Babbitt in large double trailers. The first families arrived in 1952 and the village was incorporated in 1956.

The Peter Mitchell Mine and Pilot Plant

The Babbitt mine, later named the Peter Mitchell Mine, received a great deal of attention in the press. Numbers quoted in 1952 descriptions seemed mind-boggling, "The taconite ore body at Babbitt is about nine miles long, 2,800 feet wide and 175 feet deep at the thickest point.… It is estimated to contain at least 1.5 billion tons of magnetic taconite." What was most impressive to mining men was the fact that the deposit was virtually free of glacial drift and could be mined at a rate of 80,000 to 100,000 tons a day. Many hematite mines didn't produce that much ore in a year.[78]

Mining started east of the old Babbitt pit, where the taconite was thought to be especially good for developing concentrate.

The ore was removed by the tried and tested method of drilling and blasting. However, a new and faster method of drilling known as "jet piercing" was introduced. Using liquid oxygen and fuel oil to produce a high temperature jet, the machine literally burned its way into the taconite at a rate of 35 feet an hour. The old churn drills used by the Mesabi Iron Country couldn't make this much headway in a day. Each hole, when blasted, produced as much as 2,000 tons of broken rock, which were picked up by electric shovels, loaded into trucks and hauled two miles to the pilot plant at the old Mesabi Iron Company site.[79]

Beginning in 1952, the remodeled buildings and rebuilt machinery of the old Mesabi Iron Company plant served as a test facility for the full-scale production plant already under construction on the north shore of Lake Superior. At the Babbitt site, broken rock from the mine was crushed into marble-sized pieces and fed into a rod mill which reduced the ore to the consistency of coarse powder. It was then sent to a magnetic separator designed to separate the iron from the rock.

From there, the material passed through a classifier and a second "wet magnetic separator," which removed even more waste, and the concentrate then went to balling drums and a newly developed pelletizing furnace to be turned into hard pellets assaying at a steady 64 percent to 65 percent iron. Although there were problems with the rod mill and other adjustments needed to be made, by the end of its first year of operation the Babbitt plant was operating so smoothly and effectively that the company continued using it to produce pellets until the fall of 1957. By then, the main plant at Lake Superior had been in operation for almost two years.[80]

Silver Bay

A 47-mile railroad was constructed to connect the mine to the world's first full-scale taconite pellet production plant. It was located on Lake Superior just up the shore from Beaver Bay, where nearly 100 years earlier Christian Wieland and Henry Eames had begun their expedition to Iron Country to see firsthand the mountain of iron now being mined.

With its 192 magnetic separators, 36 rod and ball mills and six pelletizing lines complete with furnaces, the plant was a marvel of modern construction. Designed to produce 3.7 million tons of pellets a year, the plant was producing almost 6 million tons a year by 1961, while sluicing 12 million tons of tailings a year into Lake Superior.[81]

A townsite was laid out nearby, planned by Pace Associates in consultation with the University's School of Architecture, the same people who planned the townsite of Babbitt. Homes were built by J.D. Harrold Company of Duluth and were similar in appearance to those in Babbitt, but were designed and laid out so the living area in each dwelling faced a landscaped area at the rear to make full use of the pre-planned recreation area. On May 1, 1954, it was announced that the lakeside town would take the name of a general store and resort that once operated in the vicinity – Silver Bay. Official incorporation followed two years later.[82]

Hoyt Lakes

Meanwhile, Erie Mining Company, backed by funding from four large steel manufacturers and the experience of managing agent Pickands Mather and Company, put together what was then the largest mining investment in history – a third of a billion dollars. At the time, Erie ownership was shared by Bethlehem Steel, Youngstown Sheet and Tube, Interlake Iron and Stelco (Steel Company of Canada). Located a few miles northeast of Aurora, Erie's concentrator and pelletizer were larger than those built by Reserve and were connected by a 73-mile-long railroad to a loading dock on Lake Superior called Taconite Harbor.[83]

Unlike Reserve, Erie did all of its processing at the mining site. Tailings were dumped into a large disposal area north of the plant, where the water was allowed to settle before it was returned and used again. The system was supplemented by a water supply drawn from the Partridge River. Experiments were conducted and proved successful in revegetating the constantly expanding tailings areas.[84]

Establishment of the Erie plant resulted in another new town. Named after Elton Hoyt II, head of Pickands Mather and Company, Hoyt Lakes, like Babbitt and Silver Bay, was entirely pre-planned before homes were built and sold to employees. The new taconite towns bore little resemblance to

HOUSING AREA
MAY 21, 1955
SILVER BAY, MINN

the old range towns but, like the earlier places, they were boom towns.

Construction of homes at Hoyt Lakes began in May 1954. By the end of the year, a town of gently curving streets, landscaped lots and 100 occupied homes had come into being. Incorporation took place in 1955 and, that December, 269 votes were cast for the first village officers. After the mine and plant went into full production, the population expanded to 3,400.

Taconite Production Expands

While all this was going on, the Oliver Iron Mining Company, financed by United States Steel, broke ground near Virginia for its own experimental taconite plants. The company named its concentrating plant "Pilotac." It had a production capacity of 500,000 tons a year. The concentrate was shipped to an agglomerating plant called "Extaca" four miles away.[85]

In 1959, the Erie and Reserve plants in Minnesota were not the only shippers of taconite pellets. Cleveland Cliffs' Eagle Mill in Michigan, Bethlehem's Lebanon plant in Pennsylvania, Pickands Mather's Hilton Mine and Marmoraton Mining and International Nickel in Sudbury, Ontario, were all shipping taconite pellets in that year. There was no doubt that a great change was taking place in the steel industry – furnace operators were turning to pellets.[86]

Still Oliver waited. There were many in mining circles who doubted the wisdom of full-scale taconite production in Minnesota – especially when there was no guarantee that the state's taconite deposits wouldn't some day be taxed like natural ore. True, the 1941 law exempted taconite from such taxation, but laws could be changed. Something stronger was needed.

Along with this, there were many in mining who were convinced that taconite

A 1955 aerial photo of Silver Bay shows the contoured, planned development of the town to make maximum use of nearby recreational and scenic attractions. LAKE COUNTY HISTORICAL SOCIETY

237

pellets could never compete with the rich deposits of foreign ores that were being discovered in Canada, Brazil and elsewhere. Erie and Reserve men heard a lot about "risky investments" in Duluth's Kitchi Gammi Club during the late 1950s – and it was true that there was not a soul alive who could say taconite pellets were competitive with foreign ores. The smelting qualities of taconite pellets had never been tested in a steel mill on a commercial scale.[87]

This test finally came in the summer of 1960. Pellets were used exclusively for several months in Armco's Bellefonte Furnace at Middletown, Ohio. The furnace was able to produce twice as much pig iron per day as it did using natural ore.[88] By September, word was out and steel companies began making plans to build more taconite plants all over the world – there was even talk about building more plants in Iron Country.

However, potential taconite producers saw a problem with investing in northeast Minnesota. In their minds, existing law exempting taconite from ad valorem taxes wasn't enough to justify a large investment of money. A guarantee that the law couldn't be changed was needed. If this could be achieved, future investment would be justified.

The kind of guarantee the companies wanted could only be achieved by a constitutional amendment. This required an act of the state Legislature to place the issue before the Minnesota public for a vote. Supporters of the amendment faced an uphill battle. A constitutional change had to be approved by a majority of the voters. This meant any voter not voting on the amendment would be counted as voting "no." Besides, the proposed amendment would never get before the public without a bill from the Legislature – and the Legislature was divided on the issue.

A lively debate followed. An attempt to pass the bill in 1961 failed. In 1963, the bill passed, an amendment could be voted on, but only with the provision that if passed, the tax guarantee would last no more than 25 years. A well-organized campaign to sell the amendment to the public followed. There were posters, advertisements in newspapers, radio and television; there were billboards, pamphlets, bumper stickers on

cars and town rallies. In 1964, the taconite amendment passed.

Investment followed. In 1966, Eveleth Taconite (EVTAC) Company opened its Thunderbird Mine and began processing taconite at its Fairlane Plant near Forbes. In 1967, United States Steel's Minnesota Ore Operations Minntac Plant began producing pellets. In 1969, Hanna Mining established its National Steel Pellet Company near Keewatin and its Butler Taconite Plant near Nashwauk. By 1972, Minntac had the largest pellet plant in America and more than 70 percent of all Mesabi ore shipments were taconite concentrate: 12 million tons from Minntac; 10 million from Erie, 9 million from Reserve, 2.6 million each from National and Butler; and 2.1 million tons from Eveleth Taconite.[89]

Taconite processing expanded rapidly and continued to sustain northeast Minnesota's mining base for the next 30 years. In 1961, processed taconite shipments from Minnesota for the first time surpassed shipments of high grade natural ore that had made the three iron ranges famous and, after 1965, shipments of taconite more than equalled all other forms of processed ore coming from the state. There were 32 plants processing ore on the Mesabi in 1970. Of these, six were concentrating taconite, but of the 54,682,000 tons of iron ore shipped from the range that year, 34 million were in the form of taconite and semitaconite concentrates.[90]

Steadily improving technology made it possible to do more and more with fewer and fewer workers. In 1970, the mines provided employment for almost 15,000 people. Twenty five years later, the number had shrunk to less than 6,000, but the remaining workforce was better educated, better trained, better paid and far more specialized than any of the mining crews in Iron Country's past. Despite its declining role as northeast Minnesota's major employer, the taconite industry remained a vital source of funding for the region's schools and communities.

The Reserve Mining Company Controversy

Mining, like other industries, experienced great changes after 1950. Worldwide economic and industrial realignments, political

upheavals, rising costs, advances in science and new discoveries about the earth's environment caused a shift in values away from the beneficial effects of what seemed, to some, an expanding technology that had somehow gotten out of hand. By the end of the 1960s, a literate, vocal and, sometimes, influential segment of the world's population began to see protection of the environment as more of a priority than improving economic conditions and raising living standards. Although conflicts and disputes were not new in the iron and steel industry, environmental concerns gave rise to controversies of a different kind. One arose in Minnesota out of a segment of the public's anxiety over suspected pollution and the process of pellet production itself.

In 1950, most experts within and outside the industry thought Lake Superior was a good place to locate a taconite plant. The lake provided the much needed supply of water and seemed a logical site for tailings disposal. To many, depositing tailings into the deep water of the lake seemed far more environmentally sound than storing them on land, where plant and animal life could be disrupted and possibilities of erosion were great.

More important at the time was the fact that no one knew for sure if pellets could economically compete with foreign ores. If the state was going to expand its tax base from taconite and the industry was going to become the "economic savior" of northeast Minnesota, Reserve Mining Company's production costs had to be kept as low as possible. Company officials based their decision to locate next to the lake on these economic factors. The state, aware of the region's economic needs, provided them with the necessary permits.

During the next three decades, everything changed. In 1965, a National Water Quality Laboratory was established in Duluth and two years later patches of green-colored water, which had alarmed some fishermen and resort owners, were found to be caused by suspended tailings from Reserve Mining Company's taconite plant. Concerns over water quality were brought to the Minnesota Pollution Control Agency (MPCA), which in 1971 was under the direction of newly appointed Grant J. Merritt, grandson of Alfred Merritt, one of the central figures in the Merritt-Rockefeller legal battles of the

1890s, and son of Glen Merritt, longtime Duluth postmaster. Because Duluth drew its drinking water from the lake, the MPCA, as part of its statutory duties, began monitoring it for possible pollution.[91]

Meanwhile, the U.S. Environmental Protection Agency (EPA) was making its own study of Lake Superior's water. In 1972, the EPA began court proceedings against the company and, in 1973, the agency's announcement of finding "asbestos-like fibers" in Duluth's drinking water launched a public outcry and a complicated, controversial and highly publicized litany of litigation that lasted for years. In the end, the company was forced to resort to an expensive "on-land tailings disposal site" at a cost exceeding $300 million.[92]

Frank D. Schaumburg, in his book *Judgment Reserved*, said this about the result:

"Environmental groups concerned about possible changes in Lake Superior … pressed their cause with such vigor that a commercial enterprise (Reserve) had to change its mode of waste disposal completely.… It is by no means certain that the concession achieved will do the most for the well being of society.[93]

The change added greatly to production costs and when the steel market went bad in the 1980s, Reserve's parent companies, Armco Steel Corporation and Republic Steel Corporation, looked for other options. In May 1987, Reserve Mining Company was officially dissolved, leaving a large number of former employees without insurance and pension plans.

Reserve wasn't the only company to run into environmental issues that totally contradicted the premise on which it was organized. The movement toward environmental protection was by this time global and enterprises the world over were forced to deal with it. At the same time, there remained many who were convinced that even though an industrial technology like mining could, from time to time, cause environmental damage and even threaten health and safety, its benefits were so great that its costs to the environment needed to be balanced against the needs of society. The Reserve controversy, litigated under standard legal procedure and settled on the basis of fines and expenditures, left the public not only with the economic consequences, but

clearly divided over the issue of balancing taconite mining's costs against its benefits.[94]

Reclaiming Abandoned Minelands

There were other concerns related to the change from hematite mining to taconite pellet production, some the same as in the days of the great Hull-Rust and Mahoning – cost of production, taxes, wages and benefits, safety, labor contracts, mine closings and loss of jobs. There were also the new concerns – assessing environmental impact, monitoring water and air quality, repairing environmental damage, dismantling outdated ore concentrating facilities and disposing of vast acreages of empty pits, abandoned railways and other mining wasteland left over from the days of hematite mining.

During the administration of Minnesota Governor Rudy Perpich, the Iron Range Resources and Rehabilitation Board from its new office near Eveleth returned to its original charge of diversifying the region's economy and dealing with the negative impact of mining when it established its Mineland Reclamation and Iron Range Interpretative programs in the late 1970s. The reclamation program sought to "reforest" and "reshape" abandoned mine properties in order to make them useful as parks, recreation areas and tourist rest stops, while the interpretative program turned the abandoned Glen Mine site near Chisholm into what later came to be called "Ironworld, USA," a complex of facilities designed to attract visitors to the region by combining the Iron Country's unique mining history and immigrant heritage with interpretive displays and entertainment. The effort, once described as "a model of what can be done with a valueless wasteland created by mining," has since enjoyed moderate success. However, high costs related to construction and maintenance of the facility and other sites owned and operated by the agency became the focus of new concerns over government spending and taxes.

Taxes – Again

The first years of the 1960s were recession years in northeast Minnesota. The depletion of hematite ores and the closing of mines brought about loss of jobs, a sluggish business climate and a steady reduction of income for Iron Country communities,

particularly the state's Iron Range Resources and Rehabilitation Commission (later IRRRB). Even after the economic climate improved following the passage of the Taconite Amendment in 1964, the IRRRC's income, based largely on natural ore occupation taxes, continued to decline. The tax on taconite mining, existing since 1941, was a five cents per ton production tax assessed only when production occurred and not earmarked for rehabilitation.[95] By 1966, it was clear that if the state Legislature did not intervene and taconite mining continued to expand as expected, the IRRRC would fade into history like the hematite mines of the past.

Once again iron range lawmakers and elected officials joined forces in a concerted effort to change the tax situation on the range, something the region's legislators had been doing for years. They were instrumental in paving the way for municipal expansion and ad valorem taxation in 1909 and, in the 1940s John Blatnik, Tom Vukelich, J. William Huhtala and others managed to get the Legislature to remove taconite from the ad valorem tax base to encourage development of low-grade ores. Again in 1964, led by Aurora's Fred Cina, range legislators were instrumental in changing the state constitution to provide a 25-year guarantee to taconite companies that they would not be taxed at rates that would exceed tax increases on other manufacturing companies in the state. Six years later, in 1970, lawmakers William Ojala, Peter Fugina and Douglas Johnson, with support from iron range communities, joined brothers George, Tony and then-lieutenant governor Rudy Perpich in an effort to divert a portion of the existing taconite production tax to the IRRRC, so that the agency could begin dealing once again with the negative impacts of mining.

In 1971, the Legislature appropriated one cent per ton to the IRRRC, a seemingly modest amount for an agency that had in the past contributed much to the development of the taconite process. However, this was just the beginning. In 1973, the Legislature also diverted a portion of the taconite production tax (a tax paid to the state based on income) to the IRRRC. By this time, with taconite production approaching 50 million tons, the various taxes were contributing more than $1 million a year to the commission's budget.[96]

By 1978, the benefits of taconite were being felt in every community in Iron Country, not just in terms of peak employment and resulting ancillary business expansions, but in recreational areas, parks, trails, tourism related facilities, business assistance, water and sewer projects, mineland reclamation and other public works programs. The 1977 Legislature had expanded the commission into the Iron Range Resources and Rehabilitation Board and given it responsibility over two important funds: the Taconite Area Environmental Protection Fund (TAEP) for immediate economic development and the Northeast Minnesota Economic Protection Fund (known as the "2002 fund," later the "2003 fund" and later still the "2006 fund"), a portion of the production tax to be invested and used later, supposedly at a time when the region's taconite resources were exhausted. In that same year, the production tax base rate, which had gradually risen to 60 cents a ton, was readjusted to $1.25 a ton. In 1986, it was again readjusted, this time to $1.90 a ton, most of which was distributed to cities, townships, school districts, counties, property tax relief with a statutory "taconite area" and to the IRRRB.

Then, after a decade of prosperity during the 1970s, the domestic iron and steel industry experienced a sudden and unexpected downturn in the 1980s. Steel companies had been slow to adopt the latest technology, expensive labor contracts had been negotiated, an energy crisis had set in, but probably more impacting was the steady rise of offshore steel competition. Steel imports flooded the American market. The demand for domestic steel declined sharply and, along with it, the demand for taconite pellets from Minnesota's Iron Country.

Since then, the advent of the global economy, with its often subsidized steel mills turning out a product so inexpensive that it is irresistible to American steel consumers, has resulted in international iron mining mergers that seem to show little interest in iron mines located within the United States. This has left Iron Country's taconite producers seeking ever greater cost and tax reductions as a way to remain viable in an increasingly competitive worldwide market. The region's schools, units of government and communities are also left with unsolved problems and declining budgets. Events in the 1990s and

early 21st century taconite industry reflect the difficulties that the national iron and steel industry has and is facing.

The Tumultuous 1990s and Early 21st Century

If a single idea can describe the iron and steel industry of the late 20th and early 21st centuries, if would most likely be turbulent. Ups and downs in the economy, consolidations and mergers, closings and reopenings were recorded with regularity, each time sending reverberations through Iron Country and the entire state of Minnesota.

Following its closure in 1986, the former Reserve Mining Company operation successfully re-opened in 1989 as Northshore Mining Company, but by then, other forces were rippling through the mining industry. Republic Steel Corporation, one of the former owners of Reserve Mining Company and all its environmental problems, experienced economic difficulties and was acquired by LTV Steel Corporation in 1993.

After reopening in 1989, Northshore Mining was acquired in 1994 by Cleveland Cliffs Inc. and has since produced a capacity of about 7 million tons of high-grade pellets per year. In May 2003, a new pilot project, Mesabi Nugget LLC, turned out its first batch of high-grade pig iron nuggets at Northshore. A joint venture of Kobe Steel of Japan, Ferrometrics Inc., Cleveland Cliffs and Steel Dynamics Inc. with substantial state funding participation, the $26 million plant began a series of test runs on a continuous basis June 7, 2003, at a rate of 2 tons per hour. The nuggets contain 96 percent to 98 percent pure iron and 2 percent to 4 percent of carbon.

Time will tell if this promising new technology has a place in the future of Iron Country, but initial reactions of those involved were positive. The first results of smelting in steelmaking furnaces have shown that it is competitive in all ways with pig iron produced from blast furnaces, making it an attractive product to feed the steel minimills that have become increasingly competitive with the major steelmakers.

Minnesota's other pioneer taconite producer, Erie Mining Company, also encountered increasingly challenging

conditions. In the late 1970s, Youngstown Sheet and Tube Company fell into financial difficulty and its assets, including its 35 percent share in Erie, went through a series of ownership changes. By the early 1990s, LTV Steel Corporation, a conglomerate built on predatory 1980s and 1990s acquisitions of the assets of financially troubled or failing steel firms, owned the former Youngstown interest in Erie. After it expanded its ownership interest, the company was renamed LTV Steel Mining Company. Although Erie/LTV never had serious infractions of environmental law like Reserve, it had other problems – notably costs and the quality of its pellets.

As LTV Steel itself ran into financial trouble, a decision was made to close the mining company in January 2001, including its loading facility at Taconite Harbor. Earlier, in a pattern familiar to Iron Rangers, the Taconite Harbor townsite that had been built in the 1950s to house dock and power plant employees was closed, as the company chose to disassemble the site to avoid costly upgrading of the sewer system to meet standards on Lake Superior shoreland.

LTV Steel Corporation itself did not long outlive the closure of the mining company and was sold at auction in February 2002 to become part of International Steel Group. The assets of the former Erie Mining company had already been sold, with Cleveland Cliffs Corporation buying the mining, production, railroad and dock facilities and Minnesota Power acquiring the power plant at Taconite Harbor.

In February 2004, an agreement was reached between Cleveland Cliffs and Polymet Mining Corporation allowing the latter company to use the former Erie/LTV plant and facilities to process non-ferrous (non-iron) ore from a mine south of Babbitt. Polymet, headquartered in Vancouver, British Columbia, Canada, intended to use the crushing and concentrating equipment of the former taconite plant as well as railroad facilities to transport and process an estimated 800 million tons of ore containing copper, nickel, platinum, palladium, cobalt, gold and silver.

Meanwhile the owners of two other significant producers of taconite pellets, National Steel Pellet Company of Keewatin

and Eveleth Taconite (EVTAC) Company of Eveleth, faced increasing financial difficulty as imported steel products ate into their markets and income. By 2003, a shutdown at National Steel Pellet was contemplated, but a May agreement by U.S. Steel to acquire National Steel Corporation appears to have averted that possibility. The plant became Keewatin Taconite Company and economies were achieved by combining some administrative functions with those at the company's Minntac Mine operations.

EVTAC was less fortunate and actually closed in early summer 2003 as two of its owner companies, Rouge Steel and Stelco (Steel Company of Canada), found themselves in increasing financial difficulty. The plant would remain shuttered until December, when a deal between Cleveland Cliffs and Laiwu Steel Group of China led to reopening the facility as United Taconite Company to produce iron ore. An agreement was reached between Cliffs and steelmaking customers in which United pellets would replace supplies from eastern Canadian mines which, in turn, would be shipped in equal amounts to China.

In late 2002, news announcements that United States Steel was selling its Minntac ore operations at Mountain Iron reverberated through the Iron Range. That this 100-year-old steel juggernaut would divest its major source of iron ore seemed almost unthinkable, since its history had always been to own every asset that was required in steel production. And, indeed, the Minntac sale did not take place and the corporation would go on to acquire National Steel, which increased its ore assets. However the divestiture by U.S. Steel of the Duluth Missabe and Iron Range Railroad and the USS Great Lakes Fleet had already taken place. After operating as subsidiaries of eastern investment firms for a couple of years, the DM&IR and Great Lakes Fleet ended up as properties of the Canadian National Railway in late 2003. Although the CN, as a foreign company, cannot operate the fleet under existing U.S. maritime law, its presence in Iron Country had been increasing through earlier decades and the acquisition significantly increased its presence in the ore transportation business. At the start of 2004, Great Lakes Fleet was scheduled to operate under management of a U.S. managing

company, maintaining the importance of the fleet in marine transportation.

In an attempt to stem the importation of steel at prices with which U.S. steelmaking firms could not compete, in March 2002 the federal government imposed tariffs designed to give domestic steelmakers a three-year window to restructure and otherwise become competitive. By November 2003, the World Trade Organization had ruled that the tariff was illegal and threatened to impose sanctions against a wide range of American exports. Shortly thereafter the tariff was rescinded well ahead of schedule.

Despite protests from domestic steelmakers and labor organizations alike, the tariffs were lifted on imports in 2004, but may have been a moot point anyway, since the domestic steel business showed little sign during 2002 and 2003 of rebounding from the downward spiral that marked the previous decade. Indeed, Bethlehem Steel Corporation, once the second largest steelmaker in America and a massive consumer and investor in Minnesota ore, ceased to exist during the time the tariff was in place. Oglebay Norton Company, another venerable company in iron ore production and transportation, entered Chapter 11 bankruptcy protection in February 2004 to restructure and begin reducing more than $450 million in debt. Although it no longer had any active iron ore mining properties, Oglebay was a significant ore transporter and within a few weeks of declaring Chapter 11, American Steamship Company showed interest in acquiring Oglebay's 12-ship fleet. As this volume went to the printer, no resolution of either the bankruptcy or disposal of the fleet was finalized.

Increasingly in the late 20th and early 21st centuries, iron ore assets were held by three large firms: U.S. Steel, Cleveland Cliffs and International Steel Group. It is impossible to predict whether this trend will continue, but the takeover by 155-year-old

Cliffs of more than 40 percent of active iron mining operations in the United States has challenged the way that unified steelmakers have traditionally done business. Cliffs also has ownership interests in both International Steel Group and the Mesabi Nugget project – which could give it advantages in future iron ore production and marketing.

The question that all this tumult raises is: Has taconite lived up to all of its promise and hoopla? It may still be too early to tell. History often falters when it attempts to draw conclusions on events that have not yet run their full course.

But one thing about taconite is clear. Vast taconite canyons stretch from Babbitt to Nashwauk. They dwarf the hematite open pits of the past and the old underground mines are lost in the rubble created by the giant electric and hydraulic shovels.

One early promise of taconite was that it would be possible to mine the entire iron formation from which the ores of Mesabi were created. It still is. But will mining continue in the region for years to come, as was promised by legislators and the promoters and developers of the taconite industry? The answer to that question seems to lie more in the areas of changing human values and the impact of the global economy on the industry than in the enormous amount of iron still remaining in the ground.

However, demand for iron ore or any reduced iron product of mining is entirely dependent on a healthy domestic steel industry and American steel producers have never faced challenges greater than the ones they were facing at the start of the 21st century. The question remains: Can the once mighty steel industry rebuild itself to compete successfully with foreign imports and thereby revive a struggling domestic mining industry? Therein may lie the fate of Iron Country and its people. ∎

Epilogue

The country north of Lake Superior has always been a harsh land of thin soils and temperature extremes, a place that for untold centuries could only now and then support a scattering of hunter-gatherer peoples.

However, the region's waterways and close proximity to Lake Superior made it a crossroad of trade and factored it early into an expanding fur industry, assuring its role as an extension of eastern-based commercial interests. Since that time it has remained a land of extractive enterprise initiated by and conducted for the economic good of people in other places. It became the domain of migrants, trappers of the trade and their families; a place foreign to settlers, government and law until 1854. Even after that, except possibly for people living on federal "Indian reserves," the hand of government was seldom felt in the region until its iron ore potential came to light in the late 19th century.

The existence of iron ore became public knowledge in 1852 and mining began 30 years later. It took billions of years for Iron Country's hematites to form yet, once discovered, they were mined out in less than a hundred, and the last of the region's marketable iron in the form of taconite continues to be removed in enormous amounts, even as demand for the region's iron declines. Iron was clearly the determining factor in shaping northeast Minnesota's communities and present-day demographics. Federal homestead and pre-emption laws, supposedly created to encourage settlement, ownership of land by small farmers and consolidation of the nation's western frontier, became in northeast Minnesota a means for mining and lumbering interests to gain control of the land, not for settlement, but for the profit of already wealthy speculators and entrepreneurs who had little interest in making the region their home.

The peopling of the Vermilion and Mesabi mining districts occurred only after mining companies and townsite developers had control of the land – and the population patterns that emerged were largely the result of commercial enterprise and often questionable acquisition practices.

On the Cuyuna, settlement preceded the discovery of iron ore and as a result this range never experienced the extensive iron land acquisitions and consolidations seen on the other two. However, on all three ranges – once the mines were operating – the communities that formed around them (and the mines themselves) remained so dependent on the eastern steel market that decisions made by executives and corporate directors in such far away places as Cleveland, Detroit and New York impacted directly on daily life in iron range towns.

Along with mining, extensive lumbering took place on both the Vermilion and Mesabi ranges, bringing large numbers of people to Tower, Winton, Virginia and Grand Rapids where some of Minnesota's most productive sawmills were located.

The advance of both mining and lumbering across the range occurred simultaneously and in many ways were interconnected. The mines brought the first railroads to the mining districts and thus provided lumbermen with access to the untouched forests north of the two ranges and a ready market for timber products. The lumber business clearly contributed to rapid settlement, but its impact on the surrounding countryside was far greater than its influence in iron range towns. On the Cuyuna, the era of intensive lumbering had passed by the time the first marketable ore was discovered.

The original populations of Iron Country towns were made up largely of immigrants, but they were not exactly like

the immigrants who populated other parts of the Midwest, like the Swedes and Norwegians, who sold their farms in the "old country," for example, to own large tracts of land in Iowa, Minnesota and the Dakotas. Instead, a majority of the migrants to the mining districts were a landless people drawn from the rural regions of Europe, often victims of oppression, government or otherwise: single men, married men, women with families joining their husbands, fugitives, runaways, people with divergent beliefs, young men in search of fortune and adventure, men and women in their late teens and twenties lured by the advertisements of steamship companies and employment agents.

The result was an inexperienced workforce and town populations composed of recent arrivals, many with little understanding of American ways. For a time, mining companies were not simply sources of livelihood, but also protectors of health and safety, promoters of community and dispensers of law and justice. In a rapidly evolving America with its growing economy, expanding educational opportunities and rising expectations, these were roles companies could not long maintain. Company attempts to maintain order and control led to repression, conflict, strikes and violence, while issues raised over property, ethnicity and human rights gave rise to a vibrant form of politics that pitted iron range politicians against the mining companies in an ongoing tug-of-war over community improvement and iron ore taxation.

Depletion of the region's natural ores after World War II changed the dynamics for a time, as politicians and mining men joined forces with geologists, engineers and chemists in a successful effort to process the low-grade taconite from the iron formation in which the natural ores were found. The result was a rapid development of taconite plants, expanded employment, new arrivals, numerous public improvements and three new towns. The new prosperity was not without controversy as issues smoldered over taxation, public spending and the impact of taconite processing on the environment. However, in the midst of all this turmoil, a growing global steel market sharply diminished the demand for the region's iron, raising new issues over taxation, public improvements, mining company survival and, once again, the future of northeast Minnesota's communities.

Coping with the unpredictable fluctuations of mining economy and forces of change, over which there seemed to be no control, became an accepted part of life for the generations who made Iron Country their home. They, like people in other single industry regions – Massachusetts' textile towns, the coal belt towns of West Virginia and Pennsylvania, Michigan's iron mining districts – came to know the hurt and anguish of mine and plant closings, loss of jobs, loss of pensions and insurance, strikes, accidents and death. They confronted turmoil and intimidation, experienced poverty and prosperity, and through it all they endured.

Somewhere along the way they became "Rangers," no longer the Finns, Austrians, Italians or whatever the ethnic background may have been, who brought their diverse ethnic ways to the Range. The change was subtle and persisted over generations. A sense of place and shared identity arose among the working people of the Range. Pride in one's ethnic heritage remained strong, but what mattered to a Ranger was not so much that one's grandfather was Croatian or Serbian, but that he was a Croatian or Serbian miner from the range. The popularity of this perception among the young is seen in the rash of Rangers' Clubs that formed on college campuses during the 1930s, '40s and '50s. Rangers today carry with them the hopes and aspirations of the immigrant peoples who found their America in the mines. Whatever challenges they may encounter, they know that their roots run deeper than the ores, and it is they who will leave their mark on the region.

There is a word that was brought to Iron Country by immigrant miners from the chalk mines of Slovenia that seems to capture the essence of what a Ranger is. The word is *tuteshi*. It means, "We are the true people from here."

Marvin Lamppa

245

Glossary of Terms

AD VALOREM TAX – A tax based on value. In the mining regions it is a tax levied on the owner of a body of ore, usually a mining company, based on the estimated value of unmined ore still in the ground.

ADIT – A nearly horizontal passage into a mine connecting the surface to an underground ore body that is being worked; used sometimes solely for drainage or ventilation or both.

BACK – The under surface of a block of ore in an underground mine. It is usually horizontal but may be inclined from side to side depending on the dip of the vein. In the Soudan Mine, where ore was mined from underground stopes, it was the unmined portion of the ore body separating two levels, after all development work had been completed.

BACK STOPING – Removal of ore from a stope after it has been prepared for production.

BARRING – Using a steel bar to drop down loose material after a blast in an underground stope mine in order to make sure that it is safe for mining crews to enter.

BENEFICIATION – Any process used to improve the iron content of lean ore.

BESSEMER ORE – Commercial grade iron ore with a phosphorous content low enough to be successfully smelted in a Bessemer converter. The Bessemer limit varied with the iron content of the ore. At the Soudan Mine it tended to be less than six hundredths of one percent.

BLASTING – An explosion of relatively small volume carefully calculated to fracture a given rock mass or a block of ore in an iron mine. Types of blasts used in mines vary according to the type of mining taking place, purpose and conditions. In modern taconite mining, they may entail several hundred thousand tons of crude ore.

BREAST – The vertical end surface of a block of ore.

CAGE – Part of the hoisting and lowering system of an underground mine used by miners to enter and exit the mine. It was always located above the skip (the container holding the ore).

CAPTAIN – An experienced miner who was given the responsibility for all work in an underground mine. He hired his own shift foremen and work crews, discharged and promoted workers at his discretion and set rates for contract pay. It was his responsibility to see that all work was properly performed and the mine was producing. The captain usually made one round of all work areas during a shift and made daily reports to the manager of the company who might have his office as far away as Duluth.

CCC – The Civilian Conservation Corps was established on March 31, 1933, as part of Franklin D. Roosevelt's New Deal program to give emergency work relief to young men 17 to 25 and to carry through a program of conservation.

CHURN DRILL – A drill invented on the Mesabi Range used to explore for iron ore where the deposits tended to be too soft to form a core in a diamond drill. It functioned by driving pressured water down a hollow rod through perforations near the drill bit forcing debris created by the action of the drill into a casing pipe through which the material was returned to the surface for inspection.

CONCENTRATE – The portion of finely ground taconite rock holding a very high iron content after the waste has been removed.

CONCENTRATOR – The area in a taconite processing plant where the iron content of finely ground taconite rock is increased.

CONTRACT SYSTEM – The traditional method of determining a miner's pay in an underground mine. As it was used in Minnesota's iron mines, a contract mining crew (usually four miners in a given "pitch," or work area) was assigned a rate of pay for either the number of feet excavated in development work or the number of ore cars loaded over a given period of time (usually a month) in production work. A close tally of the number of cars loaded, or feet excavated, was made each shift and reported to the paymaster. At the end of the month, the total earnings were divided among the crew, minus the amount drawn for supplies, which generally included explosives, fuses, caps and carbide for their lamps.

CROSSCUT – A horizontal gallery (passage) driven at right angles to the strike of a vein in an underground mine, often used to connect the vein of ore to a working shaft.

DEVELOPMENT MINING – Excavating an approach to an ore body (block of ore) and preparing it for production.

DIAMOND DRILL – A device used to explore for iron ore in areas where the deposits are hard and dense. It uses a rotating hollow feed screw with a diamond-studded bit to form a core of the material being drilled inside the hollow screw, through which it is hoisted to the surface for inspection. At the Soudan Mine, where the ore was extremely hard, it was also used in production mining to drill holes for blasting.

DINKEY – Tiny steam-powered locomotives weighing about six tons and capable of pulling 20-car trains of small wooden hand-dump cars along a narrow-gauge track, used mostly for development work in early Mesabi open pits.

DRIFT – A horizontal gallery (passage) driven along the course of a vein.

DRIVING – The act of mining horizontally to develop drifts, crosscuts and adits. Excavating any horizontal gallery (passage) in an underground mine.

EXPLORATORY DRILLING – Using a drill (diamond, churn) to locate an ore body for possible underground or open pit mining.

GANG – Four to six miners working a pitch (work area) under contract in a Mesabi underground mine. (In the Soudan Mine, the contract team was referred to as a crew.)

GOPHER HOLING – An early method of using explosives to loosen a bank of ore so it could be excavated by steam shovel in an open pit mine. A number of small excavations called "gopher holes" were made with hand shovels into the face of the bank. Several kegs of black powder were placed in each hole, covered up and set off simultaneously by means of a battery.

GRAB-AND-CARRY SYSTEM OF MINING – A mechanized system of mining attempted in places where the ore was spread out over a large area and close to the surface. It consisted of a large clamshell-like device suspended by steel cable from two towers set about a quarter of a mile apart. It was expected to pick up something like 25 tons of ore in one grab and speed it to a loading pocket located on a railroad at the edge of the pit, where it could be dumped into the ore cars of a waiting train. (It was predicted that the entire action would take about two minutes.) The system was installed at the Grant Mine near Buhl and Hale Mine near Biwabik, but it functioned haltingly in both places and was, for the most part, unsuccessful.

HALF-BREED SCRIP – Term used in the late 19th century to refer to scrip (a legal document) supposedly issued to people of mixed blood living among the Sioux and Chippewa at the time treaties were made with the federal government. The scrip was supposed to give them the legal right to locate on lands of their choice outside of the reservations. The scrip fell into the hands of speculators and investors and was used as a method to acquire timber and mining lands in northeast Minnesota.

HAND DRILL – The earliest type of drill used to explore an ore body. It is no more than a sharpened steel bar held upright and turned slowly while it is hit with sledge hammers to drive it into the ground. It requires a three-man crew: one to hold and turn the bar and two to drive it down with sledge hammers. This method of drilling was extremely slow. (It has been said that after a full 10 hours of drilling by this method into Vermilion Range iron ore, a certain drill crew had to leave a man behind holding his finger on the spot they were working so that it could be found the next morning.)

HEMATITE – For years, as the steel industry's most desirable form of iron ore, it made the name Mesabi famous. It is basically iron oxide (Fe_2O_3) and varies in color and density from the hard steel-gray found on the Vermilion Range to the red earthy masses of the Mesabi. It can have an iron content as high as 70 percent and is relatively easy and inexpensive to smelt.

HOIST – The system that brings the ore to the surface in an underground mine. Systems vary, but generally they include an engine, rope (steel cable), headframe, sheave, wheels, cage and skip. Electrically operated hoists have long since displaced the old steam and compressed air hoists in both large and small mines.

IWW – Industrial Workers of the World, an industrial union with a strong syndicalist ideology that assumed leadership of the 1916 miners strike on the Mesabi. It's influence faded after 1920.

JASPELITE – Hard irony rock found in abundance on the Vermilion Range.

JET PIERCING DRILL – A fast drilling device used in taconite mining after 1951. It burns holes into the formation using liquid oxygen and fuel oil to produce an extremely high temperature. It can drill a hole 8 inches in diameter in hard taconite at a rate of 35 feet an hour, or more.

LENSES – Term used by 19th century mine operators in Michigan and Minnesota to refer to vertical formations of iron ore both at the surface in the form of outcroppings and below ground.

LEVEL – All horizontal workings tributary to a given shaft station in an underground mine. Levels are usually numbered downward from the surface (2nd level, 3rd level, 4th level, etc.) or are designated as 100-foot level, 200-foot level, etc., according to the vertical depth from the surface.

LIMONITE – A hydrated ferric oxide form of iron ore ($2Fe_2O_3 \cdot 3H_2O$), varying in color from dark brown to yellow, found on both the Cuyuna and Mesabi iron ranges. It is considered to be an important iron ore, even though its iron content seldom exceeds 50 percent.

LOCATION – All buildings on a parcel of land held by a mining company, from the mine office to employees' dwellings. Locations varied from rude squatters' shack towns to spacious enclaves of comfortable homes complete with electricity, running water and sewage disposal. The Mesabi Range spawned more than 175 of these little towns.

MAGNETITE – A common form of iron ore (Fe_3O_4), black in color and strongly attracted by a magnet. Quantities of the ore were known to exist on the eastern Mesabi since the early days of mining, and even though its iron content can run as high as 71 percent, it is difficult to separate impurities from its iron. Therefore it is said to have "low furnace value" and has not been mined to any significant extent.

MAGNETIC SEPARATOR – A magnetic device designed to separate iron from rock in processing taconite.

MAIN LEVEL – The "main haulage" level in an underground mine. When ore mined from a level (or several levels) is dropped down to haulage level (level connected to a shaft), the haulage level is called the "main level."

MILL MINE – A system of mining that combined open-pit and underground methods. The surface materials covering an ore body were stripped away as though for open pit mining and a shaft sunk at the edge of the newly formed pit. Drifts were run from the shaft station into the ore 50 or 60 feet below the top of the ore body. Up raises were made from the drift to the surface. Through these openings ore was "milled" (dropped down) into chutes, loaded into small ore cars and trammed to the shaft where it was raised to the surface to be dumped into railroad cars for shipment. In 1904, seven percent of the Mesabi's iron ore output came from mill mines.

MILLS – Chutes through which ore was dropped from above into waiting trams on the main level of a mill or underground mine.

MOTORIZED DUMP CAR – Railroad dump cars powered by electric motors used in some of the Mesabi's deeper open pit mines to carry ore to skip hoists where it was raised to the surface. With an ore load placed directly over its drive wheels, a motorized dump car was surprisingly powerful and could pull a train of a dozen or more fully loaded ore cars to the hoist.

MUCKER – A more or less inexperienced worker in an underground mine who scrapes together loose ore accumulating around a mill chute on a haulage level and hand loads it into a tram car, or assists a crew of contract miners in scraping ore into a mill.

NATIONAL RECOVERY ACT – New Deal legislation enacted June 16, 1933, designed to speed up industrial production, spread employment, protect labor, reduce hours, raise wages and provide money for a system of public works and emergency relief through the regulation of industry and planned economy. Although it was too far reaching to last long without challenge, its recognition of a union's right to organize had a lasting impact on workers in Iron Range mines.

NON-FERROUS ORES – Ores that do not contain iron, such as those of copper, palladium, titanium and nickel.

OVERHAND STOPE MINING – Mining upward, usually in a back. The ore is broken so as to fall downward. Excavation proceeds upward from below.

PELLETIZER – The area of a taconite plant where taconite concentrate is rolled into raw pellets and solidified in a furnace.

PERCUSSION DRILL – A power drill run by compressed air that replaced hand drills in most mining operations. It operated on the same principle as the hand drill – percussion. The old "slugger" rock drills used in early mining operations fired a 60- to 80-pound hammer against a heavy steel drill rod which rotated once every six blows and made so much noise underground that "it was impossible to speak loud enough to make yourself heard at a distance of 6 inches from a person's ear."

PITCH – A place in an underground mine assigned to a gang (crew) of contract miners for production work.

PRODUCTION MINING – Breaking down a block of ore, removing it and preparing it for shipping.

PWA – Public Works Administration established in 1933 to increase employment through government spending for the construction of roads, public buildings and other projects.

RAISE – A vertical excavation in an underground mine driven upward from a drift and in an ore body. It can be used as a manway, timber chute, waste chute, ore chute or for ventilation.

RAISING – Mining upward in an underground mine, such as in excavating a raise.

ROD MILL – In taconite processing, after lean ore has been crushed to a point where the particles are approximately three-quarters of an inch in size, it goes through a final crushing in what is known as the rod mill, a series of large cylinders, each charged with 70 or more tons of smooth steel rods. When the product leaves the rod mill it is as fine as mud.

SHAFT – A vertical excavation in an underground mine of restricted cross section and of great depth used for both access and for working (lifting excavated rock and ore to the surface).

SINKING – Mining vertically downward, such as in "sinking" a shaft.

SINTERING – Beneficiation process usually designed to remove water from wet ores. It also refers to the process used in the old Mesabi Iron Company mine at Babbitt to produce a marketable form of processed taconite.

SKIP – The part of the hoisting and lowering system of an underground mine that contains the ore being lifted to the surface. It is usually the size of a medium ore car and has wheels set on tracks along one wall of the shaft to guide it to the surface. It is located below the cage in most underground mines.

STOPE – Any excavation underground, other than in development work, made for the process of removing ore. The outlines of a stope are always determined by the size and shape of the body of ore being mined.

SUBLEVEL – A level driven from a raise or manway and not directly connected to a working shaft. In most Mesabi underground mines, the ore removed at the sublevel was dropped through chutes to a main level below, trammed to the shaft and raised to the surface.

TACONITE – A very hard low grade iron ore comprised approximately of 51 percent silica and 27 percent iron, making up a large part of the formation in which the rich earthy hematite ores of the Mesabi Range were formed. It must be processed into high grade pellets before it can be turned into steel.

TAFT-HARTLEY ACT – Passed on June 23, 1947, over President Harry Truman's veto, the act banned the closed shop, permitted employers to sue unions for broken contracts and damages inflicted during strikes, required unions to abide by a 60-day "cooling off" period before striking and required unions to make public their financial statements. The act was amended in October 1951 to permit union-shop contracts without first polling employees.

TRAMMER – A worker in an underground mine assigned the task of moving the ore from a chute or place of work to the shaft station. In many early mines this was accomplished by pushing a small hand dump car along a track to the shaft.

WAGNER ACT – Also known as the National Labor Relations Act, passed July 5, 1935, creating a new National Labor Relations Board with the power to determine appropriate collective bargaining units, subject to elections it supervised at the request of workers. After this act was passed, unions organized rapidly on the Iron Range.

WPA – On April 8, 1935, the Emergency Relief Appropriations Act was passed, establishing the Works Progress Administration which eventually provided employment for more than 8$\frac{1}{2}$ million Americans who had lost their jobs as the result of the Depression. Beginning in 1939, it was called the Works Projects Administration and although most of the projects were geared to manual labor, provision was made for projects involving artists, writers, musicians and actors. Some of the works cited in this book are the result of WPA projects.

Endnotes

CHAPTER ONE [1-11]

[1]George M. Schwartz and George A. Theil, *Minnesota's Rocks and Waters,* 1954, University of Minnesota Press, Minneapolis, p. 108.

[2]*Mines and Minerals Chapters of Tax Commission Reports, Eighth Biennial Report,* 1922, St. Paul, Chapter IV, p. 4. See also Jerome Machamer, "The Geology and Mining Practices at the Soudan Mine, Vermilion District of Minnesota," May 1955, Senior Thesis, Cornell University, pp. 30-36.

[3]For a detailed description of the "Ely Trough," see *Fourth Biennial Report of the Minnesota Tax Commission,* Chapter VI, 1914, St. Paul, pp. 136-138.

[4]Schwartz and Theil, pp. 244-245.

[5]Ibid., p. 246.

[6]Ibid., p. 110.

[7]Ibid., pp. 246-248. See also Gene LaBerge, *Geology of the Lake Superior Region,* 1994, Geoscience Press Inc., Phoenix, Arizona, p. 79.

[8]W.R. Appleby, "Special Report on the Cuyuna Range," Minnesota School of Mines, May 1, 1914, *Fourth Biennial Report of the Minnesota Tax Commission,* 1914, St. Paul, Chapter VI, pp. 111-114.

[9]*Eighth Biennial Report of the Minnesota Tax Commission,* 1922, St. Paul, Chapter IV, p. 5.

[10]Gordon Peters, *Passport in Time,* 1996, video produced by the U.S. Forest Service. Peters, a U.S. Forest Service archaeologist, and his staff, working over a period of 14 years, identified more than 3,000 archaeological sites in the Superior National Forest covering 10,000 years. In this video, Peters describes the environment of northeast Minnesota 12,000 years ago. See also H.E. Wright Jr., "The Environment of Early Man in the Great Lakes Region," *Aspects of Upper Great Lakes Anthropology,* ed. Elden Johnson, 1974, Minnesota Historical Society (hereafter MHS), St. Paul, p. 8.

[11]Ibid., Peters. See also Elden Johnson, *The Prehistoric Peoples of Minnesota,* 1969, MHS, St. Paul, pp. 5-8.

[12]Peters, *Passport in Time.* Wright, "Environment of Early Man," *Aspects,* pp. 10-12.

[13]Jack Steinbring, "The Preceramic Archaeology of Northern Minnesota," *Aspects,* 1974, MHS, St. Paul, p. 72. See also Johnson, *Prehistoric Peoples,* pp. 9-12, for a description of Archaic tools.

[14]Eric W. Morse, *Fur Trade Canoe Routes of Canada/Then and Now,* 1989, University of Toronto Press, Ottawa, pp. 27-32. Steinbring, "Preceramic Archaeology," *Aspects,* p. 67. Peters, *Passport in Time.*

[15]Steinbring, "Preceramic Archaeology,"*Aspects,* p. 67.

[16]George R. Stuntz, "Evidences of Early Man in Northeastern Minnesota," read before the Minnesota Academy of Natural Sciences, Dec. 2, 1884. Copy in Northeast Minnesota Historical Center, University of Minnesota-Duluth (hereafter UMD), Duluth.

[17]George R. Stuntz, narrative of his 1865 explorations in Walter Van Brunt, ed., *Duluth and St. Louis County: Their Story and People,* Vol. I, 1921, American Historical Society, Chicago and New York, p. 344.

[18]Stuntz, "Evidences."

[19]Steinbring, "Preceramic Archaeology," p. 67.

[20]George R. Stuntz, "The Mound Builders in Northeast Minnesota: Their Occupations and Routes of Travel," *Bulletins, 1883-1891,* Minnesota Academy of Natural Sciences, Vol. 3, pp. 84-88.

[21]James B. Stoltman, "The Laurel Culture in Minnesota," 1973, Minnesota Prehistoric Archaeology Series, No. 8, MHS, St. Paul, pp. 1-11.

[22]Peters, *Passport in Time.*

[23]Johnson, *Prehistoric Peoples,* p. 13.

[24]Peters, *Passport in Time.*

[25]Johnson, *Prehistoric Peoples,* pp. 13-20. Mike Budak, Grand Mound Interpretive Center, in Peters' *Passport in Time.*

[26]James B. Stoltman, "Within Laurel Cultural Variability in Northern Minnesota,"*Aspects,* 1974, pp. 88-89.

[27]Findings of Lloyd A. Wilford, Jul. 2-29, 1940, MHS, St. Paul. With the aid of five WPA laborers, Wilford excavated 18 10-foot squares within the limits of the southern half of the mound. Much of the mound had previously been disturbed and at the time of the excavation it had the appearance of a small volcano. People living in the area had found it a convenient source of black dirt.

[28]Harold Hickerson, *The Chippewa and Their Neighbors: A Study in Ethnohistory,* 1970, Irvington Publishers Inc., New

York, pp. 40-41. Hickerson includes quotes from two eyewitnesses of the Feast of the Dead, the Jesuit, Jerome Lalemant in 1641, and Nicolas Perrot who in 1670 was sent by the French government to take possession of the western Great Lakes.

[29]Pierre Esprit Radisson's account of a 1660 Dakota "Feast of the Dead" is in *Voyages of Peter Esprit Radisson,* 1885, Prince Society, Boston, pp. 201-206, Reprint edition, ed. Gideon Scull, 1943, Peter Smith, New York, pp. 218-219. Also, in Hickerson, *Chippewa and Their Neighbors,* p. 48, is Radisson's statement: "The renewing of their alliances, the marriages according to their countrey coustomes are made; also the visit of the boans of their deceased friends for they keepe them and bestow them upon one another." See also Van Brunt, *Duluth,* Vol. I, p. 14.

[30]Stoltman, *Aspects,* p. 89.

[31]Peters, *Passport in Time.*

[32]Ibid.

[33]Ibid.

[34]Nancy S. Ossenberg, "Origins and Relationships of Woodland Peoples: The Evidence of Cranial Morphology," *Aspects,* p. 15.

[35]Ibid., p. 21.

CHAPTER TWO [12-24]

[1]George Stuntz, "Evidences," read before the Minnesota Academy of Natural Sciences, Dec. 2, 1884.

[2]F.A. Edson and R.S. Lerch, "Discovery Near Aurora, Minnesota," Jun. 4, 1936, in Charles E. Aguar, *Exploring St. Louis County's Historical Sites,* 1971, Aguar Jyring Whiteman Moser Inc., Duluth, p. 29.

[3]Mari Sandoz, *The Beaver Men,* 1964, Hastings House Publishers, New York, p. 19.

[4]Ibid., p. 59.

[5]Harold Hickerson, "The Early Saulteur and Their Ceremonies," *Chippewa and Their Neighbors,* pp. 39-41.

[6]William Brandon, *Indians,* 1987, Houghton Mifflin Company, Boston, p. 327.

[7]An account of the origin of the term "Sioux" is found in *Jesuit Relations, XVIII,* ed. Reuben Gold Thwaites, 1959, New York, pp. 231-233. See also *Voyages of Peter Esprit Radisson,* Scull, ed., pp. 201-206.

[8]Northern portion of a map drawn in 1697 by Jean Baptiste Louis Franquelin shows the lands of the Sioux of the East and Sioux of the West divided by the Mississippi River, map from the Ayer Collection, Newberry Library, Chicago, as found in Mildred Mott Wedel, "Le

Sueur and the Dakota Sioux," *Aspects,* p. 167. See also 1702 map drawn by Guillaume Delisle, *Aspects,* p. 168. The maps locate and name 10 of 11 Eastern Sioux villages.

[9]Ibid., *Aspects,* p. 166. "The Le Sueur-Delisle Extracts (1702:43)" report that most of the Sioux of the East with 'about 300 *cabanes'* were living near Mille Lacs Lake, called by the French at that time Lac des Sioux or Lac de Buade after Louis de Buade, Comte de Frontenac, on p. 170, *Mendouacanton* (Mdewakanton): *Nation du lac; 1702-Village du lac d'esprit.* See also William W. Folwell, *A History of Minnesota,* 1956, MHS, St. Paul, Vol. I, pp. 455-457, for a description of how Minnesota got its name. Also, 2004 interview with native Lakota speaker from Oglala Lakota College in Kyle, South Dakota.

[10]Wedel, p. 170.

[11]Roy W. Meyer, *History of the Santee Sioux,* 1967, University of Nebraska Press, Lincoln, p. 9.

[12]Ibid., pp. 165-171. See also Stoltman, *Laurel Culture,* pp. 10-11.

[13]See Lawrence Burpee, ed., *Journals and Letters of Pierre Gaultier de Varennes de la Verendrye and His Sons,* 1927, Champlain Society, Toronto, for map entitled *VII Carte Des Decouvertes de la Verendrye.* The upper region appears to include the Mesabi height of land and Esquagama Lake.

[14]R.E. Carey, "The Vermillion Lake Road and Indian Trail from Minnesota Point to Vermillion Lake," unpublished manuscript, Northeast Minnesota History Center (hereafter NEMHC), and Rev. Joseph A. Gilfillan, "Minnesota Geographical Names Derived From the Chippewa Language," 1885, St. Paul, as found in *The Minnesota Archaeologist,* Dec. 1976, p. 30.

[15]Wedel, *Aspects,* p. 165.

[16]Harold Hickerson, *Land Tenure of the Rainy Lake Chippewa,* 1967, Smithsonian Press, Washington D.C., pp. 44-45.

[17]William W. Warren, *History of the Ojibway Nation,* 1974, Ross and Haines Inc., Minneapolis, p. 407.

[18]Ibid., p. 83.

[19]Ibid., p. 85.

[20]Van Brunt, *Duluth,* Vol. I, p. 27.

[21]Ibid., p. 164. Hickerson, *Chippewa and Their Neighbors,* pp. 65-68.

[22]Hickerson, *Southwestern Chippewa,* American Anthropological Association, Memoir 92, Jun. 1962, pp. 65-72. Warren, *History of the Ojibway,* pp. 132-134.

[23]Hickerson, *Southwestern Chippewa,* pp. 65-72. Warren, pp. 96-97.

[24]Warren, pp. 164-165.

[25]Warren, pp. 84-85. Hickerson, *Southwestern Chippewa*, p. 67.

[26]Burpee, p. 174.

[27]Warren, p. 157. Hickerson, *Southwestern Chippewa*, p. 69.

[28]Margry, 1886, 6:78 as quoted in Wedel, *Aspects*, p. 166.

[29]Hickerson, *Chippewa and Their Neighbors*, pp. 67-71.

[30]Burpee, pp. 380-381.

[31]Warren, p. 169.

[32]Burpee, p. 238.

[33]Burpee, p. 236.

[34]Warren, p. 85.

[35]Peter C. Newman, *Caesars of the Wilderness*, 1987, Penguin Books Canada, Markham, Ontario, p. 240.

[36]Ibid., p. 9.

[37]Elliott Coues, ed., *Manuscript Journals of Alexander Henry and David Thompson, 1799-1814*, 1897, 1965, Minneapolis, Vol. I, pp. 80-81.

[38]For lists of North West Company employees in 1804 see L.R. Masson, ed., *Les Bourgeois de la Compagnie du Nord-Ouest* (Origin, journals, narratives, letters, etc. relating to the North West Company), 1889, Quebec, Reprint Edition 1960, Antiquarian Press, New York, Vol. I, pp. 395-413. See also Newman, pp. 29-30 and Grace Lee Nute, *The Voyageur's Highway*, 1941, MHS, St. Paul, pp. 45-46.

[39]Duncan Cameron, "The Nipigon Country, 1804" in Masson, *Les Bourgeois*, Vol. II, pp. 242-243. See also Martin Hunter, *Canadian Wilds*, 1935, A. R. Harding, Columbus, pp. 24-29. Hunter, a former Hudson's Bay Company trader, describes that company's traditions and procedures, northern natives and methods of hunting and trapping.

[40]Hunter, p. 28.

[41]See "Reminiscences" by Roderick McKenzie in Masson, Vol. I, pp. 9-56.

[42]Ibid., p. 66.

[43]Ibid., p. 65.

[44]Peter Grant, "Sauteux Indians," about 1804 in Masson, Vol. II, pp. 307-366.

[45]Newman, p. 7.

CHAPTER THREE [25-38]

[1]Grant, "The Sauteux Indians," about 1804, Masson, Vol. II, p. 309.

[2]Cameron, "Nipigon Country," in Masson II, p. 240.

[3]Grant, "Sauteux," Masson, Vol. II, p. 309.

[4]Ibid., pp. 307-308.

[5]Ibid., p. 313.

[6]Grace Lee Nute, "Posts in the Minnesota Fur-Trading Area, 1660-1885," *Minnesota History*, Dec. 1930, MHS, St. Paul, pp. 353-354.

[7]Ibid., pp. 353-385.

[8]See Hickerson, *Rainy Lake Chippewa*, pp. 48-52; also Hickerson, "Ethnohistory of Chippewa of Lake Superior," *Chippewa Indians III*, 1974, Garland Publishing Inc., New York and London, p. 20.

[9]Nute, "Posts in Minnesota," pp. 357, 362, 371. Henry R. Schoolcraft, *Narrative Journal of Travels Through the Northwestern Regions of the United States*, 1821, Albany, New York, p. 203, notes the ruins of a North West fort at Fond du Lac and on p. 218 describes in detail the North West fort at Sandy Lake, which was then occupied by clerks of the American Fur Company.

[10]Hiram Hayes in Van Brunt, Vol. I, p. 42.

[11]John S. Pardee in Van Brunt, Vol. I, p. 43.

[12]Bruce M. White, "Give Us a Little Milk, Economics and Ceremony in the Ojibway Fur Trade," May 1985, M.A Thesis, McGill University, Montreal, pp. 33-36, provides insight into the significance of traders' rum to Ojibway people. See also pp. 53-55.

[13]Folwell, Vol. I, pp. 91-97.

[14]Ibid., p. 98.

[15]Louis A. Tohill, "Robert Dickson," *Minnesota History*, Dec. 1925, MHS, St. Paul, pp. 336-338.

[16]Warren, pp. 368-369.

[17]Tohill, p. 337.

[18]Edmund Jefferson Danziger Jr., *The Chippewas of Lake Superior*, 1978, University of Oklahoma Press, p. 72., notes that "American Fur Company traders counseled their customers about political matters and often acted as liaisons with the United States government," and that the "Indian headmen and federal treaty commissioners accepted this function may be found in the agreements which traders helped to negotiate. In the land cession treaties of 1837 and 1842, for example, the Chippewas sold the northern half of Wisconsin. From the proceeds of the land sales, they granted debt claims to traders of $70,000 and $75,000."

[19]Folwell, Vol. I, p. 132.

[20]Schoolcraft, p. 203.

[21]D. 4/116, in Hudson's Bay Company Records, Manitoba Provincial Archives, Winnipeg, Canada (hereafter HBC).

[22]"Roderick McKenzie to George Simpson," Dec. 18, 1821, "McKenzie to Simpson," Mar. 18, 1822, D. 4/116, HBC.

[23]B. 105/a/8, HBC.

[24]The list of U.S. Trader Licenses for the year 1822 includes one issued to "Youngs L. Morgan" at Sault Ste. Marie "to trade on Lac Vermillion" from Jul. 29, 1822, to Aug. 1, 1823, by H.R. Schoolcraft, "bond $867.75; U.S. Serial No. 93," MHS. See Youngs L. Morgan "Diary of an Early Fur Trader," 1822-23, as found in *Inland Seas*, Great Lakes Historical Society, Winter 1962-Winter 1963.

[25]B. 105/a/9, HBC.

[26]B. 105/a/8, HBC.

[27]U.S. Traders Licenses, 1822-1847, MHS Collection, St. Paul.

[28]See Hickerson, *Rainy Lake Chippewa*, p. 54, for comparisons of Indian populations at Rainy Lake and Lake Vermilion during the years 1821-1834.

[29]Hickerson, *Chippewa Indians III*, pp. 98-99. Grace Lee Nute, *Voyageur's Highway*, p. 45.

[30]Folwell, Vol. I, pp. 500-501.

[31]*House Executive Document 451*, 25th Congress, 2nd Session, Washington, D.C.

[32]Folwell, Vol. I, p. 50.

[33]W.E. Culkin, unpublished manuscript at NEMHC.

[34]Folwell, Vol. I, pp. 495-502.

[35]James Norwood in David D. Owen, *Report of a Geological Survey of Iowa, Minnesota, and Wisconsin Territories*, 1852, Philadelphia, p. 315.

[36]"Treaty with the Chippewa, 1826," in Charles J. Kappler, LL.M., *Indian Affairs, Laws and Treaties*, Vol. II, 1904, Government Printing Office, Washington, D.C., p. 268.

[37]"Treaty With the Chippewa, 1854," in Kappler, pp. 648-651.

[38]Ibid.

[39]Ibid.

[40]Luther Webb notes at a council with Bois Forte at Grand Portage, Oct. 16, 1865, in "Letters Received, Office of Indian Affairs, National Archives" 1824-81 (hereafter LR, OIA, NA), Washington, D.C.

[41]David A. Walker, "Lake Vermilion Gold Rush," *Minnesota History*, Summer 1974, MHS, St. Paul, p. 44. See also N.H. Winchell, "Historical Sketch of Explorations and Surveys in Minnesota," *Geological and Natural History Survey of Minnesota*, 1889, St. Paul, Vol. I, pp. 95-97.

[42]Thomas Clark, *Report of the State Geologist. Augustus H. Hanchett, MD*, 1865, Fred Driscoll, Incidental Publisher, St. Paul.

[43]Walker, "Gold Rush," p. 44.

[44]Helen Wieland Skillings, *We're Standing on Iron! The Story of the Five Wieland Brothers 1856-1883*, 1972, St. Louis County Historical Society, Duluth, p. 49.

[45]*St. Paul Pioneer*, Dec. 14 and 21, 1865, St. Paul.

[46]"J.N. Treadwell to J.C. Bush," Jul. 20, 1858, MHS Collection, St. Paul.

[47]Henry H. Eames, *Report of the State Geologist on the Metalliferous Region Bordering on Lake Superior*, 1866, St. Paul. Ruth M. Elliot, "Vermilion Gold Rush of 1865," 1923, unpublished manuscript, MHS Collection.

[48]*St. Paul Pioneer*, Dec. 14 and 21, 1865.

[49]*Cleveland Herald*, Oct. 10, 1865, Cleveland, Ohio.

[50]*St. Paul Daily Press*, Sep. 19, 1865. Elliot, "Vermilion Gold Rush."

[51]*St. Paul Pioneer*, Oct. 25, 1865.

[52]Elliot, "Vermilion Gold Rush." *St. Paul Pioneer*, Oct. 31, 1865, May 15, 1866. *Gazette*, Dec. 16, 1865, Superior, Wisconsin.

[53]Elliot, "Vermilion Gold Rush." *Gazette*, Oct. 21, Nov. 11, 1865, Superior. See also Folwell Vol. I, pp. 470-478, for description of Chippewa half-breed scrip and Folwell Vol. I, p. 482-486, for description of Sioux half-breed scrip.

[54]*Gazette*, Oct. 21, 1865, Superior.

[55]*Gazette*, Nov. 11, 1865.

[56]*Gazette*, Jan. 20, 1866.

[57]Ibid.

[58]Van Brunt, Vol. I, p. 344.

[59]*Gazette*, Jan. 20, 1866.

[60]Ibid.

[61]*St. Paul Daily Press*, Feb. 22, 1866.

[62]*St. Paul Pioneer*, May 9, 1866. *St. Paul Daily Press*, May 19, 1866. Elliot, "Vermilion Gold." Eric C. Peterson, "Gold Mining in Northern Minnesota," unpublished manuscript, 1954, UMD, Department of History.

[63]"Mining Laws of the Vermillion Lake Mining District, Minnesota, adopted in convention of miners at Vermillion Lake, Mar. 10, 1866," as found in "Articles of Association, Report of Trustees, Vermillion [sic] Lake Mineral Land Company," Richard Eames papers, MHS, St. Paul. *St. Paul Pioneer*, May 15, 1866.

[64]*St. Paul Pioneer*, May 15, 1866.

[65]Elliot, "Vermilion Gold." *St. Paul Pioneer*, May 15, 1866.

[66]Jas. V.Z. Blaney to Martin Ryerson, Robert H. Foss and Charles H. Oakes, trustees of the Vermillion Lake Mineral Land Company, Nov. 14, 1866, Chicago, as found in "Articles of Association," Richard Eames papers, MHS.

[67]*St. Paul Pioneer*, Apr. 7, 1866.

[68]Ibid.

CHAPTER FOUR [39-53]

[1]Today called Everetts Bay.

[2]John A. Bardon papers, 1845-1880, MHS.

[3]Luther Webb to D.N. Cooley, Dec. 12, 1865, LR, OIA, NA.

[4]Webb to Cooley, Nov. 8, 1865, LR, OIA, NA, Washington, D.C.

[5]Morrison to Cooley, Nov. 8, 1865, LR, OIA, NA.

[6]Stephen Miller to D.N. Cooley, Nov. 13, 1865, LR, OIA, NA.

[7]Ibid.

[8]Bois Forte chiefs to Cooley, commissioner of Indian Affairs, Feb. 24, 1866, LR, OIA, NA. See also "Treaty with the Chippewa – Bois Forte Band, 1866," in Kappler, LL.M., *Laws and Treaties*, Vol. II, pp. 916-918.

[9]Ibid., pp. 916-918.

[10]Shubael P. Adams, J.C. Ramsey, John G. Webb to L.V. Bogey, "Commissioners Report to Set Off a Reservation for the Bois Forte," Jan. 22, 1867," LR, OIA, NA. George Stuntz to Indian Agent Luther Webb, Jan. 31, 1867, LR, OIA, NA.

[11]"Commissioners Report," LR, OIA, NA.

[12]Ibid.

[13]Ibid.

[14]Stuntz to Luther Webb, Dec. 31, 1866, LR, OIA, NA.

[15]*Gazette*, Mar. 28, 1868.

[16]Ibid., May 30, 1868.

[17]Ibid., Aug. 22, 1868.

[18]Ibid.

[19]Ibid.

[20]Ibid., Sep. 26, 1868.

[21]Ibid.

[22]John R. Carey, in Van Brunt, Vol. I, p. 348.

[23]George Stuntz autobiographical comments in Dwight E. Woodbridge and John S. Pardee, eds., *History of Duluth and St. Louis County: Past and Present*, 1910, C.F. Cooper and Company, Chicago, Vol. I, pp. 229-235.

[24]George Stuntz interview, *Vermilion Iron Journal*, Nov. 5, 1891.

[25]Ibid.

[26]Ibid.

[27]Ibid.

[28]Stuntz narrative in Van Brunt, Vol. I, p. 345.

[29]*Vermilion Iron Journal*, Nov. 5, 1891.

[30]Van Brunt, Vol. I, p. 345.

[31]*Statutes at Large of the United States of America, XVII*, as quoted in Fremont P. Wirth, *The Discovery and Exploitation of the Minnesota Iron Lands*, 1931, Torch Press, Cedar Rapids, Iowa, p. 36.

[32]Ibid., p. 39.

[33]Ibid., p. 208.

[34]For a vivid description of the Keweenaw copper boom, see Russell McKee, *Great Lakes Country*, 1966, Thomas Y. Crowell Company, New York, pp. 177-180.

[35]Ibid., p. 181.

[36]David A. Walker, *Iron Frontier: The Discovery and Early Development of*

Minnesota's Three Ranges, 1979, MHS, St. Paul, p. 8, and McKee, p. 185.

[37]Skillings, *We're Standing on Iron!*, p. 51.

[38]Ibid., p. 3.

[39]Ibid.

[40]Ibid., p. 49.

[41]Ibid., p. 50.

[42]Ibid., pp. 51-52.

[43]Ibid., pp. 51-52. See also E.W. Davis, *Pioneering With Taconite*, 1964, MHS, St. Paul, p. 8.

[44]Davis, p. 8.

[45]Ibid., p. 9.

[46]Ibid., p. 10.

[47]Ibid., pp. 10-11.

[48]Ibid., p. 12.

[49]Ibid., pp. 11-12 Davis draws the figures from abstracts and deeds to property eventually occupied by the Reserve Mining Company, Babbitt and Silver Bay.

[50]Here and the following paragraph from Ibid., pp. 12-13. See also Frank A. King, *The Missabe Road*, 1972, Golden West Books, San Marino, California, pp. 12-13.

[51]Van Brunt, Vol. I, p. 351. Davis, p.14.

[52]Walker, *Iron Frontier*, p. 24.

[53]Ibid., pp. 24-25.

[54]Ibid., p. 25.

[55]Albert H. Chester in Van Brunt, Vol. I, p. 351.

[56]Ibid.

[57]Hal Bridges, *Iron Millionaire*, 1952, University of Pennsylvania Press, Philadelphia, pp. 99-103.

[58]Albert Chester, "Romance of the Ranges," a paper contributed to the Old Settlers' Association of the Head of Lake Superior, quoted in Van Brunt, Vol. I, p. 352.

[59]Ibid., pp. 352-353.

[60]Ibid., p. 252.

[61]Ibid., p. 253. Davis, p. 14.

[62]Van Brunt, Vol. I, p. 355.

[63]John Mallmann to Newton H. Winchell Mesaba, Sept. 27, 1890, in Newton H. and Horace V. Winchell, *Geological and Natural Survey of Minnesota, Bulletin No. 6, Iron Ores of Minnesota*, 1891, Minneapolis, p. 175.

[64]Chester in Van Brunt, Vol. I, p. 353.

[65]Ibid., p. 356.

[66]Ibid.

[67]Z.J. Brown is listed as "Farmer to the Bois Forte Bands at Vermilion Lake," date of employment, Mar. 24, 1877, "List of Employees, La Pointe Agency," LR, OIA, NA. See also Van Brunt, Vol. I, p. 356.

[68]Fremont P. Wirth, *The Discovery and Exploitation of the Minnesota Iron Lands*, 1931, Torch Press, Cedar Rapids, Iowa, pp. 138-139. Van Brunt, Vol. I, p. 357.

CHAPTER FIVE [54-73]

[1]Bridges, *Iron Millionaire*, pp. 156-157, 159.

[2]Wirth, pp. 136-137. Van Brunt, Vol. I, pp. 358-359. Bridges, pp. 156-160. Stone's

letters to Tower are quoted explaining the then-accepted use of fraudulent entrymen to gain access to public lands.

[3]Bridges, pp. 160, 225.

[4]Wirth, pp. 135-136.

[5]Walker, *Iron Frontier*, pp. 32-33. See also Wirth, p. 137.

[6]Van Brunt, Vol. I, p. 359.

[7]The names of entrymen and descriptions of property located by them are listed in *U.S. General Land Office, Tract Book*, National Archives, Washington, D.C., Vol. 60, pp. 61-72.

[8]Walker, p. 37. Bridges, p. 166.

[9]Wirth, pp. 132-133. Van Brunt, Vol. I, p. 374.

[10]Wirth, p. 134.

[11]Bridges, p. 170. King, p. 16

[12]Samuel P. Ely letter to George C. Stone, Feb. 7, 1883, quoted in Walker, p. 59; partially quoted and commented on in Bridges, pp. 225-226.

[13]See Bridges, pp. 172-186, for details.

[14]Franklin Prince to Charlemagne Tower Letters, Oct. 1883-Mar. 1884, Minnesota Mines Collection, United States Steel Corporation, copy in Iron Range Research Center, Chisholm (hereafter IRRC).

[15]Bridges, pp. 210-211.

[16]Prince to Tower, Nov. 1883, IRRC.

[17]Ibid., Jan. 1884.

[18]Van Brunt, Vol. I, p. 361.

[19]Ibid., p. 358.

[20]Bridges, p. 191.

[21]Ibid. Walker, p. 54.

[22]Bridges, pp. 177, 191.

[23]See King, *Missabe Road*, p. 17, for an account of McGonagle's work in laying out the final survey for the line. See also Bridges, p. 192.

[24]Bridges, pp. 192-193.

[25]Van Brunt, Vol. I, p. 361.

[26]King, pp.17-18. Bridges, pp. 185-186.

[27]Prince to Tower, Oct. 1883. Folwell, Vol. IV, p. 15.

[28]Bridges, pp. 194-197. See also Hugh E. Bishop, *By Water and Rail: A History of Lake County, Minnesota*, 2002, Lake Superior Port Cities Inc., pp. 20-32.

[29]Quote is from Walter Havighurst, *Vein of Iron, The Pickands Mather Story*, 1958, World Publishing Company, Cleveland, p. 73.

[30]Van Brunt, Vol. I, pp. 422-423. Walker, p. 88.

[31]King, pp. 23-24. Bridges, pp. 198-199. Bishop, *Water and Rail*, p. 29.

[32]King, p. 18. Bridges, p. 186.

[33]For construction problems, see Bridges, pp. 214-217. Ely to Tower Jr., May 15, 1884, quoted in Walker, p. 57.

[34]Van Brunt, Vol. I, p. 374.

[35]Ibid.

[36]Van Brunt, Vol. II, p. 980. Carlton C. Qualey, "The Cornish: A Mining Elite," *Entrepreneurs and Immigrants: Life on the Industrial Frontier of Northeast Minnesota*, 1991, IRRC, p. 76. *Duluth*

News Tribune, Feb. 1, 1884, Mar. 14, 1884, and Mar. 21, 1884.

[37]Prince to Tower, Mar. 1884. Bridges, pp. 201-204. Van Brunt, Vol. I, p. 365. *Duluth News Tribune*, Mar. 21, 1884.

[38]Prince to Tower, Mar. 1884.

[39]Prince to Tower, Jun. 1884. Bridges, p. 206.

[40]Prince to Tower, Jul. 1884, IRRC.

[41]King, p. 24. Bridges, pp. 218-219.

[42]King, pp. 24-25. Bridges, p. 220.

[43]Bridges, p. 221.

[44]Charlemagne Tower Jr. to Charlemagne Tower Sr., Aug. 2. 1884, quoted in King, p. 25.

[45]Bridges, pp. 220-223. King, p. 25. Elisha Morcom Jr., "The Discovery and Development of the Iron Ore Industry," 1926, unpublished manuscript, copy in IRRC.

[46]Bridges, p. 224. King, p. 25. "Tower-Soudan," *Missabe Iron Ranger*, the Duluth, Missabe & Iron Range Railway magazine, Jul. 1954, Duluth, p. 5.

[47]Bridges, pp. 224-225. King, p. 26.

[48]Walker, p. 59. Bridges, pp. 230-232.

[49]Bridges, pp. 233-239. Walker, p. 65.

[50]Bridges, pp. 244-245. Van Brunt, Vol. I, pp. 370-371. *Vermilion Iron Journal*, Jan. to Jul., 1888; Walker, pp. 65-67. N.H. Winchell & H.V. Winchell, *Iron Ores of Minnesota*, p. 187.

[51]See Bridges, pp. 267-269.

[52]Ibid., p. 269.

[53]Ibid., p. 270.

[54]Ibid., p. 269.

[55]Ibid., p. 273.

[56]Ibid., pp. 273, 278.

[57]Friction between Captain Elisha Morcom and George Stone over management of the mine; Charlemagne Tower Jr.'s criticism of Stone's alleged "haphazard accounting methods" and "easy going bookkeeping;" and Stone's efforts to block the Republican Party endorsement of Tower Jr. as a candidate for the State Senate are described in Bridges, pp. 258-264. See also, p. 280.

[58]*Vermilion Iron Journal*, Sep. 8, 1887.

[59]Ibid.

[60]Kenneth Duncan, "The Soudan Mine and the Minnesota Iron Company," *Skillings Mining Review*, Nov. 4, 1967, p. 22. "D.H. Bacon Resigns," *Tower Weekly News*, Dec. 28, 1900.

[61]Winchell and Winchell, *Iron Ores*, pp. 27-36.

[62]Ibid., p. 188.

[63]Ibid., p. 187.

[64]Ibid., p. 188.

[65]Ibid.

[66]Ibid.

[67]Ibid., pp. 178-179.

[68]Ibid., p. 180.

[69]*Vermilion Iron Journal*, Jun. 20, 1889.

[70]Winchell and Winchell, *Iron Ores*, pp. 193-196.

[71]J. Morgan Clements, *The Vermilion Iron Bearing District of Minnesota*, 1903,

U.S. Geological Survey, Monographs No. 45, Washington, D.C, p. 242.

[72] Hilliard Larson, recollections of a Soudan miner in the 1920s, as interviewed by Michael Karni, Aug. 1981. Tape without transcript is on file at IRRC.

[73] *Vermilion Iron Journal*, Jul. 26, 1888.

[74] J.R. Leifchild, *Cornwall: Its Mines and Miners*, 1857, Longman, Brown, Green, Longmans and Roberts, London, p. 138.

[75] Hilliard Larson, Karni interview.

[76] Minnesota Bureau of Labor, Biennial Report, 1901-1902, as found in Minnesota, Executive Documents, 1903, Vol. 2, St. Paul, p. 879, on file at IRRC. See also G.O. Virtue, "Minnesota Iron Ranges," *Bulletin of the Bureau of Labor* No. 84, Sep. 1909, U.S. Department of Labor and Commerce, Washington, D.C., p. 386.

[77] Donald H. Bacon, "System of Filling at the Minnesota," *Vermilion Iron Journal*, Jul. 31, 1892.

[78] See George J. Young, *Elements of Mining*, 1946, New York, pp. 338-349 and pp. 554-568 for an understanding of "overhand stope mining," and Donald H. Bacon, "Development of Lake Superior Ores," *Transactions*, American Institute of Mining Engineers, Vol. XXI, 1892, pp. 299-304, for descriptions of underground methods used in the Soudan Mine during the Bacon era.

[79] Van Brunt, Vol. I., pp. 363-364.

[80] Ibid., p. 364. *Vermilion Iron Journal*, May 18, 1893.

[81] *Vermilion Iron Journal*, May 18, 1893, and May 18, 1906.

[82] Winchell and Winchell, *Iron Ores*, pp. 335-349.

[83] Van Brunt, Vol. I, p. 365. Walker, p. 69.

[84] Winchell and Winchell, *Iron Ores*, p. 199.

[85] Van Brunt, Vol. I, p. 367. Walker, p. 69.

[86] Van Brunt, Vol. I, p. 367. Winchell and Winchell, *Iron Ores*, pp. 196-198.

[87] Van Brunt, Vol. I, p. 367.

[88] Winchell and Winchell, *Iron Ores*, pp. 186, 196.

[89] See Winchell and Winchell, *Iron Ores*, p. 187, for a detailed description of the underground method of mining used at the Chandler in 1889.

[90] Van Brunt, Vol. I, pp. 382-383.

[91] Winchell and Winchell, *Iron Ores*, pp. 335-349.

[92] The Northeast Minnesota Mining Company was incorporated in Minneapolis by A.C. Bruce, J.G. Emery Jr. and J. Paulson on Apr. 27, 1887, according to Winchell and Winchell, *Iron Ores*, p. 343.

[93] *Vermilion Iron Journal*, Apr. 20, 1893.

CHAPTER SIX [74-101]

[1] Van Brunt, Vol. I, pp. 376-378, 381. *Vermilion Iron Journal*, Jul. 11, 1889. It should be noted, however, that official census figures for Tower never exceeded 1,400. Prince to Tower, Oct. 1883-March 1884, from vertical file Minnesota Mines Collection, United States Steel Corporation, IRRC.

[2] Will Harrington's comments are from the *Vermilion Iron Journal*, Sep. 15 and Sep. 22, 1877.

[3] Peter Schaefer, "History of the Vermilion Range Press," unpublished manuscript presented to the first annual convention of the St. Louis County Historical Society, Virginia, Minnesota, Aug. 7, 1923, as filed in the archives of MHS.

[4] *Vermilion Iron Journal*, Oct. 13, 1887.

[5] *Vermilion Iron Journal*, Feb. 4, 1888.

[6] Schaefer, "Vermilion Range Press," p. 2.

[7] *Vermilion Iron Journal*, Jan. 3, 1889.

[8] Schaefer, "Vermilion Range Press," p. 2.

[9] Ibid., pp. 5-6.

[10] Van Brunt, Vol. I, p. 375.

[11] Ibid., p. 375.

[12] Ibid., p. 376.

[13] "An Irishman Passing Through Tower," *Vermilion Iron Journal*, Jun. 20, 1887.

[14] *Vermilion Iron Journal*, Sep. 1887-Jul. 1888.

[15] Ibid., Jul. 26, 1888.

[16] Ibid., Apr. 21, 1892.

[17] Ibid.

[18] Ibid., Dec. 6, 1888, and Apr. 21, 1892.

[19] Ibid., Feb. 18, 1892.

[20] Van Brunt, Vol. I, pp. 377-378, and Vol. II, pp. 575, 586, 588.

[21] Agnes M. Larson, *History of the White Pine Industry*, 1949, University of Minnesota Press, Minneapolis, p. 253.

[22] For areas logged, see Miron Heinselman, *The Boundary Waters Wilderness Ecosystem*, 1996, University of Minnesota Press, Minneapolis, pp. 99-100. A good description of Howe Mill improvements is found in the *Vermilion Iron Journal*, Jan. 19, 1893.

[23] "Tower-Soudan," *Mesabi Iron Ranger*, Jul. 1954, Duluth, p. 11.

[24] Heinselman, p. 100.

[25] *Mesabi Iron Ranger*, Jul. 1954, p. 11. Frank H. Gillmor, superintendent of logging operations for the Virginia and Rainy Lake Lumber Company, interview by Lucile Kane, Jul. 24-25, 1948, MHS.

[26] Aguar, *St. Louis County's Historical Sites*, p. 42. Gillmor, MHS. See also *Mesabi Iron Ranger*, Jul. 1954, p. 11.

[27] *Vermilion Iron Journal*, Nov. 18, 1890. See also Walker, *Iron Frontier*, p. 62 and Schaefer, "Vermilion Range Press."

[28] *Vermilion Iron Journal*, Nov. 7, 1889.

[29] Hans R. Wasastjerna, ed., *History of the Finns in Minnesota*, 1957, Minnesota Finnish-American Historical Society, Duluth, p. 358. See also Michael Karni, "Finnish Temperance and Its Clash with Emerging Socialism in Minnesota," in *Finnish Diaspora II: United States*, Michael G. Karni, ed., 1981, pp. 163-172. The Multicultural History Society of Ontario, Toronto.

[30] *Vermilion Iron Journal*, Mar. 22, 1894-Mar. 14, 1895. Schaefer, "Vermilion Range Press."

[31] *Vermilion Iron Journal*, Jul. 1888-Jul. 1892. See also Arnold Alanen, "From Tower to Soudan: Townsites and Locations on the Vermilion Iron Range," *Entrepreneurs and Immigrants*, 1991, Michael Karni, ed., IRRC, p. 33.

[32] Van Brunt, Vol. I, pp. 381, 390.

[33] Ibid., pp. 370-373. *Vermilion Iron Journal*, Sep. 8 and Nov. 1, 1887.

[34] *Vermilion Iron Journal*, Nov. 1, 1888.

[35] Van Brunt, Vol. I, pp. 370-373. Interviews Jul. 25, 1979, with Elina Sipola Saari, resident of Soudan, 1900-1979; Jul. 4, 1979, Helen Sipola Lamppa, resident of Soudan, 1900-1920; Jul. 23, 1981, Carl Soderberg, resident of Soudan, 1907-1981.

[36] Saari, Sipola and Soderberg interviews.

[37] *Vermilion Iron Journal*, Apr. 18, 1895.

[38] Ibid., Feb. 4, 1892.

[39] Ibid., Aug. 10, 1893. Also Saari, Sipola and Soderberg interviews.

[40] *Vermilion Iron Journal*, Aug. 10, 1893.

[41] Ibid., Aug. 3, 1893.

[42] *Polk Directory*, Soudan, 1901, 1903, 1907, IRRC. Van Brunt, Vol. I, pp. 372 and 381. See also *Tower Weekly News*, Jan. 6, 1905, for story of mine closing.

[43] The story of the strike is taken from the *Vermilion Iron Journal*, June 23, 1892.

[44] Van Brunt, Vol. I, pp. 382-383.

[45] Ibid., p. 385.

[46] "Beginnings of Ely," *The Ely Miner*, Jul. 4, 1930. *Vermilion Iron Journal*, Sep. 8, 1887. Van Brunt, Vol. I, p. 382.

[47] Van Brunt, Vol. I, p. 382. *Vermilion Iron Journal*, Mar. 15, 1888.

[48] Lee Brownell, early resident of Ely, collected photographs of Native Americans in the streets of frontier Ely, interview Jul. 28, 1972; Frank Teutloff, Bois Forte tribal member, born in the Ely area in 1911, recalled a native village and cemetery in the vicinity, interviewed by tribal member Jerry Pete, *Vermilion Lake Bois Forte History Project*, Dec. 17, 1996, tape and transcript on file at IRRC. Ernestine Hill, Bois Forte tribal member, was born on Basswood Lake, her mother was a trapper, her father a commercial fisherman, undated interview by tribal member Jerry Pete, tapes and transcripts at IRRC.

[49] Van Brunt, Vol. I, pp. 369-370. See also Aguar, *St. Louis County's Historical Sites*, pp. 38-39.

[50] A.K. Knickerbocker, "The Contract Wage System for Miners," *Mining and Scientific Press*, Apr. 3, 1920. See also G.O. Virtue, "The Minnesota Iron Ranges," p. 389.

[51] John Somrock and Lee Brownell, *A History of Incredible Ely*, 1976, Ely, p. 7.

[52] Issues of *The Ely Miner*, 1895-1916, and *Vermilion Iron Journal*, 1888-1895, report numerous fatalities and injuries in mines of the Ely area.

[53] *Ely Iron Home*, Dec. 23, 1890.

[54] Ibid., Dec. 30, 1890.

[55] See Winchell and Winchell, *Iron Ores*, pp. 196-201, for detailed description of the earliest workings at the Chandler, Pioneer and Zenith mines at Ely. See also *Eighth Biennial Report of the Minnesota Tax Commission*, 1922, St. Paul, Chapter IV, p. 4, for a description of the iron formation at Ely.

[56] Van Brunt, Vol. I, pp. 382-385.

[57] Ibid., p. 383.

[58] Ibid.

[59] Ibid.

[60] "Municipal Court Records, City of Ely, 1888-95," at IRRC.

[61] Van Brunt, Vol. I, pp. 383-384.

[62] *Ely Iron Home*, Apr. 7, 1891.

[63] Ibid.

[64] Ibid., Mar. 30, 1900.

[65] "A Gentleman of the City," *The Ely Miner*, Mar. 30, 1900.

[66] "Captain Pengilly," *The Ely Miner*, Jan. 1, 1904.

[67] "Captain Charles Trezona," Van Brunt, Vol. III, pp. 1,206-1,207.

[68] Wirth, *Minnesota Iron Lands*, p. 58.

[69] Ibid., p. 59.

[70] Ibid., pp. 60-61.

[71] Ibid., pp. 56-79. *Ely Times*, Dec. 23, 1892. M.D. Harbaugh, *Lake Superior Iron Ores*, 1952, Cleveland, p. 226.

[72] *Tower Weekly News*, Jun. 1, 1906. Harbaugh, p. 226.

[73] Jennie Hari, "Section Thirty" *Roaring Stoney Days*, Jul. 1958, Ely-Winton Historical Society, Ely, p. 63.

[74] Larson, *White Pine Industry*, p. 297.

[75] Ibid., pp. 265-288.

[76] *Vermilion Iron Journal*, Jan. 21, 1892.

[77] Ibid., Dec. 3, 1891. See also Larson, pp. 273-275.

[78] The Knox Lumber Company notice of incorporation was published in the *Duluth Evening Herald*, Oct. 15, 1893.

[79] *The Ely Times*, Jan. 5 and Mar. 16, 1894.

[80] See Larson, pp. 263-264.

[81] *The Ely Times*, Jan. 19, 1894. Larson, pp. 262, 392. Heinselman, p. 101.

[82] Larson, pp. 255, 259. King, p. 36.

[83] *The Ely Miner*, Jul. 24, 1895.

[84] Ibid. Also *Ely, Since 1888*, 1988 souvenir publication, *Ely Echo*, p. 20.

[85] Larson, pp. 185, 255. Heinselman, p. 100.

[86] *Ely Miner*, Sep. 28 and Oct. 6, 1898. The relationship between Simpson and Brown and Swallow and Hopkins is explained as follows: "The firm (Simpson and Brown) will only log and saw the

timber on contract, but their contract covers nearly the entire tract containing about 100,000,000 feet of white pine. The contract also calls for the delivery of the lumber on cars at Ely for shipment to Eastern and Western markets." See also *Ely, Since 1888*, pp. 21-22.

[87]See Larson, pp. 349-371, for a description of economic transformations and technical changes taking place in the lumber industry during the 1890s and early 1900s. See also Larson, p. 365, for comment on Swallow and Hopkins. See also *Ely, Since 1888*, pp. 21-22, and Heinselman, pp. 101-103.

[88]*Ely, Since 1888*, p. 21.

[89]Mr. and Mrs. Huxley Pelkola, "History of Winton," *Roaring Stoney Days*, Jul. 1953, Ely-Winton Historical Society, p. 56.

[90]Van Brunt, Vol. II, pp. 711-712.

[91]*Ely, Since 1888*, pp. 20-21.

[92]Ibid., p. 21.

[93]Harold Snabbi, interviewed Feb. 5, 1962.

[94]Pelkola, p. 59.

[95]Heinselman, p. 102.

[96]John Wesley White, *Historical Sketches of the Quetico-Superior*, Vol. XII, Superior National Forest Service, U.S. Department of Agriculture, at IRRC.

CHAPTER SEVEN [102-121]
[1]Van Brunt, Vol. 1, p. 397.

[2]Ibid.

[3]Donald L. Boese, *John C. Greenway and the Opening of the Western Mesabi*, 1975, Itasca Community College, Grand Rapids, pp. 2-3.

[4]John Stone Pardee, "At the Foot of the Rainbow; Fighting for the Crown; In the Treasure Country," p. 9, quoted in Wirth, *Minnesota Iron Lands*, p. 158. See also Van Brunt, Vol. I, p. 444.

[5]Havighurst, *Vein of Iron*, p. 77.

[6]Grace Lee Nute, ed., *Mesabi Pioneer: Reminiscences of Edmund J. Longyear*, 1951, MHS, St. Paul, p. 7. Van Brunt, Vol. I, p. 394.

[7]U.S. General Land Office, *Tract Book, Minnesota, Vol. 64*, pp. 205-228, quoted in Wirth, p. 155.

[8]Larson, *White Pine Industry*, p. 302. Wirth, pp. 218-219.

[9]Nute, ed., *Mesabi Pioneer*, p. 23. Wirth, pp. 156-157.

[10]Larson, pp. 270, 277. Van Brunt, Vol. I, pp. 250-251, and Vol. II, pp. 548-549, 747. King, *Missabe Road*, pp. 70-71.

[11]Walker, *Iron Frontier*, pp. 218-219.

[12]Larson, p. 252. Also see Wirth, pp. 162-164. Walker, *Iron Frontier*, pp. 218-221. Van Brunt, Vol. I, pp. 250-252.

[13]Wirth, p. 162. *General Laws of Minnesota for 1887*, Minneapolis, as quoted in Wirth, p. 169: "… No corporation other than those organized for the construction or operation of railroads, canals or turnpikes shall acquire, hold or own, over five thousand (5,000) acres of land, so hereafter acquired in this state." According to Wirth, "It is probable that the different holding companies were organized in order that the Great Northern Iron Ore Properties would not be in conflict with the law."

[14]Larson, p. 273. Wirth, p. 157.

[15]Larson, pp. 272-282. Wirth, pp. 159-160.

[16]Wirth, pp. 173-174, quotes Matthias, Nordberg, Orfield, *Federal Land Grants to the States*, 1915, Minneapolis, p. 148: "Federal land grants to the State fall into nine well-defined classes, distinguished from one another primarily by the difference in the purpose to which they might be applied. These nine classes are the internal improvements, school, salt spring, university, public building, railroad, swamp agricultural, college and park and forestry lands." Wirth goes on to say on p. 174: "This vast area of State lands was extended by the selection of indemnity lands. In cases where the sections granted to the State by the Government had passed into private hands by purchase from the Government or by pre-emption, the State was permitted to select other lands in lieu thereof. The State in selecting its indemnity lands oftentimes wisely selected in the iron region."

[17]Winchell and Winchell, *Iron Ores*, p. 356. Wirth, p. 174.

[18]Dwight E. Woodbridge, "Discovery of Iron in St. Louis County," Aug. 6, 1923, NEMHC files. Winchell and Winchell, pp. 202-203. See also Van Brunt, Vol. I, p. 396, and Walker, *Iron Frontier*, p. 76.

[19]Van Brunt, Vol. I, p. 395. Winchell and Winchell, *Iron Ores*, p. 357. "Report of the Senate Committee Relative to Iron Ores and Peat Lands in the State of Minnesota," *Senate Document No. 2*, Jan. 1921, pp. 3-4, in *Mines and Minerals, Chapters of the Tax Commission Reports, 1910-1922* (hereafter *Senate Document No. 2*).

[20]Wirth, p. 172. Van Brunt, Vol. I, p. 396. *Act of the Minnesota Legislature of 1889: Act Regulating the Sale and Lease of Mineral and Other Lands Belonging to the State*, in Winchell and Winchell, 357-360: "State Auditor William W. Braden, a strong supporter of the 'mineral lease bill,' lobbied for its passage in the State Legislature."

[21]*Senate Document No. 2*, p. 3.

[22]Warren Upham and Rose Barteau Dunlap, *Minnesota Biographies, 1655-1912*, 1912, MHS, Vol. 14, p. 170. Winchell and Winchell, 1891, pp. 202-204.

[23]Winchell and Winchell, 1891, p. 202-204.

[24]Ibid., p. 202.

[25]Ibid., pp. 202-203. Nute, ed., *Mesabi Pioneer*, p. 13, states that Edmund Longyear calls Mallmann's mine the *Siphon Mine*.

[26]Winchell and Winchell, p. 205.

[27]Van Brunt, Vol. III, p. 933.

[28]Ibid.

[29]Ibid.

[30]David T. Adams, Dec. 7, 1920, in Van Brunt, Vol. II, p. 703.

[31]Adams, 1920, in Van Brunt, Vol. II, pp. 702-703.

[32]Ibid.

[33]Ibid., Van Brunt, Vol. II, p. 704.

[34]Van Brunt, Vol. III, p. 934. See also *Iron Ranges of Minnesota, Historical Souvenir*, 1909, *Virginia Enterprise*, Virginia, p. 41, at IRRC.

[35]Van Brunt, Vol. II, p. 703. *Encyclopedia of Biography of Minnesota*, 1909, Century Publishing and Engraving, Chicago, p. 243.

[36]Van Brunt, Vol. II, p. 703, and Vol. III, p. 934.

[37]Van Brunt, Vol. III, p. 1,232.

[38]Ibid.

[39]Ibid. See also Walker, p. 94, and Nute, ed., *Mesabi Pioneer*, pp. 20-21.

[40]Van Brunt, Vol. III, p. 1,232.

[41]Van Brunt, Vol. I, pp. 444-445.

[42]Walker, p. 76. Van Brunt, Vol. I, p. 397. Theodore Christian Blegen, *Minnesota, A History of the State*, 1963, Second Edition 1975, University of Minnesota, St. Paul, p. 365.

[43]Larson, p. 266. Alfred Merritt, "Reminiscences," 1917, typewritten manuscript at NEMHC.

[44]Ibid. Also Paul De Kruif, *Seven Iron Men*, 1929, New York, p. 34, a popular but romanticized account of the Merritt misadventures.

[45]Van Brunt, Vol. I, p. 396.

[46]Wirth, pp. 56-79.

[47]Alfred Merritt, "Reminiscences."

[48]Ibid.

[49]"Recollections of Leonidas Merritt" in Van Brunt, Vol. I, p. 396.

[50]Van Brunt, Vol. I, pp. 395-396. Alfred Merritt, "Reminiscences."

[51]Leonidas Merritt in Van Brunt, Vol. I, p. 397.

[52]Walker, pp. 84-85. DeKruif, pp. 101-102. "List of Companies Incorporated Under the Laws of Minnesota for the Purpose of Mining and Quarrying," Winchell and Winchell, p. 343. The list includes a Mountain Range Iron Company, Duluth, incorporated May 31, 1889, by L. Merritt, A. Merritt, C.C. Merritt, K.D. Chase, C. Chambers.

[53]Alfred Merritt, "Reminiscences." DeKruif, pp. 102-103. Andrus R. and Jessie L. Merritt, "The Story of the Mesabi," 1934 manuscript in MHS, p. 149 (hereafter Andrus Merritt).

[54]Walker, p. 85.

[55]Ibid., pp. 84-85. Van Brunt, Vol. I, p. 398. Winchell and Winchell, p. 343.

[56]Accounts of the actual events surrounding the discovery of iron ore at Mountain Iron vary. In some, the ore was found when the wheels of Merritt lumber wagons sank into it. See Van Brunt, Vol. I, p. 398. In others, Captain J.A. Nichols, at the insistence of the Merritt brothers, reluctantly moved his test pit crews south of where he believed good iron ore should be located and immediately bottomed into hematite. See De Kruif, pp. 104-105. An interesting account is found in Van Brunt, Vol. I, p. 418. In this account, after digging unsuccessfully in places insisted upon by the Merritts, Nichols is said to have flatly ignored their orders, moved his men and equipment to the northwest quarter of Section 3, Township 58-18, and "to have come in a day later with a bushel of ore, found at a depth of six feet."

[57]Andrus Merritt, p. 152.

[58]Horace V. Winchell, "Report on the Mesabi Iron Range," *Twentieth Annual Report of the Minnesota Geological Survey, 1891*, Part IV, 1893, Minneapolis.

[59]DeKruif, pp. 117-125.

[60]Van Brunt, Vol. I, pp. 398-400. Harlan Hatcher, *A Century of Iron and Men*, 1950, Bobbs-Merrill Company Inc., Indianapolis and New York, pp. 154-155.

[61]"J.H. James Talks," *The Great Missabe Iron Range*, special publication of the *Minneapolis Tribune*, 1892, p. 14.

[62]Van Brunt, Vol. I, p. 446.

[63]Ibid., pp. 399-400.

[64]For Leonidas Merritt leases, see Winchell and Winchell, pp. 350-353.

[65]Leonidas Merritt, testimony before the Stanley Committee on Investigation of the United States Steel Corporation, U.S. House of Representatives, 1911, Government Printing Office, Vol. III, pp. 1885-1934, quoted in DeKruif, p. 148.

[66]King, p. 46. Walker, pp. 100-101.

[67]King, p. 48, Walker, pp. 101-102.

[68]King, p. 46.

[69]Ibid., p. 47.

[70]Ibid., p. 48; *Duluth News Tribune*, Oct. 17, 1892.

[71]King, p. 49.

[72]Frederick T. Gates, *The Truth About Mr. Rockefeller and the Merritts*, 1911, G.P. Putnam, New York, p. 4.

[73]Ibid., p. 5.

[74]Van Brunt, Vol. I, p. 399. King, p. 49. De Kruif, pp. 183-187. Walker, pp. 111-112.

[75]*Duluth News Tribune*, Jan. 30, 1893. Leonidas Merritt, speaking at the Stanley Committee Hearings, quoted in Walker, p. 114. See also King, p. 49.

[76]Walker, p. 114.

[77]Ibid., pp. 103-104, 108.

[78]Henry Oliver Evans, *Iron Pioneer: Henry W. Oliver, 1840-1904*, 1942, E.P. Dutton, New York, pp.198-203.

Walker, p. 104. Van Brunt, Vol. II, pp. 575-578.

79Evans, p. 202. Van Brunt, Vol. II, pp. 575-578. Walker, p. 104.

80Walker, p. 104-105.

81Ibid., "J.H. James Talks," p. 14.

82Wirth, p. 190. Walker, p. 112.

83Wirth, p. 190. Walker, pp. 114-115.

84Van Brunt, Vol. I, p. 401. Walker, p. 115.

85Leonidas Merritt to the board of directors of the Duluth, Missabe and Northern Railroad, Feb. 7, 1893, quoted in Van Brunt, Vol. I, p. 402.

86Ibid., p. 403. Walker, pp. 140-143.

87Gates, *Truth*, p. 8. Wirth, pp. 190-191. Walker, pp. 138-143.

88Walker, p. 145.

89Ibid., p. 145. Leonidas Merritt to the "Stanley Committee Hearings" in De Kruif, p. 189.

90Gates, *Truth*, pp. 8-9.

91Walker, p. 151. Wirth, pp. 192-194.

92Wirth, pp. 192-194

93Walker, pp. 160-162.

94Ibid., pp. 178-181.

95Evans, p. 211.

96Andrew Carnegie to Henry Frick, Mar. 16, 1894, quoted in Walker, p. 207-208.

97Ibid., p. 210.

98Ibid., pp. 211-218.

CHAPTER EIGHT [122-143]

1"Log of the First Diamond Drill Hole on the Mesabi, 1890," as found in Grace Lee Nute, ed., *Mesabi Pioneer*, pp. 102-109. See also Winchell and Winchell, *Iron Ores of Minnesota*, pp. 171-175.

2Ibid., Nute, ed., *Mesabi Pioneer*, pp. 8-9. See also Davis, *Pioneering with Taconite*, pp. 30-31.

3Nute, ed., *Mesabi Pioneer*, pp. 8 and 109.

4Ibid., p. 42.

5E.J. Longyear, "Explorations on the Mesabi Range," read at a meeting of the American Institute of Mining Engineers in Jul. 1897 and published originally in 1898 in the Institute's *Transactions*, 27: 537-541, as reprinted in Nute, ed., *Mesabi Pioneer*, pp. 95-100. Charles Van Barneveld, *Iron Mining in Minnesota*, 1912, University of Minnesota, Minneapolis, p. 43.

6Nute, ed., *Mesabi Pioneer*, p. 20. David E. Perry, "Exploratory Diamond Drilling on the Mesabi 1890 to 1910," *Range History*, Fall 1980. *The Mesaba Range*, Sep. 22, 1892 and Aug. 3, 1893. "List of Early Contract Drillers and Exploration Sites," compiled by David E. Perry, Mar. 2, 1976, unpublished manuscript, in the files of the Iron Range Historical Society (hereafter IRHS), Gilbert.

7Van Barneveld, pp. 26-27.

8Ibid., p. 24.

9C.R. Emerson, "Drilling on the Mesabi in 1908," *Skillings Mining Review*, Mar. 22, 1975, p. 13.

10Harold Dean Cater, "Foreward," in Nute, ed. *Mesabi Pioneer*. Perry, "Exploratory Diamond Drilling."

11Harlan Hatcher, *A Century of Iron and Men*, pp. 158-159.

12Nute, ed., *Mesabi Pioneer*, pp. 14 and 20.

13Ibid., p. 29.

14Ibid., p. 30.

15Ibid., pp. 48-49. "Edmund J. Longyear and the First Drill Hole on the Mesabi Range," *Longyear News Bits*, Jul.-Aug. 1975, pp. 6-8.

16Nute, ed., *Mesabi Pioneer*, p. 31.

17Ibid., pp. 8 and 14. Van Brunt, Vol. 1, pp. 345-347, 356.

18Nute, ed., *Mesabi Pioneer*, p. 13.

19Ibid., p. 14.

20Van Brunt, Vol. I, p. 422.

21"Ghost Towns of the Arrowhead," *Duluth News Tribune*, Oct. 28, 1931.

22Van Brunt, Vol. II, p. 854.

23Ibid., Vol. I, p. 435. *The Mesaba Range*, Oct. 6, 1892.

24*The Mesaba Range*, Jun. 8, 1893. According to the *Fourth Decennial Census of the State of Minnesota, 1895*, Mesaba Village had a population of 184; the *Twelfth Census of the United States*, taken in 1900, lists a population of 117 for Mesaba Village; and the *Fifth Decennial Census of the State of Minnesota*, 1905, shows Mesaba Village with a population of 46.

25Van Brunt, Vol. II, p. 705.

26Ibid.

27Mrs. Emma Braaten, resident of Mesaba Village from 1911-1928, interviewed Feb. 5, 1962.

28Frank King, *The Missabe Road*, p. 90.

29"Ghost Towns," *Duluth News Tribune*, Oct. 28, 1931. Charles Walberg, resident of Mesaba Village, interviewed by Grove Wills, *Mesabi Daily News*, Jul. 9, 1960.

30Captain Willard Glazier, *Down the Great River*, 1887, quoted in Donald L. Boese and Richard R. Cain, *Grand Rapids Companion*, 1991, Grand Rapids Centennial Committee, p. 4.

31Agnes M. Larson, *White Pine Industry*, pp. 172-173. Boese and Cain, p. 14.

32Boese and Cain, p. 14.

33Ibid., p. 11.

34Richard Cain, *La Prairie, The Road Back*, 1990, City of La Prairie by Paragraphics Inc., Deer River, Minnesota, pp. 54-56.

35This story appears in John M. Carmody, *Logging Town, The Story of Grand Rapids, Minnesota*, 1941, Works Progress Administration project, Grand Rapids, p. 32.

36Boese and Cain, p. 56.

37*Logging Town*, p. 13.

38Larson, p. 367.

39Nute, ed., *Mesabi Pioneer*, pp. 31, 29.

40George Chanak, early resident of Carson Lake Location, "Farewell to Poverty and Happiness," unpublished manuscript, IRRC.

41Arnold Alanen, "The Locations: Company Communities on Minnesota's Iron Ranges," *Minnesota History*, Fall 1982, p. 97.

42Virtue, "Minnesota Iron Ranges," Sep. 1909, pp. 357-358.

43Alanen p. 95.

44Nute, ed., *Mesabi Pioneer*, pp. 46-47.

45Alanen, p. 95.

46Ibid., p. 97. According to Alanen, "The third settlement form was the model location. No more than 10 of these settlements existed throughout the entire Lake Superior region, but the mining companies, perceiving them as highly visible examples of benevolent paternalism, invested rather heavily in such locations. The management of both the company and model locations was quite similar, although the later were laid out in a more attractive manner, contained higher quality housing and were intended primarily for supervisory personnel and highly valued employees."

47In 1892, town developers advertised Merritt lot sales in Duluth, Ely, Tower and Merritt newspapers. Merritt was consistently portrayed as "The Future Metropolis of the Mesaba [sic] Iron Range, surrounded by the Biwabik, Cincinnati, Hale, Canton, Shaw, Kanawha and other iron mines, shipments from which will be made as soon as railroad facilities are afforded.... No better chance to make money."

48Van Brunt, Vol. I, pp. 431-432.

49Marion Stuart Cann, *Is This Hand Worth Playing? A Problem for Investors*, 1891, Duluth Stock Exchange, Duluth, p. 26.

50Van Brunt, Vol. I, p. 431. *The Mesaba Range*, Jul. 14, 1892.

51"Historical Data as to the Surveying and Building of the line of the Duluth and Iron Range Railroad to Merritt and Biwabik," quoted in Aguar, *St. Louis County's Historical Sites*, p. 28. See also Van Brunt, Vol. I, p. 436.

52Van Brunt, Vol. I, p. 432.

53*The Mesaba Range*, Jul. 14, 1892.

54Fred M. Seely, "History of Biwabik," *Biwabik Times*, Mar. 31, 1961.

55Ibid.

56*The Mesaba Range*, Sep. 22, 1892.

57Ibid., Sep. 15, 1892.

58Ibid., Jul. 14, 1892.

59Ibid., Oct. 6, 1892.

60 Van Brunt, Vol. I, p. 436.

61Ibid., pp. 432, 439, 424-425. *The Mesaba Range*, Jun. 22, 1893.

62Van Brunt, Vol. I, p. 433.

63Ibid., pp. 452-453.

64Ibid., p. 453.

65The Elba mine was the result of the discovery of "an enormous body of ore" by Merritt test pit crews under the direction of Wilbur Merritt. Two other mines, the Roberts and Corsica, opened a few years later, gave longevity to the location, which was later renamed Elcor (a combination of Elba and Corsica). See Walker, p. 94. According to Mildred R. Alm, *University of Minnesota Mining Directory*, Mar. 1964, University of Minnesota, p. 81, the Elba mine was operated by the Minnesota Iron

Company from 1898-1900 and by the Hobart Iron Company from 1901-1926.

66Alex Sipola, resident of Elba as a boy, 1896-1899, letter to author, Feb. 5, 1961.

67*Biwabik Times*, May 17, 1907. Van Brunt, Vol. I, p. 462. Sipola, letter.

68Van Brunt, Vol. I, p. 435.

69Ibid., pp. 436-437.

70Ibid., p. 437.

71*The Mesaba Range*, Dec. 28, 1893.

72Van Brunt, Vol. I, p. 436.

73Nute, ed., *Mesabi Pioneer*, p. 51.

74Horace V. Winchell, "The Iron Rangers of Minnesota," 1895, Lake Superior Mining Institute, a guide written for members before they gathered on the Mesabi Range for their third annual meeting, as quoted in Van Brunt, Vol. I, p. 447.

75Van Brunt, Vol. I, pp. 447-451.

76The names of ethnic saloons are from a list of "remembered names on saloon fronts" as part of "Biwabik – Past and Present," *Biwabik 1892-1967*, Diamond Jubilee Historical Souvenir Booklet, 1967, prepared and edited by Kathryn Coombe, Biwabik, p. 5.

77*The Mesaba Range*, Nov. 8, 1893.

78Van Brunt, Vol. I, pp. 441, 447.

79Ibid., pp. 438-442.

80Coombe, *Biwabik Historical Souvenir*, p. 9.

81*Sanborn Maps of Biwabik* in 1906, 1912, Sanborn Map Company, Broadway, New York.

82Van Brunt, Vol. II, p. 587.

83Ibid., p. 586. *Duluth Evening Herald*, Sep. 15, 1892.

84Van Brunt, Vol. II, pp. 586-588.

85*The Mesaba Range*, Aug. 25, 1892.

86Ibid.

87Van Brunt, Vol. II, pp. 586, 590.

88Ibid., p. 590.

89Ibid., pp. 590-591.

90Ibid., pp. 579, 582, 584. *The Virginia Story, Historical Souvenir Booklet 1897-1967: Celebrating Virginia's Diamond Days*, 1967, Diamond Jubilee Publications Committee, Virginia, p. 12.

91Van Brunt, Vol. II, p. 593.

92"Virginia." *R.L. Polk & Company Directory of the Range Towns*, 1899, Duluth, p. 519.

93*Virginian*, Aug. 17, 1907, Virginia.

94The *Sanborn-Perris* map of Virginia, dated Oct. 1900, four months after the

fire, records a population of 3,800 and several all brick and stone blocks along Chestnut street. So fast did Virginia recover from the fire. (Hereafter *Sanborn Map*)

[95]Van Brunt, Vol. I, p. 423.

[96]Ibid., p. 424.

[97]Ibid.

[98]"An Early Review of the Village" in Van Brunt, Vol. I, p. 424, states that "a school was opened the same fall, with Miss Richardson as principal and Miss Sharp as her assistant. The first church was built by the Methodists, but it, together with the schoolhouse, burned down June 20, 1893. The balance of the town was threatened with destruction at the same time, but was saved by diligent labor on the part of most of the population, adjacent buildings being covered with blankets soaked in water drawn from the spring near the sawmill...."

[99]*Fourth Decennial Census of the State of Minnesota, 1895.*

[100]Van Brunt, Vol. I, p. 422.

[101]Ibid., pp. 428-429.

[102]Ibid., p. 426.

[103]Ibid., pp. 427-429.

[104]*The Mesaba Range*, Oct. 6, 1892.

CHAPTER NINE [144-171]

[1]LeRoy Hodges, special agent and geographer, former U.S. Immigration Commission, "Immigrant Life in the Ore Region of Northern Minnesota," *The Survey*, Sep. 7, 1912, p. 703.

[2]"Mesabi Ore Shipments, 1892-1915," data from the U.S. Bureau of Mines, see Marvin Lamppa, "Historical Survey of Iron Range Communities," Dec. 1984, IRRC, p. 17

[3]Grover Cleveland, 1888 presidential campaign.

[4]Virtue, "Minnesota Iron Ranges," p. 340: "This union of mining and transportation interests, which was begun by the building of the Duluth and Iron Range Railroad in 1892, has become an established feature of the industry on both the Vermilion and Mesabi ranges. [Editor's note: The D&IR was actually begun in 1883 and completed in 1884.] With the movement for the control of ore supplies by eastern iron and steel manufacturers which marked the decade 1890 to 1900, not only the Vermilion mines, but the newly discovered deposits on the Mesabi Range quickly passed by purchase of lease into the hands of a few concerns

which were primarily steel producers rather than producers of ore.... While the printed list of mining companies on the Mesabi is large, it should be understood that the number of interests concerned is very much less...."

[5]Hodges, p. 703.

[6]Van Brunt, Vol. 1, p. 446.

[7]Ibid.

[8]Van Barneveld, *Iron Mining in Minnesota*, p. 168. See also "Iron-Mesaba Range," *The Engineering and Mining Journal*, Aug. 26, 1893, p. 222, and Wirth, *Iron Lands*, p. 364.

[9]John H. Hearding, "Pioneer Mining Man Describes Early Days in Eveleth District," *Skillings Mining Review*, Aug. 18, 1923, p. 1. "Mines and Quarries," from *Thirteenth Census of the United States*, 1910.

[10]Robert Marsh, *Steam Shovel Mining*, 1920, New York, pp. 27-28.

[11]Virtue, p. 364.

[12]See W.F. Schwedes, "Mechanical Shovels," *Proceedings of the Lake Superior Mining Institute*, Vol. 28, 1930, p. 107.

[13]Ibid.

[14]Bill Beck, *Northern Lights, An Illustrated History of Minnesota Power*, 1985, Minnesota Power, Duluth, p. 237.

[15]"The present tendency in design is to increase power relative to dipper size, thus giving greater speed in swinging, crowding and hoisting. A 5 yard shovel may be equipped with a 4-4.5 or 5 yard dipper; the harder the digging, the smaller the bucket. In loading iron ore upon the Mesabi, electric shovels give average and maximum loading rates per 8-hr. shift as follows: $1^{1}/_{4}$-yd., 1,600-3,000 long tons; 3 yd., 2,500-5,000; 4-yd., 4,000-5,000 long tons, with power consumption ranging from 0.2 to 0.33 kw.-hr. per ton." George J. Young, *Elements of Mining*, 1946, New York, p. 407.

[16]Earl E. Hunner, "Some Recent Developments in Open Pit Mining on the Mesabi Range," 1930, *AIME Yearbook*, p. 4. Hearding, *Skillings*, p. 1.

[17]Hearding, *Skillings*, p. 1. King, *Missabe Road*, pp. 137-147.

[18]Hunner, pp. 4-6.

[19]Ibid., p. 104. King, p. 142.

[20]Beck, p. 237.

[21]*Skillings Mining Review*, Feb. 28, 1938, p. 2.

[22]Beck, pp. 231-233.

[23]See Polk Directory of the Range Towns, 1913, Duluth, for electric utility systems in Hibbing, Virginia, Eveleth, Chisholm, Buhl, Biwabik. See also Beck, pp. 164-167.

[24]For this and the following three paragraphs, see Beck, pp. 159-169 and 229-244.

[25]Ibid., pp. 113-114.

[26]Ibid., pp. 114-116.

[27]"Stripping of Embarrass Iron Ore Property," *Skillings*, May 1, 1943, p. 1. C.R. Burton, "Powerplants for Production Trucks on Mesabi Range,"

Skillings, Nov. 18, 1950, p. 1.

[28]*Skillings*, Jan. 5, 1945, p. 9.

[29]Virtue, p. 367. J.A. MacKillican, "History and Present Status of Mining in Minnesota," *Skillings*, Feb. 23, 1946, p. 10. According to Van Barneveld, *Iron Mining in Minnesota*, p. 44, "Open pit mining called for a longer development period and for greater outlay of capital than was required for the development and equipping of an underground mine." This was particularly true during the first two or three decades of mining on the Mesabi. As power shovels improved and machinery for moving the ore became more sophisticated, the open pit method became less expensive and was often the most profitable way to mine Mesabi ore. However, this was not always the case.

[30]Virtue, p. 367.

[31]MacKillican, *Skillings*, p. 4. Young, pp. 568-570. Virtue, p. 366.

[32]"Memoirs from the Minnesota Iron Ore Mines," told from the point of view of a Finnish miner, translated by Vienna C. Maki, undated, unpublished document, IRHS. Virtue, "Number of Employees Fatal Accidents and Rate Per 1,000 Employees, By Years, 1898 to 1903," p. 368: "What the loss of life actually was prior to 1905 will never be known." Information used by Virtue for his table was collected after 1897. According to Virtue, p. 369, "There is little doubt that were the statistics complete they would reveal a loss of life higher than these incomplete returns indicate." See also MacKillican, *Skillings*, pp. 4-5.

[33]Virtue, p. 366. MacKillican, pp. 4-5. Young, pp. 579-583.

[34]Virtue, p. 366.

[35]Although stockpile shipments were made in 1962 and 1963, actual underground mining at the Godfrey conducted by the Snyder Mining Company ended in 1961. Mildred R. Alm and W.D. Trethewey, *University of Minnesota Mining Directory*, p. 81.

[36]Virtue, p. 365. Young, pp. 443-446.

[37]Virtue, p. 365.

[38]Ibid.

[39]Ibid.

[40]From "Population in the Chief Mining Communities of St. Louis County, Minn., 1895, 1900, 1905," as found in Virtue, p. 343. *Fifth Decennial Census of Minnesota, 1905*, p. 42. Paul H. Landis, *Three Iron Mining Towns*, 1938, Edward Brothers, Ann Arbor, Michigan, p. 19: "Eveleth bade fare to become the largest town on the range, as it then exceeded Hibbing in population."

[41]Braaten interview.

[42]Virtue, p. 362. Hodges, "Immigrant Life," pp. 706-707. Landis, p. 19.

[43]*Virginia Enterprise*, Apr. 29, 1904.

[44]Landis, p. 21.

[45]1905 Bovey Village minutes quoted in Donald L. Boese, *John C. Greenway and the Opening of the Western Mesabi*, p. 26.

[46]Hodges, p. 707.

[47]Ibid., p. 703. Matti E. Kaups, "The Finns in the Copper and Iron Ore Mines of the Western Great Lakes Region, 1864-1905: Some Preliminary Observations," as found in Michael G. Karni and Douglas J. Ollila Jrs., eds., *The Finnish Experience in the Western Great Lakes Region: New Perspectives*, 1975, Institute for Migration, Turku, Finland, p. 75.

[48]Virtue, pp. 343-353.

[49]A Mesabi Range pioneer woman, in Landis, p. 71.

[50]Ibid.

[51]Folwell, *History of Minnesota*, Vol. 4, pp. 53-56.

[52]Landis, pp. 79-86.

[53]C.M. Atkinson, ed., *Mesaba Ore*, 1902, in Van Brunt, Vol. II, p. 552.

[54]Van Brunt, Vol. II, p. 542 and Vol. III, p. 1,234.

[55]Van Brunt, Vol. II, pp. 553-555.

[56]Ibid., pp. 541-549.

[57]"Hibbing," *Polk Directory*, 1907, p. 436.

[58]"Historical Survey of Iron Range Communities," prepared by author for the Iron Range Interpretative Center, Dec. 1984, Table 3; "Business and Store Front Construction, 1908-1912," p. 45; and Table 4, "Wood Frame Building Heights, 1908-1912," p. 46, copy at IRRC.

[59]Van Brunt, Vol. II, p. 563.

[60]Ibid., p. 559. For list of businesses, see *Polk Directory*, 1910, pp. 344-475.

[61]*Hibbing on the Move, Since 1893*, 1991, Hibbing Book Committee, Hibbing, pp. 20-21.

[62]Van Brunt, Vol. II, pp. 517-519.

[63]Ibid., pp. 523-526. Hearding, "Early Days in Eveleth," *Skillings*, p. 1.

[64]Van Brunt, Vol. II, p. 517.

[65]Ibid., David T. Adams, p. 516.

[66]*The Mesaba Range*, Jun. 20, 1893. Neil McInnis, Eveleth pioneer, in Van Brunt, Vol. II, p. 514.

[67]Hearding, p. 1.

[68]McInnis, Van Brunt, Vol. II, p. 518.

[69]*Fourth Decennial Census of Minnesota*, 1895.

[70]Van Brunt, Vol. II, p. 522.

[71]*The Eveleth News*, Apr. 3, 1909.

[72]"Eveleth," *Polk Directory*, 1915.

[73]Hearding, p. 1. Virtue, pp. 378-379.

[74]Virtue, pp. 378-379.

[75]*Chisholm Herald*, Apr. 7, 1905.

[76]Van Brunt, Vol. I, p. 497, identifies Oliver Iron Mining properties in 1919 as the Burt (3), Chester, Chisholm, Clark, Crescent, Croxton, D'Autremont, Duncan, Forster, Glen (2), Hartley-Burt-Palmer, Hartley-Burt, Humphreys (2), McGilvary, Monroe, Monroe (Tener), Myers, Niles, Oliver Reserve (3), Pillsbury, Pettit, Pontiac (2), St. Clair, South Meyers and Twin City; Shenango Furnace Company mining properties as the Pillsbury No. 2, Shenango, South Tener and Tioga; Hanna Mining

Company properties as the Alexandria, Alexandria-Snyder, Leonard and Leonard-Burt; Tod-Stambaugh Company properties as the Billings and Dunwoody; Meridan Iron Company property as the Pearce; Inter-State Iron Company property as of 1910 as the Jordan; and International Harvester property as the West Mesabi Reserve.

[77]Ibid., pp. 497, 499.

[78]*Fifth Decennial Census of Minnesota, 1905.*

[79]Van Brunt, Vol. I, p. 500.

[80]*Chisholm Herald,* Sep. 9, 1908.

[81]Ibid.

[82]Ibid., Sep. 18, 1908.

[83]Recollections of Sanford P. Bordeau, resident of Sparta as a boy, unpublished manuscript written in 1975, IRHS. *Fifth Decennial Census of Minnesota,* 1905. Mark Nolan, "Early History of Sparta and Gilbert," manuscript prepared for the St. Louis County Historical Society, Dec. 18, 1929, IRHS. "Sparta-Gilbert," *Iron Ranges of Minnesota, Virginia Enterprise,* 1909, pp. 25-26.

[84]*Biwabik Times,* May 1, 1908.

[85]Van Brunt, Vol. I, p. 456. Nolan manuscript.

[86]John S. Domanoski, resident of old Sparta as a boy, interviewed on Mar. 26, 1962. *Iron Ranges, Virginia Enterprise,* 1909, p. 25. Van Brunt, Vol. I, p. 456. Quote from Nolan manuscript, IRHS.

[87]Van Brunt, Vol. I, pp. 456-457.

[88]Ibid., pp. 457-458. *Iron Ranges, Virginia Enterprise,* 1909, p. 26.

[89]Van Brunt, Vol. I, pp. 457-458. Nolan manuscript.

[90]Van Brunt Vol. I, p. 458. Nolan manuscript. *Gilbert, 1909,* Sanborn Map.

[91]Van Brunt, Vol. I, pp. 458, 469.

[92]Ibid., pp. 458-459. Nolan manuscript.

[93]*Gilbert Herald,* Sep. 9, 1920.

[94]Van Brunt, Vol. I, pp. 462-463.

[95]Landis, pp. 51-53.

[96]Ibid.

CHAPTER TEN [172-196]

[1]See Arundel Cotter, *United States Steel, a Corporation With a Soul,* 1921, Doubleday, Page and Company, New York, pp. 63-67. Hatcher, *Century of Iron and Men,* p. 192.

[2]United States Steel's first annual report for 1901 is found in Cotter, p. 192. William Appleby, *Mining Directory,* 1920, pp. 131, 133, 137-140.

[3]Van Brunt, Vol. I, p. 486. Van Brunt, Vol. II, p. 585. Appleby, 1920, pp. 130, 134; 1923, p. 167.

[4]See Peter Bolf, "The Pioneering Butlers," *Range History,* Dec. 1979, for details on Butler Brothers activities on the Mesabi Range.

[5]Larson, *White Pine Industry,* p. 278. Van Brunt, Vol. I, pp. 471-472. See also Nute, ed., *Mesabi Pioneer,* pp. 23-36.

[6]Van Brunt, Vol. I, p. 471.

[7]Alm, *Mining Directory* 1964, lists 31 mining properties, along with shipping

dates and operators, for Township 58-19 (the vicinity of Buhl).

[8]See author's "Gamble at the Grant," *Range History,* Sep. 1977, for a description of the grab system at the Grant Mine. Also see "The Grab System of Mining at the Grant Mine, Buhl, Minnesota." *The Iron Trade Review,* Mar. 14, 1907, p. 424. The quote on electric shovel mining at the Wabigon is from Cotter, p. 263.

[9]Van Brunt, Vol. I, p. 480.

[10]Origin of the name, "Great Scott," is in Warren Upham, *Minnesota Geographic Names: Their Origin and Historic Significance,* 1969, MHS, St. Paul, p. 484.

[11]Van Brunt, Vol. I, p. 480.

[12]Ibid.

[13]"Buhl," *Sanborn Map,* 1909.

[14]*Virginia Enterprise,* Nov. 11 and Nov. 20, 1914. *Chisholm-Tribune Herald,* Oct. 13, 1914; Oct. 15, Oct. 20 and Dec. 4, 1915.

[15]Steve Hecimovich, *A Town is Born, A Historical and Pictorial Review of Buhl, Minnesota,* 2002, Buhl 100-Year Anniversary, pp. 7-8.

[16]Ibid.

[17]Van Brunt, Vol. I, p. 471.

[18]See *University of Minnesota Mining Directory* Issues, 1928-1962, for descriptions and shipping dates of mines in the vicinity of Aurora.

[19]Van Brunt, Vol. I, p. 487.

[20]Ibid.

[21]Alm, *Mining Directory,* Minneapolis, 1964, pp., 100, 121, 188, 199. "Nashwauk," *Iron Ranges of Minnesota.*

[22]Ibid., *Iron Ranges.*

[23]Ibid. "Nashwauk," *The Minnesota Arrowhead Country,* 1941, Arrowhead Association Inc., Chicago, reprint edition by MHS, St. Paul, 1988, pp. 146-147. *From Timber to Taconite, The Story of Nashwauk,* compiled by the 75th Anniversary Book Committee, 1978, *Eastern Itascan,* Nashwauk, p. 5. Larson, p. 278. Upham, *Names,* suggests Nashwauk "has an Algonquin name, from Nashwauk river and village near Fredericton, New Brunswick ... probably allied with Nashua, 'land between.'" *Fifth Decennial Census of the State of Minnesota,* 1905.

[24]"Estimates covering the ore bodies lying west of the village of Nashwauk – crossing ranges 23, 24, 25, 26 and 27 – a distance of 35 miles, involving the consideration of ore bodies containing washable ore and also merchantable ore are made on similar lines to the Lyndale mine ... These bodies contain standard ore and washable ore. The standard ore can be shipped direct, that is, is merchantable. The washable ore material must be treated in some way to make the ore merchantable." *Mines and Minerals,* from the *Fourth Biennial Report of the Minnesota Tax Commission,* 1914, St. Paul, Chapter VI, p. 131.

[25]*Mines and Minerals, Third Biennial Report,* 1912, Chapter V, pp. 74-78.

Fourth Biennial Report, 1914, Chapter VI, pp. 135-136.

[26]"Nashwauk," *Iron Ranges,* 1909. *Fourth Biennial Report,* 1914, pp. 134-135. *Timber to Taconite,* p. 47.

[27]"Nashwauk," *Minnesota Arrowhead Country,* pp. 137-138. *From Timber to Taconite,* p. 5. See also fire insurance map of buildings in Nashwauk in 1920, Sanborn Map, 1921.

[28]"Keewatin," *Minnesota Arrowhead Country,* pp. 137-138.

[29]Mine opening dates are listed in Alm, *Mining Directory,* 1964, pp. 48-49, 88, 141, 171. See *Keewatin 1906 to 1956,* 1976, Bicentennial Committee, Fred J. Raniele, chairman, Keewatin, p. 5. See also "Keewatin," *Minnesota Arrowhead Country,* p. 137.

[30]See *Keewatin 1906 to 1956,* 1956, Bicentennial Committee, Fred J. Raniele, chairman, Keewatin, Minnesota, for biographical information on entrepreneurs and businessmen locating in Keewatin.

[31]Ibid. See also Sanborn Map, 1921.

[32]Boese, *Opening of the Western Mesabi,* pp. 4, 132.

[33]Ibid., pp. 5-6. Van Brunt, Vol. III, p. 1,187.

[34]Boese, p. 6. *Skillings,* Jan. 21, 1920, p. 5. See also Walker, *Iron Frontier,* pp. 232-233.

[35]Boese, p. 15.

[36]Ibid., pp. 12-17, for biographical information in this and the following paragraph. See also Van Brunt, Vol. I, p. 415 and Walker, pp. 232-233.

[37]Boese, pp. 16-17. Walker, p. 233.

[38]Boese, pp. 21-41 for a more detailed history of Bovey.

[39]Ibid., pp. 25, 34-35.

[40]Ibid., pp. 26-27.

[41]*Grand Rapids Herald Review,* Oct. 21, 1905.

[42]Ibid.

[43]*Itasca Iron News* quote is in Boese, p. 41.

[44]Alm, *Mining Directory,* 1964, pp. 53, 65, 78, 99, 103, 106, 201.

[45]For biographical information on John C. Greenway, see Boese, pp. 43-61.

[46]Ibid., pp. 67-69.

[47]Ibid., pp. 131-134.

[48]*Fourth Biennial Report of the Minnesota Tax Commission,* 1914, Chapter VI, pp. 132-133.

[49]Boese, pp. 85, 89. "Coleraine," *Iron Ranges,* 1909.

[50]Boese, p. 89.

[51]"Coleraine," *Iron Ranges.*

[52]Boese, pp. 168-179.

[53]Ibid., p. 173.

[54]Ibid., p. 162.

[55]John C. Greenway in Boese, p. 163.

[56]"Calumet 1910," Sanborn Map.

[57]Boese, pp. 104-111.

[58]Appleby, *Mining Directory,* 1924. Alm, *Mining Directory,* 1964.

[59]According to Anna Himrod, ed., *The Cuyuna Range, A History of a Minnesota Iron Mining District,* 1940, Works Progress Administration (WPA) sponsored Minnesota Historical Records Survey Project, St. Paul, pp. 105-106, from Jan. to Apr. 1904, Oliver Iron Mining Company sank 12 drill holes in T 46-25 and T 47-25 and in 1906 sank a shaft in Sec. 30, T 47-28. The Cuyuna Range portion of this chapter relies heavily on the WPA-sponsored study prepared under the direction of Anna Himrod. For detailed information on the Orelands Mining Company and Kennedy Mine, see pp. 32-33.

[60]"Special Report on the Cuyuna Iron Range," *Fourth Biennial Report, 1914,* Chapter VI, pp. 111-118. See also Frank F. Grout and J.F. Wolff Sr., *The Geology of the Cuyuna District,* 1955, University of Minnesota, Minneapolis, pp. 19-38.

[61]Himrod, ed., *The Cuyuna Range,* p. 3.

[62]Ibid., p. 6.

[63]*Deerwood Enterprise,* May 9, 1930: "Pajari's dip needle was reportedly later found by more successful entrepreneurs." See also Arvy Hansen, ed., *Cuy-una! ... A Chronicle of the Cuyuna Range,* 1976, Bicentennial Publication, *Crosby-Ironton Courier,* Crosby, p. 4.

[64]Himrod, ed., *The Cuyuna Range,* pp. 11-12.

[65]"How the Needle of a Compass Pointed the Way to Fortune," *American Magazine,* Feb. 1922, in Hansen, ed., p. 5.

[66]Ibid., p. 13. *Skillings,* Dec. 3, 1932, p. 3. See also Walker, pp. 248-249.

[67]Walker, p. 249. Himrod, ed., *The Cuyuna Range,* p. 17. *American Magazine,* 1922, quote in Hansen, ed., p. 6.

[68]Hansen, ed., p. 7.

[69]Himrod, ed., *The Cuyuna Range,* pp. 22-26.

[70]Ibid., p. 26. *Duluth News Tribune,* Oct. 25, 1908. Walker, p. 252. *Duluth Evening Herald,* Jul. 8, 1905.

[71]C.K. Lieth to Anna Himrod, Dec. 6, 1937, quoted in *The Cuyuna Range,* p. 20.

[72]Ibid., pp. 22-26. Hansen, ed., pp. 19-20.

[73]*Brainerd Dispatch,* Sep. 18, 1908.

[74]Ibid., Apr. 21, 1911.

[75]Walker, p. 254.

[76]Ibid., pp. 254-255.

[77]*Eighth Biennial Report,* 1922, Chapter IV, p. 13.

[78]"Manganese and Its Metallurgical Use," and "Cuyuna Range Manganiferous Iron Ore," *Sixth Biennial Report*, 1918, Chapter VIII, pp. 146-149.

[79]Himrod, ed., *The Cuyuna Range*, pp. 80-81. Berger Aulie, *The Milford Mine Disaster*, 1994, Virginia, pp. 132-133. Frank Hrvatin Jr, the 14-year-old miner who survived the mine disaster, taped interview in IRRC.

[80]Hrvatin interview. *Duluth Herald*, Feb. 7, 1924. *Crosby Courier*, Feb. 8, 1924. *Skillings*, Feb. 9, 1924. For information on each of the deceased miners see Aulie, pp. 68-126.

[81]Himrod, ed., *The Cuyuna Range*, pp. 80-81.

[82]Ibid.

[83]"Findings of the committee appointed to investigate the causes of the Milford Mine Disaster, 5 Feb. 1924," in Aulie, pp. 149-153.

[84]Appleby, *Mining Directory*, 1924. *Eighth Biennial Report*, 1922, St. Paul, Chapter IV, pp. 27-28.

[85]Hansen, ed., p. 68.

[86]Himrod, ed., *The Cuyuna Range*, pp. 80-81. Hansen, ed., *Cuy-Una!*, pp. 38-51.

[87]*Duluth Herald*, Nov. 14, 1910.

[88]Hansen, ed., p. 50.

[89]Ibid.

[90]Ibid., p. 31.

[91]George Crosby, *Crosby, The Metropolis of the Cuyuna*, promotional booklet published in about 1914.

[92]Ibid.

CHAPTER ELEVEN [197-218]

[1]*Polk Directory*, 1915, Duluth, pp. 51, 71, 288, 358.

[2]Ibid., pp. 462-472.

[3]Duane Krenz, "An Historical Geographic Study of the Virginia and Rainy Lake Company, the Last White Pine Operation in the Great Lakes Region," May. 1969, Masters Degree Thesis, Mankato State College, p. 49.

[4]John E. Haynes, "Revolt of the Timber Beasts, IWW Lumber Strike in Minnesota," *Minnesota History*, Spring 1971, p. 164. Frank H. Gillmor, superintendent of Logging Operations for the Virginia and Rainy Lake Lumber Company, interviewed by Lucile Kane, Jul. 24 and 25, 1948, MHS.

[5]Duane Krenz, "Northern Timber," *Range History*, Jun. 1979, p. 5. *Arrowhead Country* lists the following buildings in Cusson: Minnesota and

Rainy Lake office buildings, a coal dock, several ice houses, a boiler house, warehouse, hay shed, timber shed, pumphouse, doctor's office, a general store, schoolhouse, theater, recreation building and machine shop, along with several rooming houses and private residences. Discussion of the Duluth, Rainy Lake and Winnipeg Railroad is found in Agnes Larson, *The White Pine Industry in Minnesota*, p. 362, and indicates that it was built specifically to haul logs. Once the largest logging road in Minnesota, it later entered the ranks of regular railroads.

[6]Gillmor-Kane interview. Aguar, *Exploring St. Louis County's Historical Sites*, pp. 51-52.

[7]Larson, *The White Pine Industry in Minnesota*, pp. 234, 400.

[8]See Russell L. Olson, *The Electric Railways of Minnesota*, 1976, Minnesota Transportation Museum Inc., Hopkins, Minnesota, pp. 445-467, for a detailed history of the Mesaba Inter-urban Electric Railway from its inception in 1911 to its final run in 1927.

[9]Ibid., p. 447.

[10]Ibid., pp. 447-449.

[11]J.O. Bergeson, timekeeper during construction of the streetcar line and later assistant treasurer and auditor, wrote a history of the Mesaba Railway, 1911-1923, unpublished manuscript in NEMHC. Rodney L. Halunen, "Ghost Towns and Locations of the Mesabi and the Inter-urban Electric Streetcar Line," 1966, Graduate Paper, University of Minnesota, p. 103.

[12]Olson, p. 448.

[13]John S. Domanoski of Gilbert lived in Sparta as a boy and often rode the streetcar, interview, Mar. 26, 1962.

[14]Peter Volden, streetcar motorman and conductor, in Halunen, p. 108.

[15]Olson, pp. 450-457.

[16]Ibid., see map of Mesaba Railway, pp. 453-459.

[17]Olson, pp. 449-450.

[18]Ibid.

[19]Hilda V. Anderson, "A History of the Beginnings of the Bus Industry with Grass Roots in St. Louis County," 1954 manuscript at IRRC, pp. 5-8. Margaret Walsh, "Tracing the Hound, The Minnesota Roots of the Greyhound Corporation," *Minnesota History*, Winter 1985, p. 312. "1914 Revised," *Go Greyhound*, Nov. 1, 1985, pp. 6-8.

[20]Violet Maryland Weckman, "Victor Maryland: Pioneer Bus Man on the Range," *Mesabi Daily News*, Oct. 3, 1976.

[21]Walsh, "Tracing the Hound," pp. 312-313. Arthur W. Bacon, "Everything Happens on a Bus," *Saturday Evening Post*, Apr. 20, 1946.

[22]Walsh, p. 314.

[23]Ibid., Hilda Anderson, pp. 5-8. Bacon, "'Everything Happens."

[24]Walsh, pp. 316-321. LeRoy Wilkerson, "History of the Mesaba Transportation

Company," undated, unpublished manuscript in NEMHC.

[25]*Hibbing Tribune*, Apr. 26, 1906. Van Brunt, Vol. III, p. 970.

[26]Rudolph Pinola, "Labor and Politics on the Iron Range of Northern Minnesota," 1957, Doctoral Dissertation, University of Wisconsin, pp. 148-149.

[27]Van Brunt, Vol. II, p. 359.

[28]According to the *Fifth Decennial Census of the State of Minnesota*, 1905, the population of Hibbing was 6,566 and the foreign-born population was 3,537, or 53.9 percent.

[29]Pinola, p. 149.

[30]Ibid., p. 150.

[31]*Hibbing Tribune*, Dec. 1, 1909.

[32]Pinola, p. 150. *Duluth Herald*, Apr. 6, 1916. *Hibbing Tribune*, Apr. 7, 1926.

[33]Edmund L. DeLestry, *Western Magazine*, 1916, quoted in Pinola, p. 156.

[34]Pinola, p. 151. See also Van Brunt, Vol. II, pp. 562-563, for annexations and additions.

[35]John Syrjamaki, "Mesabi Communities, a Study of their Development," 1940, Doctoral Dissertation, Yale, pp. 341-352. Pinola, pp. 145-160. *Eveleth, Minnesota, Where Mines and Towns Meet*, 1921, Eveleth Commercial Club Publication, pp. 39-41.

[36]Paul Landis, *Three Mining Towns*, 1938, Edwards Brothers, Ann Arbor, Michigan, p. 253.

[37]Pinola, pp. 158-160. Syrjamaki, pp. 353-358.

[38]Syrjamaki, p. 353. Pinola, pp. 160-163.

[39]Virtue, "Iron Ranges," p. 369.

[40]Ibid., pp. 346-351.

[41]Ibid., p. 344.

[42]Ibid., pp. 367-377. Also on p. 372 is a table based on data drawn from the biennial reports of the Bureau of Labor indicating that there were 96 fatal accidents in St. Louis County iron mines in 1906, 81 in 1907, 54 in 1908 and 61 in 1909. According to Karni in "Finnish Temperance," *Diaspora II*, p. 166: "During 1905-1906, the death rate on the Mesabi was approximately 7.5 workers per thousand employed...."

[43]Joe Potocnik, immigrant Elcor businessman, who worked for a time at the Genoa Mine, Bill Potocnik, "Saga of a Supermarket, *Range History*, Summer 1983.

[44]For wages paid by Oliver Iron Mining Company in St. Louis County mines during the years 1902-1909, see Virtue, p. 387; for contract pay system, see pp. 388-389.

[45]Michael Karni's Aug. 1981 interview with Hilliard Larson, miner at Oliver's Soudan Mine during the years 1917-1963.

[46]Hodges, "Immigrant Life in the Ore Region of Northern Minnesota," *The Survey*, Sep. 7, 1912, p. 706.

[47]Ibid.

[48]Memorandum quoted in Robert M.

Eleff, "The 1916 Minnesota Miners' Strike Against U.S. Steel," *Minnesota History*, Summer 1988, p. 65.

[49]*Duluth News Tribune*, May 5, 1894. Matti Kaups in *The Finnish Experience*, p. 87, quotes a contemporary report: "Deputy Sheriff Al Free fatally shot a Finnish striker and agitator named Mattson at Mountain Iron yesterday evening ... the leader of the Finns at Mountain Iron who are the only ones causing trouble here."

[50]*Eveleth Mining News*, Jun. 3, 1904. "4 Major Mine Strikes Recalled," *Hibbing Tribune*, Jun. 29, 1946. John Syrjamaki, "The People of the Mesabi Range," *Minnesota History*, Sep. 1946, p. 204. Pinola, pp. 12-21 for descriptions of early strikes, including those at Ely. According to Pinola, p. 17, "In June 1904, 400 men walked out at the Drake and Stratton stripping operation at the Fayal Mine near Eveleth.... " From p. 20, "On the third day of the strike a clash took place between strikers who had been sent to the works to protect 'life and property.' Two strikers were taken to the hospital, one with a bullet in his head and another with a jagged shell in his chest. Many others were wounded by the deputies of Sheriff Butchart." Quote of "Slovenian miner" from *Glas Svobode* as found in Hyman Berman, "Education for Work and Labor Solidarity: The Immigrant Miners and Radicalism on the Mesabi Range," unpublished manuscript presented at a conference on the role of education on the Mesabi Range, sponsored by the University of Minnesota, Oct. 18-19, 1963, p. 37, copy at IRRC.

[51]Neil Betten, "Strike on the Mesabi – 1907," *Minnesota History*, Fall 1967, p. 341. Richard O. Boyer and Herbert M. Morais, *Labor's Untold Story*, 3rd Edition, 1976, United Electrical, Radio and Machine Workers of America, New York, p. 146.

[52]Berman, p. 38: "In the summer of 1906, recognizing that effective organization of the Minnesota iron mines was needed in order to prevent scabs from breaking into the unionized western fields – the WFM (Western Federation of Miners) appointed Italian Socialist Teofila Petriella, as special organizer."

[53]Ibid., p. 38. Betten, p. 341.

[54]Betten, p. 342. *Virginia Enterprise*, Jul. 19, 1907.

[55]Hans Wasastjerna, ed., *History of the Finns* p. 256. Boese, *Western Mesabi*, p. 127.

[56]Betten, p. 342. Pinola, p. 21.

[57]Betten, pp. 342-343. Pinola, p. 23.

[58]Betten, p. 344. *Virginia Enterprise*, Jul. 26, 1907.

[59]Syrjamaki, p. 217. Betten, p. 345. *Eveleth News*, Jul. 24, 1907.

[60]*Labor World*, Aug. 17, 1907. Mary Harris Jones "obituary quotes" in Elizabeth Janeway, ed., *Women, Their Changing Roles*, 1973, New York Times Company, New York, pp. 166, 167.

[61]Betten, p. 344.

[62]Wasastjerna, ed., p. 454.

[63]Betten, p. 345. Syrjamaki, p. 217.

[64]*Eveleth News*, Aug. 24, 1907.

[65]Ibid. *Labor World*, Aug. 23, 1907; Attitude of mining company officials related to Montenegrins and other immigrant arrivals in 1907 and 1908 is expressed in Virtue, p. 356 and also Berman, p. 45.

[66]*Virginian*, Aug. 23, 1907. *Labor World*, Aug. 31, 1907. *Eveleth News*, Jul. 24, 1907.

[67]Lumbering continued to be an important employer on the range until 1910 but after that, it was important only in the Virginia area. See Syrjamaki, p. 183. The exodus of Finnish families from the mining districts to such nearby rural communities as Makinen, Palo, Embarrass, Hutter, Sax, Forbes, Alango and Zim is well-documented. "The Finns were motivated much less by the instinct for self-preservation and health than they were by the mining strikes of 1907 and 1916. The consequence of these strikes was the shutting off of the main possibility of gainful labor from the majority of the Finns in this region of mines and there was not much of a choice left: either leave the mining region or settle down as farmers," according to Wasastjerna, ed., p. 539.

[68]*Biwabik Times*, Jan. 24, 1908, reported that the captain, his wife, three sons and 16-month-old baby all miraculously escaped death. "Two local Austrians" and "a man who claimed to be the husband of socialist lecturer Elizabeth Gurley Flynn" were immediately arrested and blamed for the incident. Note: All three were later found innocent and freed.

[69]Himrod, ed., *The Cuyuna Range*, p. 55.

[70]Arthur Puotinen, "Copper Country Finns and the Strike of 1913," *Finnish Experience in the Western Great Lakes Region*, 1975, Institute for Migration, Turku, Finland, pp. 143-153, for analysis of the Michigan copper strike and resulting "Italian Hall tragedy" and the role played by syndicalist ideology as inspiration for "industrial war."

[71]Philip S. Foner, *History of the Labor Movement in the United States*, 1965, International Publishers, New York, Vol. 4, pp. 492-493. Eleff, p. 64.

[72]Part of the Federal Industrial Relations Committee Report printed in the *Duluth Herald*, Nov. 21, 1916, is quoted in Douglas Ollila Jr., "Ethnic Radicalism and the 1916 Mesabi Strike," *Range History*, Dec. 1978.

[73]Foner, p. 490: "… it was the callous, driving attitude of the bosses that the miners most resented. They pushed the men to the limit day-in and day-out. 'Always they are driving us in all manners of way,' protested an Eveleth miner … it was a common saying on the range that five years in the mines was enough to ruin any man in body and spirit, however strong he was physically …"

[74]Harrison George, "Victory on the Mesabi Range," *International Socialist Review*, Jan. 1917, pp. 429-430. Foner, p. 490. *Duluth News Tribune*, Jun. 6, 8 and 12, 1916.

[75]Melvyn Dobofsky, *We Shall Be All: A History of the Industrial Workers of the World*, 1969, Quadrangle Books, Chicago, pp. 324-325.

[76]Foner, pp. 493-495. George, pp. 429-430.

[77]Foner, p. 495. Marion B. Cothren, "When Strike-Breakers Strike," *Survey*, Aug. 26, 1916, p. 535. Pinola, p. 29.

[78]Foner, p. 495.

[79]Foner, p. 499.

[80]Ibid., p. 497.

[81]Leslie H. Marcy, "The Iron Heel on the Mesaba Range," *International Socialist Review*, Aug. 1916, pp. 75-76. Foner, p. 500.

[82]Foner, p. 496. Cothren, p. 535.

[83]Marcy, p. 75.

[84]Eleff, p. 70.

[85]Ibid. Foner, p. 497.

[86]Otto Christenson, "Invading Miners' Homes," *International Socialist Review*, Sep. 1916, pp. 161-162.

[87]Ibid. Foner, pp. 500-502. Elizabeth Gurley Flynn, *The Rebel Girl – An Autobiography*, 1955, International Publishers, New York, pp. 207-208.

[88]Christenson, p. 162. Foner, p. 501.

[89]Berman, p. 53. Eleff, p. 71. Foner, p. 503.

[90]Michael Karni, "Elizabeth Gurley Flynn and the Mesabi Strike of 1916," *Range History*, Winter 1981.

[91]Mary Heaton Vorce in Boyer and Morais, *Untold Story*, p. 175. See also Karni, *Range History*.

[92]Foner, p. 507. See also Karni, *Range History*.

[93]Ibid., p. 513.

[94]Christian Hakala, "The Greatest Nation's Greatest Playground: Building a Community Through Sports in Eveleth, Minnesota, 1919-1929," 1997, Masters Thesis, Truman State University, Kirksville, Missouri, p. 12.

[95]Haynes, "Revolt of the Timber Beasts," *Minnesota History*, pp. 163-166.

[96]Jussi Hinkhanen, "The Speak English Movement in the St. Louis County Rural Schools," *Koti*, Mar. 1922, p. 6. Genevieve Anderson, "Americanizing the Immigrant Woman Through the Home Teacher," in Catherine Rukavina, "Americanization Classes," *Range History*, Sep. 1978.

[97]Frank L. Palmer, *Spies in Steel, An Expose of Industrial War*, 1928, The Labor Press, Denver. The publication includes photostatic copies of reports from informers kept by Oliver Iron Mining Company on political activities of individuals, anti-company statements and pro-union sentiment among employees. It also includes the names of persons involved, along with places and dates.

CHAPTER TWELVE [219-243]

[1]"Mineral Industries," 1939, Series E214, *Sixteenth Census of the United States, 1940*, pp. 599-600. See also *Mining Directory Issues* for the years 1929, 1930, 1931, 1932.

[2]"Along the railroad embankment, beside the garbage incinerator, in the city dumps there appeared towns of tar-paper and tin, old packing boxes and old car bodies…. Symbols of the New Era, these communities quickly received their sardonic name: they were called Hoovervilles." Arthur M. Schlesinger Jr., *The Crisis of the Old Order: The Age of Roosevelt 1919-1933*, 1957, Houghton Mifflin, Boston, p. 177.

[3]Foner, Vol. 4, p. 511. Pinola, "Labor and Politics," p. 161.

[4]Pinola, "Labor and Politics," p. 166. *Ely Miner*, Nov. 2, 1934.

[5]Franklin Delano Roosevelt, *Inaugural Address*, Mar. 1933.

[6]John Craig, ed., *Mining Directory*, 1936, p. 200. Pinola, p. 82. *Virginia Daily Enterprise*, Oct. 20 and 21, 1936.

[7]Arundel Cotter, *United States Steel*, p. 249.

[8]John Syrjamaki, "Mesabi Communities," p. 226.

[9]Pinola, pp. 82, 169.

[10]Ibid., p. 168. John DeGraaf, "John T. Bernard," *Tribute to John T. Bernard*, Jun. 1977, Tyomies Society, Superior, Wisconsin.

[11]John P. Jacobson, "The Merger of the Democratic and Farmer-Labor Parties in Minnesota," Jul. 1966, Masters Thesis, Bemidji State University, p. 8.

[12]British Prime Minister Winston Churchill, Mar. 11, 1940.

[13]"Annual Shipments by States, 1900-1951," in *Lake Superior Iron Ores, Mining Directory and Statistical Record*, 2nd Edition, Cleveland, 1952, p. 275.

[14]From Cabell Phillips, *The 1940s: Decade of Triumph and Trouble*, 1975, MacMillan, New York, p. 76: "… There were by the beginning of 1941 clear signs of incipient industrial chaos as manufacturers and producers attempted to sandwich defense orders into the booming demand for civilian goods. Many were reluctant to sacrifice a sure thing to gamble on the uncertainties of military procurement, to retool and convert their factories and to allocate steel and scarce metals to turn out guns and airplane engines instead of automobiles and vacuum cleaners. For a time, cantankerous old Henry Ford, a devout isolationist and Anglophobe, refused to accept war orders offered by a British purchasing mission."

[15]*Lake Superior Iron Ores*, 1952, p. 275.

[16]President Franklin Delano Roosevelt, Dec. 8, 1941.

[17]Geoffrey Perrett, *Days of Sadness, Years of Triumph: The American People, 1939-1945*, 1973, Coward, McCann and Geoghagen, Toronto and New York, pp. 27-29.

[18]Frank C. Harper, *Men and Women of Wartime Pittsburgh and Environs, A War Production Epic*, 1945, Frank C. Harper, Pittsburgh, p. 22.

[19]Ibid.

[20]S.I. Rosenman, *Public Papers of Franklin D. Roosevelt*, 1942.

[21]In 1940, Iron Country mines produced 48,949,000 tons; in 1941 they produced 64,061,000 tons; and in 1942 Iron Country mines produced a record 75,300,000 tons of iron ore, with 70,280,000 from the Mesabi Range, according to *Lake Superior Iron Ores*, p. 275. Hatcher, *A Century of Iron and Men*, p. 262, states: "In sheer tonnage, the Mesabi mines far surpassed the combined output of all other ranges. In the great peak year of 1943, when the total shipments of the Lake Superior District reached 93,495,392 tons, over 70,000,000 tons came from the Mesabi."

[22]The following quote in Phillips, p. 195, succinctly describes the prevailing attitude of the time: "The logic of the case was inescapable – thousands of able-bodied GIs were tied down to desk and service and even mechanical jobs which women could perform as well or better than they – but the idea that young females should be officially introduced into the rough and celibate domain of army camps and naval stations … was socially and morally intolerable to many legislators."

[23]*Lake Superior Iron Ores*, pp. 212-219.

[24]Pinola, pp. 52-54.

[25]Ibid., p. 54.

[26]Ibid., pp. 56-59.

[27]Ibid., pp. 59-64.

[28]In Van Brunt, Vol. I, pp. 482-483, are the following comments related to a range school: "The Buhl High School … erected in 1912-1913 … ranks well with the magnificent schools of the Mesabi Range, where can be found, it is generally conceded, more complete educational facilities for elementary and high school students than are provided in any other part of the United States, not even excepting the very large cities. The wealth of the school districts of the Mesabi mining towns makes it possible to offer such salaries to educators that the most skilled of the profession are attracted into service. And in equipment, the large schools of the range are wonderfully complete."

[29]Edward W. Davis, *Pioneering with Taconite*, 1964, MHS, St. Paul, p. 93.

[30]Ibid., p. 96. See also "R.C. Allen Talks of Oliver Ore Sales Departure," *Skillings*, Feb. 3, 1940, p. 1.

[31]See Dana H. Miller, *The Iron Range Resources and Rehabilitation Board: The First Fifty Years*, 1991, Iron Range Resources and Rehabilitation Board, Eveleth, Minnesota, for details related to the establishment of the IRRRB and a review of its various initiatives and projects.

[32]Ibid., p. 7. *Minnesota Statutes,* Sec. 298.22.

[33]Miller, p. 10.

[34]*Iron Range Resources and Rehabilitation Commission Biennium Report, 1945-1947. IRRRC Biennium Report, 1948-1950:* The state legislature transferred substantial amounts of money from IRRRB (Then called IRRRC) funds to the University of Minnesota Mines Experiment Station during the years 1942-1968. According to Miller, p. 9: "With the creation of the IRRRB, the Mines Experiment Station and Davis found a consistent and generous supporter of its research. The agency's first transfer, in 1942-44, totalled $40,000 and reached a high in the 1962-64 biennium, when the Legislature committed $390,000. All told, more than $2.5 million found its way to the Mines Experiment Station...."

[35]Havighurst, *Vein of Iron,* p. 204. "Taconite," *IRRRC Biennium Report,* 1943-45, pp. 68-69. Walter G. Swart, E.M., on geology, in "Report on Mesabi Iron Company" at Babbitt, 1931, pp. 15-24, IRRC.

[36]Swart, pp. 15-24. See also Davis, pp. 1-5.

[37]Davis, pp. 16-17.

[38]Ibid., pp. 18-19.

[39]Ibid., p. 24.

[40]Ibid., p. 36.

[41]Swart, p. 25. Davis, p. 27.

[42]Davis, pp. 27 and 21.

[43]Walter G. Swart's "Report on the Magnetic Deposits of the East Mesabi Range," Jul. 1915, p. 27.

[44]Ibid., pp. 27-28.

[45]Ibid., p. 29: The quote is from Arthur B. Parsons, "Operations of the Mesabi Iron Company," *Engineering and Mining Journal Press,* Jan. 25-Feb. 2, 1924, p. 6.

[46]Ibid., p. 5. Davis, pp. 38-39, 42.

[47]Davis, p. 42.

[48]Ibid., p. 42.

[49]Ibid., pp. 46-47.

[50]Ibid., pp. 47, 51.

[51]Ibid., p. 52.

[52]Ibid., pp. 50-52.

[53]Parsons, p. 5.

[54]The additions are shown on a map made by Johnson and Higgins of New York, Jun. 5, 1924. Copy in MHS. See Davis, pp. 44, 52.

[55]Davis, p. 52

[56]Ibid., pp. 50-51.

[57]According to Swart in his "Report on Mesabi Iron Company," 1931, p. 29, Iron Lake was a natural lake from which water was pumped over a low ridge into Argo Lake, an artificial lake created by throwing a small earthwork dam across the outlet of an old cedar swamp. Although the two lakes provided some of the water for the plant, mostly during the summer, the only consistent source of water was Birch Lake located in the Hudson Bay watershed.

[58]Parsons, p. 6.

[59]"Eastern Mesabi District – Beneficiation by Magnetic Separation – Babbitt Plant," *Eighth Biennial Report,* 1922, Chapter IV, pp. 29-32. Swart, p. 253. Details of crushing, magnetic cobbing and meshing are also found in Parsons, pp. 9-15. See also Davis, pp. 48-49 for "Mesabi Iron Company Babbitt Plant Original Flow Sheet."

[60]Swart, 1931, p. 253.

[61]Davis, pp. 60-61.

[62]Ibid., p. 55.

[63]Swart, pp. 228-229. *Lake Superior Iron Ores,* 1938, p. 300.

[64]*Iron Ores,* p. 129.

[65]Swart, 1931, pp. 228-229. Davis, p. 57.

[66]See Swart, 1931, p. 228, for details related to penalties and increased costs of transportation and storage.

[67]Davis, pp. 58-59.

[68]Jackling to Swart, Jul. 17, 1931, in Swart "Report on Mesabi Iron Company," IRRC.

[69]Davis, p. 64.

[70]Ibid., pp. 65-68.

[71]Ibid., pp. 84-89.

[72]Ibid., p. 90.

[73]"Taconite Plans of Erie Mining Company," *Skillings,* Feb. 23, 1952, pp. 1-2.

[74]Ibid. "Erie Mining Company Taconite Development," *Skillings,* Jul. 7, 1956, p. 2.

[75]"Taconite Pilot Plant Contract Awarded to Ohio Firm," *Skillings,* Jun. 9, 1951, p. 2.

[76]Davis, pp. 109-111.

[77]Ibid.

[78]"Reserve Mining Co. Starts a Taconite Plant at Babbitt," reprint from *Engineering and Mining Journal (EMJ),* Nov. 1952. For details on primary and secondary taconite crushers, see "Reserve Mining Company: Mining and Crushing at Babbitt, Minnesota," *Skillings,* Jan. 26, 1957, p. 3.

[79]"Reserve Starts Taconite Plant," *EMJ* 1952. Davis, pp. 154-155.

[80]"Reserve Crushers at Babbitt," *Skillings,* Jan. 26, 1957, p. 3. See also Davis, pp. 161-166.

[81]Davis, pp. 178-181.

[82]"Pelletizing Taconite Ore," *Skillings,* Feb. 9, 1957, p. 1. Davis, pp. 172-174.

[83]Havighurst, pp. 209-210. "Erie Taconite Development," *Skillings,* Jul. 7, 1956, p. 2.

[84]*Skillings* Jul. 7, 1956, p. 2.

[85]See "Oliver Begins Taconite Program at Mountain Iron," *Skillings,* May 19, 1952, p. 4.

[86]"Shipment of Iron Ore Pellets in North America," *Skillings,* Mar. 12, 1960, p. 4.

[87]Davis, p. 190.

[88]Ibid., p. 191.

[89]David N. Skillings Jr., "1972 Activity at Minnesota Iron Ore Mines and Plants," *Skillings,* Jun. 3, 1972, p. 1.

[90]Ibid.

[91]The MPCA had recently replaced the former Water Pollution Control Commission and assumed all of its authority in administering and enforcing all laws relating to water pollution in the state, plus additional responsibilities in the fields of air pollution, solid waste disposal and pollution-related land use planning. It should be noted that Michigan and Wisconsin, along with a number of independent environmental groups, also became concerned about the quality of both water and air in the vicinity of the Reserve plant and involved themselves in the controversy.

[92]United States vs. Reserve Mining Company (hereafter RMC), U.S. District Court District of Minnesota (hereafter D. Minn.) 1972. Armco Steel Corporation vs. United States, 8th Cir. 1974. United States vs. RMC, D. Minn. 1974. RMC vs. United States, 8th Cir. 1974. Minnesota vs. RMC, 418 U.S. 911 1974. Minnesota vs. RMC, 419 U.S. 802 1974. United States vs. RMC, D. Minn. 1974. RMC vs. EPA, 1975. Minnesota vs. RMC, 420 1975. RMC vs. Lord, 1976. United States vs. RMC, 408 F. Supp. 1212 D. Minn 1976. United States vs. RMC, 412 Supp. 705 D. Minn. 1976. United States vs. RMC, 417 F. Supp. 789 D. Minn 197.United States vs. RMC, 417 F. Supp. D. Minn. 1976.

[93]Frank D. Schaumburg, *Judgment Reserved,* 1976, Reston Publishing Co., Reston, Virginia.

[94]See Robert V. Bartlett, *The Reserve Mining Company Controversy: Science, Technology, and Environmental Quality,* 1980, Indiana University Press, Bloomington and London, for an in-depth study of the causes and effects of the Reserve Mining Company controversy.

[95]Peter Kakela, "The Minnesota Taconite Production Tax," *Engineering and Mining Journal,* Mar. 1, 1999.

[96]Miller, *Iron Range Resources,* p. 13.

Bibliography

BOOKS AND ARTICLES

Aguar, Charles E., *Exploring St. Louis County's Historical Sites*, 1971, St. Louis County Historical Society, Aguar, Jyring, Whiteman Moser Inc., Duluth.

Alanen, Arnold, "The Locations: Company Communities on Minnesota's Iron Ranges," *Minnesota History*, Fall 1982.

Alanen, Arnold, "From Tower to Soudan: Townsites and Locations on the Vermilion Iron Range," *Entrepreneurs and Immigrants,* Michael Karni, ed., 1991, Iron Range Research Center (IRRC), Chisholm.

Appleby, W.R., "Special Report on the Cuyuna Range," Chapter VI, *Fourth Biennial Report of the Minnesota Tax Commission,* St. Paul.

Aulie, Berger, *The Milford Mine Disaster*, 1994, DeWitt and Caroline Van Evera Foundation Grant, printed by W.A. Fisher Company, Virginia, Minnesota.

Bacon, Arthur W., "Everything Happens on a Bus," *Saturday Evening Post*, Apr. 20, 1946.

Bacon, Donald H., "Development of Lake Superior Ores," *Transactions*, Vol. XXI, 1892, American Institute of Mining Engineers.

Bacon, Donald H., "System of Filling at the Minnesota," *Vermilion Iron Journal*, Jul. 31, 1892.

Bartlett, Robert V., *The Reserve Mining Controversy: Science, Technology, and Environmental Quality*, 1980, Indiana University Press, Bloomington and London.

Beck, Bill, *Northern Lights, An Illustrated History of Minnesota Power*, 1985, Minnesota Power, Duluth.

Betten, Neil, "Strike on the Mesabi-1907," *Minnesota History*, Fall 1967.

Bishop, Hugh E., *By Water and Rail: A History of Lake County, Minnesota*, 2000, Lake Superior Port Cities Inc., Duluth.

Blegen, Theodore Christian, *Minnesota, A History of the State*, 1963, 2nd Edition, 1975, University of Minnesota, Minneapolis.

Boese, Donald L., *John C. Greenway and the Opening of the Western Mesabi*, 1975, Itasca Community College, Grand Rapids, Minnesota.

Boese, Donald L., and Cain, Richard, *Grand Rapids Companion, 1891-1991*, Grand Rapids Centennial Committee, Grand Rapids.

Bolf, Peter, "The Pioneering Butlers," *Range History*, December 1979.

Boyer, Richard O., and Morais, Herbert M., *Labor's Untold Story*, 1976, United Electrical, Radio and Machine Workers of America, 3rd Edition, New York.

Brandon, William, *Indians*, 1987, Houghton Mifflin, Boston.

Bridges, Hal, *Iron Millionaire: Life of Charlemagne Tower*, 1952, University of Pennsylvania Press, Philadelphia.

Burpee, Lawrence J., ed., *Journals and Letters of Pierre Gaultier de Varennes de la Verendrye and His Sons*, 1927, The Champlain Society, Toronto.

Burton, C.R., "Powerplants for Production, Trucks on Mesabi Range," *Skillings Mining Review*, Nov. 18, 1950.

Cain, Richard, *La Prairie: The Road Back*, 1990, City of La Prairie by Paragraphics Inc., Deer River, Minnesota.

Cann, Marion Stuart, *Is This Hand Worth Playing? A Problem for Investors*, 1892, Duluth Stock Exchange, Duluth.

Carmody, John M., admin., *Logging Town, The Story of Grand Rapids, Minnesota*, 1941, Works Progress Administration Project, Grand Rapids.

Christenson, Otto, "Invading Miners' Homes," *International Socialist Review*, Sep. 1916.

Clark, Thomas, *Report of the State Geologist, Augustus Hanchett*, 1865, Fredrick Driscoll, Incidental Publisher, St. Paul.

Clements, J. Morgan, *The Vermilion Iron-bearing District of Minnesota*, Monograph of the United States Geological Survey, No. 45, 1903, Washington, D.C.

Coombe, Kathryn, ed., "Biwabik – Past and Present," *Biwabik 1892-1967*, 1967, Diamond Jubilee Historical Souvenir Booklet, Biwabik, Minnesota.

Cothren, Marion B., "When Strike-Breakers Strike," *Survey*, Aug. 26, 1916.

Cotter, Arundel, *United States Steel: A Corporation With a Soul*, 1921, Doubleday, Page & Company, New York.

Coues, Elliott, ed., *Manuscript Journals of Alexander Henry and David Thompson, 1799-1814*, Vol. I and II, 1897, Reprint edition 1965, Ross and Haines Inc., Minneapolis.

Crosby, George, *Crosby: The Metropolis of the Cuyuna,* promotional booklet published in about 1914.

Danziger, Edmund Jefferson Jr., *The Chippewas of Lake Superior,* 1978, University of Oklahoma Press, Norman.

Davis, E.W., *Pioneering With Taconite,* 1964, Minnesota Historical Society, St. Paul.

DeGraaf, John, "Tribute to John T. Bernard," Tyomies Society, Jun. 1977, Superior, Wisconsin.

De Kruif, Paul H., *Seven Iron Men,* 1929, Blue Ribbon Books, Harcourt Brace & Company, New York.

Dobofsky, Melvyn, *We Shall Be All: A History of the Industrial Workers of the World,* 1969, Quadrangle Books, Chicago.

Duncan, Kenneth, "The Soudan Mine and the Minnesota Iron Co," *Skillings Mining Review,* Nov. 4, 1967.

Eames, Henry H., *Report of the State Geologist, Henry H. Eames, on the Metalliferous Region Bordering on Lake Superior,* 1866, Fredrick Driscoll, State Printer, St. Paul.

Eleff, Robert M., "The 1916 Minnesota Miners' Strike Against U.S. Steel," *Minnesota History,* Summer 1988.

Emerson, C.R., "Drilling on the Mesabi in 1908," *Skillings Mining Review,* Mar. 22, 1975.

Encyclopedia of Biography of Minnesota, 1909, Century Publishing and Engraving, Chicago.

Evans, Henry Oliver, *Iron Pioneer: Henry W. Oliver, 1840-1904,* 1942, E.P. Dutton, New York.

Eveleth, Minnesota: Where Mines and Towns Meet, 1921, Eveleth Commercial Club Publication.

Flynn, Elizabeth Gurley, *The Rebel Girl, An Autobiography,* 1955, International Publishers, New York.

Folwell, William W., *A History of Minnesota,* Vols. I-IV, 1956, Minnesota Historical Society St. Paul.

Foner, Philip S., *History of the Labor Movement in the United States,* Vol. 4, 1965, International Publishers, New York.

From Timber to Taconite, The Story of Nashwauk, 1978, Seventy-fifth Anniversary Book Committee, *Eastern Itascan,* Nashwauk.

Gates, Frederick T., *The Truth About Mr. Rockefeller and the Merritts,* 1897, The Knickerbocker Press Reprint Edition, G.P. Putnam, 1911, New York.

George, Harrison, "Victory on the Mesabi Range," *International Socialist Review,* Jan. 1917.

Gilfillan, Rev. Joseph A., "Minnesota Geographical Names Derived From the Chippewa Language," *The Minnesota Archaeologist,* Vol. 35, No. 4, 1976, Minnesota Archaeological Society, St. Paul.

Grout, Frank F., and Wolff, J.F. Sr., *The Geology of the Cuyuna District,* 1955, University of Minnesota, Minneapolis.

Hansen, Arvy, ed., *Cuy-una! A Chronicle of the Cuyuna Range,* 1976, Bicentennial Publication, *Crosby-Ironton Courier,* Crosby, Minnesota.

Hari, Jennie, "Section Thirty," *Roaring Stoney Days,* 1958, Ely-Winton Historical Society, Ely.

Harper, Frank C., *Men and Women of Wartime Pittsburgh and Environs, A War Production Epic,* 1945, F.C. Harper, Pittsburgh.

Hatcher, Harlan, *A Century of Iron and Men,* 1950, Bobbs-Merrill Company Inc., New York.

Havighurst, Walter, *Vein of Iron, The Pickands Mather Story,* 1958, World Publishing Company, Cleveland.

Haynes, John E., "Revolt of the Timber Beasts: IWW Lumber Strike in Minnesota," *Minnesota History,* Spring 1971.

Hearding, John H., "Pioneer Mining Man Describes Early Days in Eveleth District," *Skillings Mining Review,* Aug. 18, 1923.

Hecimovich, Steve, *A Town is Born, A Historical and Pictorial Review of Buhl, Minnesota,* 2002, Buhl 100 Year Anniversary, All Class Reunion Committee, Buhl.

Heinselman, Miron, *The Boundary Waters Wilderness Ecosystem,* 1996, University of Minnesota Press, Minneapolis.

Hibbing on the Move Since 1893, 1991, Hibbing Book Committee.

Hickerson, Harold, "Ethnohistory of Chippewa of Lake Superior," *Chippewa Indians III,* 1974, Garland Publishing Inc., New York.

Hickerson, Harold, *Land Tenure of the Rainy Lake Chippewa at the Beginning of the 19th Century,* 1967, Smithsonian Press, Washington, D.C.

Hickerson, Harold, *Southwestern Chippewa: An Ethnohistorical Study,* Memoir 92, 1962, The American Anthropological Association, Menasha, Wisconsin.

Hickerson, Harold, *The Chippewa and Their Neighbors: A Study in Ethnohistory,* 1970, Irvington Publishers Inc., New York.

Himrod, Anna, ed., *The Cuyuna Range: A History of a Minnesota Iron Mining District,* 1940, Minnesota Historical Records Survey Project, Works Progress Administration, St. Paul.

Hinkhanen, Jussi, "The Speak English Movement in the St. Louis County Rural Schools," *Koti,* Mar. 1922.

Hodges, LeRoy, "Immigrant Life in the Ore Region of Northern Minnesota," *The Survey,* Sep. 7, 1912.

Hunner, Earl E., "Some Recent Developments in Open Pit Mining on the Mesabi Range," 1930, American Institute of Mining and Metallurgical Engineers, Tech. Pub. No. 333.

Hunter, Martin, *Canadian Wilds,* 1935, A.R. Harding, Columbus, Ohio.

James, J.H. "J.H. James Talks," *The Great Missabe Iron Range,* 1893, *Minneapolis Tribune,* Minneapolis.

Janeway, Elizabeth, ed., *Women, Their Changing Roles*, 1973, *New York Times*.

Johnson, Elden, ed., *Aspects of Upper Great Lakes Anthropology*, 1974, Minnesota Historical Society, St. Paul.

Johnson, Elden, *The Prehistoric Peoples of Minnesota: Minnesota Prehistoric Archaeology Series*, 1969, Minnesota Historical Society, St. Paul.

Kakela, Peter, "The Minnesota Taconite Production Tax," *Engineering and Mining Journal*, Mar. 1, 1999.

Kappler, Charles J., LL.M, *Indian Affairs: Laws and Treaties*, Vol. I and II, 1904, Government Printing Office, Washington, D.C.

Karni, Michael, "Elizabeth Gurley Flynn and the Mesabi Strike of 1916," *Range History*, Winter 1981.

Karni, Michael G., ed., *Finnish Diaspora II: United States*, 1981, Multicultural History Society of Ontario, Toronto.

Karni, Michael G., Kaups, Matti E., Ollila, Douglas Jr., eds., *The Finnish Experience in the Western Great Lakes Region: New Perspectives*, 1975, Institute for Migration, Turku, Finland, in cooperation with the Immigration History Research Center, University of Minnesota, Minneapolis.

Keewatin 1906-1956, 1956, Bicentennial Committee, Fred J. Raniele, chairman, Keewatin.

King, Frank A., *The Missabe Road*, 1972, Golden West Books, San Marino, California.

Knickerbocker, A.K., "The Contract Wage System for Miners," *Mining and Scientific Press*, Apr. 3, 1920.

Krenz, Duane, "Northern Timber," *Range History*, Jun. 1979.

LaBerge, Gene, *Geology of the Lake Superior Region*, 1994, Geoscience Press, Phoenix, Arizona.

Lake Superior Iron Ores, Mining Directory and Statistical Record, 2nd Edition, 1952, Lake Superior Iron Ore Association, Cleveland.

Lamppa, Marvin, "Gamble at the Grant." *Range History*, Sep. 1977.

Landis, Paul H., *Three Iron Mining Towns*, 1938, Edwards Brothers, Ann Arbor, Michigan.

Larson, Agnes M., *History of the White Pine Industry of Minnesota*, 1949, University of Minnesota Press, Minneapolis.

Leifchild, J.R. *Cornwall: Its Mines and Miners*, 1857, Longman, Brown, Green, Longmans and Roberts, London.

MacKillican, J.A., "History and Present Status of Mining in Minnesota," *Skillings Mining Review*, Feb. 23, 1946.

Marcy, Leslie H., "The Iron Heel on the Mesaba Range," *International Socialist Review*, Aug. 1916.

Marsh, Robert Jr., *Steam Shovel Mining*, 1920, McGraw-Hill Book Company, New York.

Masson, Louis Rodrigue, ed., *Les Bourgeois de la Compagnie du Nord-Ouest* (Original journals, narratives, letters, etc. relating to the North West Company), Vol. I-II, 1889, Quebec, Reprint Edition, 1960, Antiquarian Press, New York.

McKee, Russell, *Great Lakes Country*, 1966, Thomas Y. Crowell Company, New York.

Meyer, Roy W., *History of the Santee Sioux*, 1967, University of Nebraska Press, Lincoln.

Miller, Dana H., *The Iron Range Resources and Rehabilitation Board: The First Fifty Years*, 1991, IRRRB, Eveleth.

Mines and Minerals Chapters of Tax Commission Reports, 1910-1922, St. Paul.

Minnesota Arrowhead Country, 1941, Arrowhead Association Inc., Minnesota Historical Society reprint, 1988, St. Paul.

Morgan, Youngs L., "Diary of an Early Fur Trader," *Inland Seas, Quarterly Journal of the Great Lakes Historical Society*, Winter 1962 to Winter 1963.

Morse, Eric W., *Fur Trade Canoe Routes of Canada/Then and Now*, Second Edition, 1989, University of Toronto Press, Ottawa, Ontario.

Newman, Peter C., *Caesars of the Wilderness*, 1987, Penguin Books Canada, Markham, Ontario.

Nute, Grace Lee, "Posts in the Minnesota Fur-trading Area, 1660-1885," *Minnesota History*, Dec. 1930, Minnesota Historical Society, St. Paul.

Nute, Grace Lee, ed., *Mesabi Pioneer: Reminiscences of Edmund J. Longyear*, 1951, Minnesota Historical Society, St. Paul.

Nute, Grace Lee, *The Voyageur's Highway*, 1941, Reprint Edition 1969, Minnesota Historical Society, St. Paul.

Ollila, Douglas Jr., "Ethnic Radicalism and the 1916 Mesabi Strike," *Range History*, Dec. 1978.

Olson, Russell L., *The Electric Railways of Minnesota*, 1976, Minnesota Transportation Museum Inc., Hopkins, Minnesota.

Owen, David D., *Report of a Geological Survey of Wisconsin, Iowa, and Minnesota*, 1852, Lippincott, Grambo & Co., Philadelphia.

Palmer, Frank L., *Spies in Steel, An Expose of Industrial War*, 1928, The Labor Press, Denver, Colorado.

Parsons, Arthur B., "Operations of the Mesabi Iron Company," *Engineering and Mining Journal*, Jan. 25 and Feb. 2, 1924.

Pelkola, Mr. & Mrs. Huxley, "History of Winton," *Roaring Stoney Days*, 1958, Ely-Winton Historical Society, Ely.

Perrett, Geoffrey, *Days of Sadness, Years of Triumph: The American People, 1939-1945*, 1971, Coward, McCann and Geoghagen, Toronto and New York.

Perry, David E., "Exploratory Diamond Drilling on the Mesabi, 1890-1910," *Range History*, Fall 1980.

Phillips, Cabell, *The 1940s: Decade of Triumph and Trouble*, 1975, Macmillan, New York.

Potocnik, Bill, "Saga of a Supermarket," *Range History*, Summer 1983.

Qualey, Carlton C., "The Cornish: A Mining Elite," *Entrepreneurs and Immigrants: Life on the Industrial Frontier of Northeast Minnesota*, 1991, Iron Range Research Center, Chisholm.

Rukavina, Catherine, "Americanization Classes," *Range History*, Sep. 1978.

Sandoz, Mari, *The Beaver Men*, 1964, Hastings House Publishers, New York.

Schaumburg, Frank D., *Judgment Reserved*, 1976, Reston Publishing Co., Reston, Virginia.

Schlesinger, Arthur M. Jr., *The Crisis of the Old Order: The Age of Roosevelt 1919-1933*, 1957, Houghton Mifflin, Boston.

Schoolcraft, Henry R., *Narrative Journal of Travels, Through the Northwestern Regions of the United States Extending From Detroit Through the Great Chain of American Lakes to the Sources of the Mississippi River*, 1821, Reprint Edition, 1970, E.&E. Hosford, Arno Press Inc., Albany, New York.

Schwartz, George M., and Thiel, George A., *Minnesota's Rocks and Waters*, 1954, University of Minnesota Press, Minneapolis.

Schwedes, W.F., "Mechanical Shovels," *Proceedings of the Lake Superior Mining Institute*, Vol. 28, 1930.

Scull, Gideon, ed., *Voyages of Peter Esprit Radisson*, 1943, Peter Smith, New York.

Seely, Fred M., "History of Biwabik," *Biwabik Times*, Mar. 31, 1961.

Skillings, Helen Wieland, *We're Standing on Iron! The Story of the Five Wieland Brothers 1856-1883*, 1972, St. Louis County Historical Society, Duluth.

Somrock, John, and Brownell, Lee, *A History of Incredible Ely*, 1976, Cyko Art Print-Craft, Ely.

Stoltman, James B., *The Laurel Culture in Minnesota*, 1973, Minnesota Prehistoric Archaeology Series No.8., Minnesota Historical Society, St. Paul.

Stuntz, George R., "The Mound Builders in Northeast Minnesota: Their Occupations and Routes of Travel," *Bulletins*,Vol. 3, 1883-1891, Minnesota Academy of Natural Sciences.

Syrjamaki, John, "The People of the Mesabi Range," *Minnesota History*, Sep. 1946.

The Virginia Story, Historical Souvenir Booklet, 1892-1967, Celebrating Virginia Diamond Days, 1967, Diamond Jubilee Publications Committee, Virginia.

Thwaites, Reuben Gold, ed., *Jesuit Relations, XVIII*, 1959, Pageant, New York.

Tohill, Louis A., "Robert Dickson," *Minnesota History*, Dec. 1925, Minnesota Historical Society, St. Paul.

Upham, Warren, *Minnesota Geographic Names: Their Origin and Historic Significance*, 1969, Minnesota Historical Society, St. Paul.

Upham, Warren, and Dunlap, Rose Barteau, *Minnesota Biographies, 1655-1912*, 1912, Minnesota Historical Society Collections, St. Paul.

Van Barneveld, Charles, *Iron Mining in Minnesota*, 1912 and 1913, University of Minnesota School of Mines, Minneapolis.

Van Brunt, Walter, ed., *Duluth and St. Louis County, Their Story and People*, Vol. I-III, 1921, American Historical Society, Chicago and New York.

Virtue, G.O., "The Minnesota Iron Ranges," *Bulletin of the Bureau of Labor*, No. 84, 1909, U.S. Department of Commerce and Labor, Washington, D.C.

Walker, David A., "Lake Vermilion Gold Rush," *Minnesota History*, Summer 1974, Minnesota Historical Society, St. Paul.

Walker, David A., *Iron Frontier: The Discovery and Early Development of Minnesota's Three Ranges*, 1979, Minnesota Historical Society Press, St. Paul.

Walsh, Margaret, "Tracing the Hound, the Minnesota Roots of the Greyhound Corporation," *Minnesota History*, Winter 1985.

Warren, William W., *History of the Ojibway Nation*, 1974, Ross and Haines Inc., Minneapolis.

Wasastjerna, Hans R., ed., *History of the Finns in Minnesota*, 1957, Finnish-American Historical Society, Duluth.

Weckman, Violet Maryland, "Victor Maryland: Pioneer Bus Man on the Range," *Mesabi Daily News*, Oct. 3, 1976.

Winchell, Newton H., and Horace V., *Geological and Natural Survey of Minnesota, Bulletin No. 6, The Iron Ores of Minnesota*, 1891, Harrison and Smith, State Printers, Minneapolis.

Winchell, Horace V., "Report on the Mesabi Iron Range," *Twentieth Annual Report of the Minnesota Geological Survey 1891*, 1893, Minneapolis.

Winchell, Newton H., "Historical Sketch of Explorations and Surveys in Minnesota," *Geological and Natural History Survey of Minnesota*, Vol. I, St. Paul; Thirteenth Annual Report, State of Minnesota, 1889.

Wirth, Fremont P., *The Discovery and Exploitation of the Minnesota Iron Lands*, 1931, Torch Press, Cedar Rapids, Iowa.

Woodbridge, Dwight E., and Pardee, John S., eds., *History of Duluth and St. Louis County, Past and Present*, Vols. I-II, 1910, C.F. Cooper and Company, Chicago.

Young, George J., *Elements of Mining*, 1946, McGraw-Hill, New York.

PERIODICALS

American Magazine
Biwabik Times
Brainerd Dispatch
Chisholm Herald
Chisholm-Tribune Herald
Cleveland Herald
Crosby-Ironton Courier
Deerwood Enterprise
Duluth News Tribune
Duluth Evening Herald
Duluth Herald
Ely Echo
Ely Iron Home
Engineering and Mining Journal
Eveleth News
Eveleth Mining News
Gazette (Superior, Wisconsin)
Gilbert Herald
Go Greyhound, Greyhound Corporation magazine
Grand Rapids Herald Review
Hibbing Tribune
IRRRC Biennium Reports
Itasca Iron News
Labor World (Duluth)
Lake Superior Iron Ores
Longyear News Bits
Mesabi Daily News
Missabe Iron Ranger, Duluth Missabe & Iron Range Railroad magazine
Minneapolis Tribune
Skillings Mining Review
St. Paul Pioneer
St. Paul Press
St. Paul Daily Press
The Ely Miner
The Ely Times
The Eveleth News
The Iron Trade Review
The Mesaba Range
Tower Weekly News
University of Minnesota Bulletin *Mining Directories*
Vermilion Iron Journal
Virginia Daily Enterprise
Virginia Enterprise
Virginian

INTERVIEWS AND LETTERS

*Indicates a tape and/or transcript is available at Iron Range Research Center, Chisholm, Minnesota.

Emma Braaten, resident of Old Mesaba 1911-1928. By author, Feb. 5, 1962.

*Lee Brownell, resident of Ely and local historian. By author, Jul. 28, 1972.

John S. Domanoski, recollections of Old Sparta 1906-1910. By author, Mar. 26, 1962.

*Ernestine Hill, Bois Forte tribal member born on Basswood Lake, talks about commercial fishing on border lakes and lumber camps. By Jerry Pete, undated.

*Frank Hrvatin Jr., survivor of Milford Mine disaster 1924. By Joe Drazenovich, May 11, 1976.

*Frank H. Gillmor, By Lucile Kane, transcript, 1948.

*Helen Sipola Lamppa, recollections of Soudan Location 1900-1920. By author, Jul. 4, 1979.

*Hilliard Larson, recollections of a Soudan miner from 1917-1963. By Michael Karni, Aug. 1981.

Elina Sipola Saari, resident of Soudan, 1900-1979. By author, Jul. 25, 1979.

Alex Sipola, recollections of Elba Location 1896-1899. Letter to author, Feb, 5, 1961.

Harold Snabbi, recollections of Ely and Winton during lumber era. By author, Feb. 5, 1962.

*Carl Soderberg, resident of Soudan, 1907-1981. By Michael Karni, Jul. 23, 1981.

*Frank Teutloff, Bois Forte tribal member and Ely resident, recalls Indian village and cemetery in vicinity. By Jerry Pete, Dec. 17, 1996.

Interview with native Lakota speaker from Oglala Lakota College in Kyle, South Dakota. By Konnie LeMay, 2004.

DOCUMENTS AND MANUSCRIPTS
FROM COLLECTIONS

House Executive Document 451, 25th Congress 2nd Session, Washington, DC.

Iron Range Historical Society Collections, Gilbert, Minnesota.

Bordeau, Sanford P., "Recollections of Sparta as a Boy," unpublished manuscript, 1975.

Maki, Vienna C., "Memoirs from the Minnesota Iron Ore Mines," unpublished manuscript, undated.

Nolan, Mark, "Early History of Sparta and Gilbert," unpublished manuscript, Dec. 18, 1929.

Perry, David E., "List of Early Contract Drillers and Exploration Sites," unpublished manuscript, March 2, 1976.

Iron Range Research Center, Chisholm, Minnesota.

Chanak, George, "Farewell to Poverty and Happiness," unpublished manuscript, undated.

Directories of Minnesota Iron Range Towns, R.L. Polk & Company, Duluth, 1899-1930.

Insurance maps of Iron Range towns, 1892-1937, Sanborn-Perris and Sanborn Map Company, Broadway, New York.

Anderson, Hilda V., "A History of the Beginnings of the Bus Industry with Grass Roots in St. Louis County," typed manuscript by the wife of Andrew Anderson, Hibbing, 1954.

Iron Ranges of Minnesota Historical Souvenir, 1909, *Virginia Enterprise*, Virginia.

Lamppa, Marvin, "Historical Survey of Iron Range Communities," prepared for the Iron Range Interpretative Center, Dec. 1984.

Minnesota Bureau of Labor, Biennial Report 1901-1902, Minnesota Executive Documents, Vol. II, 1903, St. Paul.

Morcom, Elisha Jr., "The Discovery and Development of the Iron Ore Industry," unpublished manuscript, 1926.

Municipal court records, Ely, 1888-95.

Swart, Walter G., "Geology," in "Report on Mesabi Iron Company," at Babbitt, Minnesota, 1931.

Swart, Walter G., "Report on Magnetic Deposits of the East Mesabi Range," 1915.

United States Steel Corporation, Minnesota Mines Collection.

U.S. District Court and Court of Appeals, 8th Circuit Records (Reserve Mining Company, 1972-1976).

White, John Wesley, *Historical Sketches of the Quetico-Superior*, Vol. XII, Superior National Forest, U.S. Department of Agriculture.

Manitoba Provincial Archives, Winnipeg.

Hudson Bay Company Records, 1821-1839 (microfilm).

Minnesota Historical Society Collections, St. Paul.

Bardon, John A., papers, 1845-1880.

Eames, Richard, papers, 1866.

Elliot, Ruth M., "Vermilion Gold Rush of 1865," unpublished manuscript, 1923.

Ely, Edmund F., and family papers, 1820-1904, 1927.

Gillmor, Frank H., By Lucile Kane, transcript, 1948.

Merritt, Andrus R. and Jessie L., "The Story of the Mesabi," unpublished manuscript, 1934.

Rice, Henry M., papers, 1816-1895.

Schaefer, Peter, "History of the Vermilion Range Press," unpublished manuscript, 1923.

Treadwell, J.N., personal letter to J.C. Bush, July 20, 1858.

Wilford, Lloyd A., findings, Jul. 2-29, 1940.

United States Traders Licenses, 1822-1847 (Allen Woolworth notes).

National Archives, Washington, D.C.

Office of Indian Affairs, Letters Received, 1824-81 (microfilm).

Presidential Executive Order creating the Vermilion Lake Reservation, Dec. 21, 1881.

United States General Land Office, *Tract Book* Vol. 60.

Northeast Minnesota Historical Center, Duluth.

Bergeson, Jay O., papers, general passenger and freight agent for the Mesaba Railway, company records 1911-1923.

Carey, R.E., "The Vermillion Lake Road and Indian Trail from Minnesota Point to Vermillion Lake," unpublished manuscript, 1936.

Culkin, William E., papers, 1908-1942.

King, Frank A., railroad papers 1884-1967.

Merritt, Alfred, "Reminiscences" manuscript, 1917.

Stuntz, George R., papers 1852-1888, 1907.

Wilkerson, LeRoy, "History of the Mesaba Transportation Company," undated, unpublished.

Woodbridge, Dwight E., "Discovery of Iron in St. Louis County," manuscript, 1923.

University of Minnesota-Duluth Archives.

Nute, Grace Lee, papers.

Peterson, Eric C., "Gold Mining in Northern Minnesota," unpublished manuscript, Department of History, 1954.

U.S. Census Records.

Third Decennial Census of the State of Minnesota, 1885.

Fourth Decennial Census of the State of Minnesota, 1895.

Fifth Decennial Census of the State of Minnesota, 1905.

Twelfth Census of the United States, Population Schedules, St. Louis County, 1900.

Thirteenth Census of the United States, Mines and Quarries, 1910

Sixteenth Census of the United States, Population Schedules, St. Louis County, 1940.

DISSERTATIONS, THESES, SCHOLARLY PAPERS

Berman, Hyman, "Education for Work and Labor Solidarity: The Immigrant Miners and Radicalism on the Mesabi Range," manuscript prepared for conference on the role of education on the Mesabi Range, Oct. 18-19, 1963, University of Minnesota.

Hakala, Christian, "The Greatest Nation's Greatest Playground: Building a Community Through Sports in Eveleth, Minnesota, 1919-1929," M.A. thesis, 1997, Truman State University, Kirksville, Missouri.

Halunen, Rodney L., "Ghost Towns and Locations of the Mesabi and The Inter-urban Electric Streetcar Line," graduate paper, Jun. 1966, University of Minnesota.

Jacobson, John P., "The Merger of the Democratic and Farmer-Labor Parties in Minnesota," M.A. thesis, Jul. 1966, Bemidji State University.

Krenz, Duane A., "An Historical Geographic Study of the Virginia and Rainy Lake Company, the Last White Pine Operation in the Great Lakes Region," masters thesis, May 1969, Mankato State College.

Machamer, Jerome, "The Geology and Mining Practices at the Soudan Mine, Vermilion District of Minnesota," senior thesis, May 1955, Cornell University.

Pinola, Rudolph, "Labor and Politics on the Iron Range of Northern Minnesota," doctoral dissertation, Jun. 1957, University of Wisconsin.

Stipanovich, Joseph, "Report of the Historical Survey of Iron Range Communities," Dec. 1984, Iron Range Interpretive Program, Iron Range Resources and Rehabilitation Board.

Syrjamaki, John, "Mesabi Communities, A Study of their Development," Jun. 1940, doctoral dissertation, Yale University.

White, Bruce M., "Give Us a Little Milk, Economics and Ceremony in the Ojibway Fur Trade," M.A. thesis, May 1985, McGill University, Montreal.

DOCUMENTARIES.

Peters, Gordon, "Passport in Time," documentary video produced by United States Forest Service, 1996.

Index

About the Author

Known widely as writer and host of "Iron Country," WDSE-TV 8's popular 12-part video documentary series, Marvin Lamppa has spent a lifetime researching and teaching the history of northeast Minnesota and its iron mining districts. Born and brought up in Embarrass in the heart of Iron Range country, he received his undergraduate degree from the University of Minnesota-Duluth, graduate degree from the University of Minnesota and taught history in Iron Range schools and community colleges for many years. He also developed and taught a course in the history of Minnesota's mining districts for Bemidji State University before becoming director of the Iron Range Interpretative Program in 1977.

During his time as director, the author served as a member of the State Historical Records Advisory Board and was instrumental in bringing about the Iron Range Research Center, a state of the art archives and research facility in Chisholm, Minnesota. Among his publications are "Embers of Revival: Laestadian Schisms in Northeast Minnesota, 1900-1940," in *Finnish Diaspora II: United States,* 1981, Toronto; "Ashawiwisitagon, The Land Where Rivers Run Two Ways," in *Range History,* Winter 1983; "Preservers of a Faith: American Influences on Laestadian Congregations in Northern Minnesota, 1870-1950," in *Finns in North America,* 1988, Turku, Finland; and "From Art to Science: Mining at Soudan, 1882-1924," in *Entrepreneurs and Immigrants,* 1991, Chisholm, Minnesota.

Marvin and his wife, Carolyn, live in Babbitt, Minnesota.

Publications of Lake Superior Port Cities Inc.

By Water and Rail:
A History of Lake County, Minnesota
by Hugh E. Bishop
Hardcover: ISBN 0-942235-48-7
Softcover: ISBN 0-942235-42-8

Haunted Lake Superior
by Hugh E. Bishop
Softcover: ISBN 0-942235-55-X

The Night the Fitz *Went Down*
by Hugh E. Bishop
Softcover: ISBN 0-942235-37-1

Superior Way, Third Edition
by Bonnie Dahl
Softcover: ISBN 0-942235-49-5

Michigan Gold, Mining in the Upper Peninsula
by Daniel R. Fountain
Softcover: ISBN 0-942235-15-0

Minnesota's Iron Country:
Rich Ore, Rich Lives
by Marvin G. Lamppa
Softcover: ISBN 0-942235-56-8

Shipwrecks of Isle Royale National Park
by Daniel Lenihan
Softcover: ISBN 0-942235-18-5

Betty's Pies Favorite Recipes
by Betty Lessard
Softcover: ISBN 0-942235-50-9

Lake Superior Journal: Views from the Bridge
by James R. Marshall
Softcover: ISBN 0-942235-40-1

Shipwrecks of Lake Superior
by James R. Marshall
Softcover: ISBN 0-942235-00-2

Once Upon an Isle:
The Story of Fishing Families on Isle Royale
by Howard Sivertson
Hardcover: ISBN 0-9624369-3-3

Schooners, Skiffs & Steamships:
Stories along Lake Superior Water Trails
by Howard Sivertson
Hardcover: ISBN 0-942235-51-7

Tales of the Old North Shore
by Howard Sivertson
Hardcover: ISBN 0-942235-29-0

The Illustrated Voyageur
by Howard Sivertson
Hardcover: ISBN 0-942235-43-6

Haunted Lakes (the original)
by Frederick Stonehouse
Softcover: ISBN 0-942235-30-4

Haunted Lakes II
by Frederick Stonehouse
Softcover: ISBN 0-942235-39-8

Shipwreck of the Mesquite
by Frederick Stonehouse
Softcover: ISBN 0-942235-10-X

Julius F. Wolff Jr.'s Lake Superior Shipwrecks
by Julius F. Wolff Jr.
Hardcover: ISBN 0-942235-02-9
Softcover: ISBN 0-942235-01-0

Lake Superior Magazine (Bimonthly)

Lake Superior Travel Guide (Annual)

Lake Superior Wall Calendar (Annual)

Lake Superior Mini Wall Calendar (Annual)

Lake Superior Wall Map

Lake Superior Map Placemats

For a catalog of the entire Lake Superior Port Cities
collection of books and merchandise, write or call:

Lake Superior Port Cities Inc.
P.O. Box 16417 • Duluth, MN 55816
1-888-BIG LAKE (244-5253) • 218-722-5002
FAX 218-722-4096 • E-mail: guide@lakesuperior.com